BANDIT NARRATIVES
IN LATIN AMERICA

ILLUMINATIONS:
Cultural Formations of the Americas Series

John Beverley and Sara Castro-Klarén, *Editors*

BANDIT
NARRATIVES
IN LATIN AMERICA

FROM VILLA TO CHÁVEZ

JUAN PABLO DABOVE

University of Pittsburgh Press

Published by the University of Pittsburgh Press, Pittsburgh, Pa., 15260

Cataloging-in-Publication data is available from the Library of Congress

ISBN 13: 978-0-8229-6435-3
ISBN 10: 0-8229-6435-X

Cover art: Alberto Breccia (1919–1993), *El fin*, 1993. Acrylic paint on canvas,
50 x 70cm. Reproduced by permission of the heirs of Alberto Breccia.
The painting was inspired by a short story by Jorge Luis Borges ("El fin").

Cover design by Laurence Nozik

To my son, Tomás. For the many, many hours that we played ball and games, and swam and talked and drove and walked and read and watched movies together, and invented silly words for silly games. The memory of those hours, of the undivided joy they were (and are, and will be for many years still), will be with me until the end.

To my wife, Susan, whose love never ceases to impress me as an undeserved gift.

And to Alba and Celeste. For those evenings in the backyard, in San Nicolás, in the unseasonable warmth of May.

CONTENTS

Acknowledgments   ix

Preamble: Porfirio Díaz's Paradox   xi

Introduction   1

PART I. BANDITRY, SELF-FASHIONING, AND THE QUEST FOR LEGITIMACY

1. *Speculum Latronis*: On Villa's *Retrato autobiográfico*   19
2. Hugo Chávez, Maisanta, and the Construction of
   an Insurgent Lineage   42

PART II. BANDITRY AND THE EPIC OF THE NATION

3. The Burning Plains: On *Las lanzas coloradas*   65
4. "Bodies for the Gallows": On *¡Vámonos con Pancho Villa!*   86
5. The Andean Western: On *Cuentos andinos*   104
6. Borges and the Melancholic *Cultor del Coraje*   122

PART III. BANDITRY AND THE LATIN AMERICAN LEFT

7. Dangerous Illusions and Shining Utopias: On *Seara Vermelha*   143
8. The Heart of Darkness: On José Revueltas   170

PART IV. BANDITRY AND THE DILEMMAS OF LITERATURE

9. Borges and Moreira: Inglorious Bastards   191
10. Language, the Devil, and the (Out)law: On *Grande Sertão:*
    Veredas   211
11. An Abundance of Hats and a Scarcity of Heads:
    On *La guerra del fin del mundo*   227
12. Banditry, Neoliberalism, and the Dilemmas of Literature:
    On *Plata quemada*   245
13. What Is a Bandit?   261

    Notes   277
    Works Cited   339
    Index   379

ACKNOWLEDGMENTS

A FEW CLOSE FRIENDS helped me to keep the faith during the long, sometimes difficult process of writing this book. I would like to express my profound gratitude to them: Pablo Makovsky, Peter Elmore, Juan Pablo Canala, Annick Louis, Alejandra Laera, and Susana Rosano. My life would be poorer without them.

A number of friends and colleagues were crucial to this book, by providing inspiration, sharing knowledge, helping me with specific aspects of my research, inviting me to participate in events and projects and to share my work in talks, or just by reminding me with their presence what the university should really be about: Rob Buffington, Mabel Moraña, Ignacio Sánchez-Prado, Mary Long, Elías Palti, Adela Pineda, Idelver Avelar, Emilio Bejel, Benigno Trigo, Gisela Salas-Carrillo, Donna Goldstein, Doreen Delisle, Joshua Lund, Anne Garland, Julio Ramos, Laura Rosato, Germán Alvarez, Rafael Olea Franco, Nina Gerassi-Navarro, Jill Kuhnheim, Ori Preuss, John Slater, Max Parra, Gustavo Faverón Patriau, Wladimir Márquez, Alberto Moreiras, José Luiz Villacañas Berlanga, Francisco Ángeles, Enrique Foffani, Héctor Hoyos, Christopher Conway, Juan Carlos Galdo, Paula Sozzi, Sandra Contreras, Rafael Acosta, Francisco Ramírez Santacruz, Ana Peluffo, Daniel Attala, José Ramón Ruisánchez Serra, Alejandro Cortazar, Amy Robinson,

Amelia Barilli, Leila Gómez, Pedro Mairal, Robert McKee Irwin, and Mónica Szurmuk.

Special thanks to John Beverley, Sara Castro-Klarén, Peter Kracht, and Joshua Shanholtzer at the University of Pittsburgh Press for their generosity in providing (again) a home for my work. And to Alex Wolfe, also at the University of Pittsburgh Press, and Eric Levy for their superb job producing the book and copyediting the manuscript, respectively.

And to the memory of Mirta Susana Thobokolt, the librarian who, many years ago, when I was a kid, sad and lonely and lost, in my first week of high school, gave me Emilio Salgari's books to read. She (with the help of Sandokan and Yanez and the rest of the Tigers of Mompracem) saved me then, and unbeknownst to her, she saved me many times in the years since. Wherever you are, thank you.

PREAMBLE

PORFIRIO DÍAZ'S PARADOX

Legislators and leaders of men, such as Lycurgus, Solon, Mahomet, Napoleon, and so on, were all without exception criminals, from the very fact that, making a new law, they transgressed the ancient one, handed down by their ancestors and held sacred by the people, and they did not stop at bloodshed either.

RASKOLNIKOV IN DOSTOYEVSKY'S *CRIME AND PUNISHMENT*

IN A MESSAGE dated May 25, 1911, Porfirio Díaz (1830–1915) submitted his resignation as president of the Mexican Republic to the House of Representatives (Cámara de Diputados). This occurred in the wake of the taking of Ciudad Juárez, in the state of Chihuahua, by revolutionary forces led by Francisco Madero (1873–1913) on May 10, 1911.[1] Díaz's resignation ended more than three decades of rule (1877–1880 and 1884–1911). The Porfiriato, as his long stint in power was called, was in many respects the best representative of the late nineteenth-century Latin American formula of rule: ostensibly liberal and formally republican, but in fact authoritarian, oligarchical, and decisively bent on a project of export-led macroeconomic growth, nation-state building, and social transformation according to Eurocentric models, inspired by positivist philosophy. Because of the length and the emblematic nature of his regime, Díaz's fall inaugurated the twentieth century in Mexico (and, to a degree, in Latin America).[2] The text of the resignation itself can be considered more than the mere fulfillment of a legal requirement. It can be considered the epitaph of an era and the first glimpse into another, delivered by the eminent protagonist of a past perceived to be in dissolution.[3] It is also (and, for our purposes, mainly) a brief meditation, by a seasoned political mind, at a crucial juncture in history, on certain political paradoxes that have plagued the Latin American postcolonial experience. The initial portion of the text reads:

> The Mexican People [*el Pueblo mexicano*], that people who has so generously filled me with honors, who proclaimed me its leader [*caudillo*] during the Wars of Intervention, who patriotically seconded me in all my efforts directed to promote industry and commerce in the Republic; that same people, distinguished Representatives, has risen up in millenarian armed gangs [*bandas milenarias armadas*], making clear that my presence at the helm of the Supreme Executive Power is the cause for the insurrection.
>
> I am not aware of any deed [*hecho*] of which I can be held responsible that could have originated this social phenomenon [*fenómeno social*]. But allowing—without conceding—that I could be guilty of something for which I have no knowledge, this very possibility makes me the less qualified person to reason or to make a pronouncement regarding my own culpability. As a result, and respecting, as I have always done, the will of the people, and in conformity with article 82 of the Federal Constitution, I come before the Supreme Representative body of the Nation to unconditionally resign from the charge [*encargo*] of Constitutional President of the Republic, a position with which I was honored by the people of the nation. (Spanish text in Krauze 1987, 151; a different English version in Garner 2001, 219)[4]

Díaz tersely states that the Mexican People (note the use of the capital "P" in "the People," which in Spanish is used to name the People as sovereign—as in "we the People"—as opposed to the people as "the common folk") had placed him in the highest office of the land, and had supported him in that office since 1876.[5] But now, that same People (Díaz's oratorical periods emphasize the identity: *el Pueblo, ese pueblo, ese pueblo*) had "risen up in millenarian armed gangs" (that is to say, the opposite of the People). Therein lies the paradox: Díaz simultaneously acknowledges and denies the legitimacy of the uprising.

It is important to pay attention to the line of reasoning. The rebellion, says Díaz, was carried out by "the Mexican People," the undisputed source of sovereignty in a liberal regime (and Díaz's regime was, at least nominally, a liberal one).[6] "People" is used throughout the text without any qualifiers, and it is not replaced with any of the alleged synonyms usually wielded to justify nondemocratic authoritarian rule. The People is not the *chusma* (the rabble), the *populacho* (the mob), the *masa* (the crowd) that has to be either wiped out or subjected to years of iron rule in order to actually become a People. The People in Díaz's message is also not the innocent victim of foreign ideologies or dark agitators (another common charge used to delegitimize insurrections, strikes, or any form of popular activism).

That Díaz would speak about the people in this way is surprising, since he was not a stranger to the authoritarian, paternalistic notion of the-people-as-yet-unable-to-rule as a justification for his own perpetuation as president. A prominent (but, by far, not the only) example of the use of this authoritarian notion can be found just two years before his resignation, in a fateful interview granted to James Creelman for *Pearson's Magazine*. (This long interview, tellingly titled "President Díaz, Hero of the Americas," created the expectation that Díaz was not going to run for another term.[7] This set in motion the events that ended with Madero's uprising.) Díaz explained to Creelman, "I received this Government from the hands of a victorious army at a time when the people were divided and unprepared for the exercise of the extreme principles of democratic government. To have thrown upon the masses the whole responsibility of government at once would have produced conditions that might have discredited the cause of free government" (Creelman 1908, 236). In the interview, Díaz immediately equated the people with "the masses." The decision to rule the masses while excluding them was made for the masses' own benefit as well as for that of the republican system in general. The masses have no will but unbridled passions; they are not sovereign. The people (as a plurality of individuals) are not yet the People (as a single, sovereign collective will). The latter has to be promoted into existence (through education and coercion) out of humbler materials, a creature or an artifact of the ruler and the state. This is what the interview with Creelman says.

Yet in Díaz's message of resignation the conceptual architecture that the parting ruler employs is different. The People is addressed as a full political body, whose claim to sovereignty antedates Díaz's. Díaz resigns because he respects "the will of the people," even if it is threatening or incomprehensible. Faced with the performance of no confidence (the uprising itself), Díaz cannot even plead innocence, just ignorance ("I am not aware . . ."). By doing this, he is conceding the crucial point in the Plan de San Luis Potosí, Madero's manifesto that called for a generalized insurrection. In Madero's text, "Pueblo" (in plural, "los Pueblos") is the first noun to appear. The text has a (partially) narrative form, since the uprising's claim to legitimacy is built upon an account of recent political developments (rigged, violence-ridden elections) that, in Madero's argument, made violent confrontation unavoidable. In Madero's narrative, the main character is the Mexican People, victim of Porfirian tyranny and *primum movens* of the uprising (it is the people "as only sovereign" that endows Madero with the mission to lead the uprising).

In Díaz's resignation, the uprising in 1910 was, by definition, outside the law, as all revolutions are, including the rebellion that brought him to power in 1876. Perhaps this reveals an awareness that his own revolutionary roots are at the heart of this surprisingly nuanced presentation of the uprising. But, as Díaz explains, the revolution exceeded the capacity for legal judgment by a mere appointee of the People ("this very possibility makes me the less qualified person to reason or to make a pronouncement regarding my own culpability"). The People has charged him "with the task [*encargo*] of Constitutional President of the Republic,"[8] so he is a creature of the People, and the latter occupies the position of a political sublime vis-à-vis the limited perspective of a mere president. It is significant that Article 82 of the 1857 Constitution that Díaz invokes as the justification for his resignation has nothing to do with rebellion. The article—linked to Article 79—only spells out the rules of succession in the case that the executive branch of government should be temporarily or permanently vacant. Díaz's reference to the Constitution is not an attempt to justify or even to explain away what pertains to the extralegal (the constituent power rising up in arms), but rather a deliberate move to reterritorialize it in the realm of the legal (since it is a reference to the constituted powers).

However, this is only part of Díaz's reasoning. The People carried out the revolution. But it was a People that had devolved into armed gangs. (This is a reiteration of a rather common charge made by the Porfirian press, the federal military [Katz 1998, 95], and Díaz himself, who accused the revolutionaries of banditry and cattle rustling [87].) Interestingly, the People is not represented (or misrepresented) by the armed gang (as a military or political vanguard). The People *have become* armed gangs, making any principle of representation impossible (e.g., the principle of representation as delegation or trust that justified Díaz's rule—in his eyes).[9] Díaz thus touches upon the core of the paradoxes surrounding all revolutionary events. The People in a revolutionary situation is, as mentioned above, a sort of political sublime. That is, the People is beyond representation, in both senses of the term, since the revolution is an interdiction of the accepted means of representation. This means that, for all practical purposes, the People ceases to be a People (purported origin of the constitutional order, but, as an object of representation, a creation of that constitutional order) and becomes a Multitude. This is a well-known paradox in Western political thought, but one that only comes to the fore, in full force, in revolutionary situations. Therefore, it is impossible for a mere president (as Díaz himself said) to decide whether the subject of the revolution is indeed the People in arms, or a diabolical mimicry of the People (a bandit gang, a criminal band, a terrorist organization). This same paradox can be seen at work in the Western ambiguities and uncertainties surrounding the Arab Spring of 2012 and its equivocal developments. Are the insurgents the People, waking at last, or are they common criminals disguised as militias, shredding any discernible principle or authority, or just terrorists linked directly or indirectly to Al-Qaeda, or plunderers and racketeers like ISIL? (And the vagaries of Western policies toward the region bespeak the uncertainties regarding the actors of current developments.) Answering this question (and this question has to be answered; there is no body politic without it) entails some sort of unavoidable epistemological violence. This violence is at the very core of any form of politics, since constituent power needs to be individuated as some sort of collective, transformed (and thus denied) into some political identity that already depends on a constituted paradigm: the People, the Nation, the Working Class, the Indian, the Speakers of the True Language—or, if the attempt is to delegitimize said constituent power, it becomes the Crowd, the Gang, the Band, the Tribe, the Terrorist Network, the Regime. To put it differently: answering this question is not a matter of empirical proof, but of going back to the unavoidable dogmatism at the heart of the very idea of law (Supiot [2005] 2012), to the irrecoverable moment of the decision that founds the political realm (Schmitt [1922/1934] 1985).

In 1911, invoking the specter of banditry, as Díaz does, was nothing new in Mexico. Vanderwood (1992) has amply shown how Porfirian rule based a significant portion of its claim to both national and international legitimacy on its capacity to provide "order." By this, Díaz and his supporters meant the capacity of the central state to exert (or at least aspire to exert, or pretend to exert) an effective monopoly on territorial violence and to claim the legitimacy of that monopoly. The purported elimination of banditry (or any form of rural nonstate violence that challenged the state, and was therefore labeled banditry) was thus a cornerstone and a showcase in the process of acquiring (or aspiring to acquire) this monopoly.[10]

The scaffold of agrarian capitalism in Mexico was erected on four posts: the local political bosses, the telegraph, the railway, and the Rurales (Knight [1986] 1990). The Rurales were a rural constabulary created with the explicit mission of quashing or co-opting banditry. Rural banditry had been a growing problem in Mexico since the end of the eighteenth century, born out of demographic pressures on land as well as a growing economy and regional exchanges that increased the opportunities for robbery (Taylor 1982; Archer 1982). As such, it was part of the century-long agrarian crisis that extended from the eighteenth century well into the twentieth (Tutino 1989). The generalized disruptions brought about by the decade-long War of Independence and the collapse of *imperium,* as well as the struggles among caudillos and armies of centralist or federalist, liberal or conservative persuasions, the impact of the Mexican-American War and the French intervention, and Indian rebellions such as the Cruzob in Yucatán, meant a general collapse of the (already contested) capacity of the central state to exert effective territorial sovereignty. This inability defined most of the nineteenth century in Mexico, and the Rurales were a part of the strategy to correct that.

But they were also (and, to a degree, primarily) a means to shore up the federal government, since the corps was under the direct control of the presidency, allowing the president to keep other vectors of violence in check, either through co-optation, collaboration, or coercion. These vectors were the landowners (and their private militias and henchmen), rural insurgents of all stripes, local caudillos, disaffected governors, and the army. Local and regional autonomy, the overlapping of different political or judicial jurisdictions, and competing power holders were always the ideal ecosystem for banditry (as Hobsbawm reminds us), and the suppression of both banditry and local autonomy marched hand in hand.[11] In this respect, the Rurales were strikingly similar to other rural constabularies throughout history. In the Hispanic world, the Santa Hermandad in medieval Spain or the Acordada in colonial Mexico come to mind (Lunenfeld 1970; MacLachlan 1974). This double purpose was not lost on the contemporaries of these state-led efforts, neither in Mexico nor in other national contexts.[12] Porfirio Díaz's rule was, consequently, a constant balancing act between the demands of landowners for relative autonomy and the intangibility of property rights, and Díaz's tight control of any event on the ground that could overtly challenge centralized rule. Mobilized in the realm of political discourse, "banditry" as a trope was both a legitimating tool and a political weapon. This legitimating tool was used fully in the Creelman interview quoted above, which contrasted Porfirian rule with the prior state of affairs. Creelman comments that Díaz "found Mexico bankrupt, divided, infested with bandits, and prey to a thousand forms of bribery. Today life and property are safe from frontier to frontier of the republic" (1908, 252).

In his resignation Díaz highlights banditry as the factor that brought down his regime. This admission is more than an easy justification or a muted confession of historical failure (if, after three decades of rule justified by nation-state making, the People has devolved into armed gangs, these would have been three lost decades). It is above all a blunt identification of the paradox inherent in constituent power. This paradox is located in the undecidable oscillation of insurgent violence between founding epic (which could be called "the dramatic decision by the Mexican People to divest Díaz of his mandate") and entropic criminality (which could be called "the uncontrolled anarchy brought about by armed millenarian gangs"). Díaz doesn't make a decision about the nature (or the meaning, which is the same thing) of revolutionary violence, since he cannot: the very act of presenting a formal resignation, instead of just fleeing, is an implicit recognition of the legitimacy (not necessarily the right) of the uprising. A resignation, as a speech act, is unequivocal in this respect. Resigning, even in the face of overwhelming force (one can imagine Díaz resigning on the battlefield in front of Madero, after losing the battle), has as its "felicity conditions" (Austin 1962) the recognition of the interlocutors as symmetrical, as both legitimate contenders for power. (This is why Salvador Allende, in his last message to the Chileans, clearly stated that he was not going to resign. Resignation would have been an acknowledgment of the political—as opposed to the criminal—nature of Pinochet's coup, something that Allende was not going to make.) Díaz is trapped in a situation in which he is acknowledging, by the mere act of resigning, the legitimacy beyond the law of the power that divests him of his power. By invoking the "People" he shows that he is not fooling himself in this respect. But by also asserting that the People, in its sovereign splendor, is or can be identical to an armed gang, he is also able to point out that the decision regarding the meaning of violence is a battle as crucial (and as "material") as any fought in the field.

This decision bespeaks the entirely contingent (unfounded) nature of political arrangements, their perennially disputable character, and, above all, the cultural nature of these disputes. The difference between bandit (or terrorist, or criminal) and sovereign is forever elusive. (If the caliphate that ISIL is fighting for triumphs, takes hold, and is eventually recognized by the international community, the plundering and racketeering and murdering currently taking place would be resignified—retold—as the birth pains of a new state.) Each particular conflict enacts this indeterminacy all over again. Or, to put it in other terms: revolutionary or insurgent situations interdict the dogmatic assumptions upon which the law (the language that is the connecting tissue of any human society) is based. In his resignation, Díaz allows the moment of indecisiveness, a moment essential to all revolutions, to resonate in his own discourse. Nothing embodies this anxiety regarding the identity of such oppositions more than a well-known passage from Saint Augustine. In *De civitate Dei* (The City of God), borrowing from Cicero, he ponders,

Justice removed, then, what are kingdoms but great bands of robbers? What are bands of robbers themselves but little kingdoms? The band itself is made up of men; it is governed by the authority of a ruler; it is bound together by a pact of association; and the loot is divided according to an agreed law. If, by the constant addition of desperate men, this scourge grows to such a size that it acquires territory, establishes a seat of government, occupies cities and subjugates peoples, it assumes the name of kingdom more openly. For this name is now manifestly conferred upon it not by the removal of greed, but by the addition of impunity. It was a pertinent and true answer that was made to Alexander the Great by a pirate whom he had seized. When the king asked him what he meant by infesting the sea, the pirate defiantly replied: "The same as you do when you infest the whole world; but because I do it with

a little ship I am called a robber, and because you do it with a great fleet, you
are an emperor." ([413–426] 1998, 58)

Saint Augustine had divine justice as the guarantee that there was an ultimate,
unequivocal distinction between bands of robbers and kingdoms. This is why
he begins his reasoning with the premise "justice removed" ("Remota itaque
iustitia quid sunt regna nisi magna latrocinia"), meaning that the argument
that follows depends entirely on an impossible situation, namely, the removal
of divine justice; hence the necessary reference to a pre-Christian anecdote.
Secular states such as Mexico were deprived of that guarantee. In the absence
of a transcendent value or set of values that would anchor the law as justice,
politics becomes the never-ending dispute to decide upon the exception (and
to decide what is politics), and the lines between outlaw and sovereign would
be forever blurred. This happens, for example, in Friedrich Schiller's *Die
Räuber* (*The Robbers*, 1781) and in Heinrich von Kleist's *Michael Kohlhaas*
(1808), where the outlaw is also the "avenging angel" intent upon delivering
a divine—or at least a higher—justice. The intervention of the avenging angel
is the apparition of the unfathomable excess from the law, the embodiment
of the distance between law and justice, since divine justice is beyond com-
prehension. This is why the avenging angel is difficult to distinguish from the
devil; or, as posited by Altamirano in his novel *El Zarco*, the killer of bandits
who use terror to deliver justice is difficult to distinguish from the fearsome
bandit himself (Altamirano 1901).

   Returning to the epigraph that opened these pages: when Dostoyevsky's
Raskolnikov states (repeating what he had written in a journal article) that
legislators and leaders are always criminals, since they act beyond the law,
Razumihin (the policeman who is questioning him as a suspect in the murder of the old money lender) comes back with a crucial question: if that is
true, how does one distinguish these extraordinary people from the ordinary
ones? There is no definitive, "grounded" answer to this question, although
each political conjuncture demands and compels one. This lack of distinction
between banditry and the state is a recurring motif in Western literature and
thought, at least from the Romans on.[13] But Díaz's case is not a dialectical, literary, or academic exercise, but rather an answer to a "real" pressing situation,
articulated by the person whose very identity as leader is called into question
(and ultimately destroyed) by the enactment of the paradox.

Consider one example that starkly illustrates Díaz's paradox. In March of 1912, Pascual Orozco, dissatisfied with Madero (who had not given him the prominent civil or military position to which Orozco aspired) and lured by the promises of northern conservatives (in particular the Terrazas/Creel clan), led an uprising against the president. Orozco was, at the time, a prestigious leader who was able to muster a sizable force. (Ironically, Orozco and his Colorados were dubbed bandits by the Maderista press when news of the uprising reached the capital. Former victims, they now used the same discursive tactics that the Porfirian press and military had directed against Madero [Meyer 1967, 54–55].) After the first Battle of Rellano (March 24, 1912), Orozco came to be in control of most of Chihuahua.[14] Once he was in possession of a crucial branch of the northern railroads, Orozco's advance toward Torreón (and later toward Mexico City) seemed certain. For a moment, it was feared that Villa would join Orozco's insurgency. Legend has it that Orozco rejected Villa's aid in the rebellion because "he did not accept bandits in his forces" (Meyer 1967, 68). But Villa remained loyal to Madero and to Abraham González (governor of Chihuahua, and the person who had recruited Villa in the first place). In fact, he fled Chihuahua City, where he had retired to become a butcher and cattle wholesaler (at which time he was accused of rustling many of the cattle that he killed), only later to organize a loyalist force in Parral, a town in southern Chihuahua that was to become the epicenter of Villismo. (Regarding the depth of Villista sentiment in Parral, Nellie Campobello provides a most telling account in her text *Cartucho* [1931].) Villa at this moment became an irregular fighter (since he had not been officially recalled to active service), operating in an area ceded—for all practical purposes—by the federal government. He lacked the "regular" means to arm and equip his men and was thus obligated to supply his army with forced contributions. To man his forces, Villa requisitioned horses, weapons, and 150,000 pesos.[15] He provided receipts for these. An additional 50,000 pesos was requisitioned (without receipt or commitment of repayment) from the Banco Minero owned by the Creel/ Terrazas clan, Orozco's supporters and instigators. The expropriation was as much driven by the need to supply his troops as by a retaliatory impulse (which Villa would fully acknowledge) against the Creel/Terrazas interests, an animosity that predated this conflict and, it seems, even the revolution.

As in most cases of rural insurgents (or even "regular" armies), this is the grain of truth that provides the anchor for the bandit trope. Rebel (and regular) armies usually lacked regular lines of supplies. It was a long-sanctioned practice to sustain them by plundering stores or haciendas that belonged to the enemy faction, or by demanding ransoms in cash, cattle, lodging, or supplies. The same coerced extraction was carried out with the allies; however, it was not retaliation, but rather a "patriotic contribution," or a loan to be repaid in an entirely hypothetical future. The line that separated plundering or extortion from the patriotic contribution was blurry, but very real. It determined, above all, the level of exaction, not its occurrence (and that level was rarely random or arbitrary; instead it was determined by a more-or-less strict "moral economy"). And of course, more often than not, well-to-do store and hacienda owners contributed to both sides of any given struggle (as seen, for example, in Fernando de Fuentes's film *El compadre mendoza* [1935]), since it was a sure way to curry favor with whichever faction ended up on top. As long as the predatory practice was carried out with a certain restraint, it was considered the price of doing business, not much different from mob protection. Therefore, police and armed forces, until well into the twentieth century in some cases, were not entirely different from bandits or racketeers when it came to the material aspect of certain practices. The difference was in how those practices were articulated to a legality not yet completely defined or enforced, and in how the actors on the ground (i.e., its perpetrators, its victims, the population at large) perceived it. For example, in such an unexpected place as the "Plan de San Luis Potosí," Madero establishes that "for war expenses, voluntary or forced loans will be secured. Forced loans will be secured only from Mexican citizens or Mexican institutions. There will be a scrupulous record of these loans and promissory notes will be issued to the interested parties so that the loan can be canceled when the revolution triumphs" ([1910] 1976, 11). Villa was, then, tapping into a clear precedent, articulated by none other than Madero, a figure above suspicion of bandit practices.

With the aforementioned resources, Villa garrisoned Parral and supplied his troops as well as the circumstances allowed. Orozco could not advance east or (more importantly) south without the risk of being flanked by Villa. Thus, he had to rethink his plan and deal with him. He laid siege to the city, and after some resistance (Villa repelled the first assault), Parral fell. But the waste of time and ammunition (which was hard to replace, given American neutrality and the embargo of all weapons shipments), compounded by the abuses against life and property that the Orozco forces committed in occupied Parral, proved fatal to the fortunes of his faction. Deprived of the element of surprise, drained of prestige, and with his ammunition depleted, Orozco was soundly defeated at the Second Battle of Rellano (May 22, 1912).

Villa's unexpected stand in Parral had saved Madero. Villa was made an honorary general (and mocked by the career generals who considered him a rustic and a clown, something that he remembered bitterly). But he was still not completely trusted. He was immediately commissioned by Madero to fight Orozco as part of the federal División del Norte (not to be confused with Villa's own División del Norte, 1913–1915), under the leadership of Díaz-era general and would-be dictator Victoriano Huerta (Taibo [2006] 2010, 141). Huerta hated Villa. A year earlier, both men were on opposite sides, one as a general defending the Díaz regime,[16] the other as a prominent revolutionary leader. Villa tried to ingratiate himself with Huerta and his fellow generals, to no avail. In June of 1912, Huerta managed to imprison Villa on trumped-up charges of horse stealing (he allegedly stole a mare that belonged to a businessman of the area) and insubordination. Huerta wanted Villa shot on the spot, but Villa was saved in the nick of time by General Rubio Navarrete and Emilio Madero (a picture survives of that momentous occasion: Villa in front of the firing squad). Villa was sent to Mexico City instead, to face trial while sitting in jail. When it was obvious that the initial charges of horse stealing and insubordination were weak and would not stand up in court, the judge changed the case so that the main charge would be the "sacking of Parral" (Taibo [2006] 2010, 157).

Surprisingly, Madero failed to free, to support, or even to contact Villa directly in his hour of need. It has been suggested that he did not consider Villa a bona fide revolutionary, but rather merely a talented *condottieri* (Katz 1998). This is why, for example, in his letter to Villa in April 1912, when commending him for his actions against Orozco, he insisted on a monetary reward (Osorio 1985, 4). Prior to this, in 1911, after the revolution had deposed Díaz, Madero also insisted on a monetary reward for Villa. Taibo ([2006] 2010, 115) even mentions a document in which this reward was contingent upon Villa leaving Mexico for the United States. Personal distrust or animosity aside, it is certain that Villa's ambiguous reputation as an erstwhile bandit was not erased by his revolutionary accomplishments. This dubious reputation seems to have been an important consideration for Madero (who had previously defended Villa publicly), at a time when the collapse of the state monopoly on violence had triggered an epidemic of banditry that greatly concerned Madero. In fact, he had asked Congress in December 1911 (that is, just a month after taking office) to grant him the power to suspend due process for bandits, a notable throwback to the nineteenth-century traditions of dealing with outlaws (Vanderwood 1992, 162). However, it is surprising that Madero treated Félix Díaz's rebels (who tried to stage a counterrevolutionary insurrection) with more leniency than that with which he treated Villa (Knight [1986] 1990, 1:477). Even Tomás Urbina, Villa's subordinate and *compadre* from their bandit days (and all along unequivocally and exclusively bent on personal profit), was able to secure a better deal for himself than Villa did (Holguín 2000).

In his correspondence with Madero, Villa emphatically maintained that his actions were both legitimate and legal. His requisitions in Parral, he insisted, were justified because of the need to fight Orozco. He claimed that he had been authorized to do so by González, and that personal gain did not guide his actions. And finally, his requisitions had specific targets: only prominent members of the reactionary camp were given the squeeze (Osorio 1985, 21, 22, 23, 37). (The bulk of the correspondence with Madero, however, comprises emotional pleas for a fair hearing, as well as lamentations about the ingratitude and slander that he was suffering.) But Madero refused to side with Villa against a real general—a "son of Chapultepec." He never even personally answered Villa's letters (his secretary did, and the tone is unmistakably noncommittal, if not downright hostile), something that stung Villa deeply. Failing to support his most able military leader was a fateful mistake, and a glaring act of ingratitude, which eventually cost Madero his life. Villa, seeing the futility of his attempts to vindicate himself in court or to secure Madero's support, and aware that a coup was in the making (and that his head would roll in that case), decided to escape from prison with the help of a young lawyer named Carlos Jáuregui (the reach of and the participants in the plot to aid Villa's escape were never fully elucidated). Villa escaped, in true mythical bandit fashion, disguised as a lawyer, by just walking out the jail's front door. Also in true mythical bandit fashion (or like Ivanhoe returning from his imprisonment in Palestine to fight for the cause of King Richard against the usurper

John), he escaped to the United States and then crossed back into Mexico, riding to the rescue of the true sovereign. However, unlike Ivanhoe, he arrived too late. The coup had already happened, and Madero was already dead.

In any case, Villa extracted resources by force or the threat of force, from the well-to-do of Parral, with armed agents who lacked a clear official mandate (not a written one that could be produced in his defense). Just like in the alternative posited by Díaz in his message of resignation, the expropriations can be considered either a legitimate, although extralegal, act of state, carried out in a situation of pressing need, or an act of out-and-out banditry. In fact, his actions follow, to the letter, the minimalist definition of banditry as provided by social historians such as Richard Slatta or scholars such as Gillian Spraggs: "Banditry is the taking of property by force or by the threat of force" (Slatta 1994, 76), "the taking of property in front of the owner by creating fear" (Spraggs 2001, 4). But, by the same token, Villa's actions were not carried out in order to secure any economic profit for himself or his men (although he was accused of this); they took place in the defense of the legal state government, challenged by a glaringly illegal counterrevolutionary coup. Villa understood his actions as an emergency measure, when he was faced with a clear and present danger to the constituted authorities. Villa, as a colonel in the revolutionary army, could also claim a certain clout for doing this. It should also be noted that the deportment of Villa's troops was correct, something that could not be said of all troops involved in this stage of the conflict—revolutionary, Orozquista, or federal.

Villa escaped from jail before his trial was completed, and soon afterward, Madero fell and was killed. In the fight and chaos in Mexico City that was the run-up to the coup (the so-called "Decena Trágica"), the files of Villa's trial disappeared in a fire in the prison (Taibo [2006] 2010, 172). So there was never an "official" pronouncement regarding what transpired in Parral. But we can be sure of this: the decision about the meaning of his actions (i.e., the guilty verdict or the one upholding his innocence) would have been an entirely political act. By political I do not mean "removed from truth" or "distorted by particular interests" (as in the current distinction between "politics" and "policy," the second one conceived as rational, data- or fact-based, nonpolitical). The decision regarding Villa could *only* have been a political one, because there is no option between political and nonpolitical when it comes to a judgment about meaning, but there is always a political pronouncement because the grounds for the decision do not lie in the nature of the act, but in the interplay of forces that produce truth.[17] "Banditry" (like "paramilitarism") is one of those tropes that bring to the fore the contested, contingent nature of all of these pronouncements. Some of those interplays of forces are studied in this book.

INTRODUCTION

ANY DEBATE ABOUT what banditry is, who a bandit is, or what a bandit and his supporters, sympathizers, and enemies want, is part and parcel of a debate on representation. What and who do bandits represent, if anything at all? On the other hand, who represents (who defines, depicts, and/or narrates) bandits, and how, and in which contexts, and for what purposes? Studying bandits and studying how these figures were represented assumes (perhaps controversially) that there is no way to tell the bandit—the "real" bandit—apart from his representation. This is what I have called elsewhere, using the terms of an old philosophical debate, the "nominalist approach" (as opposed to the "realist approach").[1] According to the nominalist approach, a bandit is defined as whoever was called or labeled a bandit and treated as such. This would cancel (or reposition) some of the problems that have nagged bandit scholars for decades. The first problem is that the rubric applies to such a wide array of actions as to make a simple, unequivocal definition either impossibly complex or artificially simple, and that the rubric "bandit," in all its lexical variations,[2] has been applied to a wide array of rural insurgents—from the humble peasant highway robber (armed perhaps with a machete) to a leader of thousands or tens of thousands of men fighting a war of international resonance, such as Augusto César Sandino or Francisco Villa, or from a band of murdering sociopaths to a group of high-minded revolutionary fighters. It is not crucial in my approach to decide once and for all if a particular man or woman was "really" a bandit, or if his particular action was "really" an act of banditry; rather, the importance lies in the examination of why, how, and for what purpose and with what effect the label was used, and how it was contested, contradicted, or accepted by the bandit himself, by his contemporary allies and enemies, and by posterity, in relation to similar or different problems than those that gave rise to the original labeling act.

This is the larger problem that frames this book. In tackling it, however, many different approaches are possible, depending on disciplinary training, theoretical perspective, the problem emphasized, or the genre or cultural form chosen. This study has a very defined scope. It explores the uses of the bandit character as a cultural trope in literature (novels and short stories, mostly) and in discursive practices that do not belong to literature proper, but that tap into literature's authority and prestige (such as Pancho Villa's autobiography and some of Hugo Chávez's public interventions). At a minimum, then, this is a thematic (and necessarily fragmentary) mapping of how banditry was variously depicted, during a specific period, by a number of intellectuals in twentieth-century Latin America. This book studies how men of letters bodied forth their desires regarding literature's place and authority and, perhaps more prominently, how they embodied their anxieties regarding the increasingly problematic place and role of literature within national cultures (and, complementarily, the increasingly problematic place of the very notion of national culture). These desires and anxieties are both given expression, at the level of the narrative plot, in the conflicted relationship between bandits and men of letters.

I would like to emphasize, then, that this book is not about bandits per se. It is about how men of letters articulated the bandit trope, in order to reflect upon their own practice, their own place in society, or to carry out a particular literary or political project. The self-referential use of the bandit trope, as a tool for either the legitimation or the critique of the ideology regarding the role of modern literature in national societies (or of particular literary and political projects within those societies), is perhaps the most important point I address. By contrast, the two chapters in which this preoccupation is not present (chapter 1, on Pancho Villa's autobiography, and chapter 2, on Hugo Chávez's construction of his own persona as the culmination of an insurgent lineage) are the two chapters in which the importance and value of lettered practices is more unequivocally affirmed, and rather taken as a given.

The self-referential use of the bandit trope arises, I would venture, from the perception of a crisis in the literary institution, a loss or lack of legitimacy of its social standing and its mission (and a need for the redefinition of both), and an erosion of its prestige and authority. To put it succinctly, it was a crisis regarding representation, in both senses of the term: how adept was literature at depicting individuals and societies, and how legitimate was literature's claim to represent individuals and societies? One can say, with reasonable certainty, that the avant-garde movements in Latin America were the first to articulate this sense of crisis as crucial to the (self-)perception of literature as an institution. This book will not focus on how "real" this crisis was (even if it could be quantified), or on whether crisis equals decline, as in Jean Franco's expression "the Decline and Fall of the Lettered City." It will focus, instead, on how modern Latin American literature was defined, to a significant degree, by this perceived crisis, and how the most important literary efforts of the period tried either to overcome this challenge, to deny it, to embrace it, or to tread some middle path between the previous options.

Things were quite different during the long nineteenth century, when literature (as conceived and practiced in national literatures), and the writing practices and disciplines associated or competing with literature, were struggling but ascendant social institutions. Perhaps literature as a practice was devoid of economic or institutional support, its professionalization hindered or stunted, its practitioners attacked or persecuted or ignored. But very few (and least of all, very few men of letters) doubted the crucial role of literature (and increasingly, within literature, of prose narrative) in the constitution of the national cultures of Latin America. Literature was, if I may be allowed the hyperbole, sovereign. Writers and educated heroes could be brutalized, mocked, or even killed (like the young *unitario* in *El matadero*), but the dignity and importance of the lettered practice remained unpolluted. This is the meaning of the (by now mythical) scene of young Sarmiento leaving Argentina to eat the bitter bread of banishment, but literally writing on stone his core conviction: "On ne tue point les idées" ("Ideas should not be killed" was Sarmiento's preferred translation). The fact that the quotation is in fact a misquotation—as Ricardo Piglia ([1980] 2002) has noted and reasoned—is as telling as the ironclad conviction that motivated the inscription.

This conviction about the centrality of the lettered practice has a long lineage in Latin America, and it is, in fact, one unifying trait within Latin

American culture (as Ángel Rama has proved in his seminal *La ciudad letrada*). In the postcolonial era, however, this conviction became less of an administrative fact—the mastering of a technology, a place in a bureaucracy—and more of a moral and epistemic position. The man of letters would have been the one who knew, mapped, and diagnosed the present, the one who could recover and animate and interpret the past, and who could predict, figure out, or fend off the future. This can be traced to the European Romantic revolution (William Blake: "Hear the voice of the Bard! / Who Present, Past & Future, sees") and its uncomfortable adaptation to the Latin American milieu. It was romantic in origin, but over the years it intersected and superseded ideologies and literary schools. Through many metamorphoses, many academic and political lexicons, many displacements and revisions and reinventions, this ideology is still with us today even though, as this book seeks to prove, a consciousness of its dilemmas and shortcomings underpins some of the best literary efforts of the last century.

How does banditry fit into this scheme? During the long nineteenth century both conservative and liberal writers used the bandit trope to legitimize or criticize the social order (or specific aspects of it). At the same time, banditry served as a point of contrast or a reservoir of cultural capital that helped writers to legitimize their own practice: its place, its necessity, and its sovereignty within the nation-state in the makings (see my commentary on Fernández de Lizardi below for a kind of "primal scene" of this relationship where the national writer is born in the face-to-face with the body—the corpse—of the outlaw). This manner of articulating the bandit trope has not disappeared in the twentieth century; the bandit trope (or tropes, referring to the forms of nonstate violence that have replaced it, or at least displaced it, in the cultural landscape: the terrorist, the drug trafficker, the urban criminal—*motochorro, pirata del asfalto, secuestrador express, pibe chorro*) still embodies or gives expression to conflicts that have little to do with actual outlawry. (Take as an example the controversy and media hype on the topic of "urban insecurity" and "the narco" as a crucial political arena in Argentina.) Banditry is indeed mobilized in order to create narratives of legitimation or to criticize such narratives, and twentieth- and twenty-first-century authors still draw on the authority of literature in order to craft and impose those narratives. But the standing of literature within the social realm, and the very notion of

what literature is, have changed decisively since the beginning of the twentieth century.

Even within a narrative project that ends up affirming the power and status
of literature, the interrogation, I would contend, is always there, and more
often than not, the dilemma resurfaces in one way or another (when it is not
the driving force of the narrative project). This book traces a number of cases
in which this affirmation/interrogation is conducted through a face-to-face
between a bandit and a man of letters. The scene that puts the bandit and the
man of letters face to face, either to confront or to collaborate, in horror or
in awe, is not just a topic among others, but the topic that gives expression
to one of the deep undercurrents of the entire postcolonial cultural process.
Allow me to present two scenes of this face-to-face that I hope will make the
thrust of this book clearer. One of them belongs to the nineteenth century,
but I would argue that its relevance as an emblem extends into the present.

It can be said that Latin American postcolonial literature begins with the rotten corpse of a bandit. This rotten corpse appears in book 5 of *El periquillo sarniento* (1816), a Mexican novel by Joaquín Fernández de Lizardi, considered
the first Latin American postcolonial novel (although it was written in the
midst of the Mexican independence wars). Perico, the son of decent parents
turned rogue and criminal, is its protagonist. At a late point in the narrative,
Perico is down on his luck after a brief stint with a gang of highway robbers.
The Acordada, the colonial corps in charge of providing security in Mexican
caminos reales (king's highways), had stamped the gang out of existence.
Perico was the only survivor. This would seem like just another episode in
his adventurous life, but something else happens this time. Riding away from
the scene of the ambush, he spots the bloated corpse of Januario, executed as
a brigand chief, hanging from a tree. Januario was Perico's childhood friend,
and a partner in and sponsor of his early misdeeds. Perico understands that
this is no chance meeting. This is a "lesson" that the dead Januario "loudly
voices." How Perico reacts to this rather ghastly sight is significant: he composes a sonnet and carves it into the very tree from which Januario's dead
body hangs. This encounter, as I have argued elsewhere (see Dabove 2007;
Dabove and Hallstead 2009), is, although brief, the axis of the novel. Because
of this encounter, Perico realizes that he must redeem himself sincerely and
for good. He abandons his criminal career and becomes Don Pedro: a model

citizen, a husband, a father, and an owner. But above all, he becomes a writer—
the writer of the autobiographical narrative that is *El periquillo sarniento*, dictated *in articulo mortis* to El Pensador Mexicano, Fernández de Lizardi's nom
de plume and, here, his fictional alter ego.

There are two dimensions of this scene that I would like to highlight. The
first one is the decisive role of the state in the production of the man of letters. Januario probably did not die by hanging, but was most likely shot by a
firing squad or killed during a skirmish and later hanged (as so happens, for
example, with the execution of el Zarco in Altamirano's novel *El Zarco*). The
state's posthumous assault on the body (the refusal of a burial, the theatri-
cal display) is a *plus*, not of violence, but of meaning. It shows that in Januario's dead body there is a message. This is what was called a "theater of the
law," the deliberate communicative/performative techniques through which
elites reasserted their hegemony when challenged from below.[3] The assault
dispossessed Januario of his voice (the hanging by the neck could not be more
symbolic in this respect), and animated what was the empty carcass, the dead
flesh, with the state's own voice. Januario thus becomes a talking corpse that
repeats the law ad infinitum: the one, anteceding any actual laws, that makes
the bandit an enemy of mankind, bound to be killed on the spot. Perico hears
that voice, he feels that it interpellates *him*, since Januario is a mirror image
of his own self, and this act of "hearing" the state's voice is the origin of the
novel, in a very literal sense (reinforced by the fact that Perico's first reaction is to write a poem on the very fatal tree from which Januario is hanging).
But additionally, the state provided the event that organized Perico's aimless
wandering into a "life," a time with meaning, a politically and ethically relevant learning process. Don Pedro provides the raw facts, but the state has
provided the meaning, the narrative framework of which the raw facts are
only illustrations. Don Pedro's memories (*El periquillo sarniento*) want to be
a life lesson for his offspring. But Don Pedro is less the author of that lesson
than the translator into words of the lesson that the state taught him through
the dead body of the bandit.[4]

The second scene was conceived in the other extreme of Latin America. In
1967, at the height of the revolutionary tide that swept Latin America and
the world, Pablo Neruda (1904–1973) published *Fulgor y muerte de Joaquín
Murieta*. It is a play that has a half-serious, half-humorous tone, perhaps

in the path of John Gay (*The Beggar's Opera*, 1728) and Bertolt Brecht (*The Threepenny Opera*, 1928). This is to say that *Fulgor* is a play in which humor never distracts from the project of a scathing critique. Neruda traces the life of Murieta (spelled by him with one *r*, in the Chilean tradition). Murieta is, in Neruda's account, a Chilean *roto* who goes to California following the elusive promise of golden riches, only to become a bandit of the avenger variety and to find a violent death at the hands of early Californian justice (*injusticiado* is the neologism Neruda plays with). His head is severed from his body, and it seems to have a life in the entertainment industry as a display piece, just like the head of Lampião, almost a century later, taken on a tour of the Brazilian northeastern backlands by his slayers (Grunspan-Jasmin 2001). The head eventually disappears, entering the realm of legend and speculation, much like the head of Pancho Villa, stolen from his grave in Parral shortly after his death and never to be found again.

Fulgor y muerte does not rank among the best of Neruda's works. However, the play closes with two telling moments. One is the soliloquy of the severed head of Murieta (of which I reproduce here a fragment):

> *I speak as a Head bled of its force and inflection.*
> *The voice that I summon is strange; the lips are not mine.*
> *What can the Dead say? The Dead with no other direction*
> *Than that which the wind takes as it works in the void of the rain?*
>
> *To whom is it given to know? What intruder*
> *Or friend, tracing the naked truth in the snow,*
> *Shall interpret my story or sing it in truth, in the end?*
> *My time is a hundred years hence. My lips shall be Pablo Neruda. (171)*

The final chorus (after this monologue) intones a poem that ends with these lines:

> *Joaquín, return to your nest: gallop the air toward the south on your blood-*
> *colored stallion.*
> *The streams of the country that bore you sing out of silvery mouths. Your poet*
> *sings with them,*
> *Your fate mingled bloodshed and gall, Joaquín Murieta; but its sound*

is still heard. Your people repeat both your song and your grief, like a tolling bell
struck underground. The people are million. (175)

Murieta, the bandit, is not merely a man of the people, but through his death
he becomes the point around which a People coalesces, acquires its identity
and its self-consciousness. The People is not merely the People of the Nation,
but a transnational, class-based identity, spanning from Chile to California to
Republican Spain (mentioned in the song too) to Vietnam, mentioned at the
end, and whose sufferings are equated with the sufferings and death of Murieta (79). By making Murieta a Chilean, Neruda not only follows an established
tradition (see Leal 1999), but also disengages Murieta as an icon of frontier
culture, of Chicano culture, and makes him an icon of the Third World and of
peasants everywhere. And the man of letters (Neruda) is the one who would
put the voice of the bandit into words, a voice that otherwise would have been
deep but lost in the unintelligible voices of the river or the wind. Neruda's
voice—Neruda as a character of the play—is the voice of the People because
Neruda is the only way for the People to acquire a voice. Neruda is the one who
is endowed with superior knowledge (endowed by the bandit head), capable
of leading the People out of the "fog" of ideology.[5]

Murieta's head was cut off as a trophy (and for its cash value). Decapitation as a penalty was not contemplated in American penal codes, and in any
case he was already dead when the decapitation occurred. Its decollation and
exhibition was intended to show that Murieta was indeed dead, and to serve as
an object lesson to would-be insurgents (like the photographing of Guevara's
body more than a century later). When it comes to banditry, this use—exhibit-
ing the head or the corpse of the dead outlaw—survived long, long after it was
superseded in the rest of the West. American Western iconography supplies
many obscure instances. But more famous examples of this can be found in
the treatment of Conselheiro's corpse and head after the defeat of Canudos in
1897, Jesse James's corpse after his murder in 1882, the aforementioned destiny of Lampião's head after his death in Angicos in 1938, and Sangre Negra's
corpse (airlifted by the Colombian army in a tour of the area's villages in order
to prove that he was indeed dead). However, Murieta's head later acquired a
meaning that was not explicitly contemplated in Janes's (2005) classification: the decollated head as commodity and spectacle for market consumption.[6] This is perhaps its most famous avatar, since the poster referring to the

exhibition of Murieta's head has been amply reproduced (Neruda dutifully reproduces the poster in the first edition of *Fulgor*). Neruda transforms the head into a sort of "ancestor head." It is not a trophy displayed by the vanquisher, but rather the emblem of a spirit of a precursor that guides the community toward the future, by the promise of eventual emancipation.

Thus we have a talking corpse (Januario) and a talking head (Murieta). Both speak to the fictional alter egos of the authors (to Perico, and through him to El Pensador Mexicano; to Neruda). Both scenes have optimistic overtones, but for opposite reasons. Perico defines himself, his place, and his task, as a (forced) ally of the state that displayed and wrote the corpse. Neruda (the Neruda that appears in the text) defines himself, his place, his task, as an ally, heir, and voice of the bandit that fought the state and the racist, imperial oppressor. In both cases, the man of letters translates the corpse's message into words of enduring appeal. And the triad is the same: the state that dealt with the bandit, the bandit himself, and the man of letters. The legitimacy and the nature of the bond among the three positions is different, however. In both cases, the state's violence is productive. But in Fernández de Lizardi, it produces a citizen-writer allied with the state and defined by this alliance. In Neruda, it produces a collective popular subject opposed to the state and defined by this opposition, and a writer—not a citizen—allied with said popular subject.

These are just two examples. My intent in this book is, precisely, to provide others and to reflect upon them. Of course, this face-to-face (head-to-head) is not exclusive to Latin American literature. Sir Walter Scott's hugely influential highland novels present the same pairings: the English aspiring writer Francis Osbaldistone is saved by the highland rebel (and robber, and smuggler, and racketeer) Rob Roy MacGregor (*Rob Roy*, 1817), and bookish Edward Waverley and Fergus Mac-Ivor forge an enduring friendship that will last until Fergus's exalted execution (*Waverley*, 1814).[7]

In the chapters that follow I examine cases from Mexico, Argentina, Peru, Brazil, and Venezuela. I make occasional references to other national contexts as well, such as Ecuador, the Dominican Republic, Chile, Nicaragua, Cuba, and Colombia. Also, as has always been the case in the "field" of bandit studies (if such a thing exists), numerous comparisons are drawn from contexts both outside Latin America and outside the specific period under study.[8]

This volume is divided into four parts. Part I ("Banditry, Self-Fashioning, and the Quest for Legitimacy") analyzes the way in which two revolutionaries, at the beginning and at the end of the chronological arc that this book covers (roughly from the Mexican Revolution to the so-called Bolivarian Revolution), fashion their public images by embracing an outlaw past. On the one hand, Pancho Villa (1878–1923), in his *Retrato autobiográfico* (posthumously published), surprisingly embraces his prerevolutionary outlaw career in order to find, in that period of his life, not the negation of his revolutionary present, but its condition of possibility. Villa constructs himself as a "mirror of bandits," the social bandit par excellence, and his outlaw stint as the military, political, and cultural school for his revolutionary stint. This allows him to create a triple identification between himself, the People (defined in a sui generis fashion), and the Fatherland, to therefore erect himself as the only loyal and possible mediator between the just ruler (Madero) and the sovereign (the People). This is possible by a double appeal to the authority of literature. First, he recruited a traditional intellectual (Manuel Bauche Alcalde) who received his confidences and heavily edited the written version of those confidences. Second, Villa tapped into preexisting traditions (both written and oral) of bandit narratives.

Hugo Chávez (1954–2013), the second case to be studied in this section, legitimized his socialist agenda by highlighting, in speeches, interviews, and performances, that he was a descendant of a rural insurgent, Pedro Perez Delgado, also known as Maisanta (1881–1924), the so-called "last man on horseback." Maisanta was an outlaw and rebel from the *llanos* (Venezuela's legendary cattle frontier) who fought against the long dictatorship of General Gómez (1908–1935), the president responsible for creating the modern oil-dependent Venezuela. By highlighting this ancestry, Chávez linked himself to a lineage of "anti-imperialist" insurgents that dated back to the sixteenth century and the Indian rebellions against the Spaniards, through the llanero insurgents of the nineteenth century (in particular the popular Federalist leader Ezequiel Zamora). This lineage allowed him to construct an image of the "real" (and only) Venezuela, as one of the contenders in a prolonged conflict against "empire," a conflict that encompassed all the realms of the social. This strategy justified the mixture of legalism and exceptionalism that defined Chávez's presidency.

Part II ("Banditry and the Epic of the Nation") examines how the bandit trope played a significant role in the crafting of twentieth-century nationalism. *Las lanzas coloradas* (1931), by Antonio Uslar Pietri (1906–2001), is, together with Rómulo Gallegos's *Doña Bárbara* (1929), one of the most important Venezuelan (and arguably, Latin American) novels of the first half of the twentieth century. *Las lanzas* focuses on the 1813–1814 llanero insurgency and its deleterious effects on the Creole hacendado class, in order to construct a synthetic/dialectic version of the national subject and the national leader (Bolívar, as a synthesis of *mantuano* enlightenment and llanero martial prowess). The Mexican Rafael Muñoz (1899–1972), on the other hand, uses the Villista epic of 1913–1914 with a purpose that is similar, but only to a certain degree. He creates a version of a popular subject (the group of fighters called the Leones de San Pablo), but, at one point in the novel, he disassociates Villa from *Villismo*, thus uncoupling the popular leader from the popular subject, in order to create a narrative of the revolution congruent both with its myth of origin (as a peasant revolt) and with the triumph of the authoritarian faction to which Muñoz belonged. However, once the disassociation of Villa (and his loyal follower, Tiburcio) from the popular subject takes place, the novel ceases to be a war novel and it becomes a bandit novel. By "bandit," however, the novel means the ethical or epistemological distance between the man of letters (i.e., the American sergeant), his worldview, and the premodern rural warrior, incomprehensible, but an unavoidable presence.

The Peruvian Enrique López Albújar (1872–1966) takes yet another path in the concoction of a "popular" subject out of rural violent subjects. López Albújar is usually read (following the early indications of José Mariátegui) as either a precursor or a founder of literary indigenism, a condition that has ensured him a solid (albeit minor) place in Peruvian literary history. Perhaps López Albujar should be read as a writer of frontier adventure stories instead, in the line of Jack London, Bret Harte, or Guy de Maupassant and his short stories of Corsican theme. It is not that López Albújar did not have the "national problem" in mind. But instead of addressing banditry as part of what I will call "narratives of crisis," that is, symptoms or testimonies of the impossibility that Peru faced of coalescing into a cohesive nation, I argue that López Albújar tried to put together a sort of minor frontier epic, an Andean Western of sorts, in which the "Indian problem" (but not the Indian) disappears.

At the same time that López Albújar was writing *Cuentos andinos*, Jorge Luis Borges (whose work I examine initially in chapter 6) also had something of a minor epic in mind. Gauchos, *guapos,* and *orilleros* (the nomenclature is deliberately vague) were its main characters and Borges (1899–1986) developed a series of short stories in the 1930s and 1940s to that effect. But his case is vastly different from that of López Albújar. Borges had to contend with a well-established version of the gaucho as Argentina's epic hero, and thus he polemically deals not with national heroes, but with *malevos,* deserters, orilleros, runaways whose only luxury is an unblemished reputation of courage (a different kind of heroes, then, the so-called *cultores del coraje*). In order to do this, he intersects the illustrious epic with a minor product: Eduardo Gutiérrez's dime novels. Borges's minor epic (the term is deliberately a contradiction in terms) is also singular because, unlike the classic epic hero, who is one with his community and one with the epic law, Borges's men of courage experience their destiny as a burden, an invisible jail from which they will never escape (because that destiny is what they are). This is why I propose in this chapter the idea that Borges's tales of men of courage should be read as a melancholic epic, assessing both the political and the aesthetic value of the term.

Banditry and the politics and thought of the Left have a long, shared history. The bandit label was used as a badge of infamy to apply to leftist movements, assimilating one with the other. In other cases, the threat of leftist insurgency replaced banditry in the cultural imaginary, as well as in policy making (this is presented in narrative form in "Complot," a short story by the Chilean Lázaro Baeza). In other cases, for either derogatory or encomiastic purposes, a genetic relationship is posited, with banditry blooming into full-scale revolutionary war. This is the case with Eric Hobsbawm, whose whole theory of social banditry is predicated upon establishing a link between "prepolitical" peasant protest and full-fledged class struggle. Latin American Marxists were not absent from this debate. Part III ("Banditry and the Latin American Left") presents two (hopefully emblematic) case studies in order to show how Latin American writers of Marxist affiliation examined, in fictional form, and reflected upon an intellectual and political issue of utmost importance for the Latin American Left at the time: that of the revolutionary potential of the peasantry, and its relationship to the Communist Party and the modern Marxist intellectual in particular. This issue was always present in Marxist thought, especially in the cases of the Andean countries (witness, for example, Mariátegui's *Siete ensayos* [1928]) and in the context of the Mexican Revolution. But it acquired a renewed emphasis with the Chinese

Revolution and the Asian and African anticolonial wars from the 1940s on. I examine this in detail in the chapters on Jorge Amado (Brazil, 1912–2001) and José Revueltas (Mexico, 1914–1976). Even though both authors' points of departure are similar (both were party loyalists and two of the most important Marxist writers in Latin America), their conclusions are starkly divergent. Amado successfully incorporates premodern peasant outlawry into a narrative of the transformation of the premodern peasant into a modern rural proletarian, transformation that would herald, in his view, a modern Communist Party–led revolution. The opposite transformation occurs in Revueltas. The militant, fascinated by the power and moral authority of the outlaw (Ventura), "goes native." He does not abandon Marxism. He abandons Marxism as a set of dogmas, a defined vision of a comprehensible world, in favor of a hybrid version of Marxism as the gateway to an aesthetic/ethical revelation (of the sublime in the abject) infused with Christian motifs but devoid of any transcendentalism.

In the last part of the book ("Banditry and the Dilemmas of Literature") I consider how the bandit trope helps certain writers (Jorge Luis Borges, João Guimarães Rosa [1908–1967], Mario Vargas Llosa [1936–], and Ricardo Piglia [1941–2017]) to engage in a prolonged self-reflection on the epistemological and political limits and possibilities of literature as a cultural practice. As I mentioned earlier, this entire book is, in one way or another, about this. But in the works specifically analyzed here, this problem acquires another level of urgency, centrality, and self-awareness. João Guimarães Rosa's *Grande Sertão: Veredas* (1956), the best Brazilian novel of the century (possibly of all time), is our first case study. It is well known that the novel is a sort of cultural laboratory where all the trends, all the disparate aspects that compose Brazilian and Western cultural identity, appear. It is also well known that the novel is a sustained reflection on the nature of language (and national language) as well as a glimpse of an impossible, utopian language, made out of archaisms and neologisms, localisms and foreign words, anomalous constructions and quotes from the classics. This Babelic feat happens in the voice of a rural outlaw, the *jagunço* Riobaldo Tatarana, usually considered less a jagunço and more a synecdoche for the rural subject, the *comarca oral* (oral hinterland) (Pacheco 1992). This may be true. But it is not irrelevant that Riobaldo is an outlaw. He is not any *sertanejo* (inhabitant of the *sertão*, the rural hinterland) or just a more representative or colorful or recognizable sertanejo. The novel is a reflection on language, but on a particular aspect of language: its role as a vehicle of the law, and also the place where the law finds its limits. The possibility (or impossibility) of the pact with the devil (which is what allows Riobaldo to become a bandit chief) is the most extreme aspect of this. So perhaps the merit of my analysis is its attempt to link together the formal aspect and the thematic one, and what it means that this utopian language is the language of an outlaw, whose most important life event, the pact with the devil, happens outside of language (and hence may or may not have happened).

Chapter 6 has already explored how Borges crafted a melancholic epic to reignite the literary value of the gaucho and the orillero against both the liberal and the authoritarian state-centered nationalism of the 1920s–1940s. By doing this, he refashioned the images of the gaucho and the orillero in Argentine culture. In chapter 10, "Borges and Moreira: Inglorious Bastards," by contrast, I examine the "late" Borges (although some of the texts that I mention are from at least the 1940s). Borges, a staunch opponent of both Peronism and Marxism, revisits the topic of the gaucho malo. This revision is double. It is a critique, on the one hand, of nationalist populism (in particular, left-wing populism, influential in Peronism from the 1960s on), but also, and perhaps more decisively, of his own literature. Both aspects are presented emblematically in the short story "La noche de los dones," a rewriting of Eduardo Gutiérrez's *Juan Moreira* (1879) influenced by Borges's admiration for another of Gutiérrez's novels, *Hormiga Negra*. For Borges, the adoption of the orillero and the gaucho malo as centerpieces of his literature was both a political and an aesthetic mistake. One could call it willful blindness toward history. If in *El idioma de los argentinos* (1928) he affirmed that "the pampa and the slums [*suburbios*] are gods" and that "the future is the most secure, cherished possession of the Argentines," by the late 1940s he was able to sorely experience that the future was in fact an ominous reenactment of the past, and the telluric gods were not the gentle deities of a *locus amoenus*, but the bloody insatiable gods of a barbarian cult.

The shortsighted journalist who is the protagonist of Mario Vargas Llosa's *La guerra del fin del mundo* (1981) makes the same mistake. The journalist wants to be the Brazilian Oscar Wilde. If Dorian Gray, in search of unusual experiences and edgy thrills, went slumming, the journalist goes to the backlands embedded in the army charged with quashing the millenarian movement in Canudos, deep in the Bahian sertão. While there, he becomes separated from the army (which has been utterly routed by the jagunços), gets lost, and spends the war among the jagunços. There, the sought-for experience and the thrills indeed happen. But they are experiences, not of knowledge and enlightenment, but of blindness and loss; and the thrill is that of sheer terror, not of excitement. Paradoxically, it is in that loss that he finds the conditions of possibility for his future work, that he becomes a true twentieth-century writer. Just like in Guimarães Rosa, it is through an excursion (and an experience of loss) deep into the premodern sertão that modern literature is possible.

Journalists and bandits close the final section of the book. *Plata quemada*, the commercially successful (and controversial) 1997 novel by Ricardo Piglia, tells a story not of rural bandits, but of an urban gang of bank robbers (based on a true story). However, it is my contention that the novel stands (in Borgesian fashion, perhaps) as a revival of sorts of the nineteenth-century popular novels of gauchos malos. If *Respiración artificial* (1980), the novel that secured Piglia's place in the Latin America literary canon, was fashioned by Piglia as a twentieth-century *Facundo* (Domingo Faustino Sarmiento, 1845), *Plata quemada* was the twentieth-century *Juan Moreira*, a tale of outlaw resistance to the (post)modernizing leap of the 1990s, when it seemed that neoliberalism and the Pax Americana were here to stay.

Finally, the book's final chapter takes up some of the topics presented explicitly in the preamble and implicitly throughout the book. I present there a reflection on the always-elusive meaning of the word "bandit."

PART I

BANDITRY, SELF-FASHIONING, AND THE QUEST FOR LEGITIMACY

SPECULUM LATRONIS

On Villa's *Retrato autobiográfico*

Torn from the society of all he held dear on earth, the victim of secret ene-mies, and exiled from happiness, was the wretched Verezzi.

PERCY BYSSHE SHELLEY, *ZASTROZZI*

The question is, am I a monster, or am I myself a victim? And what if I am a victim?

RASKOLNIKOV IN DOSTOYEVSKY'S *CRIME AND PUNISHMENT*

And if the misfortune of my misadventures reaches that extreme, I will accept my role as a victim.... If my bad luck has me in jail, I have to endure it with patience, because that is the way humankind is. I was born to suffer in this world, but I was not born to be a traitor, and for this, I feel very happy; happy to the bottom of my heart.

PANCHO VILLA, LETTER TO ABRAHAM GONZÁLEZ,
FROM THE MEXICO CITY PENITENTIARY, NOVEMBER 7, 1912

THE REVOLUTIONARY STINT of Doroteo Arango Arámbula, also known as Pancho Villa (1878–1923), superbly exemplifies how the Mexican Revolution was a war fought not only on a military front, but on a discursive one as well. The now-fabled Northern Revolution's battlefields were the sierras and the plains. However, the arena of discourse was a battlefield that was less bloody but not less viciously disputed. On this battlefield, adversaries engaged each other not to occupy a city or to control a railway line, but to dispute an even more elusive target: legitimacy. Legitimacy meant local, national, and international recognition for oneself as a bona fide contender in a bona fide war—a *hostes* as opposed to a *latro*, conducting *bellum* as opposed to *latrocinium* (Grünewald [1999] 2004). Legitimacy also meant the capacity to define (or try to define) the enemy, not only as wrong and perhaps evil, but also as somebody of a lesser political, moral, and even ontological status: a usurper, a tyrant, a counterrevolutionary, a criminal, or (as happened to Villa) a bandit fighting for profit or to indulge an innate penchant for violence. The bandit label is still used in the context of civil wars—for instance, in Libya by the Qaddafi regime as well as initially in Syria by the Assad regime, or in the civil war in South Sudan—but the terrorist label enjoys a wider currency, to the point of having largely replaced the outlaw in the global imagination, even when in some cases, such as that of ISIL, "bandit" is a more appropriate label than "terrorist" since although ISIL is made up of global jihadists, and it has (just recently) started to carry out bona fide (i.e., Al-Qaeda-style) terrorist acts, it finances itself successfully through territorially based plundering and racketeering.[1] In Mexico, these two wars (the military and the discursive) were, of course, inextricably linked, although, while the first one largely ended in the 1920s, the second one took decades more to be resolved, as Ilene O'Malley (1986), Friedrich Katz (1998), Thomas Benjamin (2000), and Max Parra (2005), among others, have aptly shown.

Throughout the 1910s, Villa fought both wars doggedly, and in the end, he lost both. The measure of his defeat in his struggle for legitimacy was the impossibility of his shedding (until his posthumous rehabilitation, almost a half century after his death) his image as a bandit.[2] Francisco Villa was the name Arango had adopted sometime in the 1890s, for reasons that are still debated.[3] In his heyday, many hyperbolic variations accompanied his name. He was the Mexican Eagle, the Mexican Napoleon, the Centaur of the North, the Latin Sir Galahad (as the American secretary of state William Jennings Bryan put it), the south-of-the-border Robin Hood, and the avenger of the downtrodden Mexican peasant. However, these epic designations never completely obliterated the humbler "Doroteo Arango": cattle rustler, occasional highway, hacienda, and mine robber, and murderer (when necessary). Of course, Villa's enemies made sure that "Arango" never disappeared from sight. Álvaro Obregón, Villa's nemesis and vanquisher, consistently referred to him in public and in private, in written and oral form, as Arango (see, for example, Obregón's *Ocho mil kilómetros en campaña*), a gesture replicated by the factional literature written during Villa's life (e.g., John Kenneth Turner's *¿Quién es Pancho Villa?*) and after (e.g., Celia Herrera's *Pancho Villa ante la historia* and Rodrigo Alonso Cortéz's *Francisco Villa, el quinto jinete del Apocalipsis*).[4] This ambiguous reputation would enhance his visibility and his romantic appeal to this day, making him a feature of myriad movies, novels, *corridos*, and short stories (see Parra 2005). *Mutatis mutandis*, the Villa legend, is the closest thing there is in Latin America to a "Greenwood Matter" or an "Arthurian Matter" or a "Carolingian Matter": an ever-changing body of stories loosely anchored in an ever-receding historical reality that is increasingly difficult to discern from myth, and which is subject to unceasing political wrangling.

As Katz (1984) notes, this interest would also prevent, until quite recently, the serious historical study of Villismo as a social phenomenon. In addition, at many junctures in his revolutionary career, his reputation presented a significant, even insurmountable, obstacle to many of his goals or ambitions, and for decades (in fact, until the 1960s–1970s) it delayed his incorporation into the revolutionary pantheon (O'Malley 1986). Early on, Madero had to defend Villa in the international press, to fend off the charges directed against Villa—and by extension against him and his camp—in the Porfirian and American press. An important instance of this defense is the letter that Madero sent to the *El Paso Morning Times*, establishing a neat distinction between outlaw (avenger of the family honor and defender of the poor) and bandit (professional criminal). This defense created conflicts with several of Madero's early officers, and prompted complaints shortly after the revolution's triumph, when Villa returned to private life as an entrepreneur (Taibo [2006] 2010, 121). Orozco and his allies used the excuse of the (entirely imaginary) Villista threat to Chihuahua City to trigger the 1912 rebellion (133, 138). The reader will remember Villa's feud with Huerta, and his imprisonment and near execution on robbery charges. The bandit label was a ubiquitous motif in the Huertista press in 1913–1914, as well as the centerpiece of a well-orchestrated campaign by Carranza's intelligentsia aimed at discrediting Villa nationally and internationally (after the Villa/Carranza breakup, a time when U.S. recognition, linked to an essential supply of arms and logistical support, hung in the balance). Villa's reputation as bandit provided the crucial legal argument for justifying Pershing's 1915 Punitive Expedition. A nineteenth-century treaty allowed for the crossing of international borders in order to pursue marauders and Apaches; the treaty was revived to authorize a military intervention—disguised as a police operation—without violating Mexican territorial sovereignty, something that Carranza opposed and that was politically toxic. It also provided legal cover for the bloody counterinsurgency campaign waged against Villa by Francisco Murguía (made infamous by his policy of hanging Villista sympathizers from trees and leaving the corpses to rot under the public eye) and his successors. In fact, there was a reward on Villa's head, dead or alive.

Villa's status as a bandit was one of the main sticking points at the time of the 1920 peace negotiations between Villa and President Adolfo de la Huerta. Obregón steadfastly opposed peace with a bandit (Taibo [2006] 2010, 762). Villa, on the other hand, refused a pardon, which entailed an assumption of guilt for a crime, and he demanded an armistice, with its implicit assumption of equal status between the contenders.[5] Nonetheless, Villa was never able to shed his bandit image and he acknowledged this defeat with good humor. A couple of days after the peace agreement had been signed, Villa and his companions and escorts made a stop in San Pedro de las Colonias, the former site of one of the battles of the División del Norte in its southward thrust to dislodge Huerta from power. A group of Mexican and American journalists were waiting for him. The journalists pressed him for a statement about the momentous occasion: peace (that was the hope, at least) after a decade of uninterrupted and increasingly vicious fighting. Villa replied, "Well, you can say through the press that the war is over, and that the bandits"—pointing at himself—"and the honest men"—looking all around him—"are all mixed up [revueltos]" (Jaurrieta 2009, 229). One could read this as a good example of self-effacing folk humor. But it can also be read as the exact reversal of Díaz's resignation. Both cases are simultaneously an admission of defeat and also the deliberate effort to locate that defeat in an impossible-to-decide terrain that lowers a veil of doubt upon the act that is taking place or has just taken place (just like Díaz, who did not decide whether the subject of the revolution was the sovereign People or criminal armed millenarian gangs).

Revueltos means mixed up with an undistinguishable mass. The war, and each camp in the war, aspired to keep bandits and honest revolutionaries apart. Now they were one and the same. The peace process (i.e., the final enactment of the Constitution of 1917, and the reconstruction of the Mexican state under Obregón) was to be predicated upon this lack of distinction of which a number of dissident intellectuals of the 1920s and 1930s, such as José Vasconcelos and Martín Luis Guzmán, were acutely aware. Vasconcelos's *La tormenta* and Guzmán's *El águila y la serpiente*, which flatly equated the triumphant Sonoran faction with a gangster state, are perfect examples. Carranza's only enduring contribution to the Spanish language, notes Guzmán, was the coinage of the word *carrancear*: to plunder and to conduct extortion as the main goal of a military operation/occupation—a charge amply corroborated by both anecdotal and historical testimonies. Carranza's generals (including those, like Mungía, in charge of chasing the "bandit" Villa) were (in)famous for blatant greed. Emblematic (but not unique) in narrative fiction is Artemio Cruz, the Carrancista officer turned tycoon in Carlos Fuentes's eponymous novel. So Villa accepted his defeat, but with the caveat that bandits were now ubiquitous, revueltos with everybody else.

Villa's damaging reputation did not materialize out of thin air. He was indeed a cattle smuggler and robber from the mid-1890s until Abraham González recruited him in late 1910. Many questions, however, remain unanswered. First of all, what was the true extent and nature of his bandit activities? Villa himself claims that he was a famous outlaw, well known in at least Chihuahua and Durango before 1910, and that he was the scourge of Porfirian-era law enforcement. (Madero, in the aforementioned letter to the El Paso newspaper, seems to subscribe to this, thus giving credibility to what Katz [1998, 2–4] has called the "epic legend.") The archival evidence for it, however, seems to be scant, and is not always consistent with this judgment. Villa seems to have been more of a minor outlaw, and not the epic figure he pretended to be (Katz 1998, 64). It also seems that his relationship with the law was much more fluid than he admitted. He was in the employment of several American and English businessmen as a trusted leader of men, and Katz has uncovered evidence that, as late as 1910, Villa petitioned the authorities on the matter of some restitution of property (including his guns). This was hardly the attitude of a hunted fugitive.

The second question that comes to the fore is, what did it mean to be a bandit in that area, and at that time? Much like in other cattle frontiers before and after (i.e., the Venezuelan llanos, the Argentina pampas, and the Brazilian northeastern *sertão*), both Chihuahua and Durango comprised vast expanses of unfenced land devoted to extensive cattle ranching. The ownership of both the land and the cattle was heavily disputed since much of the land had been recently appropriated by the landed elite at the expense of the independent peasants who had been former allies (of the same elite) in the fight against the common enemy: the Apache. (The better-known case is the appropriation, by the Terrazas clan, of land granted to the military colonies in Chihuahua, from peasants who had been Terrazas's clients and protégés during the Apache wars.) This conflict over land and over the autonomy of erstwhile military colonies was one of the factors that made Chihuahua into the "cradle of the Revolution" (Katz 1998). So, even though it seems indisputable that Villa took and slaughtered cattle not bearing his mark (he himself had no mark during those years), or bearing no mark at all, to call this "theft" is at least contestable (30). Furthermore, even though in many rural societies theft is more serious an offense than murder, to take cattle claimed by large landowners may have elicited sympathy among many in the rural North (including commercial entrepreneurs, who benefited from the brisk smuggling of cattle toward the United States, where cattle was in high demand).

And a final question arises: how did Villa's outlaw past influence his revolutionary career? His time riding in the sierra was the school where he acquired his marksmanship, his horsemanship, and his extended network of contacts, as well as his unsurpassed knowledge of the land. But how did this experience influence his military strategies, his political consciousness, his behavior toward prisoners, civilians, foreigners, and the elite? To his enemies (and his enemies were legion) Villa never ceased to be a mere bandit. At best, they considered him a profiteering bandit, a condottieri, or a provocateur, in the pay of either the Germans or the Americans working in the shadows (for different reasons) toward a new Mexican-American war.[6] At worst, he was considered a phenomenon (either a bizarre development—a monster—or a symptom, an expression of a given state of affairs, i.e., the oppression of the Porfiriato). As a phenomenon, he could act, but he could not express himself (i.e., acquire consciousness of his situation in history, or of the larger implications of his actions). Some of Villa's former supporters can be counted in this camp; a prime example is Martín Luis Guzmán, who was never a follower, even though he wrote two of the most important books on Villa (the aforementioned *El águila y la serpiente* and *Memorias de Pancho Villa* [1936–1951]).

Villa's more unequivocal supporters, on the other hand, deny any connection between these two periods in Villa's life. Pérez Rul and Nellie Campobello deny that he was ever a bandit; like Madero, they draw a fine distinction between outlaw and bandit. This last debate also permeates contemporary scholarship. On the one hand, there are those who read Villa's career through the prism of his bandit identity. Perhaps the most prominent among them is Alan Knight. As a political program, Villismo in government was for Knight "institutionalized social banditry: a regime weak on ideology and studied 'structural' reform, but strong on generous gestures and hand-outs, and thus a regime enjoying genuine popularity and relying on legitimacy more than coercion" ([1986] 1990, 2:125). Knight explains Villa's military strategy (and in particular his fatal flaws in the 1915 battles of Celaya and León) as the limitations of a regional guerrilla fighter confronting a general with a modern, national outlook and up-to-date military tactics (in particular, the newly developed trench warfare, which proved fatal to Villa's signature cavalry charges). Finally, Knight considers Villa's actions in Mexico City in 1914, as well as the increasingly bloody turn the war took after 1915, a reversion to his "true" bandit identity.

On the other hand, there are those who vigorously argue that Villa's outlaw past did not project into his revolutionary career. Katz is a prominent figure in this camp. According to Katz (1998), prior to 1910 Villa was a bandit *among many other things*. In a frontier society such as Chihuahua at the turn of the century, there were many occupations for a man of strength, contacts, and resources, and the limit between the law and outlawry was blurred for all, including the members of the cattle, mining, and commercial elite who hired Villa for various assignments. Katz also points out that from 1910 to 1914 Villa's army was (when compared to other armed factions) a model of discipline, organization, and deportment, and that the excesses in which he and some of his officers indulged from late 1914 on (i.e., bloody retaliation, extortion, execution of prisoners) were behaviors not exclusive to Villa and his followers, but symptoms of a universal degradation of social bonds after more than five years of continuous civil war. When Villa started charging protection to miners, in order to allow for continuous operation and transport, he was not reverting to "old ways," but rather was developing new tactics to finance the survival of his military enterprise, when other streams of revenue had dried up or had become impossible. So this last question is perhaps unanswerable, and the debate will likely go on. But Villa himself was not indifferent to it. His own intervention in this debate is the topic of the remainder of this chapter.[7]

As a testimony of this discursive battle, there is perhaps no text as important as *Pancho Villa: Retrato autobiográfico, 1894–1914*. Autobiographies and testimonial narratives by outlaws of all stripes (*sicarios*, guerrilla fighters, *narcos*) have since become a fashionable genre. But at the time they were a rarity: most outlaws in Latin America were complete or functional illiterates (Villa wasn't—but in spite of the favorable picture that Dumas paints of Luigi Vampa as a erudite bandit, this was exceptional). If not, they lacked continuous or even regular access to media outlets or to intellectuals willing and able to engage with "their side" of the story. And unlike in the United States, there was not a strong journalistic industry only beholden to the reading (and buying) public that could make the lurid stories into best-selling items.

Even though the *Retrato* cannot be considered an autobiography (and many questions about the text are still unanswered), it is one of Villa's (very mediated) intended interventions in the dispute. (Other forms of intervention were the interviews that Villa granted, the movie on which he collaborated, the work of intellectuals affiliated with him, and, very importantly, the letters that Villa sent to Madero, which I have mentioned in the preamble.)[8] *Pancho Villa: Retrato autobiográfico* is the facsimile and transcription of the five notebooks penned by Manuel Bauche Alcalde (1881–1929), a journalist, literary and drama critic, and officer in the Federal Army turned Maderista, then (briefly) Villista, then Carrancista.[9] The notebooks record a number of meetings between Bauche Alcalde and Villa,[10] which took place during either January or February of 1914,[11] and during the sessions (it is not clear how many there were, or who came up with the idea of the dictation), Villa gave an account of his life, from his becoming an outlaw to 1914. Guadalupe Villa (2004, 25), following Bauche Alcalde's own statement, maintains that Bauche Alcalde persuaded Villa to dictate his memoirs. However, Bauche Alcalde arrived at the Villa headquarters in December 1913, according to Aguirre Benavides (1964, 89). Guadalupe Villa proposes an even later date of February 1914. It is not altogether clear how a new arrival in the Villista camp could have been trusted with the sensitive task of crafting Villa's public image. This transition from newcomer to confidant remains to be elucidated. José Vasconcelos knew Bauche Alcalde when they were both youngsters in Piedras Negras. He explains that his position in Villista circles was due to his being from Mexico City. Vasconcelos states, derisively, "[Bauche Alcalde] could pass as a writer among the uneducated groups of [northern] revolutionaries . . . only because, being from the South, he had an average level of education [*cultura mediana*] and he had fashioned himself as a leader in a land of the blind" ([1937] 2000, 57).

The manuscript's prologue makes clear that it was intended for publication. But it remained in manuscript form during both Villa's and Bauche Alcalde's lifetimes, even though it was known before its publication and was referred to and used by several scholars, journalists, and writers, such as Elías Torres (*Vida y hechos de Pancho Villa*, 1975), Ramón Puente (*Villa en pie*, 1935), and Federico Cervantes (*Francisco Villa y la revolución*, 1959), among others. The most important writer to put the manuscript to use was Martín Luis Guzmán, who used it as a partial source for his *Memorias de Pancho Villa*. *Pancho Villa: Retrato autobiográfico* was eventually published in 2003.[12]

Villa's account should be read as a literary artifact. It is an intervention that is fully consistent with Villa's needs at that unique moment: the zenith of Villa's military prestige and achievements after the battle of Torreón and right before the battle of Zacatecas, his most celebrated one, which dealt the final blow to Huerta's regime—and sealed his break with Carranza. I mentioned that Villa's war was both military and discursive. Villa was obviously more than able to take care of the first one, but he needed a coherent document, crafted in literary form, by a man of letters (albeit a minor one like Bauche Alcalde), to effectively intervene in the second one. Villa was indeed in sore need of asserting his revolutionary credentials. Even though he was one of the earliest armed revolutionaries and even though he played a crucial role in the military defeat of the Federal Army in both 1911 and 1913–1914, he had no prerevolutionary credentials as a leader of a military colony, as a labor organizer (even though he worked as a miner and as a mason), or as a member of the anti-reelection movement. Therefore his undeniable military prowess was not embedded (or anchored) in a preexisting narrative that would unequivocally distinguish his actions from that of a profiteering bandit or a successful mercenary. He thus had to fashion an insurgent narrative

to socialize his pre-1910 actions and establish a strong link between outlaw
and revolutionary, precisely at the moment, and for the same reasons, that
his opponents wanted to emphasize the mutual exclusion between these two
forms of nonstate violence.[13] Villa acknowledges (in fact embraces) his violent
bandit past, thus conceding this crucial point of the argument to his enemies.
But at the same time that he acknowledges it, he also decisively challenges
what it means to be a bandit. In particular, Villa challenges the relationship
between banditry and revolution. When addressed from this point of view,
the narrative exhibits remarkable consistency and a clear totalizing impulse.
Villa not only presented himself as a noble bandit; he presented himself as *the*
noble bandit, as a sort of living compendium of noble bandit motifs, motifs
embedded in a unique narrative framework.

The manuscript claims to give us Villa's true voice and the true account
of his life—something that many claim to have done since the early 1910s,
usually for either political or commercial reasons. This text is perhaps closer
to (but is still impossibly far from) that elusive target. Bauche Alcalde heavily
overwrote Villa's words during the interviews, not always felicitously. There
are a number of easily noticeable editorial inconsistencies,[14] contradictions,
and elisions.[15] But the main challenge is to decide whether it is necessary to
engage in the arduous (and ultimately impossible) task of trying to fully discern what "belongs" to Villa from what "belongs" to Bauche Alcalde.[16]

Faced with this challenge, there are at least three options. One is to gloss
over these problems and to claim that "this is Villa" at last (something which,
to a degree, Taibo [2006] 2010 does). Another option is to dismiss the text
entirely as yet another concoction by a second-rate intellectual looking to
score a commercial success on the coattails of Villa's feats—and the lack of
strong scholarly interest in the text so far seems to suggest that this is the
choice of most academics, although this assessment may be proven wrong or
premature. A last option would be to argue that, although disparate in many
ways, both "voices" display a remarkable consistency of purpose, and that both
should be evaluated at this level, but not for truthfulness. This is Friedrich
Katz's understanding. He examines the text (still in manuscript form in 1998,
when Katz's monumental *The Life and Times of Pancho Villa* appeared) less
as a source of historical information and more as cornerstone of the "white
legend" on Villa (Katz 1998, 5). Three decades earlier, Hobsbawm (who read
Guzmán's book, which, as I mentioned, used the memoirs) had also referred

in passing to Villa's self-fashioning as his "robin-hoodization,"[17] and went on to compare Villa's self-Robin-Hoodization to that of Salvatore Giuliano, the Sicilian bandit ([1969] 2000, 151).[18]

Following this line of analysis, these pages will examine Villa's text as an intervention in the then-ongoing debate on Villa himself, a counternarrative whose goal was to legitimate his position as the very embodiment of the northern popular revolution and not as a regrettable anomaly that polluted the entire movement. Villa tried to accomplish this not by rejecting the accusations of banditry, but by fully embracing his outlaw past. Significantly, the bulk of the text is devoted to the outlaw years, while it could have been devoted to his far less problematic revolutionary years. Not only does Villa make this outlaw past compatible with his revolutionary present, but he also makes this past the very condition of possibility for his legitimation. Since it is impossible to fully discern Villa from Bauche Alcalde, I would like to emphasize a distinction: there is Pancho Villa, commander in chief of the Northern Division of the Constitutionalist Army, who, during some irretrievable days in the winter of 1914, dictated his memoirs to Manuel Bauche Alcalde. And then there is "Pancho Villa," the textual figure who is a composite of Pancho Villa's and Bauche Alcalde's voices. In what follows, I will be referring to the textual figure, in its triple (and problematic) nature as author, narrator, and character of the *Retrato*, unless it is otherwise obvious that I am talking about the historical figure.

First-person accounts by former rural outlaws, featuring a "strategic use of the truth," are not unheard of. Some of the best-known examples in Latin America are the letters written by Manuel García, the Cuban outlaw, published in Cuban newspapers (Poumier-Taquechel 1986; Perez 1989), as well as the famous interview given by Lampião in Juazeiro, in which he (like Villa, as we will see) mourns the bad turn that his life has taken, and justifies his actions as revenge for his father's killing during a feud in the backlands of Pernambuco.[19] Like Villa, Lampião gave the interview at the peak of his career—1927—when he had been commissioned to fight the Prestes Column on behalf of the government forces and the state landowners. (He was issued an honorary military degree, as well as arms and munitions, and thus came closer to respectability than he had ever been before or would be after.[20])

One could also mention the testimonial narrative of the slave, turned runaway slave, turned bandit, turned revolutionary Esteban Montejo (*Biografía*

de un cimarrón, 1968, dictated to and edited by Miguel Barnet), who spends
a significant amount of his narrative reconciling those not-always-compati-
ble stints, and explaining away some dubious (but most surely unavoidable)
associations and behaviors. Finally, as yet another example, one could think
of Cipriano Benítez, a 1820s montonero in Buenos Aires Province (whose
depositions before the law are superbly presented and analyzed in Fradkin
[2006]), who engaged in rather subtle discursive strategies to change the
definition of *montonera* from that of a *gavilla de salteadores* (gang of highway
robbers) to that of a full political body acting on behalf of the Federalist cause.
But perhaps the example that comes closest to Villa's case can be found in
the United States, in the history of collaboration between Jesse James and
John Newman Edwards, founder of the *Kansas City Times*. Newman was a
major in the Confederate Army who briefly fled to Mexico following General
Jo Shelby. When he returned, he became a vocal defender of the cause of the
former Confederacy in local Missouri politics. As part of that effort, he was a
staunch advocate for James (he published, edited, and, it has been suggested
in some cases, authored letters by James), portraying him not as a bandit, but
as a Confederate insurgent, a victim of the North's perceived brutality and
arrogance (Stiles 2002). In any case, the fascination with the "real voice" of
the bandit runs deep in Western culture.

In order to turn his bandit years into the foundation of his revolutionary
career, "Villa" frames the narrative in a particular way. He narrates his bandit
years as part of a melodramatic plot, a story guided mainly by moral and sentimental imperatives, in which the characters and situations are distributed
without ambiguity and without possibility for change in one of two morally
(not necessarily politically) defined camps. In this melodramatic plot, destiny
(i.e., the "cosmic" interplay of forces as enacted in human destinies) is more
important than history. It is, in fact, history's engine. Villa commits many acts
in the *Retrato*: he shoots and robs and rides and helps and leads armies to
victory. However, at another level (the "moral occult" that Brooks [1976] mentions), he is a character devoid of agency. He *has* to act when *forced* to do so,
and he spends his life as an innocent victim chased by an inimical destiny that
gives him no quarter. This destiny assumes the forms of persecution, treason,
and temptation. The presentation of Villa as victim allows the articulation of
his individual story with the history of the people and that of the fatherland (*la*

patria). Villa (as I will explain later) is a representative; he is a *speculum latronis*, but not because he is a champion of his community against the oppressors, but rather because he is, to an extreme degree, a victim of those same oppressors. He represents himself not as the depository of trust, but as the equal of other downtrodden peasants, through the trope of victimization.

The weapons that the melodramatic character has at his disposal emerge from a strict (and unavoidable) adherence to the prescriptions of the moral code of the rural community. They are the defense of female honor as the cornerstone of a male's persona, and a moral economy of violence (never to kill, unless provoked or betrayed; never to kill treacherously; never to kill when enjoying numerical superiority). The same code defines rules for robbery (never to rob to enrich oneself, never to rob poor folk unless imperative, never to rob violently unless provoked), and it also defines a sense of horizontal solidarity (to help and to be helped by the rural folk), loyalty beyond measure and beyond calculation to both his equals and to the just sovereign (Madero), and a complete trust in the *oral* alliance, in particular with the just sovereign. This alliance is moral and affective, not political or economic. As part of that loyalty to the sovereign, Villa is the mediation (the living link) between the sovereign and the rural folk, as well as the avenger, following the betrayal and death of the true sovereign (Madero, who was deposed and killed by Huerta).

Allow me to explain how this plays out. The *Retrato* is, from a certain viewpoint, disappointing. It certainly does not provide what Villa aficionados expect and want. How could this be? Villa is one of the most colorful characters in Latin American history. Both his personal and his military lives were full of events that are the seeds of legend. His horsemanship, his marksmanship, his wild moods and his staunch loyalty, his bravery, his feats of cunning in and outside of battle, his moments of military brilliance as well as his phenomenal blunders, his uncanny knowledge of the terrain, his almost preternatural memory, his womanizing: all of these make for a larger-than-life persona. Furthermore, his life still harbors mysteries seemingly taken out of a nineteenth-century serial novel. Are there any money or arms—of the many hidden caches that Villa had—still out there? Who was the secret mastermind behind his assassination? Who stole his head from his grave? Where is it now? How many wives (and offspring) did he really have (Villa was an unapologetic polygamist)? What really happened on that fateful afternoon of 1894 that began his story? Why did he really attack Columbus? Was some foreign power behind this attack?

The *Retrato*, however, does not read, as it could have read, as an adventure story, as do other historical or fictional autobiographies of outlaws. It does not have the cynical bravado and jubilant cruelty of the (supposed) autobiography of the Afghani outlaw Bachchah-i Saqaw, writing as the self-styled Amir Habibullah (*From Brigand to King: Autobiography of Amir Habibullah*), who describes, with glee, the original method that he devised for impaling his enemies (or the victims of his extortions). The *Retrato* does not feature the colorful events and the staunch self-assurance of the autobiography by Greek klepht Theodoros Kolokotrōnēs (*Memoirs from the Greek War of Independence, 1821–1833*),[21] or the unrepentant brashness of the supposed Indian thug informant in *Confessions of a Thug*, by Philip Meadows Taylor (who narrates murders as jokes), or the ethnographical wealth, local color, and mixture of insight and mean-spiritedness of *Biografía de un cimarrón*. It is not the ribald (and sometimes nightmarish) story of *My Confession*, by Samuel Chamberlain, war veteran and scalp hunter in the infamous Glanton Gang, the text upon which Cormac McCarthy based perhaps the best bandit novel ever written, *Blood Meridian*.[22]

Horses, in particular Siete Leguas, Villa's better-known mare, are not mentioned in the *Retrato*, even though, as "the "Centaur of the North," Villa's military legend was based on the cavalry charge and almost unbelievable feats of horse-enabled mobility. (In the *Retrato* there are no episodes like Dick Turpin's "Ride to York," in which Black Bess, Turpin's mare, played a crucial role [Sharpe (2004) 2005, 157].) There are some "trickster" episodes (a staple of bandit narratives), but again, there is no decided emphasis on this aspect at all.[23] There is nothing in the *Relato* about Villa's relationships with women, either, even though Villa (like John Gay's Macheath, in *The Beggar's Opera*) was a famous womanizer and a polygamist. The only woman of any significance in the narrative—after the mention of the assault on his sister, who appears in the narrative not as a person, but as an object to be debased or defended in an all-male conflict—is his mother.[24] The explanation may be straightforward. At a time when Villa was striving for respectability in the nation-state as a military general, he was likely hoping to distance himself (at least in this particular medium, a book) from these more picaresque aspects of banditry in order to focus on the moral ones.

Indeed, Villa's autobiography reads like a melodrama. It is a mostly dis-jointed (i.e., episodic) and repetitive tale in which a suffering hero (Villa) recounts, from the vantage point of maturity and wisdom, his early travails at the hands of a ubiquitous, evil, and capricious power bent on persecution and exploitation. The narrative begins, "The tragedy of my life begins on September 22, 1894, when I was sixteen years old" (Francisco Villa 2004, 75). Villa was then a hardworking, entrepreneurial teenager who, upon returning to his humble abode, found Don Agustín López Negrete trying to force himself upon Villa's sister.[25] In the ensuing scuffle he shot (but did not kill) the offender. He fled and took to the hills, and became a robber and cattle rustler. In spite of all his efforts to resume an honest life, he continued to be persecuted in Durango and Chihuahua, until 1910 when he was recruited by Abraham González to fight for the revolutionary cause.

As a result of the unyielding persecution by the Durango and Chihuahua landed elite he was forced to kill a number of people: Rurales, informants, traitors, and vigilantes. "Herdsman, huntsman, bandit, general" (*pastor, venator, latro, dux*), the various stages of Villa's career, mirror those of Viriatus, the archetypal bandit-turned-epic-hero, as narrated by Roman historians (Grünewald [1999] 2004, 36). But while Viriatus's story was an epic, and hence Viriatus became a mirror into which the Roman emperor could look at himself, and perhaps find himself lacking,[26] Villa narrates a tragedy. Not because it is a sad story (although Villa states that the life of the outlaw is a life of misfortune), but because it is unavoidable: the surrendering of the tragic hero to the power of destiny, between the rock of elite abuse and the hard place of an ironclad, uncompromising moral code. Villa's tale is not one of "becoming what he always was" but rather one of the unending travails of a reluctant hero (in which he becomes who he is, but reactively, so to speak).

The offense upon masculine honor, through the mediation of the female body, by a rich or powerful man (state official, landowner, military officer), an offense that forces the young male to shed blood and later to take to the bush (*prendre le maquis, darsi alla macchia*) is a classic motif of bandit narratives. There are abundant examples: Joaquín Murieta's wife is gang-raped by Anglo miners intent on scaring Murieta away from his claim (*The Life and Adventures of Joaquín Murieta*, by Yellow Bird); Demetrio Macías's wife is the victim of unwelcome sexual advances by a federal officer (*Los de abajo*, by Mariano Azuela); Juan Moreira's wife Vicenta is lusted after by Don Francisco, the *teniente alcalde*, and becomes the cause of a feud that will end in death (*Juan Moreira*, by Eduardo Gutiérrez); Cruz's wife willingly or grudgingly cheats on him with the local judge (*El gaucho Martín Fierro*, by José Hernández); Fiero Vásquez's wife Gumercinda is gang-raped by the *gendarmes* (*El mundo es ancho y ajeno*, by Ciro Alegría); Zárate's mother dies after being abused by Bustillón (*Zárate*, by Eduardo Blanco).[27] Villa (like all of the aforementioned characters) *had* to retaliate or he would have lost all honor, and hence all identity—he would have been condemned to the ghostly existence of the *coronel* Custódio, the landowner in José Lins do Rêgo's *Cangaceiros* (1953), who fails to exact bloody revenge for the death of his only son, and who lives the rest of his life as a brooding shadow, obsessively going back to the point where his life went wrong. As Pitt-Rivers reminds us for the Andalusian (and the larger Mediterranean) case, he who has lost his honor has "no shame" and his social identity is irrevocably damaged, nullified: "Structurally the opposite of the bandit, he is within the law but beyond the pale, as far as the 'moral community' goes" (Pitt-Rivers [1954] 1971, 185).[28]

Tragedy, I have said, names the ineluctable destiny of Villa. But at the same time, tragedy is another name for corrido (or, more strictly, for a type of corrido). Thus, in the *Retrato*, tragedy means both the moment in which Villa's suffering begins and the moment in which his life becomes narratable according to a well-known narrative pattern. This is not to say that Villa's narrative was consciously modeled after corridos. But Villa was indeed aware of the *corridos de bandidos* and their potential for constructing an insurgent narrative—as shown, for example, in Puente (1919). But bandits (particularly when mingled with larger insurgencies) were often aware of the nuances of public perception and the effects it could have upon their careers. Jonathan Wild, the famous English outlaw, was found to have (and to have read) books on bandits (Fielding [1743] 2010, 247); Billy the Kid was an avid reader of chapbooks featuring bandit stories (Utley 1989, 29); Jesse James was a contemporary of chapbooks devoted to his own story, a fact that he exploited to pursue his own career. Legend has it that Antônio Silvino, the Brazilian cangaceiro, commissioned popular poets to write poems to sing of his feats, as it is said that contemporary Mexican and Colombian narcos do. This resonates in *Los trabajos del reino*, by Yuri Herrera, the story of a "court poet" who composes *narcocorridos* for "the King."

In any case, the offense against masculine honor is a defining event in Villa's narrative. But this poses more questions than answers. First, its verisimilitude is dubious. How was Villa able to gain access to a *hacendado* while carrying a weapon (not even his own weapon), when five of López Negrete's bodyguards were in the immediate vicinity (Francisco Villa 2004, 80)? Why was Villa not killed on the spot after shooting the hacendado? Why was he allowed to leave the scene unimpeded? In addition to these internal inconsistencies, there are other versions of the event, either narrated by Villa to others or circulated by others around him, that contradict or correct the one in the *Retrato*.[29] And, in fact, it is unknown whether the assault happened in the first place.[30]

Whatever the truth of the episode, its goal is beyond doubt. It frames the conflict in moral terms, above ethnic, cultural, or class-based ones.[31] By disrespecting the Arangos' household, the hacendado violates the patrimonial compact of the hacienda. It appeals to the well-known familial-sexual narrative that Sommer (1991) famously dubbed the "national romance." The attempted rape is the opposite of the romance, of course: if love is a form of naturalization of the cultural makeup of the aspirational nation and its possible integration, rape is a naturalization of the conflicts that make the nation impossible.

But Villa's sister is only an extension of Villa's honor; the narrative forgets her almost immediately. The real victim of the assault is Villa. This, and the persecution that ensues (we do not know if López Negrete continued his lusting after Martina), allows for a double identification: Villa as representative of the People, and Villa as representative of the Patria. This double identification is posited (in the abstract) in the prologue written by Bauche Alcalde ([1914] 2004). But it becomes forged into Villa's image as a direct consequence of the assault. Villa can be a representative of the People. But not like Díaz, who fashioned himself as a delegate, a trustee—as we saw in the message of resignation referenced in the preamble of this book—or as a stern leader. Villa posits himself as a fellow victim. His predicament resonates with that of the fatherland, because Mexico's founding trope (that of La Malinche) is the original scene of seduction/rape of the innocent female by the powerful male (and the arc of continuity between Spanish conquerors and Porfirian elites is posited and emphasized in the *Retrato*). The trope of victimization (emblematized in the

sexual victimization) is thus an "anchor signifier" that allows Villa to construct a larger identity defined by violence—not as violence delivered (Villa as
either a noble warrior or an ignoble wild beast), but first as violence suffered.[32]

A hopefully enlightening comparison can be made with another autobiography ([1867] 1888) of another Centaur (in this case not of the sierra, but of the
plains), José Antonio Páez (1790–1873). At the same age that Villa was when
he had the scuffle with the hacendado that would mark his destiny, Páez had
his own "coming of age" moment. In 1807, his mother sent him from Guama
to Patio Grande, carrying some papers and a considerable sum of money to a
lawyer in the latter location. While he was crossing Mayuripí Mountain, four
highwaymen who knew about the money and who clearly thought that the
youngster was easy pickings, jumped him. But Páez shot and killed the leader
of the gang, and, armed only with an old sword, charged the three remaining
bandits and made them flee. In spite of his efforts to keep the episode under
wraps, he was soon identified as the hero of the day. Both Villa and Páez enter
adulthood as defenders of the family (either female honor or prized posses-
sions). But Páez does it as a hero who stands his ground against bandits. Villa
does it as a victim, who himself had to become a bandit.

The trope of victimization operates by saturation (i.e., repetition). Villa
never fully accepts his life as an outlaw. He wants to leave it and rejoin society
as a productive member (this is one of the key features of the noble bandit
theme), but time and again the violence of the rich and their arm—that is, the
state—forces him to go back to crime: he tries his hand as a tanner, as a miner,
as a mason, as a butcher. Each and every time, his relentless persecutors catch
up to him and force him to flee his newfound peace (Francisco Villa 2004, 107,
109, 113, 114, 121, 203). Villa was not born a leader; he had to become one in
the school of suffering of the outlaw life. Thus, the link Villa-nation-father-
land excludes (and opposes) the nation-state (the creature of the Porfirian
era), either as the origin or as the point of articulation (not necessarily as its
ultimate goal) of a "popular" identity, and it is not a given. In the *Retrato*, popular identity and consciousness are not immemorial, as in the primordialist
nineteenth-century version, but created during and by Villa's outlaw stint.
This is why Villa emphasizes, ad nauseam, the (much discussed, at the theoretical level) bandit-peasant link.[33] Since the thrust of the entire narrative
is to present the outlaw as a moral subject, outlawry has to be described as a
moral lifestyle embedded in a larger moral community.

But while in many versions of the myth, the community precedes the bandit, in the *Retrato*—much like in the Robin Hood stories—the community and the outlaw come into being at the same time. Outlawry becomes the origin and locus of a community that can be easily equated with the national community as *formed from below* (not as in the aforementioned Porfirian narrative, in which the People is created from the top, as an artifact of the state [see the preamble]). Villa's criminal feats are always narrated in a vague fashion. This imprecision contrasts with the precision with which Villa describes the support (in the form of supplies, information, and refuge) that he gives to and receives from his *compadres*, relatives, and friends.[34] The examples are too numerous to mention. Suffice it to say that even though Villa emphasizes his isolation as victim, his bandit stint was never "his," but part of a larger collective *modus vivendi*, guided not by the perspective of shared gain, but by the cultural and moral bond of shared values. The opposite of this moral community is the Porfirian elite. Using a well-known reversal (common from Roman times to socialist and anarchist literature) the Porfirian elite is dubbed the true (i.e., nonsocial) criminal organization, the real bandit gang, thus enacting, against the elite, the divorce of law from legitimacy.[35] Rural popular outlawry is contrasted to "patrician" banditry, whose organized form is the Porfirian state and its associates: the church and the political, legal, and financial classes (Francisco Villa 2004, 89, 122, 124, 127, 128).[36]

The meaning of Villa's robberies depends on this identification. He has no misgivings about stealing, since these acts are not considered robberies *stricto sensu* but acts of reparation governed by a strict moral economy. This is central to Villa's attempt to become the emblematic social bandit, as is the fact that Villa conflates his own image with the four varieties of social bandit proposed by Hobsbawm ([1969] 1981): the avenger, the noble robber, the expropriator, and the haiduk (with the addition of "trickster" features, one category that Hobsbawm does not mention in his famous book).[37] However, Villa takes pains to justify property's changing hands. He never robs in order to get rich, or out of pure greed. He robs out of necessity, or to settle a score (as negative reciprocity [Blok 1983]), or to help the community. In the particular case of cattle rustling (Villa's main activity), there is a defined "politics of naming" (Bhatia 2005). Villa was a cattle rustler and a dealer in stolen cattle meat. When talking about appropriating cattle, he never says "to steal," but rather appeals to a metonymical displacement: he refers to the slaughter of the cows and the selling of their by-products, but not to the origin of the cattle (Francisco Villa 2004, 87, 98, 102). When robbery has to be given its name, it is always presented as a means to a moral end. The young Villa has to steal a number of mules, for example, but exclusively as a test to which Parra (the bandit chief who educated him in the bandit life) subjects him, so that he can prove his mettle and his worthiness as a member of a male society (90).

Robbery can also be an occasion to show filial love. When Villa receives the money that he is due for the sale of the stolen mules, he gives the money in its entirety to his mother in need; she accepts the money but chastises him for his devious ways (Francisco Villa 2004, 92–93). Robbery can be the occasion for the classic Robin Hood scene as well. When Villa receives fifty thousand pesos (his portion of the bounty from a hit on a mine owner), he distributes what he robbed among family, friends, and people in need until he exhausts all of the bounty (95). (Antonio Retama, one of the beneficiaries of this largesse, will provide much-needed refuge later on [101].) Robbery can be committed out of necessity, as when stealing the horse from a rancher (105), or as a form of negative reciprocity, as when robbing a hacendado who insulted him for no reason (106), or a judge of the Acordada (117). During Villa's revolutionary stint, the figure of the expropriator acquires even more relevance. Villa acknowledges confiscating resources, but takes great pains to point out that he never did so for himself, and that he never took more than was strictly necessary: horses (158), milk (162), clothing (162), weapons (200), and money (but not in excessive amounts) (159, 277). (As we saw in the preamble, this is the same justification that he used for the forced contributions in Parral.) This moral economy shines through, Villa claims, to the point that hacendados and administrators contribute "voluntarily" to the war effort (160).

A moral economy of killing is the complement to a moral economy of robbery. Villa emphasizes his dozens of killings, many of which are unaccounted for in the historical record (Francisco Villa 2004, 87, 98, 99, 100, 102, 118, 135, 135). However, they are not random: he only kills Rurales, vigilantes, or traitors. Unwarranted killing would be beyond the pale. When members of his first gang kill an old man without reason, he immediately abandons the gang (openly, as would be considered proper), severing all further ties (101). When confronted with situations of violence, he rarely attacks first. He kills in fair fights, in fact, showing off the risks he is taking, as in the killing of Claro Reza (a former outlaw turned informant) whom Villa kills in plain sight in the middle of Parral. After the killing, Villa, like Martín Fierro after killing the Moreno or Juan Moreira after killing a police officer, does not flee, but leaves the scene at a leisurely pace, implicitly challenging anybody to dispute the fairness of the deed. Another pillar of this economy of violence is the lack of venality. Villa does not kill for money. Moreover, when he fights, he is almost always outnumbered—always himself, with a couple of partisans, fending off entire units numbering in the dozens (when not in the hundreds) (93, 97, 103, 118, 166).

Throughout his outlaw career, Villa is beset by treason, usually (but not exclusively) committed by an accomplice or an associate who reports him to the authorities (Francisco Villa 2004, 86, 93, 97, 100, 104, 166, among other instances). This is the lowest form of breach of the rural code of honor (Pitt-Rivers [1954] 1971, 178), but also of the melodramatic code of honor. The traitors in the *Retrato* belong to two categories: those who betray for no reason (out of sheer perversity) and those who betray for money (like Judas—a metaphor or sobriquet that the narrative uses abundantly). Villa's retaliation is presented only as a reaction, and fully in line with (in fact, a necessary enforcement of) the code of rural male honor. Just as the trope of victimization serves the purpose of making Villa a representative of the People (in a process of co-creation that involves a common fight, and a common enemy), the trope of treason establishes the other crucial identification, that between Madero and Villa as both victims of treason, prolonging a lineage of betrayed heroes from Hidalgo to Juárez. (I will show, in chapter 2, how this same trope operates in the case of Chávez's discourse.) Madero is betrayed on numerous occasions: first by Pascual Orozco, then by Creel-Terrazas, then by Huerta. Orozco, in fact, has an oversized role in the narrative. He is the figure that links Villa (Orozco betrays Villa three times: 118, 224, 239), and Madero (whose original treason sets in motion the events that will culminate with Madero's own death). Orozco is dubbed "Judas," since treason is not a political act but a "cosmic" disposition, and all treasons resemble the original one (202). By the same token, loyalty is not a political virtue, but a moral trait that completely defines identity, and that goes above and beyond the calculations of loss or advantage and even the ideological definitions of an alliance. (Melodrama, as we know, admits no middle ground [Brooks 1976, 18].)

If treason is potentially the paramount moral pitfall for the hero, the hero's moral mettle has to be tested through temptation (again, the Christian/

Christic motif). Villa's world is a dangerous place, but not because he could be killed (although he could indeed be killed). It is a moral minefield, and the temptation to betray is the ubiquitous trap. Villa is invited, time and again, to betray Madero (Francisco Villa 2004, 216, 217, 223). In the last instance, while in prison, Antonio Tamayo comes to his cell to offer him the opportunity to join the imminent coup against Madero. Villa not only rejects the offer, but falls into a frenzy (262). Villa reacts this way not because the offer is unconscionable, or because as a prisoner he cannot punish the tempter, but because he does not understand why he is constantly being tempted. And the almost gothic or sentimental motif should be noted: Villa is the innocent hero, imprisoned, and offered his freedom at the steep price of losing his soul—a scene reminiscent not of Robin Hood, but rather of *Zastrozzi* (Percy Bysshe Shelley, 1810), *The Mysteries of Udolpho* (Anne Radcliffe, 1794), or *Pamela, or Virtue Rewarded* (Samuel Richardson, 1740).

Loyalty is the precondition for the other major statement of the text: the alliance between bandit and sovereign (Villa and Madero). This is a vertical alliance but since it is not motivated by money or the mutual need for survival, it does not contradict or diminish the horizontal one. In fact, it complements it as its logical conclusion in the constitution of an organic body politic. Consider, as an example, Robin Hood, who goes from outlaw to royal archer and trusted retainer of Richard the Lionhearted. But the pact does not happen between them exclusively, as self-interested individuals. The pact is predicated upon both the existence of the merry men of Sherwood (as a synecdoche of the loyal Saxon community) and Sherwood as an alternative space of sovereignty. The pact is the encounter of the long-lost true king and the long-forlorn true subjects. Outlawry is the condition of possibility of the constitution of a community of true subjects. This community will support and avenge the king.[38] Villa, similarly, never becomes an ideological Maderista. He becomes the follower of a man: a man who is brave (bravery was the shared code of masculinity that trumped class, ethnicity, and education), and one with whom an oral pact can be established (Francisco Villa 2004, 174, 176, 178, 211–12). (The locus of the alliance of outlaw and sovereign is the voice and the face-to-face contact. The written medium is the locus of misunderstanding, treason, and loss.)[39]

The oral pact posits another form of relationship between Villa and Madero. Villa is the only link, the symbolic mediation, between Madero and the peasant community. In the *Retrato* he is Madero's only supporter who comes from a rural popular milieu, the other Maderistas being false ones (Orozco, Huerta), city folk (Abraham González), or foreigners who pretend to have virtues and skills that they, in all reality, do not possess (Garibaldi, Viljoen [Francisco Villa 2004, 184–87]). As such, Villa can become the avenger of Madero, when Madero is killed. This is the last figure of Villa that emerges in the narrative: Villa as avenger of the true king, killed by a usurper. Here, the link between the moral and the political becomes complete. From the humble hut in the hacienda to the epic storming of cities at the head of thousands of soldiers, the story is one, the melodrama of treason and revenge, against the many embodiments, the many names (López Negrete, Orozco, Huerta), of a single (im)moral principle.[40]

TWO

HUGO CHÁVEZ, MAISANTA, AND THE CONSTRUCTION OF AN INSURGENT LINEAGE

HUGO CHÁVEZ (1954–2013), the late president of the Bolivarian Republic of Venezuela, elicited and still elicits strong passions from both ends of the political spectrum. Chávez generated (and demanded) undivided loyalty, which after his death has come to border on religious idolatry.[1] He also provoked (and provokes) unrelenting hatred, and cruel mockery and spite, with undeniable racist and classist overtones.[2] That most of the opinions on Chávez inhabit these extremes, with little middle ground, is evidence of the fact that Chávez (like Villa) was indeed a fascinating figure. "Fascinating," not in its current diluted English sense of "very interesting" or "quite appealing," but in the strong sense of something that ignites an inextricable mix of horror and admiration, fear and attraction—something that is regarded simultaneously as abject and as admirable, something undeniably powerful that commands attention, but for reasons that somehow escape the beholder. One can feel an immediate connection with something fascinating, but it also reserves a darker, incomprehensible, and probably threatening side. This fascination is the flip side of charisma, its darker twin brother. I would like to suggest that this fascination has to do with the way that Chávez was able to craft a public persona not just as mere head of state according to the law (the head of the executive branch, enforcing the laws that have another origin), but as a sovereign outside (beyond) the law, a law giver. But Chávez was also able to craft a narrative in which this position was historically legitimated, since he was the culmination of a genealogy of popular leaders.

When, in 1999, Chávez took the oath as president, he did so in a seemingly bizarre fashion. He changed the oath, in order to deny and interdict the validity of the constitution that was actually making him president. (The constitution upon which Chávez was sworn in was the 1961 Constitution, contemporary of the Pacto de Punto Fijo, which for Chávez embodied all of the lost opportunities of Venezuelan democracy.) He said, "I swear before God, I swear before the fatherland, I swear before my people that above this moribund Constitution [*sobre esta moribunda Constitución*] I will push for the necessary democratic transformations so that the republic can have a new founding document [*carta magna*] according to the new times that we are living. I swear."

According to Chávez's rationale, his becoming president is legitimized not by the constitution, whose validity he denies, but by the insurrection of February 4, 1992 (or 4-F, as it is commonly known), which allowed him one minute of public media exposure that turned him into an instant celebrity. Chávez thus builds his image as that of a subject of legitimate violence outside the law. In that sense, as I explained in the preamble, "outlaw" is the flip side of the sovereign, since both inhabit a space of exception. Chávez places himself by his oath in the position of the sovereign who declares the old law defunct. And since the new law is not yet born, he is a sovereign who, just like social bandits, claims a legitimacy that is exterior to and predates the law, a legitimacy that inhabits an in-between space of sovereignty. What differentiates Chávez from the classic praetorian *golpista* military man of the second half of the twentieth century is not the personality cult he spawned, but rather the fact that his legitimacy is purportedly traced to the "people" ("my people," as it appears in the variation of the oath that he takes), and that this "people" has a genealogy that Chávez strove to create in narrative form.[3]

This narrative is the child of what could be called Chávez's *poietic potency*, meaning his ability to create (or recreate), consistently and convincingly, a totalizing narrative about the nation, and his own place in it, as well as his ability to do so by tapping into a double source of cultural capital: that of the popular classes and that of the lettered classes.[4] In other words: his ability to be a "man of the people" as well as a heterodox species of intellectual. Perhaps some contrasts from the United States will clarify: the Yale-educated

scion of a powerful family, George W. Bush was able to portray himself as a
"man of the people"—the candidate with whom you would have a beer, as the
famous poll stated. But his real or perceived utter lack of information and
smarts bedeviled his image throughout his presidency. Obama is the opposite.
He is undeniably well read, thoughtful, and articulate, but, like Al Gore (the
man with whom you would not have a beer), his political fortunes were beset,
to a degree, by his inability to abandon his professorial style. Chávez was a
powerful and unique synthesis of both styles: he was able to speak (to lecture)
for hours, but always in a way in which what came through was not what he
knew or pretended to know. What came through was that Chávez was also able
to establish both an emotional and a cultural connection with his audiences,
present and remote.[5]

Chávez was a well-read man. There are numerous testimonials to his early
and enduring fervor for solitary reading. Even as president, he always made
time for reading, something that set him apart from his political adversaries,
supposedly more educated and sophisticated than he, and from most Latin
American contemporary politicians, who pay lip service to literacy but have
no taste or vocation for reading—or learning. (Perhaps the most blatant example was that of Carlos Menem, president of Argentina from 1989 to 1999, and
for a time the hero of the Argentine neoliberal Right. Menem confessed that
he found instruction, inspiration, and solace by always keeping the writings
of Socrates, the Greek philosopher, on hand!) But Chávez had more than just
a genuine passion for reading—and not just an imagined one, as in Menem's
case. He had a strong belief in the power and authority of books. (Recall that
when Chávez greeted an obviously uncomfortable Obama in 2009, at the
Summit of the Americas in Trinidad, Chávez chose to mark the momentous
occasion by presenting Obama with a book: *Las venas abiertas de América
Latina*, the 1971 essay by Eduardo Galeano that, not by chance, offers a totalizing vision of Latin American history. The book went on to become an Ama-
zon best seller for some time.) That belief in the power of books permeated
his oral performances: he spoke about books often, at length, and with gusto.
Chávez's orality, however, had a Calibanesque quality. Even if informed by
ample readings, his performances were deliberately presented as the voice of
the rural, nonwhite, popular "barbarian"—because, like Caliban, Chávez presented himself as the barbarian who threatened to defeat his better-educated
adversaries at their own game, with their own words.

In the pages that follow I will elaborate on one aspect of that poietic potency, as a cornerstone of Chávez's rule: his ability to construct a narrative that linked his persona and style of rule with a long tradition of rural, popular insurgents. In particular, Chávez made this link with (and through) one outlaw/revolutionary: Pedro Pérez Delgado, also known as Maisanta (1881–1924). In order to do this, Chávez appropriated (in his oral performances) the authority and prestige assigned to literature. In particular he identifies with one specific literary work, in which he found a figure of his own destiny: *Maisanta: El último hombre a caballo*, written by José León Tapia ([1974] 1976). This link worked in unison with the better-known Chavista legitimating narrative, that is, the Bolivarian one. While Villa needed the help of a traditional intellectual in order to lend his narrative authority and "coherence" (i.e., adherence to the standards of a written autobiography), Chávez used some of his oral performances to construct his persona as a unique hybrid: an armed insurgent (the heir and embodiment of the legacy of Maisanta, and through Maisanta the legacy of Ezequiel Zamora, and through Zamora the legacy of Bolívar, as I will explain later), but also an intellectual able to give meaning and narrative coherence to the events of which he was the main character.

Hugo Chávez liked to talk. In fact, the image with which we are most likely to identify Chávez is that of a man talking. And even though Chávez was not averse to participating in the classic populist scene of the leader addressing the gathered masses at energized rallies in vast open spaces, I suspect that this was not the only classic Chavista scene. The classic Chavista scene was also that of a private monologue (e.g., the many interviews that he gave throughout the years) or a public one.[6] In the public monologues, he talked for minutes (or *a* minute, like the one that was accorded to him by Carlos Andrés Pérez in the wake of the failed 4-F uprising, which marked Chávez's entrance into Venezuela's public imagination) or for hours, both to audiences right in front of him (with which he usually engaged in some kind of dialogue) and to those watching him on TV. He talked digressively, incessantly, with unrelenting passion. He visited any topic that came to his mind, from God to peas, sharing with his audience his vision of history as well as providing advice on the number of minutes that a person should spend in the shower in order to conserve water. He lectured, confessed, challenged, read, sang, insulted, mused aloud, told jokes and anecdotes. Frequently he did this with intelligent folksy humor and piquancy. Sometimes he seemed to lack any sense of timing or propriety. Enlightening, amusing, or embarrassing, this verbosity was certainly part of his charisma.

Ana Teresa Torres (2009) points out, insightfully, that it is not by chance that one of Chávez's favorite books was Victor Hugo's *Les Misérables* (1862), which Chávez once proposed as the key to understanding Latin American contemporary social reality. In reading *Les Misérables*, one finds quite a few features that likely resonated with Chávez. These similarities are not limited to Chávez's identification with the character of Jean Valjean, the outlaw who sets out to redeem his people, but are also found in a narrative voice that moves from one topic to the next in a seamless but completely associative fashion, as well as the totalizing impulse that defines it (like Chávez, Victor Hugo also visits any topic with abandon and generosity, from the history of Paris sewers to the Battle of Waterloo). This trust in the power of (popular) literature belongs more in the nineteenth century than in the late twentieth century, since it is more akin to the one held by liberal intellectuals of the first independent century than those of postmodern ones. In particular, this trust does not have to do with literature's pedagogic potential but its political/poetical power: its power to create genealogies, and identities as part of those genealogies, that is, "national narratives."

Allow me to provide one small example of this that will also lead to the topic of Maisanta and llanero outlawry. Around the middle of the last decade, in one of his many televised appearances, Chávez once again touched upon one of his favorite topics: George W. Bush. But he did not talk about Bush—he addressed Bush directly. A segment of the speech follows, with italicized text indicating that which Chávez delivered in English (except in the case of *pajarito* and *de lo peor*):

> You tried to mess with me, little birdie [*pajarito*]. You tried to mess with me, didn't you? You do not know much about history. You do not know much about anything, you know? You suffer from a huge ignorance. You are an ignorant man, Mr. Danger. You are an ignorant man. You are an ass, Mr. Danger. You are an ass, Mr. Danger. Or to say it in my bad English, in my *bad English, you are a donkey, Mr. Danger. You are a donkey*. To dispel any doubts: I am talking about *Mr. George W. Bush. You are a donkey, Mr. Bush.* . . . I am going to tell

you something, Mr. Danger. You are a coward, you know? You are a coward. Why don't you go to Iraq to lead your armed forces? It is easy to command them from afar. If you happen to conceive the crazy scheme of invading Venezuela, I will be waiting for you in these plains, Mr. Danger. *Come on here, Mr. Danger. Come on here.* [Applause] *Come on here, Mr. Danger.* Coward, mass murderer, mass murderer, mass murderer. You are a mass murderer. You are an *alcoholic*, Mr. Danger. This is to say, you are a drunkard. You are a drunkard, Mr. Danger. You are an immoral being, Mr. Danger. You are the worst of the worst, Mr. Danger. [Addressing the audience] How do you say *de lo peor* in English? [Inaudible response from the audience] *The last! You are the last!* [pronounced "Shu arr the last"][7]

The video was a success on YouTube,[8] with a number of spoof versions also posted, most with sampling and the addition of a soundtrack in order to make Chávez's discourse into a song whose chorus would be, "Te metiste conmigo, pajarito" (You tried to mess with me, little birdie).

Both the original and the spoofs are funny. But behind the humor in the original, a serious point is made. There are a number of features of this performance that are worth mentioning and that I consider emblematic of Chávez's performative mode of rule (and an important line of legitimation of this rule). Whereas in the Western political tradition, states communicate among themselves mainly in *written* form—treaties, declarations of war, international law, passports, visas—and whereas orality is reserved for ceremonial niceties or backroom deals, Chávez makes the oral medium the privileged medium of political exchange. This address to Bush assumes the form of a challenge. In this dramatic enactment the oral duel between Chávez and Bush is the core of the scene. The real audience—those who are there with Chávez in the *hato* (cattle ranch), those who are watching him on TV—is not the "real" audience, because Chávez is not talking to these people. They are, rather, only spectators of a drama of historical proportions, the challenge of one president to another, like the Greek foot soldiers witnessing the challenge of one Homeric hero to another.

This challenge rests on a supposedly shared code of masculinity: Chávez calls Bush a coward (the ultimate offense against masculinity) and a drunkard—and here drunkard does not mean "someone who drinks" but "someone who cannot hold his liquor." And Chávez is not challenging Bush as the president of Venezuela to the president of the United States; rather, he is challenging him as one llanero, a man of the plains, to a Texan, also a man of the plains, both southwesterners. (Bush was born in New Haven, Connecticut. He was admitted to Yale largely, it seems, because his father went there also. But he crafted his public persona of a straight-shooting, no-nonsense Texas rancher, drawl and swagger included. Chávez accepts Bush's largely concocted public persona in order to establish the conditions of the challenge. This challenge would be impossible in the case of Obama.) To challenge Bush, Chávez cleverly prefers the condescending tone of the masculine rural challenge ("Te metiste conmigo, pajarito") to the angry tone of the fundamentalist (that of other Bush nemeses, such as Kim Jong-il or Mahmoud Ahmadinejad). Chávez is not challenging him to a war between states and armies, but to a duel, a variation of the singular combat. And that duel should occur in a very particular place: the llanos of Venezuela, the locus of Venezuelan nationhood.

But there are certain complexities that make this much more than a mere display of macho bravado. Chávez frames his challenge in a peculiar fashion: he appropriates the prestige of the literary institution, by calling Bush "Mr. Danger," the character of the American interloper in the ultimate nationalist novel: *Doña Bárbara* (Rómulo Gallegos, 1929). And he does this as a heterodox appropriation of literary authority: Chávez wants to display his literary knowledge (something that he did quite often, witnessed in this particular instance by the fact that the desk from which he is talking is cluttered with books, pens, notebooks), as much as he wants to display his distance from it. He pronounces "Mr. Danger" with exaggerated disregard for English phonetics ("Míster Dan-sher"), he calls Bush "a donkey" instead of "an ass," and he mistakenly translates *lo peor* as "the last" instead of "the worst." I don't know how much English ("Eenglich") Chávez knew. I do know that he was an intelligent and superbly astute person, and that he knew very well that he was displaying a deliberate butchering of the English language. But this butchering, in a country whose elite prided (and prides) itself on its ability to mimic American ways, is a performance of strong cultural value by itself. He even asks the audience, "How do you say *de lo peor*?" An unidentified member of the audience responds, "The last." Chávez dutifully repeats, "Mr. Danger, you are the last." One would imagine that Chávez is making a fool of himself. But this is not the case at all. By appropriating this mistake, he incorporates "popular" (i.e., anonymous) orality into his own voice. And by doing that, he incorporates popular orality into the historical drama of which Chávez is the protagonist. His own voice becomes not only the expression of his own (strong) passions, but a conveyor of the passions of the People. And Chávez becomes not only a leader, but also the ultimate image of the intellectual, who, in his own voice, accomplishes a cultural synthesis of popular and elite cultures. (Of course, this is a performance effect. It is impossible to know if Chávez conceived himself as such, or in such terms in this particular instance.)

But Chávez's speech begins with a rather enigmatic reference to history ("Tú no sabes mucho de historia. Tú no sabes mucho de nada ¿sabes?"). The topic is seemingly abandoned later on. But is it? I would propose that history is what frames the challenge, because this allocution is much more than another instance of Chavez's personal obsession with Bush. It is the culminating point of a historical narrative. This narrative organizes the social realm around a protracted conflict that unrelentingly divides this realm into two opposing camps. These camps have a few proper names as their emblems. On the one hand, empire: Diego de Losada (the conquistador who founded Caracas in 1567); the Spaniards and Creoles who opposed patriots during the War of Independence and who later on were able to co-opt it; José Antonio Páez, who (according to Chávez) betrayed Bolívar's dream of hemispheric unity; Antonio Guzmán Blanco and the oligarchy that betrayed the popular Federalist dream; Juan Vicente Gómez, who squandered the national wealth by selling it off to Shell and Exxon; the signers and beneficiaries of the Pacto de Punto Fijo; the opposition to Chávez; and, of course, "W."

On the other hand, we have an insurgent lineage that begins with Guaicaipuro (chief of the Teques and Caracas tribes and leader of the rebellion against the Spaniards in the Caracas Valley);[9] Bolívar (and his mentor, Simón Rodríguez); Ezequiel Zamora, the leader of popular Federalism in the mid-nineteenth century, and coiner of one of Chávez's favorite phrases: "Horror to the oligarchy" ("Horror a la oligarquía"); Cipriano Castro, the forerunner of a nationalist oil policy (according to Chávez); Maisanta, who for years fought Gómez; and, predictably, as the culmination and synthesis of this historical lineage, Chávez himself. This narrative locates the conflict that defines Venezuela in a completely mythical fashion, since Guaicaipuro and his descendants (the "real Venezuela") had no notion whatsoever of something called Venezuela, while the "nonreal Venezuelans," the evil agents of empire, were the ones who actually created the name Venezuela (from "Little Venice," it

seems, since the stilt houses in Lake Maracaibo reminded the conquistadors of Venice). This insurgent lineage has carried out a protracted anti-
imperialist and class- and race-based struggle, and this anachronistic attribution of origin is a defining feature of nationalism.

But what is important is that this lineage relies entirely on the power of the
intellectual who is able to see and to articulate a complete historical development in narrative form. In the case that occupies this study, that intellectual
was Chávez himself, the one who, in a way, speaks for the dead.[10] At the same
time, this narrative suppresses a central feature of nationalist narratives—
that of the reassuring effect of the fratricide (Anderson [1983] 1996)—since
Chávez refused to consider the history of Venezuela as part of a family drama
(even a dysfunctional family drama, as in the case of Mexico, marked by the
seduction of la Malinche by Cortés) in which the enemies, without their
knowledge, still belong to the same imaginary whole, which can only be recognized as a whole by the nationalist intellectual. That is why Chávez's national
narrative pitted the nation against a morphing empire (Lozada, Morillo,
Exxon, Royal Dutch, Bush), that is, an "other" who is completely alien to the
self. It is an "other" that needs to be suppressed and excluded. In this light, if
there is no family drama, there is no political body, and the entire Venezuelan
history is not the development of an original identity, but a time of exception defined by an unfinished (and probably endless) conflict, the struggle for
emancipation with no compromise.[11] This struggle legitimated ad infinitum
Chávez's authoritarian populism. That *poietic* potency, eminently exerted in
incessant, unending discourses, was at the same time the most admirable and
the most irritating feature of Chávez's rule. And in the twenty-first century,
when macro narratives had been declared defunct, or the tools of fundamen-
talists or cynics, it is surprising to witness the efficacy of a narrative decidedly
nationalistic, totalizing, teleological, and rooted in an appropriation of the
prestige of literature that is at the same time worshipful and eccentric.

A genealogy of insurgents, of rebels, of outlaws defines "true" Venezuelan history and identity. But there is also a locus where the true nation lives. That
locus is the llanos. The llanos of Venezuela is the region of subtropical plains
that encompasses areas of the states of Apure, Barinas, Portuguesa, Cojedes,
Guárico, Anzoátegui, and Monagas. Since colonial times, the main economic
activity of this area has been extensive cattle ranching. This gave rise to a

distinctive frontier culture. The llanos's geographical position away from the coastal urban centers and plantations that formed Venezuela's political and economic core, as well as its economic and cultural unity with the Colombian llanos, contributed to a sense of identity different from the national identity at large. The llanos were ethnically composed of a mixture of poor whites (*blancos de orilla*), Canarios (who were considered not quite whites, not quite Spaniards), whites in trouble with the law, runaway slaves trying to evade the (already tenuous) reach of the colonial state, and indigenous peoples.[12] In a society that was firmly organized around racial lines, this "savage" miscegenation stigmatized the llaneros as a group. Also, cattle ranching in the llanos catered to the needs of a highly developed smuggling economy of cattle products that bypassed the tight regulations for colonial commerce established by the Crown. This, coupled with the fact that in the llanos there was, at best, a vague sense of land and cattle property, created the perception of the llanos as a land of outlaws. The very term "llanero" came to be for a time practically synonymous with "bandit" (Izard 1983, 1987, 1988; Izard and Slatta 1987). This phenomenon is parallel to what happened in other cattle frontiers in Latin America, such as the Argentine pampas and its gauchos and northeastern Brazil and its jagunços.

Either in spite of this or because of it, llaneros loom large in Venezuelan history and culture. The cattle culture formed the basis of a frontier culture that prized strong and able riders with an unmatched knowledge of the land. In the low-capital, low-tech civil wars of nineteenth-century Venezuela, the llanero cavalry charges, armed with lance and machete, were fearsome and effective. Indeed, llaneros were the main military actors in certain phases of the War of Independence (an international as well as a civil war, with race, class, and cultural overtones).[13] Throughout the nineteenth century, llanero insurgents played a major role in the civil wars that prevented, until the advent of Venezuela's oil economy, the emergence of a state that was able to exert true sovereignty. At the same time, the llanos were the arena where some of the bloodiest uprisings against the decades-long Gómez dictatorship were fought (and defeated). Hence, as a conceptual character, a cultural signifier, the image of the llanero is split between that of the bandit, the monster vomited from hell who makes a nation-state impossible, and that of the hero of the national and popular epic; between that of the bloodthirsty robber and

murderer who makes the nation impossible, and that of the popular freedom
fighter. (Stuart Hall [1997] reminds us that this split nature is characteristic of
all tropes of otherness, and this is shown, just to give two prominent examples,
in the two most important novels in modern Venezuelan literary history: *Las
lanzas coloradas* (1931), by Arturo Uslar Pietri—which I will examine later in
this book—and the aforementioned *Doña Bárbara*.)

Maisanta: El último hombre a caballo was published in 1974 by the physician
and writer José León Tapia (1928–2007). The book had modest success when
it appeared, but has since achieved national renown, with seven editions in
print by the time Tapia died. The book tells the story of the "last" llanero caudillo, Pedro Pérez Delgado, also known as Maisanta, "El Americano," and,
posthumously, "The last man on horseback." Maisanta (a strict contemporary
of Villa, something that Chávez himself remarked upon) was a minor caudillo
who, between 1898 and 1921, took part in a number of llanero uprisings. Maisanta entered the life of an insurgent as an officer of Mocho Hernández in the
Revolución de Queipa against Joaquín Crespo and Ignacio Andrade. In 1901
he joined the Revolución Libertadora, the last stand of the caudillos against
Cipriano Castro. The caudillos' defeat signaled their irreversible decline as
a national political force. In 1914 and again in 1919 and 1921 he joined rebellions against Gómez. These rebellions ended, somewhat predictably, with
Maisanta and his fellow revolutionaries defeated and in exile. Disenchanted
with the revolutionary option, he later reconciled with Gómez (whose officer he had already been before 1914), and traded the role of revolutionary for
that of chaser of revolutionaries. In 1922, however, his long-standing enemy
Febres Cordero accused him of complicity in yet another rebellion. He was
apprehended and confined to the horrendous prison of Puerto Cabello, where
he died in 1924 of a heart attack.

   This story is, again, eerily similar to portions of Villa's story in 1912–1913
and the episode in Parral that I examined in the preamble: the insurgent
who later on becomes a chaser of insurgents, but who is never forgiven by
his erstwhile enemies (now allies) who put him away on concocted charges.
Villa was lucky, though, and evaded his enemies, while Maisanta, Tapia maintains, died of septicemia, since he had been fed powdered glass mixed with
his meals, a diet that caused internal hemorrhages and a painful and inevitable death. Maisanta always denied participation in the 1922 uprising, and he

wrote repeatedly to Gómez to that effect. Like Villa in his letters to Madero, he claimed to be the victim of treason by dark operators. He also claimed enduring loyalty to Gómez. Just like in the case of Villa, these letters went unanswered (Botello 2005, 207–14).

El último hombre a caballo was an inaugural attempt to shape into a single narrative what had been scattered between oral sources, which Tapia uses amply,[14] and written testimonies, some of which were unpublished or had very little impact at the time of the novel's release.[15] Since then, Oldman Botello has published a very well documented, largely encomiastic biography (2005).[16] Preceding all of them, of course, is Andrés Eloy Blanco's "Corrido de caballería," a poem that Chávez knew by heart, and that he quoted and sang frequently in public (he recited it to his troops when he was a young officer [Guerrero 2013, 59]) and in private (e.g., love letters to Herma Marksman [Marksman 2004, 310]).

Tapia's book is a hybrid of regionalist novel, collective testimonial narrative (in the vein of *La noche de Tlatelolco*), and exercise in regional oral history. The book also hybridizes political and intellectual traditions of diverse relevance. On the one hand, it is the book of a local intellectual, a liberal professional turned regional history buff (in this case, the history of Barinas and the llanos) and fiction writer. With certain caveats, which I will discuss later, the book also belongs to the vigorous Latin American tradition of testimonial narrative (of a national-populist orientation, in Tapia's case). When published, the work established Tapia as a respected regionalist author. Tapia would later become a writer of national visibility, and probably the most influential Latin American regionalist writer of the last few decades at least, when considered from the point of view of the influence of his most devoted reader and promoter, Hugo Chávez. Chávez was a llanero himself, born and raised in Sabaneta in Barinas state. And he was a descendant of Maisanta— his great-grandson, on his mother's side. As a child and a teenager, Chávez vaguely knew about his great-grandfather. But Maisanta was an ancestor of ill repute ("that murderer," "that brigand," Chávez recalls overhearing when he was a child [Blanco-Muñoz 1998, 29]), which was then the official vision of Maisanta, not the one that survived in the memory of the area. Chávez discovered that Maisanta was something different from a shameful family memory when reading Tapia's book in 1974 (29, 59, 65). So the construction by Chávez of an insurgent lineage, one that inspired and justified his own insurgency (i.e., the attempted coup that was Chávez's entry into the national imagination) seems to have been fostered or framed by the book's vision, since the story of Maisanta provides an essential link in the construction of the Bolivarian narrative, which, in truly *personalista* style, revolves around Chávez's biography, his body, his voice. This appropriation did not happen with Tapia's full endorsement. In fact, Tapia seemed to have been uncomfortable with his unofficial role of legitimating intellectual. He even declined the 2004 Premio Nacional de Literatura, in order to avoid his work being considered political propaganda.

Perhaps there is no better place where Chávez put forward this lineage than in the Theater Teresa Carreño, when in November 2006 Chávez presided over the act of "graduating" the "lancers" of the Misión Vuelvan Caras.[17] Since this took place on the anniversary of Maisanta's death, Chávez devoted time to a long narrative on Maisanta's life and significance, a narrative that was crowned by a lively rendition of the "Corrido de caballería."[18] Here, Chávez clearly delineates his own position in Venezuelan and Latin American history, by making Maisanta (Tapia's Maisanta—Chávez mentions Tapia with great respect) the axis of a two-dimensional narrative. On the one hand, he narrates the story of Maisanta; of Maisanta's father, Pedro Pérez (who fought in Zamora's army); and of how the nineteenth-century struggle of Pedro Pérez is the same as that of Maisanta, which is the same as his own (Chávez's). "We are the same," he declares. "There, our grandparents, and here us, their children, their grandchildren, their blood, their spirit" conduct "the last cavalry charge against the empire." On the other hand, it is Maisanta who allows Chávez to link his own struggle to that of his ancestor's contemporaries, all of them dubbed bandits at the time: Pancho Villa, Augusto César Sandino, Emiliano Zapata.

Tapia remembered receiving a passionate letter by a young lieutenant at the time his book was published. And Chávez, inspired by the book, engaged in the project of writing a biography of Maisanta, a task for which he traveled to the places where Maisanta lived and fought in Venezuela and Colombia. The book was never written, but it seems that Chávez's incursion into Colombia, which he entered carrying weapons and grenades, cost him several days in jail (Blanco-Muñoz 1998, 29, 30, 60). According to Herma Marksman, Chávez's lover throughout the 1980s and early 1990s, his reverence for Maisanta was always emphatic. The first gift that Chávez presented to her, on one of their first dates, was Tapia's book (Marksman 2004, 86). While commander of a secondary garrison, Chávez demanded, from the soldiers under his command, daily demonstrations of reverence to Maisanta, together with the more official ones to Bolívar (both pictures adorned his office there).

But sometimes this reverence bordered on the supernatural. After a fight, Chávez mentioned to Marksman that Maisanta was happy because they were able to make up (Marksman 2004, 87). Marksman also refers to how, when a certain Adarmes, a political and personal enemy, died in a car accident, Chávez mentioned that Maisanta had administered justice. Additionally, there are controversial testimonies about occurrences of Chávez's "posses-sion" by Maisanta's disembodied soul, while he was in prison after the 1992 coup attempt (87). Also well known is Chavez's use and repeated exhibition of Maisanta's scapular of Our Lady of the Socorro. Maisanta's mother gave this scapular to Maisanta's son after he was forced to flee because of a (justi-fied) murder. Maisanta invoked the protection of the Virgin before every war action by calling on "Mai Santa" (for Madre Santa), or used the expression for emphasis. The contraction, in time, replaced "Maisanta's" real name, much like in the case of Ernesto Guevara, also known as "Ché." After reading Tapia's book, and an article by Botello that mentioned that Maisanta's daughter was still alive, Chávez contacted this daughter. After the 1992 coup she gave him the relic, which he wore around his neck and displayed on public occasions. This relic, according to Chávez, protected him against both assassinations and coups (it is not entirely clear if this protection was afforded by the Virgin depicted in the relic, or by Maisanta, the former owner of the relic).

Because of this legacy, Chávez belongs not only to an insurgent family, but to a llanero insurgent family. The llanos were displaced from their political and economic place in Venezuela by the rise of the oil economy, thus turning the llanos into an economic backwater. But in the Venezuelan imaginary, oil has an ambiguous place: it is infinite wealth that belongs to everybody, that is right there for the taking, like a new El Dorado (Coronil 1997). But it is also a deleterious influence that attracted imperial adventures and brought about corrupting luxury and the destruction or forgetting of the real, rural warrior "Venezuela," and with that, the "people" as depository of Venezuelan identity. (The pernicious influence of the almost total reliance on oil wealth can be seen in the current calamitous state of the Venezuelan economy.) To claim a llanero ancestry is to claim an origin that is older and more legitimate than modern Venezuela, the pre-oil Venezuela.

Of course, Chávez's ambitious agenda could only be sustained with the revenue derived from oil, and from oil exported to Chávez's avowed enemy, the United States (PDVSA, the state-run oil company, is the sole owner of Citgo, the Houston-based chain of American refineries and gas stations). History provides interesting parallels. Chávez rose in 1992, against President Carlos Andrés Pérez, during Pérez's second stint as president (1989–1993). Pérez's political identity was fixed to that of the "Saudi Venezuela" of the 1970s (he was president during the boom years, 1974–1979), and the memory of that bonanza helped him coast into a second term. Chávez rose against this embodiment of the evils of oil dependency, just like his great-grandfather had risen up in arms against the architect of oil-dependent Venezuela. Maisanta's wealth was destroyed by the oil economy (the family hacienda, La Marqueseña, was expropriated, since it belonged to a rebel [Blanco-Muñoz 1998, 49]).[19] Therefore, Chávez could claim a symbolic independence from the corrupting influence of oil (Torres 2009, 117). And in fact, the way in which Chávez redistributed oil revenue, through the so-called "missions" that bypassed state standards for accountability, reminds us less of the state populism of the 1930s through the 1950s of Cárdenas, Vargas, or Perón, and more of the outlaw modus operandi, in which the rich (the "oligarchy") are dispossessed and the bounty is redistributed to the poor, in a *personalista*, not bureaucratic, fashion, and the distribution is less an investment in the future than a reward for loyalty. (Of course, Chávez was unable to move Venezuela away from its reliance on oil, and the drop in crude prices—as well as gross mismanagement of prior oil revenue—is punishing the country severely.)

So Tapia's work is where Chávez found the mirror of his destiny. There are a number of features in Tapia's work that allowed for its appropriation as a decisive piece in the Bolivarian narrative. While Maisanta was alive, his image oscillated between that of an insurgent *jefe grande* and that of a rural bandit. Maisanta's enemies considered him a plunderer who adopted a political veneer to obtain legitimacy and protection, much like Vanderwood's nineteenth-century profiteering bandits. In all official communications between Gómez and local officials, Maisanta and his associates are always called *bandidos, bandoleros, cuatreros*, and *gavilleros*.[20] And of course, he met the end of a bandit. He was apprehended without warrant, jailed without trial, and died without a sentence. This labeling is a classic procedure that delegitimizes rural insurgency in Latin America as well as elsewhere, as I explained earlier. But Tapia, even when denying the bandit label, emphasizes motifs that define social bandit narratives (just like Villa in the *Retrato*). Maisanta begins his career after murdering Pedro Macías, a local boss (or, as Chávez retold it, "an oligarch") who had sexually abused his sister. (The similarity with Villa's plight is uncanny, but not surprising.) His mother urges him to act as the man of the house, which he does, even though he has to flee.[21] Much like Villa, Maisanta lacks an ideology articulated according to the categories around which the political, in modern terms, is defined (class, state, and so forth). He leaves with Mocho Hernández, just looking for adventure. He joins the Libertadora against Castro out of personal loyalty to a friend. He murders Colmenares, a political boss, just in order to avenge his friend Maurielo, while at the same time he remains loyal to Gómez until the death of another friend.

Maisanta does not have a huge fighting force, but relies on charisma and a sense of shared cultural capital with the rural community, which ensures the loyalty of the local population, a superb knowledge of the terrain, and masterstrokes of genius when it comes to strategy or dissimulation. His identity mixes popular Catholicism (witnessed in the use of the scapular) with implicit machismo and an undivided loyalty to family honor. His supernatural powers are a part of his prestige, and finally he could only be brought down by treason.[22] The bandit label as used against Maisanta survives to this day (see, for example, Manuel Caballero 2004).

As I mentioned at the beginning of this chapter, Chávez fashioned his legitimacy as an unmediated (extralegal) rapport with the people ("my people"). Tapia's text provides a decisive key to how "the people" is constructed. Tapia states in his foreword that he is not the author of the book, that his narrative is in the voice of "the people," and that his text is less written than transcribed. Tapia explains, "We just decided that it would be a good idea to talk with people [*la gente*] and collect legends, anecdotes or witness accounts about the things that have happened in the land of Barinas. From time to time, we hit the road and we chatted with the old folks around; there, we have found a mother lode of popular tradition" (Tapia [1974] 1976, 27). The notion that *Maisanta* represents the unmediated voice of the people (specified differently along regional, cultural, or class lines) is the inaugural gesture of almost all the criticism on the work on Tapia since the 1980s. This recuperation of the voice of the people was such a powerful gesture that even an author like Botello (2005), who explicitly relies on documentation, feels the need to legitimize his work by also claiming firsthand access to oral testimonies.

But *El último hombre a caballo*, at its most literal level, is not the voice of the People. It is the voice of a series of individuals who shared their memories with Tapia. The synthetic artifact People is a totalization by Tapia that happens *a posteriori*, and this totalization implies two operations. First it implies that individuals disappear from the narrative. Some informants are mentioned, but there is never a portion of the narrative that is linked to a particular informant, which is a suppression that causes Tapia, by default, to become the sole, unmediated narrator (since no other voices can be isolated or identified—they are undifferentiated, and this undifferentiating of singular voices is the condition of possibility of the collective exaltation). In the second operation, Tapia transforms the informants' scattered narratives into a coherent whole. This whole is inscribed into another totality: the history of Venezuela. Because of his narration, the story of Maisanta becomes an elegy of rural Venezuela, a picture of the painful transition toward an oil economy, a reflection on imperialism and the neocolonial destiny of Venezuela. The People does not preexist the novel: it is a synthesis that is created in the novel and that does not exist outside the novel (outside of the book, there are discrete individuals). To postulate its existence is a mechanism of cultural legitimation that, at the same time, affirms and denies the epistemological privilege of the man of letters as the unavoidable and immediate mediator, and transforms the murmurs and muffled voices of the multitude into a recognizable historical figure. Chávez's profuse oral interventions, the epitome of which is the TV program *Aló presidente*, hinge on the same fiction. As the title of the program indicates, the assumed origin of the dialogue, its active pole, is the people. But again, it is never the People. There are only individuals. The moment of synthesis in which the People is born is the voice of Chávez, his digressive and totalizing answers that exert an invariable interpretative privilege.

But returning to Tapia: the suppression of the voice of the individual narratives has another effect. It makes Maisanta an unequivocally epic hero. The testimonials that Tapia collects are testimonials of people who fought with Maisanta. But their actions are never mentioned (and whoever reads *Biografía de un cimarrón*, or Elena Poniatowska's *Hasta no verte Jesús Mío*, should be aware of how the elderly people who took part in memorable actions do not tend to forget their part in them). In *El último hombre a caballo,* Maisanta is the only character of any relevance. That suppression of the other biographies uses the epic shortcut, in which the hero is made into a synecdoche of the rest of the community, and that narrative suppression is balanced with a symbolic overcharge. Chávez takes this a step further, since he occupies a double position: he is a character (a descendant of Maisanta) and he is an interpreter (the creator and propagator of the Venezuelan emancipatory narrative), and as such, he is the place where the synthesis that we call "the People" comes into being. Chavista orality is popular, epic, and meta-popular all at the same time. Chávez speaks as a hero, he speaks as the people, and he speaks as an interpreter of the People. It is in his voice, in his body at risk, that (according to Chávez himself) the People comes into being. And this is not my hyperbole: in his message in front of the Constitutional Assembly, when Chávez was turning in his project for the new Constitution of the future Bolivarian Republic of Venezuela, he asserted, bluntly, that until the events of 1989–1992, there was no People in Venezuela.

Chávez adopts three more tropes from Tapia's *Maisanta*, with which I would like to close these pages. First, Maisanta was not a victorious caudillo. He won a number of encounters, but he never won a major battle and never took a provincial capital. But in Tapia's account those defeats are attributed to two factors: first, they are due to treason by the *doctores*, meaning betrayal by caudillos such as París, Vargas, or Arévalo Cedeño who were also professional politicians with formal educations. And second, they are due to the absence of a unified and legitimate leadership. Maisanta, the only qualified leader, according to Tapia, subordinated himself to unqualified leaders. But also, these tropes are elevated in Tapia's text to a status as the keys to Venezuelan history. In fact, a summary of Venezuelan history as a chain of treason and dissension that prevented Venezuela's coming into being is the political education that Elías Cordero gives Maisanta at the beginning of the text (Tapia [1974] 1976, 56).

Chávez, for his part, enters political life and becomes an overnight hero, not as the leader of a victorious uprising but as a dignified loser. I am referring to his media inauguration, when he became a popular icon: the fateful minute that was given to him in order to call for the surrender of his comrades in arms. Unlike Pancho Villa, whose charisma was based on his victories, or at least on his resilience in the face of any defeat, Chavez's charisma was born out of his defeat. Defeat, and dignity in defeat, is a signifier that simultaneously encompasses the populist leader and the People, as common victims of a historical defeat with a superlative power of interpellation. The trope of defeat by treason creates other links with the other heroes vindicated by Chavismo: Guaicuipuro, Bolívar, Zamora, and Castro. They were defeated and betrayed because, like Maisanta, they listened to the professionals and lawyers (*los doctores*). One of the most memorable moments in Maisanta's history is the cursing of the *doctores*: "Cursed be the lawyers and all of those that take advantage of the war in order to climb upon the backs of those below [Maldita sean los doctores y todo aquel que aprovecha la guerra para ver si llega arriba a costillas de los de abajo]!—I swear that I will not do anything else with these motherfuckers, that when it is time to risk everything like a real man, are only good for meetings and conversations" (Tapia [1974] 1976, 228). But again, Chávez performs a cunning sleight of hand. He assumes the position of the defeated, and connects with the audience, but he does not define his entire identity by it. This is the role of the famous "We've lost *for now*" proclaimed in his one-minute televised address.

Failure to assume leadership, falling victim to treason, mark and stunt Maisanta's destiny. They leave the historical cycle incomplete. If Maisanta as outlaw is a point of positive legitimation (to be imitated), these last tropes are a legitimating contrastive instance where Chávez completes what Bolívar, Zamora, Castro, and Maisanta left unfinished (the designation that Chávez uses to refer to his government, Fifth Republic, serves that purpose also) (Marksman 2004, 86). Chávez echoes Maisanta as identity under the form of lineage and as difference under the form of completion. He echoes Maisanta in his obsession with the unity of leadership, the historical defeat to be vindicated; in his obsession with treason and internal divisiveness; in his challenge to the authority of the lawyers (in this case, the Adecos and Copeyanos, the signatories of the Pacto de Punto Fijo). Again, we can see how Maduro prolonged this aspect of Chavista narrative beyond the leader's death: at Chávez's funeral, Maduro grabbed Bolívar's saber and boomed, "We have broken the curse of the treason to the fatherland!" (López de San Miguel 2013).

Finally, Chávez echoes Maisanta in the obsession with the exclusion of internal dissidence from the political game and the absolute need to complete a destiny. From this point of view, the indefinite extension of his rule (cut short by his death, after yet another reelection) is not presented as a personal ambition, but as a historical need. Finally, Chávez's reliance upon *El último hombre a caballo* brings to the fore one of the most disconcerting features of his leadership and his political persona: his devotion to literature, a devotion that made him posit *Les Misérables* as the key to the Latin American political present,[23] a devotion that is one of many factors that explains the disoriented mix of puzzlement, admiration, and disdain with which we cannot avoid considering this instance of the "socialism of the twenty first century."

PART II

BANDITRY
AND THE EPIC
OF THE NATION

THREE

THE BURNING PLAINS
On *Las lanzas coloradas*

War makes the real masters.
PRESENTACIÓN CAMPOS IN ARTURO USLAR PIETRI'S
LAS LANZAS COLORADAS

Nothing is created without war. In nature, perpetual war is the perpetual
creator. War forms peoples, creates nations, makes the unity and greatness
of races. . . . Like identical twins, from its womb come forth the glory of the
captain and the glory of the artist: the laurel drenched in blood and the work
of art clad in unpolluted innocence.
MANUEL DÍAZ RODRÍGUEZ, *SANGRE PATRICIA*

LAS LANZAS COLORADAS (1931), by Arturo Uslar Pietri (1906–2001),
is a great avant-garde novel.[1] But it is also a continuation of nineteenth-century
enquiries around the topic of nationhood. From this point of view, it belongs
to the same family as its contemporary *Doña Bárbara* (1929), by Rómulo Gallegos.[2] From yet another viewpoint, *Las lanzas* is a precursor of Gabriel García
Márquez's *Cien años de soledad* (1967): the story of a family that encompasses the story of a nation, or a particular sector within the nation, erased
from the face of the earth by a cataclysmic historical event. This multiplicity

is not a coincidence. In fact, *Las lanzas* strikes the reader as having an all-encompassing cast of characters of the Latin American drama (or melodrama), as they were put forth in the literature of the long nineteenth century: the conquistador, the emancipator, the bandit, and the insurgent. There is the rich Creole and the poor white; the rebellious—savage—Indian and the peaceful—noble—one; the loyal slave, meek and spineless; and the illegitimate and resentful mixed-blood. There is the obtuse Spaniard and the enlightened Englishman, the ultraconservative clergyman and the youthful iconoclast; the innocent, abused virgin and the hardy, down-to-earth woman of the people. There is the bloodthirsty caudillo and the well-meaning, but sorely out-of-touch, liberal Creole. It also reads like an archive (González Echevarría 1998) of the identity metaphors that weave Latin American cultural narratives: banditry, incest, rape, fratricidal war, romance, cannibalism, sacrifice, orphanage, illegitimacy, and trauma, among other things. The novel ties everything together in a narrative of epic breadth and moments of superb prose (for instance, the scene of the cavalry charge and the *entrevero* [close combat] during the battle of La Victoria, which in my opinion are some of the best pages of prose ever written in Latin America).

This totalizing impulse is not merely encyclopedic. It is subordinated to the presentation of a dialectical conflict, and the ensuing synthesis, in which the nation is born. In narrative terms, it is the presentation of the conflict between the Creole Fernando Fonta and the outlaw Presentación (first moment) and between Presentación and Bolívar (second moment). Bolívar, the only one alive—and triumphant—at the end of the novel, is presented as the synthetic moment of the Venezuelan experience, the resolution or overcoming (*Aufhebung*) of the opposing tendencies in the Venezuelan emancipatory process. The *mantuano* rebellion (rich in ideology, perhaps, but lacking a firm grasp of Venezuelan reality) is the Hegelian "abstract" moment, if you will, while the llanero popular rebellion (lacking in ideology but rich in existential content) is the Hegelian "negative" moment. These rebellions give way to the synthesis, the "concrete" moment that overcomes and recuperates them: Bolívar.

In the development of this dialectic, Uslar Pietri erects himself as the intellectual able to capture the process in narrative form. In true nineteenth-century fashion, he conceived of literature as a force able to heal a national culture rife with conflict.[3] This was done through what Benedict Anderson ([1983] 1996, 1992) called the reassuring effect of fratricide, that is, the construction of a narrative of the past in which war is retold as having occurred between members of an already-formed national community. Therefore, war was, in fact, a family conflict between closely (if unknowingly) linked relatives: brothers. And it was not proof of the dissolution of national bonds but, in fact, proof that those national bonds predated the conflict, or that they were forged by the war itself.[4]

Through this process, *Las lanzas* provides an image of the Venezuelan historical process that, indirectly, justifies the historical necessity of Gómez's regime. At the time of the writing of *Las lanzas*, during the twilight of Gómez's era (he would die of natural causes in 1935, still in power), Uslar Pietri was not a full-fledged regime intellectual, but a minor bureaucrat in an exceedingly comfortable position in the Venezuelan Paris Legation. His family, who spent several years in Maracay, Gómez's usual place of residence, had personal ties with Gómez's family (Uslar Pietri was a close friend of Florencio Gómez, Gómez's son, and he was a guest at the Gómez family's table and on family trips). And while Uslar Pietri did not condone the worst excesses of the regime, the novel, it seems, is an attempt to understand the historical role of the caudillo that ended *caudillismo* (as Vallenilla Lanz [1919] 1989 puts it), by fashioning a fable in which nonstate violence is superseded by a state-in-the-making that, paradoxically, had emerged from the realm of nonstate violence. I am not positing a reading that equates Uslar Pietri's Bolívar to Gómez (although around 1930, that identification would not have been beyond the pale). Rather, I propose a reading of *Las lanzas* as a narrative enactment of the uneasy transactions (and enmities) between liberal intellectuals, outlaws, and state builders.

Las lanzas is the story of the Arcedo-Fonta family, landowners and sugar planters of the Aragua Valley. The family saga began in the sixteenth century, when the ruthless Juan de Arcedo settled the area and founded the hacienda El Altar (Uslar Pietri [1931] 1993, 17). At their zenith, the Arcedo-Fontas achieved regional prominence as landowners, bureaucrats, and members of the clergy and the colonial militia. The novel, however, dwells on the decline and eventual extinction of the last scions of the clan: the weak and indecisive Don Fernando and his sister, the sensitive and naïve Doña Inés. Both are completely unprepared to face the challenges of the violent times in which they are forced to live.

The novel focuses on the years 1813–1814, when the Venezuelan War of Independence was reaching its bloody climax, although it was still far from its resolution. In 1813 Bolívar issued the Decreto de Guerra a Muerte (War to the Death decree), which was followed by the loyalist (i.e., pro–Ferdinand the Seventh) uprising.[5] Under the leadership of Asturian José Tomás Boves (1782–1814), a popular army drawn primarily from the llanos routed the patriot forces under Bolívar's leadership and quashed the Second Republic. This was not the first or the last time that popular guerrilla bandits fought or would fight under the banner of the Bourbons: they had done so in the 1790s, during the War in the Vendée and the Chouannerie in western France, in Naples during the French occupation and Murat's reign (Fra Diavolo being the better-known character in that period), and also in the 1860s, when bandits fought doggedly in southern Italy on the side of the Bourbons against unification. Also in Venezuela, using their royalist allegiance as an ethical shield, bandits would continue marauding areas of Venezuela well into the 1820s. (In his autobiography, Páez explicitly draws the analogy between the royalist bandits and the bandits who fought the French during the occupation. Prominent among these bandits was Dionisio Cisneros, "the Fra Diavolo of Venezuela" [Páez (1867) 1888, 339–40].)

The troops under Boves, however, were less intent on affirming their loyalty to Fernando or the House of Bourbon than on giving violent expression to their ethnic, regional, and class grievances against the mantuanos (Creoles belonging to the colonial aristocracy; by extension, well-to-do Creoles of "clean" racial and religious backgrounds), and in general against all whites of republican persuasion or dubious allegiances.[6] In an analogous fashion— but under the opposite political banner—the huge popular army that Hidalgo amassed in Mexico in 1810 was fighting a class and race war as much as an anticolonial war (Van Young 2001). Because of their origin in a land considered beyond the reach of the law, their composition (llaneros, runaway slaves, blancos de orilla), their fierceness that was not in accordance with European rules of law, and their living off the land, the bandit label was amply used to characterize Boves's troops (see for example, the Gaceta de Caracas during this period).

In the novel, Presentación, the mulatto foreman of El Altar, does not want to miss out on the action. Once he becomes convinced that Fernando lacks the resolution (and bravery) to join the war (Uslar Pietri [1931] 1993, 66), he leads a slave revolt, puts the hacienda thoroughly to the torch, rapes Inés, and leaves her to die in the burning manor house.[7] By raping Inés he may have committed incest, since the novel implicitly suggests that Presentación is her illegitimate (and unacknowledged) half-brother.[8] Presentación leads his forces toward the llanos, where the Boves insurgency is gaining traction. Royalist insurgency or not, this was a common path for colonial runaway slaves, as well as other characters in trouble with the law, something that added to the coastal perception of the llanos as outlaw country. Eventually, Presentación joins Boves's forces for the awe-inspiring cavalry charge that attempts to take La Victoria. (The massive cavalry charge was the signature tactic of Boves's army, and also Artigas's during the same period in the River Plate, and would be, a century later, Villa's.) Presentación is wounded while charging the city's defenses and is taken prisoner. He dies in a cellar that doubles as a prison cell, unable to face (or even to see) Bolívar, the man who (for reasons that will be explained later) he has made his nemesis (212). In the same battle, on the other side, Fernando meets a less than dignified fate under the hooves of the charging llanero horses (201).

The choice of the War of Independence as the focus of the novel is not gratuitous. For Uslar Pietri, as well as for a significant portion of Venezuelan society, the War of Independence is the most important event in Venezuelan history, the most important cultural capital of the nation, its unequivocal founding myth.[9] Within the War of Independence, the period 1813–1814 is crucial, since this was the period of "creative destruction," the bloody staging of the annihilation of the old and the emergence of the new that has a firm hold on Venezuelan cultural mythology to this day. (Fernando, when witnessing the destruction of El Altar, is conscious that this is the end of his world, an apocalypse [Uslar Pietri (1931) 1993, 111]. For a change, a character who is often wrong is, in this instance, completely right.) The late Hugo Chávez's obsession with all things Bolívar is a testimony to the preeminent place that the War of Independence continues to have. And this obsession, even in its most "extreme" manifestations (i.e., the exhuming of Bolívar's corpse in order to look into the hypothesis that Bolívar may have been murdered), is mainstream in Venezuelan culture (Pino Iturrieta 2003, 2007), in the same way that the obsession with Martí (including Martí's death) defines Cuban culture(s) on both sides of the Florida Strait (De la Fuente 2001; Bejel 2012).

The novel is, indeed, a by-product of the cult of Bolívar. On the centennial of Bolívar's death (1930), Uslar Pietri briefly entertained the idea of an avant-garde film tentatively titled *Simón Bolívar: Poema cinematográfico*. He pitched it to his friend Rafael Rivero Oramas in a letter on June 24, 1930. Probably for the best, the film never came to fruition; Uslar Pietri wrote *Las lanzas* instead.[10] In spite of its failure, the film project, as it was described to Rivero Oramas, merits examination. Uslar Pietri explains that the movie was to present the audience with shots of the following:

> [landscapes:] mountains, rivers, seas, plains, sky; the animals: tigers, serpents, condors, macaws, colts, bulls; the men: naked soldiers, soldiers with British uniforms, men sowing, fishing, riding; old men, kids, women grinding corn; and all in a wisely arranged mix, and without any connection other than the vague Bolivarian photographic theme that unites all of them. . . . Shots of maps of America interspersed with shots of mountains and bodies of water; distorted shots of the statue in Bolívar Square; pictures like the Liberator footprints: the baptism pile with the water rippling, as if the child has just been removed from it; the bed with the sheets in disarray, as if the man has just gotten up from it; the horse saddled and sweaty as if the rider has just dismounted it; the saber in a corner, as if it has just been left there; a kid crying, and an old man smiling; pictures of weapons, shots of weapons: rifles, spears, sabers, old cannons, some sailboats. Details from Tenerani's statue [of Bolívar]. The [Venezuelan] flag flying in the wind.[11]

The film would have been a montage of images and sounds without discernible narrative continuity, dialogue, unifying musical motif, or even identifiable characters. Clearly influenced by Soviet avant-garde film, such as Sergei Eisenstein's *October* (1928), its presumptive principle of intelligibility would have been that all the things seen were "elements of Bolívar's work [*obra*]." They thus share with Bolívar a metonymical or metaphorical relationship. (They are metonymical when they show the effects of Bolívar's presence—the ripples in the baptismal water, the sweat on the horse, the crumpled sheets. They are metaphorical when they somehow share a feature attributed to Bolívar—the mountain's grandeur, for example.) The signified is one: Bolívar. He is identical to the Nation, and the Nation emanates from a Bolívar who links nature and culture (nature is "national" nature, appropriated by military,

political, and economic history, whose main agent is Bolívar). This makes
entirely illusory the plurality of signifiers that the movie presents. They cease
to make a system (hence, they cease to be signifiers) because there should
be something like a non-Bolívar as an alternative signified, for a signifier to
become one, and actually signify. In its absence, the differential and opposi-
tional nature of the signifier, precisely what makes it a signifier, disappears. In
the film, Bolívar is less a signified than a Platonic Idea, an essence outside history, accessible only through the imperfect mediation of sensible stimuli (the
film images). Bolívar never appears as such in the movie. Like the Platonic
Idea, Bolívar can be captured either through reason (the Idea is an intelligible
substance) or through tropes (like the Allegory of the Cave). The movie would
make us aware that the multiplicity of images (the movie itself) is illusory: the
many images refer to the one Idea (or the Idea of the One): Bolívar.

In the novel, Bolívar is still the pivotal figure. However, he ceases to be
the ubiquitous signified to which all the signifiers refer. As in the movie, we
never see him. He is present (metonymically) in the voices and thoughts of
others: slaves and landowners, patriots and royalists, soldiers who admire and
acclaim him and soldiers who fear or despise him, and, above all, Presentación. The voices in the novel are far removed from the images in the film.
In the novel, orality is the medium of politics: "I am Bolívar"; "Death to the
insurgent!"; "Now you are going to see how a hero fights!" The spoken word
is not the popular orality of the *criollista* novel (which either consecrates the
"popular" voice as folk culture or condemns it as superstition or barbarism).[12]
The voice is the conduit of the war report, a weapon, a command ("Natividad!
Cirilo! We are charging!"), a death sentence ("Shoot them. You guarantee that
with your head"), or a statement of hierarchical difference and hatred ("Coward slave!"). Thus, in the novel, oral performances define identities and these
identities are defined as challenges ("I have the flesh of a master!"; "I am Bolívar") or as acts of subordination ("Have a great day, don Presentación!"). In
this respect, the oral medium is superior to the ineffectual written medium:
the libel against Miranda, the half-understood edition of Rousseau, the useless papers that Roso gives Fernando, the law books that make up Fernando's
education all bespeak this ineffectual nature.

Through the presence of the voice of an enemy, and the presence of voices
defined by their positions in a political and military struggle, Bolívar's figure

enters into a network of conflicts and oppositions. The Nation does not preexist these conflicts (as the naïve patriotic mantuanos imagine), and the identification Nation/Bolívar is far from a certainty. The identification Bolívar/
Nation indeed occurs at the end of the novel. *Las lanzas* is, after all, a pious
and celebratory novel.[13] However, it occurs as the product of war (and not in
reverse: war makes Bolívar, instead of being, as in the movie, part of Bolívar's
"work"—not development, but manifestation). Moreover, the narrative path
always entails risks that make the novel stray from its original pious purpose
and allow for glimpses of alternative readings. These interpretations coexist
but diverge formally and politically. Their tense coexistence is precisely what
makes the novel rich and appealing, and it is to this interpretation that I will
devote the following pages.

Fernando and Inés embody the mantuano status quo: the stale colonial order
as well as the Creole insurrection that, in spite of its ferocious rhetoric, did
not intend to deeply affect the social aspects of the colonial social edifice. The
novel presents this status quo as historically irrelevant, surviving in a sort of
meaningless stasis. In a novel full of events, Fernando hardly does anything:
he does not finish his studies, does not fall in love, does not effectively run his
hacienda, nor does he write, or ride, or hunt, or participate in the war. As the
novel puts it, Fernando had, "in an immature flesh, a shy and indecisive spirit.
When compelled to make the most trivial decision hundreds of voices beset
him, calling to him and luring him from opposite directions. He was never able
to act in a decisive fashion or follow a single purpose" (Uslar Pietri [1931] 1993,
140). Fernando's character presents some of the motifs of the bildungsroman
(a young mind looking for meaning and direction, in a world in which the fight
between the old and the new is taking place). But it is a failed development,
since all the revelations that he experiences—be they religious or patriotic in
nature—are inconsequential in terms of building a character. Even his joining the conspiracy of the Sociedad Patriótica is less a coming of age than the
acting out of a childish fantasy, his harmless foray into the world of Byronian romanticism (secret societies, passwords, night conspiracies, oaths, and
forbidden books). This is reminiscent of the "middle of the road" hero of the
classical historical novel, according to György Lukács ([1937] 1983), but there
is a significant difference: Fernando never grows up.

War destroys this mantuano status quo without rest: Fernando dies, but his death is not a consecration (he is not a martyr *ad maiorem patriae gloriam*). Rather, it is a negligible event in the sound and fury of the battle; he dies and immediately falls into oblivion.[14] El Altar is burned to the ground. Inés survives Presentación's assault but disappears in the almost infinite plains. In her misdirected search for revenge, she walks south, the same south from which another raped woman, Barbarita (Doña Bárbara), would emerge a century later also looking for revenge. But the Arcedo-Fontas are not alone in this. None of their peers achieve a full closing (thus highlighting the impossibility of integrating the old landowning class into the new nation). Luiz perishes under a collapsing building during the earthquake of 1811. Irón dies lynched by a drunken mob. Bernardo (Fernando's best friend and the one who introduces him to the patriot cause) is a man of convictions, and he is willing to die for these convictions, but he also dies without firing a single shot in the patriotic struggle. David, the British volunteer enrolled in the patriot cause, dies with Bernardo.[15]

Fernando lacks all generative power. He dies unmarried and, as far as we can tell, a virgin, without a romantic relationship or even any interest in sex. Inés does not die a virgin, but her one and only sexual encounter (as far as the novel tells us) is the rape of which she is a victim.[16] Inés may indeed be pregnant with Presentación's child (although there is no clear indication of this in the novel), but in melodrama, each act—in particular, any sexual act—is pregnant with destiny. In this case, the Arcedo-Fonta lineage will endure in an accursed way: through the mixed-blood child of rape and incest, who will not know his true name. This would be a fitting (albeit twisted) repetition of the scene of female abuse that gave origin to the Arcedo-Fonta lineage in the first place. (The Arcedos and the Fontas became a single family when José Fonta forcibly married the late Carlos Arcedo's daughter, thus making Manuel the largest landowner in the valley [Uslar Pietri (1931) 1993, 23].) Another less-than-desirable destiny for the family would be to survive through the bastard child of La Carvajala (the woman who nurses Presentación back to health after he is wounded in a skirmish, and who will become his lover), in which case the descendant of the proud lineage of Creole landowners would be a mixed-blood peasant. So the annihilation of the brothers and their world at the hands of Presentación (or the forces that Presentación emblematizes) is the fitting, perhaps inevitable end to a historical cycle.

But Bolívar supersedes Presentación. The novel begins with a yarn told by

Espíritu Santo (one of the slaves). It is the story of Matías, an Indian bandit of royalist persuasion, like the historical bandit José Dionisio Cisneros. The story's climax occurs when Matías runs into a small, unimpressive man and demands to know his name: "Me?" the man replies. "Bolívar" (Uslar Pietri [1931] 1993, 10). The bandit vanishes like a devil in the presence of an exorcist. The story is a success, but a short-lived one: "The slaves celebrated, with loud laughter, the yarn when the shadow of a body was projected onto the middle of the circle of bodies. They looked around swiftly. The foreman, in a threatening attitude, was standing in front of them. His commanding figure towered over the eight cowed slaves" (10). If Bolívar (his body and his name) exorcises the demonic presence of the bandit Matías, the shadow of Presentación, the bandit-to-be, dissipates the presence of Bolívar conjured up by Espíritu Santo's tale. The novel ends with the same triad with which it began: Presentación, Bolívar, and a "popular" voice, that is, the unending "¡Viva el Libertador!" that salutes Bolívar's arrival in the town. Bolívar manifests himself only in the voice of others. The first narrative (Natividad's) is a tall tale told by a slave to other slaves during a work break at the plantation. The latter is not a narrative, but only an interpellation, and we do not know who speaks: the voice is not marked in class, racial, or gendered terms, so it is not a voice but the Voice. It is more the abstract mode of subjectivation of (ideal) liberal citizenship, defined by the exclusion of any differentiation of the popular voice. This is why the scene is narrated from Presentación's viewpoint. Locked in a cellar, he cannot see any of the people yelling; he can only hear voices.[17]

The battle of La Victoria is the climax of the novel. This battle occurred on February 12, 1814, but Uslar Pietri's reconstruction does not follow the historical record. Although the novel suggests that this was the ultimate face-off between Boves and Bolívar, and that it changed the tide of the war, neither Boves nor Bolívar were in the battle. The battle was only a temporary setback for Boves, who was on his way to crushing the Second Republic. The novel also suggests that Boves died in the battle, which of course he did not. Boves died later on, in 1814, in an action in which Bolívar was not present. These discrepancies are not due to historical inaccuracy, but to the fact that the logic of the novel demands a face-off between Boves (and his proxy, Presentación) and Bolívar, for the enthronement of Bolívar as the culmination of the Venezuelan drama-to-happen.

The battle is Presentacion's existential climax. When Boves orders a full cavalry assault on the town, Presentación cannot contain himself. He charges with his men before his turn, while yelling at the top of his lungs, "Now you are going to see how a true hero fights!" (Uslar Pietri [1931] 1993, 200). "Hero," in the mouth of Presentación, seems strange. He conceives his participation in the war neither as part of a national emancipatory epic nor as an imperial restoration effort. So in what sense can Presentación be a hero? Certainly he could be a hero, in a vastly broad sense of a "national hero," such as that of Rivas, Bolívar, Colonel Roso, Captain David, or Bernardo. But what kind could Presentación be?

The hypothesis consistent with the dialectical reading previously put forward would consider Presentación a "popular" hero, that is, the hero of the blacks and the mixed-bloods, the hero of the poor Venezuelans, the hero of the llaneros. Thus the novel would be the narration of a conflict whose adversaries, even if they do not consider themselves affiliated with the same cultural synthesis (the nation), are resignified by the novel as brothers who ignore the fact that they are brothers. It would be a conflict between "Venezuelans" who ignore their identity as such. Presentación's death would be a metaphor of the sublation of constituent power by constituted power, the multitude by the nation-state and its subjects. It would also be an assertion of the (necessary and necessarily suppressed) place of outlaw insurgency in the transition from the colonial system to the national one. This would emphasize the role of the novel itself as the locus of the formation of a memory of the reassuring fratricide. Presentación dies ignorant of the meaning of his destiny. In fact, he does not conceive of his life as a "biography" with a "destiny." His life, for him, is a being-for-war, a becoming-lancero, and an assemblage of man, spear, and horse. Only in the novel, through the mediation of the omniscient narrator who is fully identified with the national project, does the truth of Presentación's fate emerge. Only there does the insurgency cease to be a senseless bloodbath and become a national epic (or the opportunity for a national epic), happening beyond the consciousness of its actors. Presentación, the nomadic warrior, is transformed into Presentación, the embodiment of the People, or, to put it in Herrera Luque's ([1972] 1980) terms, the first champion of democracy in Venezuela.

But Presentación has no clue about Venezuela, or any interest in it. And this does not matter. The dead *are* the truth of the nation but they cannot *say* the truth. Only through the mediation of the narrative voice, the tear in the social fabric that was the 1814 revolution becomes the necessary negative moment in a dialectic whose synthetic moment is the nation-state. Bolívar becomes "Bolívar" when faced with Presentación. Presentación has to be erased in order for the "popular" principle of the nation to endure—as negated.

It is in opposition to the lancers led by Boves and Presentación that the patriot army becomes a "national" army: a multiracial, multiregional, multi-temporal organism, composed of Indians still living in the Stone Age, as well as of units organized according to the nineteenth-century division into three branches: infantry, cavalry, and artillery. The army is thus the forge where the national community is born. Allow me to quote the novel: "There are thin men of the Llanos, round-headed men from Coro, talkative ones from the East, men from Guyana. They have arrived from all directions and the war has mixed them up. Someone tells an adventure; another one, the story of his life; a third recalls a memory that makes him sad. . . . Those men, from all corners of the land, united for the destruction of war, talked to each other, with longing, of their native places. They destroyed each other somewhat lacking full aware-ness" (Uslar Pietri [1931] 1993, 248). The war accomplishes the geographical and cultural totalizing that Fernando dreams about at the beginning of the novel. This totalizing effect is possible through the figure of Bolívar, who is simultaneously the fulfillment of the war's intent and the limit of the risks posited by it. Bolívar territorializes the war as a national war, one that is ori-ented toward the foundation of a nation-state, while he is also the resolution of the contradiction.

Boves's army, the "seven thousand lancers," are undifferentiated lancers, utterly interchangeable, and the metaphors that describe them are always col-lective ones: water out of bounds (Uslar Pietri [1931] 1993, 263), ants (263), "advancing portions of the savannah" (191), creeping, ominous shadows (263), "moving stain" (263), "amorphous mass" (172), "crowd" (172), "tempest of men" (172), "advancing tides," (263) "avalanches" (243). Bolívar becomes the formative principle only when faced with the entropic chaos, as the formative force that suppresses chaos.

Hugo Chávez is the living proof of the force and the relevance of this inter-pretation of the novel. As I explained in chapter 2, Chávez based his legiti-macy on a double source: the massive appropriation of the Bolivarian legacy (including the dead body of the liberator), and his own llanero identity and lineage via Maisanta. Chávez thus inhabited a space not inaugurated but defined by *Las lanzas*, since he (his biography, his own body) proposed itself as a synthesis of the llanero outlaw insurgency and the national epic, the two versions of the hero. Chávez would be a Bolívar (a liberator of hemispheric proportions), but a Bolívar who had within himself a Presentación (the leader of a war through which the nation is born, or reenacted).[18]

Presentación is wounded while storming the defenses of La Victoria; he falls from his horse and passes out. He briefly awakens to realize that the battle has been lost, that he is a prisoner, and that he is being carried somewhere (Uslar Pietri [1931] 1993, 205). He passes out again and awakens in the cellar where he will die (206). There, he feverishly tries to understand how his life is ending in this way.[19] He thinks and thinks about Bolívar, to whom he devotes his last thoughts and his last energies. This "obsession" is out of character. Presentación never thought about the past before. And he never harbored rancor: he dealt decisively with insults or challenges, as shown in his impromptu decision to rise up in arms (88); the rape of Inés when she called him a murderer, a traitor, and, worst of all, a coward and slave (90–93); and the immediate and casual killing of the slave who challenged his taking over the hacienda (89–90). This anomaly, however, serves a clear ideological purpose: to emphasize the fact that Bolívar is his *historical* nemesis, not (or not only) his military one. If he were to resent somebody for his fate, it should be Ribas, the one who actually defeated him. And even this would be out of character: a true warrior never resents his vanquisher, if the vanquisher is brave and the battle was fought loyally, as in this case. But the novel ends with Bolívar's *triumphus*, not Ribas's. Presentación can listen to the drums setting the rhythm of the parade (the orderly movement of the bodies, in stark contrast to the chaotic cavalry charge), and the voices acclaiming Bolívar. But he cannot see Bolívar, and he does not even know where the scene is taking place. This is because the scene is not happening in Caracas, or in a specific village somewhere in Venezuela, but in the abstract realm of history, the place where what Presentación represents surrenders its place to what Bolívar represents. But at the same time, it is the dramatic manifestation of the fact that, if Presentación has to die for Bolívar to become what he is, Presentación had to have existed for Bolívar to become what he is.

Toward the end, the drumbeat is so strong that Presentación's flesh resonates to it ("That sound makes the flesh tremble, as well as the maddened

blood inside the flesh" [Uslar Pietri (1931) 1993, 210]). The voices hailing Bolívar are so loud that it is "as if they [the voices] were inside him" (211), making
his blood boil from excitement (211). This would be the ultimate proof of the
novel's totalizing impulse: the fact that, willingly or unwillingly, Presentación
becomes, from his humble cell, from the depth of despair and defeat, one more
of the thrilled voices hailing the liberator as the embodiment of the Nation, as
the unifying obsession of Venezuela (211), as the name after which Venezuela
came into being.[20]

But Presentación has another idea of what Venezuela is: for him it is not
an abstract brotherhood of citizens, or a concrete brotherhood of comrades
in arms. Venezuela is a huge burning plain, a huge battlefield, neither a cause
nor a territory to be fought over, but simply a territory upon which to fight:

> So beautiful are the flames rising from the huts, from the villages put to the
> torch, from the big house in the hacienda. Yellow and red flags waving among
> the flames. The whole of Venezuela engulfed in the flames of war. Through-
> out the savannas horsemen charged with couched lances, in all the corners of
> the land the towns were going up in flames. He was on the ground, wounded
> and disabled. Coming out of the Orinoco; coming out from the sea; coming
> out of the Llano. All the land, all the water, all the air. Men battled. The flames
> grow as when a house burns and the house grows with the flames like when a
> mountain burns, and the mountain . . .[21] (Uslar Pietri [1931] 1993, 209)

I would like to devote the last pages of this chapter to this alternative (i.e.,
nonnational) vision of war: war not as a medium, but as an end in itself. This
interpretation, even if it partially contradicts the previous one, does not annul
it. It adds another dimension of meaning to the novel that coexists uneasily
with the other. It is in this tension that the novel acquires additional depth,
and additional relevance, to this day.

Huts, manor houses, villages on fire, are for Presentación a superb spectacle ("So beautiful are the flames rising from the huts, from the villages put
to the torch, from the big house in the hacienda. Yellow and red flags waving
among the flames"). In this penchant for arson, Presentación is one more
link in a chain of brigand arsonists such as Michael Kohlhaas in the novel of
the same name (Heinrich von Kleist, 1808) and Karl von Moor in *Die Räuber*

(Friedrich Schiller, 1781). But unlike his German counterparts, he is not acting out of lawful revenge (like the fastidious Kohlhaas, who never forgets his two abused horses, the reason for a feud that threatens the empire) or spite (like the somber Karl von Moor, deprived of his birthright by the conniving Franz). Their acts, outrageous as they are, never represent a complete break with the law of the state or the codes of the community, to which they never cease to long for readmission (once the grievances are resolved, legally or through blood). For them, the fearsome spectacle of violence is a means to an end—they are terrorists, in a way. For Presentación, on the other hand, war *is* the end. The flames are the flags: yellow (patriot) and red (royalist). The flames collapse both causes into an undifferentiated sight of destruction.

Presentación fights superbly, but he does not share any of the meanings that guide the war for the elite: it is not an ideological war (liberalism vs. corporatism), not a national war (patriots vs. royalists), not a class war (hacendados against slaves), and not a regional war (the coast against the llanos), nor is it a racial war (the blacks and *pardos* [mulattoes] of Boves's army against the mantuanos). It is not even a warrior gentleman's war, as David understands it. The Venezuelan War of Independence was all of these things, but not for Presentación. It does not entail an affiliation with a political sign, but rather the dissolution of all signs of sovereignty. The uprising of the slaves of El Altar is not intended to establish a new juridical order for Venezuela (the tricolor flag of Miranda) or to reestablish the old one (both orders had sanctioned slavery, and a deep-seated racial hierarchy). The memorable dialogue between Presentación, Cirilo, and Natividad (Presentación's lieutenants) sufficiently explains this:

—But you have not thought about something, Natividad. Which side are we going to join?

—What do you mean, which side?

—¡Guá! Which side are we going to choose? Are we going to become Royalists or Republicans. . . .

—Well, boss, and what is the difference?

—There is a great difference! Imagine asking that! Don't you see? The Royalists have a red flag and they yell, Long live the King!

—That's it.

—On the other hand, the insurgents have a yellow flag and yell, Long live Freedom!

—Oh shit, what should we choose? (Uslar Pietri [1931] 1993, 199)

This scene has been explained away as evidence of the general lack of consciousness as well as Presentación's lack of legitimate political motivations. This is a possibility. But I think this dialogue enacts a different kind of "consciousness"—that embodied in the vision of the flames as flags. (Presentación does not want land, rank, or even honors. He mentions them only occasionally, but it is clear that his passion rests elsewhere.) He does not plunder and he does not rape. He appears to even lack an idea of society outside of war. But this is not the perennial present of the animalized barbarian, unable to conceive and to prepare for the future, or to deal with the past. War for Presentación is an experience outside of time, at once fleeting and totalizing, an exaltation of his individuality and a disappearance of it: it is an aesthetic experience, not Apollonian in nature, but rather Dionysian. He does not contemplate the battle, but his body is part of it, and loses itself in it. The scene of the battle is exemplary in this respect: "Presentación Campos feels himself wrapped by the cries and the confusion of battle. . . . He does not get tired, he does not conceive that it could ever end, once it had begun. Years will go by, furiously, tearing the enemy to pieces. . . . Presentación Campos does not have eyes to see the ones that flee, nor to become aware of the defeat: for him there are only riders, riders and spears around him, against which he unleashes his destructive wrath" (Uslar Pietri [1931] 1993, 182–83). Soon afterward, it continues:

There is not a thing still; neither the land itself, nor the trees, nor the air, shaken by the cannon fire, nor the dead, trampled by the horses. . . .

Nobody is a man anymore. Each one is only a deadly thing that knows how to destroy, that longs for destruction, that does not live but in order to destroy.

The eyes do not see human beings charging, but arms with red lances, and the others do not see men charging either, but red arms, red arms with red lances.

Of the horses, they do not see but the two ears on end that float above the nervous limbs, the two ears pointed up like the lance.

For an instant, one loses the consciousness of things, of shapes, of colors, and then, the furious eyes only see other terrible eyes, hard and cold, crystallized by fury; pale deadly stares in the flight of the lances, among the dazzling shine of the lances, under the thick tree of the lances. Glassy eyes of the dead, oily eyes of the horses, piercing eyes of the man charging, who can injure with his stare or with his weapon, eyes that do not close or blink because they would make the battle disappear. . . . Sinister glare, storm of brilliance, eyes, eyes, eyes and lances, over the tempestuous cavalry. (198)

In the battle, the world seems to explode into fragments of experience. There are not even bodies, but fragments of bodies. There are not even fragments, but colors superimposed upon other colors (the blood dripping on the horse becomes a sheer burst of color, scarlet over black; the lancer riding the horse becomes a brush of brown over yellow [194]). And certainly, there is not a narrative that places the battle in the time of history, but rather an instant of sheer intensity, in which Presentación simultaneously loses himself and reaches unimaginable heights. This is why he alone charges the village defenses: out of enthusiasm, in the Dionysian sense.

The diverse modes of conceiving war, and the politics that derive from it, appear in stark relief in the episode concerning the gift that Captain David gives to Presentación (who holds a rather equivocal fascination for him). After a ride, a bath, and a conversation together, David decides to give Presentación a pair of finely wrought English pistols (Uslar Pietri [1931] 1993, 70) and this gift entails David's misrecognition of Presentación. "Furiously egalitarian," David thinks that they are equals: men of energy with a taste for war (he thinks about Boves in a similar fashion). But they are not. And Presentación (not David) names the difference and the meaning of that difference. He rejects the liberal ideology of equality, ineffectually exposed in the meeting of the Patriotic Society (52), though that was also endorsed by David. Presentación knows that he is different and why: "The Englishman was another kind of man [different from Fernando, for whom Presentación has no respect whatsoever]. But that was not enough. If he [David] liked war it was a war that he [Presentación] did not understand. It was a war with nice uniforms, with generals full of medals, with marching bands. Presentación could not understand that. For him, war was a lance and a horse; everything else was a hindrance; no uniforms, but naked from the waist up; no music but shouting; and no more generals than the one that one has inside" (80).

With the gift, David intends to impress upon Presentación an aesthetic meaning of war. But they have different aesthetics. While Presentación is Dionysian, David is Byronian. The pistol is not given as a weapon, but rather as a souvenir ("I am going to give you an excellent English pistol. With this you will remember me. . . . Keep it and remember who gave it to you" [Uslar Pietri (1931) 1993, 70]). It is an object of art, and the gift is intended as a token of an interclass, intercultural alliance (as also occurs in Jorge Isaacs's *María* [1867] when Efraín gifts his carbine to his retainer, the free peasant Braulio). Presentación rejects the meaning implicit in the gift. The lance is his weapon. He uses the pistols only twice: to show them off when he gathers the slaves of El Altar and announces that they are leaving the plantation (Uslar Pietri [1931] 1993, 193), and to shoot them in the air when they take their first village (200). The weapons disappear throughout the rest of the work. In the same way that Presentación rejects the liberal idea of equality espoused by David, he rejects the liberal idea of freedom. In order to clarify this point, allow me to provide another example, one that draws a distinction with another plain, the Russian steppes. Boym (2010, 78) explains that "Russian cultural mythologies of national identity are often based on words that were deemed untranslatable. . . . There are two words for freedom, 'svoboda' and 'volia.' 'Svoboda' appears to resemble the Western word 'freedom,' while it is claimed that 'volia' connotes a radical liberation and a 'freer freedom' rhyming with the boundlessness of the steppe and the ruthless dreams of rebels and bandits." In the Venezuelan case, while David and the patriots pursue "svodoba," Presentación pursues (and achieves) "volia."

In *Las lanzas* the plain is not a region in relation to which Boves, Presentación, and his lancers would propose a subnational (although basically similar to the national) principle of sovereignty.[22] *Las lanzas* breaks with the aesthetic of criollismo, and its treatment of landscape as a totalizing backdrop. As Miliani explains, in criollismo "the action happened on one side, and disjointed from it, slowing down its rhythm, there was the melody of the exotic landscape" (1993, 99). In *Las lanzas* the landscape (and its symbolic frame, the region) ceases to exist, because there is no difference between landscape and action.

Landscape is a metaphor, a mediation for something else: the Nation (as we saw in Uslar Pietri's film project), nature, work, race, culture, or an aesthetic ideal. It also implies a number of segmentations, in particular the ones related to the difference between subjective point of view and the object of contemplation. One is never lost in the landscape because its cultural essence is that it is a language ready to be deciphered. We can think of Santos Luzardo, the protagonist of *Doña Bárbara*, who is linked to the plains culturally (he is from the plains, and he proves that he can be a leader of men), and through ownership (he rescues his hacienda), as well as by right of military and sexual conquest (he defeats Doña Bárbara, and he makes both her and her daughter, Marisela, fall in love with him). Through conflict, Santos Luzardo turns the plain into countryside. War (i.e., the feud with Doña Bárbara) is an accident: it does not define the plain or himself. He owns the plain. Boves and his lancers, by contrast, belong to the plain, a place where no abode is possible. This is why they are always depicted in motion, always riding in a sort of uninterrupted cavalry charge from deep in the llanos to La Victoria and onto a (theoretically infinite) beyond. The llaneros do not ride the plain. They are the plain in motion, as the novel says. It is not possible to "see" the plain, because one is fighting in it. The plain is not a spectacle, but an objective, a line of flight, the no-man's-land that one has to cover under enemy fire. "Land exists so that men can fight in it," says Presentación (Uslar Pietri [1931] 1993, 295), summarizing the novel's treatment of space. Boves and Presentación belong to the plain only through war, and through the nomadism that war imposes.

Ribas and his army (and before them, Roso and his forces) are static, quartered in the town. Although the patriot army has a cavalry division, Ribas does not ride with them. He is in the fortified town, directing the defense from its very center (the proverbial main square), while Boves is at the front of (or, more accurately, among) his lancers in motion: "And close to him, Benicio the Indian, silent, restraining his horse. And a little further away, to the right, the dense cavalry, and to the left, the cavalry, and behind him, the cavalry, and above all the heads the shining of the lances, as if the stars were low upon the earth" (Uslar Pietri [1931] 1993, 172).

A radial model of war (Ribas) opposes a longitudinal one (Boves). Ribas's orders always emanate from the center, and spread to the periphery. Boves's orders emanate from a point (a rather undifferentiated point) in the line of llaneros, and are carried out by a messenger along the cavalry line ("In front of the line of riders there was a black man galloping at full speed, constantly uttering the rallying cry, like a flag, that caused the great compact masses to charge" [Uslar Pietri (1931) 1993, 179]). It is not a war between a force that just happens to be in a town and a force that happens to be in the plains. It is a war of the plain that mobilizes a war machine against the city and its juridical and administrative apparatus, but it is never identical to it. In nation-states, war machine and economic machine work in unison (ideally) but remain differentiated entities (as Tilly [1975] has examined in the European case, the military machine and the juridical-administrative mechanism reinforce and endow meaning for each other). In the case of Boves and Presentación, the war machine, the economic machine (plunder), and the political machine are one and the same: a unified machine that blurs the segmentations of race, class, and gender upon which the Creole segmentation of the social space was theretofore based.[23]

Both armies prepare for battle. But the battle is not the same thing for both armies. For Ribas and his army, history beckons. La Victoria is not for them an indifferent skirmish or a bloodbath (like the one that obliterated the forces of Roso at La Puerta), but the "Battle of La Victoria," which was a singular landmark that occurred in 1814 and that the generations (hopefully) will not forget. Essentially they aspire to the transcendent time of secular progress toward universal emancipation. The battle also relates to another space, according to a radial model. It happens in La Victoria, but La Victoria is only important as a stepping-stone (or a roadblock) on the way to Caracas and the Second Republic, which Ribas represents. For Ribas, the battle is part of the war through the mediation of meaning, and war is conceived as mediation itself. For Boves, for Presentación, there is nothing "behind" them. They do not stand for anything beyond themselves (which differentiates their violence from a "popular" violence). The battle is the war, not an episode of the war— and there may not even be a battle, since it is an uninterrupted cavalry charge from far away in the llano. Thus, war remains a pure moment of rupture, a hiatus.

The novel celebrates the emancipatory saga, no doubt. But its very title harbors an ambiguity. The title comes from a passage of Páez's *Autobiografía* ([1867] 1888, 154): "I sent sergeant Ramón Valero with eight soldiers, hand picked because of their bravery, all mounted on nimble, fast horses [to attack the enemy forces], warning all of them that they would be shot by a firing squad if they did not come back to our lines with their lances drenched in enemy blood." But the "red lance" is, vis-à-vis the emancipatory war, an ambiguous symbol (the same way that Páez, father of Venezuela and llanero warrior, is ambiguous). Both factions could exhibit the red lance (and in the novel, the royalists do so more than the patriots, and not only because the royalist flag was red). The red lance has no preexisting symbolic bent. Presentación also could see it as a flag ("The fire of the lances goes extinct. It is no longer over the heads. Now it is level with the breasts of the men, like the poles of red ragged flags" [Uslar Pietri (1931) 1993, 175]). It is not the flag of Venezuela, the red badge of courage, but a symbol entirely immanent in the struggle.[24]

Las lanzas is a celebration of the happy (albeit bloody) synthesis of Venezuelan nationality. But it presents, equally forcefully, the excess of that synthesis. War, according to this version, simultaneously constructed and destroyed an order of identity definitions (the archive of metaphors that I mentioned earlier). In *Las lanzas* we witness a conscious play with identity metaphors, but at the same time their deconstruction. This deconstruction takes place through the War to the Death in the plains. This double treatment is perhaps the feature that makes *Las lanzas*, in my opinion, key to the literature of Latin America: its possibilities, its limits, and its obsessions.

FOUR

"BODIES FOR THE GALLOWS"
On *¡Vámonos con Pancho Villa!*

Come, all my hearties,
We'll roam the mountains high,
Together we will plunder,
Together we will ride.
We'll scar over valleys,
And gallop for the plains,
And scorn to live in
Slavery, bound down by iron chains.

"THE WILD COLONIAL BOY"

Hunted from out our father's home,
Pursued by steel and shot,
A bloody warfare we must wage
Or the gibbet be our lot.
Hurrah! This war is welcome work,
The hunted outlaw knows
He steps unto his country's love o'er the Corpses of his foes.

"OUTLAWED RAPPAREE"

¡VÁMONOS CON PANCHO VILLA! is the saga of the "Leones de San Pablo" (Miguel Ángel, Máximo, Rodrigo, Melitón, Martín, and their leader and senior, Tiburcio Maya), a small group of northern rural folk of strong Villista persuasion. The novel begins just before the incorporation of the group into the División del Norte in its unstoppable southward thrust to dislodge Huerta from power. The Leones played a distinguished part in many of the major encounters in 1913–1914 (the División's heyday, and the time in which Villa's status as the most capable general of the revolution seemed uncontested): San Andrés, Chihuahua, Ojinaga, Tierra Blanca, Torreón. In each encounter, the Leones paid their blood tribute to the cause, in the form of the death of one of their members, usually in a rather gruesome fashion. Tiburcio, the only survivor of the group, deserted the División right before the battle of Zacatecas (June 1914). But he rejoined Villa's forces in late 1915, after Obregón had defeated Villa at Celaya and León, and Villa had disbanded the División. Tiburcio followed Villa in the Columbus raid in March 1916. His only son (and only living relative) was killed in the action while manning a machine gun. When Villa went into hiding in order to recover from a wound received in a minor skirmish after Columbus, Tiburcio was one of the select few allowed to care for Villa. He was captured during a food run, though, and the Apaches enrolled in Pershing's Punitive Expedition (1916–1917) flayed his feet to try to make him disclose Villa's hiding place. When it became clear that no amount of torture or enticement would be successful, the Americans handed him over to the Carrancistas. They hanged him summarily.

My reading of *¡Vámonos con Pancho Villa!* (Muñoz [1931] 1999) follows a similar pattern as the reading I suggested for *Las lanzas*. This is not only because these works have points in common beyond the most apparent similarities (both are war novels) or because of their most apparent aesthetic differences (*Las lanzas* is an avant-garde novel and *Vámonos* can be linked to both naturalist and regionalist writing). Rather, it is due to the fact that both novels were written by young writers on good terms with the powers that be. In fact, both novels can be read as (largely successful) attempts to legitimate the historical mission of said powers. In order to carry out this task, both novels deal with events that hold a foundational place in modern national cultures: the War of Independence and the Boves uprising in the Venezuelan case, considered on the whole as a national-popular revolution; and the revolution in the case of Mexico. Both novels deal with these events by focusing on rural subjects of violence who are swept away by a revolutionary tide for reasons that remain rather opaque and that cannot be fully termed ideological. In both novels, the subjects oscillate between the avenger of the downtrodden and the out-and-out nomadic outlaw. Both novels use the saga of a rural subject in order to put together a national-statist epic that presents itself as a popular one, in which the popular element is suppressed and then recuperated as suppressed. In both novels, finally, we can locate a supplement of meaning (to use Derrida's notion) that exceeds the statist epic, and that, while certainly not annulling the main thrust of the novel, leads us to a rather unreadable (but semantically dense) point: what I called the Dionysian experience of war in *Las lanzas*, and what I will call the "empowering denial" in *Vámonos*.

Perhaps the main difference stems from the fact that *Vámonos* intervenes decisively in the debates around a figure that was, at the same time, undeniable and intractable, ubiquitous and taboo: Pancho Villa. The novel, in fact, remains a major example of the ambiguities permeating Villa's memory in the period between his assassination in 1923 and his official incorporation into the revolutionary pantheon in the 1960s–1970s. By late 1920, the Sonoran faction (Adolfo de la Huerta, Alvaro Obregón, Plutarco Elías Calles) defeated the Cristero Rebellion and claimed victory in the protracted civil war that began in late 1910. In April of 1920, Alvaro Obregón and Adolfo de la Huerta led an uprising against President Carranza (who wanted to impose the loyalist Ignacio Bonillas as his successor). The uprising succeeded and Carranza was assassinated. De la Huerta would be the interim president from June to November, handing power to Obregón (1920–1924), who would in turn hand it to Calles. The latter would dominate Mexican politics from the time of Obregón's assassination in 1928 (after he had been elected to a second presidential term—nonconsecutive, following the revolutionary precepts) until Cárdenas forced the *jefe máximo* into exile in 1936. Zapata had already been assassinated in 1919, and Villa would be assassinated in 1923.[1]

Challenges still lay ahead. There were to be internecine divisions, such as the fallout between De la Huerta and Obregón that led to De la Huerta's failed uprising in 1923, and the aforementioned conflict between Calles and Cárdenas, just to mention the most significant. There were also conflicts between the Sonorans and other actors within and outside of Mexico, such as the unions, the Left, the United States, and, most importantly, the Catholic Church and the Catholic peasantry. (The latter one led to the bloody Cristero Rebellion between 1926 and 1929, and claimed President-Elect Obregón's life. *El luto humano*, the novel by José Revueltas that I will examine later, narrates a number of gory episodes of the rebellion and dwells on the longer-lasting impact it had upon some of its participants.) But the revolutionary state progressed from 1920 on its way to political, economic, and cultural consolidation. Crucial to this consolidation effort was the crafting of a coherent narrative that would explain the events of the prior decade (Benjamin 2000). And even though, by the late 1920s, such a narrative had incorporated most of the former adversaries into the "revolutionary family" (e.g., Carranza, who, as the sponsor of the 1917 constitution and a staunch nationalist, was lauded as the founder of the new Mexican state by those who were instrumental in his assassination), Villa still remained excluded from the official revolutionary pantheon. According to O'Malley (1986) and Parra (2005), he was not so much demonized (although he was also demonized, of course) as he was outright ignored: the anniversaries of his assassination were not officially commemorated—or mentioned, for that matter—and he was largely excluded from (or his role greatly diminished in) early official narratives of the events in the 1910s (O'Malley 1986, 98).

However, Villa did not vanish. Far from it. During the 1920s and 1930s he held a grip on the Mexican imagination that possibly no other political or military leader could match. As O'Malley (1986) notes, Madero and Carranza were politicians who generally lacked charisma; Zapata had fought a small-scale regional war and he did not have a knack for public performance the way Villa did; and Obregón, even if more politically and militarily accomplished than Villa (he was the one who defeated Villa, after all), had a middle-class background that wasn't the stuff of legend—his mutilated arm and his death notwithstanding. But there were several reasons for Villa's mystique that went beyond his romantic appeal. Perhaps the most important, as both O'Malley (1986) and Parra (2005) mention, was the emergence of a public eager for the thrills that the Villa legend would provide. This public emerged from the very success of policies that had been undertaken during the 1920s reconstruction: the establishment of educational and cultural systems, which created literate publics, and the state sponsorship of cultural industries such as publishing houses, newspapers, and a film industry. This, coupled with the displacement of significant numbers of people from the rural milieu to the cities, created an audience for all things Villa (O'Malley 1986, 100), including a seemingly keen obsession with his sexual and sentimental life, which was piqued by the ongoing feud between his two "main" wives: Luz Corral de Villa and Austreberta Rentería (O'Malley 1986, 100–102).[2] Also, the passage of time afforded the opportunity for many former participants in the revolutionary events to write and publish memoirs justifying or aggrandizing their own role in them. *El águila y la serpiente* (1928), by Martín Luis Guzmán, and *La tormenta* (1936), by José Vasconcelos, are two among many other self-justifying narratives in which Villa figures prominently. (Significantly, the more nuanced and insightful narratives about Villa did not obtain in their own time the relevance that they deserved. Examples of this are the books by Jaurrieta [2009] and Terrazas [(1936) 1984].)

The so-called rediscovery of Azuela's *Los de abajo* in the 1920s can be conceived, as I have argued elsewhere (2003, 2007), as a landmark of the process in which outlaw violence was acknowledged as the origin of the revolutionary state. Even though it was acknowledged, it was distanced and isolated from the present through its "natural" suppression (Demetrio, the protagonist of *Los de abajo,* is killed in battle, but the novel never actually says who killed him. Although Carrancistas—either the army or Defensos—probably killed him, the elision makes clear that History killed him, after sidelining him and rendering him irrelevant.) In an indirect fashion, the 1920s reading of *Los de abajo* was both a denial and a reterritorialization of Villista violence (Demetrio was Villista, through his affiliation with Natera). *¡Vámonos con Pancho Villa!,* written by an intellectual of open allegiance to the powers that be, is another landmark in that same process. Muñoz was a founding member of the Partido Nacional Revolucionario (PNR), the official party of the revolution (which eventually became the PRI), in which he acted as the press liaison. Additionally, he belonged to the Sindicato de Escritores Revolucionarios (Union of Revolutionary Writers), a writers' organization affiliated with the PNR, and he was also appointed editor of *El nacional,* the PNR's official organ. Parra (2005, 100) correctly points out that "Muñoz was an ideologue of official revolutionary nationalism at a time when this concept was being defined in the culture of the Mexican state." *¡Vámonos con Pancho Villa!* is, thus, an excellent case study of the cultural dynamics of the revolutionary state.

With the significant exceptions of *Se llevaron el cañón para Bachimba*

(1941), focused on the Orozco uprising of 1912 (and its demise),[3] and the biographical *Santa Anna: El que todo lo ganó y todo lo perdió* (1936), also known as *Santa Anna: El dictador resplandeciente*, most of Muñoz's works revisit Villa's exploits or those of his followers. Muñoz even wrote a biography of Villa and a (never-produced) television script devoted to Villa's assassination.[4] Muñoz also wrote a number of short stories devoted either to Villa himself (e.g., "La marcha nupcial," "El perro muerto," "Un disparo al vacío," "Una biografía," "Villa ataca Ciudad Juárez"); to some of his most famous officers and followers (e.g., "La suerte loca de Pancho Villa," "De hombre a hombre," "Oro, caballo y hombre"); or to minor historical or legendary events in the protracted Villista struggle (e.g., "El festín," "Cadalso en la nieve," "Villa ahumada," "Obra de caridad," "La cuerda del general," "Un asalto al tren").[5] However, in *¡Vámonos con Pancho Villa!*, Villa and the Leones display a complexity that is absent in most other pieces. For example, in the other short stories, Villa is unambiguously dubbed a "bandit" (either by a character, by the narrator, or by the narrator-character). And the term is used strictly in the negative sense of robber, murderer, looter, and rapist, a beast dominated by a happy (and totally unconscious) ferocity. This was in line with the dominant version of Villa as an animal or a force of nature during the 1920s and 1930s (O'Malley 1986, 99). The novel, on the other hand, goes well beyond this characterization, to interrogate what it means to be a revolutionary and/or a bandit.

The novel has two parts. The first (henceforth referred to as *Vámonos-1*) comprises eight semiautonomous chapters, each of which was written as a stand-alone story for the Sunday literary section (the *Magazine*) of the Mexico City newspaper *El universal*. Both in intent and in style (although of a far superior quality), these were much like the vignettes that, almost at the same time, Elías Torres was writing for the Mexican press (*Sucesos para todos*), which would be compiled in volumes such as *20 vibrantes episodios de la vida de Villa* (1934) and *La cabeza de Pancho Villa* (1938), among others.[6]

Each of the first eight chapters of *Vámonos-1* depicts a feat of bravery by the Leones, in or out of battle (and more often than not, the result is the death of a member of the group). The first chapter narrates the destruction of a bridge that was essential to federal military strategy. Before that, Miguel Ángel, also known as Becerrillo (the younger member of the Leones, and a superb sniper, it seems), had been taking out the bridge's sentries, one by one, night after night. These actions were undertaken under the Leones' own initiative since they had not yet joined the División, but they served to cement their credibility as fighters, thus facilitating their incorporation into the División. The narrative continues with their distinguished participation in the battle of Torreón; it then moves from the prelude at Gómez Palacios (where Becerrillo dies), to the assault of the La Pila Hill (where the *manco* [one-armed] Espinosa dies while throwing grenades at the federal fortifications,[7] and where Rodrigo Perea kills himself when, carried away by his eagerness to wrestle a rifle from a Federal, he plunges the rifle's bayonet into his own body), to the attempt at entrapping the Federales with a fake surrender. This attempt almost comes at the price of the lives of the remaining Leones, but it serves to highlight the cavalier attitude of the Leones toward death (Muñoz [1931] 1999, 50). This attitude is put to the test in the next chapter, "El círculo de la muerte," which narrates the death of Botello, who commits suicide while playing a variation of Russian roulette. He kills himself only to prove, to a group of perfect strangers, that he is not afraid to die (61).

This first part of the novel features many characters that define northern revolutionary narratives, and attitudes that will define an image of the Mexican Revolution—attitudes such as fatalism in the face of death as a central predicate of the "Mexican difference" (Paz [1950] 1997; Lomnitz 2008), as well as a Serrano masculine honor code of loyalty and solidarity (Parra 2005). The narrative also taps into the sensationalism that permeated Villa's legend. The last León to die in this first part of the novel is Máximo Perea, on the eve of the decisive battle of Zacatecas. Máximo Perea falls victim to smallpox and is burned (presumably alive) by Tiburcio, following Tomás Urbina's orders (Muñoz [1931] 1999, 68). Tiburcio, aggravated by Urbina's callousness and by Villa's indifference to the fate of his loyal fighters, and offended by Villa's fear of contracting the disease, deserts the División (81).

When Muñoz's weekly publishing commitment was canceled (the newspaper was to serialize the memories of General Juan Barragán), he conceived the idea of uniting the vignettes, extending the narrative, and publishing it as a novel (Carballo 1965, 266). *Vámonos-1* presents a particular moment in the evolution of the revolutionary myth, a moment in which there is a gesture toward creating a totalizing narrative of the events of 1910–1920. In this narrative the figure of Villa himself is exalted but ultimately excluded, and thus severed from the ultimate historical justification for the revolution. The novel acknowledges Villa's role in the popular revolutionary epic (and his place as the most colorful and charismatic figure of the revolution). But *Vámonos-1* ends with a dramatic scene that enacts a split between Villa and Tiburcio (as synecdoche of the popular subject). The novel's second part reunites Villa and Tiburcio, but in an enterprise that cannot be called epic or popular: as Tiburcio is sorely aware, they have become outlaws, and that mark (*señal*) defines their identities and their mode of (dis)association. This disparity between the two parts of the novel warrants separate treatments.

"¡Vámonos con Pancho Villa!" is the battle cry by which the path of the six friends intersects that of the revolution. The Leones (both the characters and their feats) are a composite based on stories that Muñoz claimed to have heard, much like the way Tapia composed his own narrative. As explained earlier, Tapia named—and thanked—some of his oral sources. But he did not link them to any particular portion of *El último hombre a caballo*. He thus performed a clever trick: he claimed the authority of his sources, while simultaneously making them the anonymous, nonmediated voice of the People. Since Muñoz does not even name names, the Leones are even more emphatically a synecdoche of the popular subject, not a collection of individual destinies per se.

But this popular subject really comes into its own when Villa incorporates the Leones into the División. In this scene, there is an explicit acknowledgment of a shared memory (among the Leones) of previous martial exploits (Muñoz [1931] 1999, 19, 20). The very name "Leones" precedes the revolution and their fighting skills are already well honed (as the killing of the sentries on the bridge and the blowing up of the bridge itself abundantly show). In the scene of Becerrillo's burial, the parting words of the surviving Leones also refer to a violent past that predates Villa (31). The Leones are part of a group, but their socioeconomic status is not homogenous, and neither are their stories (Tiburcio is a ranchero, or farmer, with land of his own; Becerrillo seems to be a laborer). To a certain extent, the Leones' incorporation into the revolution is not the moment in which, individually or as a group, they reach a higher level of consciousness; rather, it is more an accumulation of individual revenge agendas, of discrete acts in a long drama of violence and retribution.[8]

The river that opens *Vámonos-1* is a metaphor for this preexisting popular subject (Muñoz [1931] 1999, 10). The river does not belong to any of the war-ring factions, but rather divides them. The triumph of the revolutionaries (the blowing up of the bridge, the advance toward the south) incorporates (ter-ritorializes) the river as part of the revolutionary camp, since it allows the revolutionaries to occupy the two margins. In analogous fashion, the battle cry "¡Vámonos con Pancho Villa!" does not create ex nihilo the Leones' identity as a fighting unit: it is the statement of an alliance. However, this alliance defines, from above, the political dimension of the group and the transformation of its violence from prepolitical to fully political (i.e., revolutionary) violence. The Leones are the visible characters of the novel. But at another level, they become (since they were not always) mediations, representatives of some-thing else, whose name is the masculine warrior culture of Chihuahua; whose name is the Mexican Revolution; whose name is Mexico. This is why it is only toward the end of the first part of the novel that Tiburcio emerges as the pro-tagonist (it can also be argued that *Vámonos-1* has no individual protagonist at all). It is because of their incorporation into a larger collective enterprise whose name is "Villa" (not "revolution," which the Leones do not discuss, but "Villa" as locus of charisma and leadership) that they cease to be a group of avengers and become part of an army.[9] This is reminiscent of *El Zarco* (Ignacio Manuel Altamirano, 1901), in which it is Juárez who makes an improvised band of rancheros-turned-vigilantes into the paramilitary arm of the nascent Mexican state, thus transforming a myriad of personal vengeances into social retribution (Melgarejo Acosta and Lund 2006; Dabove 2007).

Vámonos-1 ends precisely when this totalizing effort is still viable but starts to crumble: during the opening skirmishes of the battle of Zacatecas. This was the Federal Army's last stand. It was also the zenith of the epic saga of the División. Not by chance, one of the first episodes in the Mexican state's attempt to rehabilitate Villa's memory was the unveiling of a mural that depicts this very battle. President Gustavo Díaz Ordaz and veterans of the División del Norte attended the unveiling (see Mantecón Pérez 1967, 117). The selection of this battle as the cornerstone of this rehabilitation narrative shows that this was perhaps the last nonproblematic point in Villa's career. But behind the scenes, the battle of Zacatecas was the point at which the anti-Huerta alliance began to crumble. Villa attacks Zacatecas in open defiance of Carranza's orders. Carranza, the self-styled *primer jefe*, jealous and fearful of Villa, wanted to prevent him from reaching Mexico City before his more loyal generals (Obregón and González) could. He also wanted to deprive Villa of the glory of winning the decisive battle of the campaign. Carranza assigned Natera to storm Zacatecas, with pitiful results. Much to Carranza's chagrin, Villa resigned as commander of the División del Norte, only to be reinstated to the position by his generals. Villa went on to take Zacatecas. From then on, and in spite of the effort toward conciliation at the Convención de Aguascalientes, the revolution would become an increasingly violent and muddled war among factions with clashing claims to the revolutionary mantle. It is precisely at this point that the existence of a "popular subject without contradictions" is more and more difficult to maintain. And it is precisely at this point that the novel has to choose sides, much like every general had to choose at the Aguascalientes convention, between Villa and the Conventionistas or Carranza and the Constitutionalistas.

The novel does not choose Villa. Up to this point, the novel is an undivided (if indirect) glorification of him as a popular charismatic leader (*Vámonos-1* does not emphasize Villa's violence but rather his bravery, his marksmanship, and his folksy style) and as the creator or inspirer (not through ideology, but charisma) of a fully political subject. Zacatecas has to be the point where Villa ceases to perform these functions. After Zacatecas, according to the triumphant Carrancista narrative, Villa reverts to what he had always been: a bandit allied with either the counterrevolution or the forces of barbarism. Villa is still fascinating, but he has outlived his own historical relevance. The condemnation of Villa does not amount (it cannot amount) to a condemnation of his fighters, since his fighters embody a transhistorical, transpolitical entity: the People in arms. Thus, Villa has to be symbolically severed from his fighters. This operates in the same way in which American nationalist discourse demands that everybody "support the troops," even when fighting ill-conceived or blatantly disastrous wars—that is, distinguishing Bush or Obama from "our men and women in uniform." Of course, this is an entirely misguided distinction in an all-volunteer armed force whose public image, however, still harks back to the era of the draft and the model of the citizen-soldier.

Tiburcio's desertion is the perfect emblem for this severing and it is a clever "naturalization" of the political myth of Villa in the 1930s, where the disjunction between Villa's and Villismo's popular support had to be well established in order to garner legitimation for the Institutionalized

Revolution. Throughout *Vámonos-1* the political or social aspects of Villismo do not appear. Villismo is reduced to a military phenomenon, with no civilians or civilian administration depicted. Because of this, in 1931 (when the fighting was well over, and when militarism, as a feature of Mexican politics, was about to be phased out) Villismo-as-militarism could be relegated to the past.[10]

Even the depiction of the military aspects of Villismo is not value-neutral: none of Villa's "respectable" generals (Felipe Ángeles, most prominently) has any significance in the novel.[11] Villismo leadership is reduced to Villa himself, and to the general in charge of the División in his stead, *el compadre* Tomás Urbina. Urbina rode with Villa in his outlaw years, and he remained, to a large degree, a bandit, more interested in plundering than anything else (Katz 1998). For example, Urbina had been the instigator of the infamous plunder of Durango in 1913. In the novel, he is depicted as an animal. Urbina is not like Villa, who is compared to a jaguar, a fearsome but beautiful animal. Urbina is more like a vulture, with claws instead of hands:

> [Urbina] had achieved a reputation for being a cruel and worthy companion of Villa, of whom he had been the only companion during his outlaw years. He had his arms and hands affected by a rare disease, without a doubt the onset of a paralysis. His enemies related this disease to the fact that during the sack of Durango he had dared grab some of the vases destined to the most sacred ceremonies of the Catholic religion, from which he extracted with his muscled fingers the content, hungry for gold and gems from chalices and pyxes. His ears, red and deformed, looked like two cocks' crests stuck to the big, rounded head, and in his bulky body burned a wild and merciless soul. (Muñoz [1931] 1999, 66)

He is an animal, and like Boves in *Las lanzas*, he is a sacrilegious plunderer and murderer, whose presence pollutes the entire División. Tiburcio decides to desert the División when he is ordered by Tomás Urbina to kill Máximo. Máximo is sick with smallpox, and he has no chance of survival. The Leones were not afraid to die (witness Botello) and even less afraid to die for Villa. The decision to kill Máximo is not beyond the pale. It may even be an act of mercy. After all, Tiburcio killed Becerrillo when it was clear that he too had no chance of survival. And the risk of spreading smallpox was something that either a soldier or a general could understand. After all, an outbreak of smallpox could cripple the División and have a staggering human cost (witness the Spanish influenza pandemic of 1918 and its devastating effect on troops living in close quarters in the First World War, as well as in the Mexican Revolution). The Leones were willing to die, but they expected reciprocity in the form of recognition of a shared code of honor. This was precisely the foundation of Villa's charisma: the fact that he shared a code of masculine honor based on bravery and loyalty to his troops.[12]

But Villa is unable to live up to his own code of honor and masculine loyalty, when he shuns Tiburcio out of fear of contracting the disease:

> [Villa, inspecting the hospital train,] reached Tiburcio's car. Tiburcio was sitting at the car's door, smoking despondently, not carrying weapons or a bandolier. When he saw his general coming, however, he swiftly stood up and saluted; his eyes sparkled and he felt a tremor of enthusiasm. A word, a sign, and he would rush to the enemy's trenches, to shoot them all.... [Villa, thought Tiburcio,] was a real man, and a leader of men, not like Urbina, that son of a bitch, that horse thief ... [...] But when Villa saw the train car, he shrugged involuntarily, and his fiery gaze expressed a sudden fear. He regarded Tiburcio for a while, and he moved away from the car, at a brisk pace. Inside the car, the old man was left feeling deflated [*laxo*] like an empty sack....
>
> —It's quite all right—he said.—This is the end of the line. (Muñoz [1931] 1999, 81)

This reduces Villismo to this core scene: the legitimate revolutionary (Tiburcio), bound to a strict code of loyalty and martial honor, is faced with the rapacious, monstrous bandit chief (Urbina, and Villa, who proves to be no better than Urbina). By turning Tiburcio into a justified deserter, the popular subject is saved, but only as long as it is severed from Villa's interpellation, while Villa is delegitimized as a popular leader and remains Urbina's superior, a mere bandit chieftain (Urbina will be killed by Villa, when it is apparent that his loyalties are wavering). To a significant degree, since everyone knows how the plot of the revolution continues, it is Tiburcio's desertion that dooms Villismo. Fernando de Fuentes's film version of the novel (1936) understands this well. The last scene depicts Tiburcio leaving the train formation, walking into the night, and disappearing into it.

Taibo ([2006] 2010, 856), in his biography of Villa, shares an anecdote that illustrates this cultural/political dynamic of erasing Villa from Villismo and splitting the leader from his followers as part and parcel of the legitimation of the revolutionary state. In 1956 (i.e., before Villa's full rehabilitation), the government of Chihuahua commissioned Ignacio Asúnsolo (an important sculptor of civic works) to create an equestrian statue of Villa to be publicly displayed in the state capital. Pressures that were not fully elucidated forced Asúnsolo to modify the visage of the statue, so that it was unveiled not as a memorial to Villa (whose image was still controversial, it seems), but rather as a memorial to the "soldier of the Northern Division." Muñoz spoke at the unveiling ceremony. Tellingly, he made no mention of Villa, the man to whom he had devoted his literary career.

The second part of *¡Vámonos con Pancho Villa!* (which I will henceforth call *Vámonos-2*) narrates the reenlisting of Tiburcio in Pancho Villa's forces, after the dissolution of the División. Villa's forces are only several hundred strong; they are cavalrymen devoid of artillery, infantry, or support units. They lack morale (having been poisoned by mutual mistrust and Villa's fear of treason, which pits comrades in arms against each other) and a sense of purpose. Villa has ceased to be the stern but eminently likable leader that he was in the first part of the novel. Now he is cruel, petty, paranoid, and above all self-centered and indifferent to others' suffering. This darker version of Villa comes to the fore immediately in the narrative. When arranging for Tiburcio to reenlist in his forces, he kills Tiburcio's wife and daughter in cold blood (supposedly in order to free Tiburcio of family obligations and the painful memories of those he would leave behind). To the reader's surprise, Tiburcio does reenlist, and never seeks revenge. Eventually, Villa moves on to attack Columbus, New Mexico. During the battle Tiburcio loses his remaining son to American bullets, and he is injured while saving Villa's life. Back in Mexico, in a minor skirmish outside of Guerrero, Villa is wounded, and he is forced to disband his men and hide in a cave under the care of a few loyal followers. Tiburcio is among them. Eventually the Americans capture Tiburcio, but they are unable to turn him into an informant (even though they torture and try to bribe him). Tiburcio eventually ends up in the hands of the Carrancistas, who, after additional torture (strongly reminiscent of Christ's Passion), hang him.

The meaning of this second part is vastly different from that of the first. It offers a vision of Villismo that moves away from the one posited in *Vámonos-1*, but above all, it offers a vision of Tiburcio (now the undivided focus of the narrative) that is compelling and enigmatic. Parra (2005, 102–11) notes that a "burning of bridges" precedes each scene in which Tiburcio or the Leones go with Villa. In these scenes the male cuts himself off from his civilian identity in order to enter an all-male warrior community. This is entirely true. Both scenes of "bridge burning" are different, however. Becerrillo leaves Tía Lola, his adoptive mother, when he joins the Leones (and the División del Norte) and becomes a Dorado. This is a staple in all coming-of-age narratives. Becerrillo is the counterpart of Abasolo in *Se llevaron en cañón* (Abasolo leaves the parental home to become a Colorado). It is painful for Tía Lola to experience Becerrillo's fickle and forgetful nature, but there are no serious moral dilemmas involved. In all masculinist narratives (and *¡Vámonos con Pancho Villa!* is superlatively so), this is "just what boys do": they leave the nurturing female world behind to find their own destiny. For Becerrillo that destiny will be cruel: a bullet that will blow away his jaw and force a mercy killing. But Becerrillo, like Botello and the rest of the Leones, dies "with his boots on." In any case, his act can be easily reterritorialized into a masculine identity that, in turn, can be made into an example of Mexicanness.

The second "bridge burning" scene is quite a different matter. (This scene was also very ably analyzed by Parra [2005], but from a perspective different from the one I propose here.) Villa kills Tiburcio's wife and daughter after they offer him a meal. To say the least, this is a serious breach of the rules of hospitality. I doubt there is a regional culture, warrior or otherwise, that would condone such an act, or that there is a code of masculinity that would not ask for bloody retribution. In *Vámonos-1*, a breach of the rules of the rural code justifies (actually, calls for) desertion. In *Vámonos-2*, Tiburcio rides with Villa all the same, since this part of the novel takes place in a different universe, without the symbolic anchors of the first part. Tiburcio hesitates to name what they have become:

And now, what are we? . . . Tiburcio's mind plunged into an abyss.

—We are bandits.

All of us? No! But there is a sign that makes us all the same, a mark that distinguishes us from the rest of humankind, a sign that separates and stops us. We are bodies destined for the gallows. Once we are rounded up, once we are captured, we are going to die. Those of us who do not get away, will hang from the trees. Anyone who sees us there will rejoice discovering the sign, the word branded on our foreheads. Not all of us are bandits, but those who are captured will not have time to say it, or even to implore clemency. (Muñoz [1931] 1999, 110)

Tiburcio and the rest are now outlaws, *fuera de la ley* (Muñoz [1931] 1999, 112, 113). But here, "outlaw" has two meanings. On the one hand, it is a position beyond the law of the state. That part is easy to understand. On the other, it is a position beyond language. This can only be experienced (certainly not understood) in its distance from our values, our *Weltanschauung*. And that distance cannot be named, it cannot really be treated; it can only be pointed to. Nothing makes us experience that distance like Tiburcio's last conversation with the sergeant from the Punitive Expedition that captures him. Tiburcio is in a hospital, recuperating from the torture to which he has been subjected. The sergeant tries his hand at Spanish, trying to convince Tiburcio to turn on Villa:

> At mealtime, the Sergeant who had captured Tiburcio came and sat by him, in order to have a chat. He helped Tiburcio to eat his cereal, he peeled the fruit for him and he talked about life in the United States, a place where there were many Mexicans living and working. He presented Tiburcio with the prospect of a good house, a car....
> —Are you married? Do you have kids? . . .
> —Wife? Kids? Pancho Villa killed them.
> The Sergeant's jaw dropped. He did not understand.
> —Pancho Villa killed them? And you follow Villa?
> —Yes.
> —You obey Villa? You defend him?
> —Yes.
> —You are nuts. . . .
> —Crazy . . . yes. . . .
> —Oh! I do not believe you. You have a fever again. If a man killed my wife, I would kill that man. I would not defend him.
> —I would.
> The Sergeant's surprise, his horrified eyes, his vengeful spirit, dispelled in a moment the hate of the tormented man. "I would." In those two words resided his moral triumph. Incurable, condemned to never stand up again,

imprisoned, old, hearing the sound of the spade digging his grave, he had, nevertheless, the absolute certainty of his superiority over the Sergeant, the doctors and the nurses, and over the hundreds of soldiers that he saw through the window going to and fro, between the rows of identical tents. He had the certainty of his superiority over the entire army....

—If you tell me where Villa is, we will reward you, we will avenge you.... We will give you fifty thousand dollars, one hundred thousand dollars, so that you can live in the United States, protected by the police. Nobody will be able to harm you. What do you say, eh?

—I won't.

—If we find Villa, we will force him to ask you for forgiveness. We will take a picture of him begging you for forgiveness, for having killed your wife. You would be the only man in the world in front of whom Villa fell on his knees. You will be able to humiliate him.

—No, I will not.

—We will give you whatever you ask: a ranch, horses, purebred cows. We will heal you. You will be able to walk, you will be able to live happily, like before, a rich man. You will be able to avenge the murder of your family.

—No, I will not....

—*You damn fool*! You leave that bed this very minute, for wounded American soldiers. You can go to hell, to wait for Pancho Villa. (Muñoz [1931] 1999, 201–4)

What exasperates the sergeant (what exasperates us) is not the loyalty to the bitter end (which anybody can understand), but the fact that Tiburcio has every reason *not* to be loyal. The sergeant delivers Tiburcio to his destiny: the impatient Carrancista rope with which both Tiburcio's life and the novel end. If we read this refusal as if it were coherent with the epic tale of *Vámonos-1,* then Tiburcio's attitude is an enigma only within the fictional world (only for the American sergeant), but not for the reader who is invited to admire (with a sense of identity or of inferiority) Tiburcio's dignified denial. Tiburcio is the man who, against all odds, *no se raja* (does not break). However, it is possible to read something else here, something that does not put us in Tiburcio's place (or make us experience just how inferior to Tiburcio we are). Rather, it puts us in the place of the sergeant—in the place of someone who comes from the outside into an alien territory, of someone whose good intentions barely hide greed and violence, of someone who lives in the comfort and certainties of modernity and who can barely speak to a nomadic warrior. In short, we (like the sergeant) lack any real understanding of what is actually happening.

The sergeant's exasperation is not just a reaction to Tiburcio's obstinate refusal, but also a reaction to the impossibility of giving that refusal a meaning, of linking Tiburcio's action to a known position as a subject of violence. It is the inability of the sergeant to understand what Tiburcio wants and for what reasons he is fighting. Tiburcio's answer is a denial, of course. The sergeant translates that denial into an incapacity to articulate, to forge a class and a modern political program centered on the nation-state, its territoriality, and its modes of representation. Or even worse: in Tiburcio's case, not only does class consciousness fail, but Tiburcio does not even know what's good for him in the most basic terms, nor does he know who he is. This inability calls for the suppression of the revolutionary sound and fury by an external principle of statehood (it calls for Tiburcio to be killed as part of a cruel theater of the law). But to refuse to name the war in terms of an ultimate cause can be, in fact, a fully political option. This can be a different sense of politics, since there is a conflation of the means and the ends. There is nothing to be achieved: neither peace nor freedom nor treasure nor honor. There is no communicable value that would allow Tiburcio to be a man among men. This is different from the denial itself and its immediate effects: the abandonment of the patronizing attitude by the American and the fact that he lost control. Tiburcio's denial is an event, a sheer interruption of a major language. It does not imply an absence of consciousness, but rather a subaltern consciousness (for lack of a better word to name what we ignore) opposed to the "citizen" state consciousness, and the identity built around possessive individualism.

Therefore we should not ask why Tiburcio fights. Rather, we should ask why Tiburcio keeps rejecting and denying the sergeant's interpellation. At the risk of turning Tiburcio into a bronco version of Herman Melville's Bartleby, I would say that what Tiburcio "wants" is a place beyond honor, treason, possession, or nation; he wants a place beyond all the identity trappings. This impossible place interdicts the "illusion of inevitability" on which all social order rests (Barrington Moore, quoted in Tutino 1989, 18). In *Vámonos-1*, Villa endows Tiburcio's life with meaning. In *Vámonos-2*, Villa does not give Tiburcio anything. On the contrary, he takes everything away. Villa, therefore, is not the repository of meaning that Tiburcio taps into, but the place where meaning fails. The presentation of that experience beyond the shortcuts of myth, of ethnography, of epic, is the ethic dimension of Muñoz's writing. Tiburcio's blind loyalty (which reduplicates the "meaningless" wanderings of Villa) is the place where, precisely for its lack of meaning, Muñoz allows us to read the options of the multitude, as different from (and opposed to) the People—that is, not as a new transcendent instance to which Muñoz would provide us narrative access, but as a supplement of meaning of the popular and of populism that toward the 1930s permeated Villa's legends (and Muñoz's own writing) as part and parcel of the path that the PRI was making toward the consolidation of the revolutionary state. Tiburcio makes loyalty an untreatable value, something impossible to translate. It is not moral. It is not political. Or it is political in another dimension of the political.

Tiburcio's death is an affirmation of his own identity, his own incomprehensibility. It is the "empowering denial" (*negación fortalecedora*) of which José Revueltas writes in *El luto humano* ([1943] 2003, 245), when referring to Adán, another incomprehensible character (I will discuss this later on in this book). Muñoz's statement is rather simple, rather commonplace, and at the same time impossible to maintain. The other is incomprehensible and meaningless, when it is the reflection of our own incomprehensibility and lack of meaning. We could call this the unsettling experience of the subaltern, and we would not be entirely mistaken. We could call it the ethical experience of literature, and perhaps we would be right.

FIVE

THE ANDEAN WESTERN

On *Cuentos andinos*

IN POSTCOLONIAL PERU, banditry was, for more than a century, part
and parcel of what could be called *crisis narratives*. In Peru, just like in Mexico, for politicians and intellectuals of all stripes (who were mostly in agreement on the aspirational notion of the nation-state as the dominant form of
affiliation and identity marker), banditry was the emblem of the impossibility
of the coming into being of the struggling nation. The Peruvian case shares,
indeed, a number of similarities with the Mexican one. Both countries were
pillars of the Spanish American Empire, and in both countries Creole elites
were reluctant to embrace the cause of independence. In both contexts, the
collapse of the colonial *imperium* triggered a long period of civil wars, foreign invasions, rural unrest, and caudillo rule outside major cities. In both
countries the incapacity of the emerging state to exert an effective monopoly
on violence throughout a vast and highly fragmented territory, one that was
very ethnically diverse, was apparent (Flores Galindo 1990; Taylor 1990; for a
comparative analysis see Mallon 1994). As in Mexico, outlaw rural violence in
Peru was manifold: highway robbery, cattle rustling, *montoneras*, smuggling,
feuding, and murder for hire. Banditry enacted diverse conflicts: the crisis of
slavery (Aguirre 1990), inter- and intraclass or community struggles (Walker
1990; Taylor 1987; Orlove 1980; Flores Galindo 1990), and economic and envi-
ronmental pressures (Mayer 1990; Langer 1987).[1]

It is in this context that I would like to place Enrique López Albújar (1872–1966), in an attempt to highlight the singularity of his oeuvre. López Albújar's fictional work, in particular several pieces in *Cuentos andinos* (1920) and *Nuevos cuentos andinos* (1937),[2] present the bandit as a character who is not emblematic of a crisis, but the cornerstone of a Western of sorts. None other than José Carlos Mariátegui ([1928] 1979) considered (or invented) López Albújar as a forerunner (or perhaps even a founder) of classical *indigenismo*.[3] Given Mariátegui's weight, this notion has found wide acceptance. However, I would like to think of López Albújar's short stories more as frontier narratives, an Andean Western. I do not pretend to establish a link with the American Western in its literary or cinematic form, although this is not inconceivable. I also cannot establish a positive link with the frontier novels I have just examined (*Las lanzas coloradas, ¡Vámonos con Pancho Villa!*), but the fact that they are strict contemporaries makes a compelling case for considering them as kindred narrative projects.

Other links can be established: it is possible to trace López Albújar's short stories to Guy de Maupassant's short stories on Corsican themes, or, more generally, one can link López Albújar with the French tradition of writing about Corsican and Mediterranean violence (e.g., Stendhal and Alexandre Dumas). Corsica was, after all, a frontier of sorts in the French imagination, a place outside the cultural mainstream, but one onto which the mainstream imagination projected both its fears and its desires, a place at the same time exotic and profoundly familiar, a place almost beyond the nation, but from where the ultimate national hero—Napoleon—came.[4]

López Albújar's Andean Western would have illustrious followers: Ciro Alegría with *El mundo es ancho y ajeno* (1941)—if one reads it as a frontier adventure novel, in addition to a pious novel about the misfortunes of the once-idyllic Indian community of Rumi; Miguel Gutiérrez with *Hombres de caminos* (1988); and Eliécer Cárdenas with *Polvo y ceniza* (1979) and *El árbol de los quemados* (2008). In López Albújar's stories, there are Indians, of course. But Indians are not featured as part of a reflection on an "Indian question," and not even as a reflection on the "national question," but as members of a frontier society—which is, after all, what many areas in Andean Peru were well into the twentieth century, as the Eleodoro Benel episode illustrates (Taylor 1987). In this respect, López Albújar is different from his contemporary Ventura García Calderón—in particular, García Calderón's collection of

short stories *La venganza del cóndor* (1924), which features many episodes of
Andean violence, similar on the surface to those of López Albújar. But García
Calderón's work should not be considered Western, even though the stories
take place in an area where the reach of the state is at best sporadic; rather, it
is a kind of Andean gothic. More accurately, it could be considered a kind of
Andean imperial gothic (Dabove 2009), in which Andean orientalism replaces
Asian palaces and Egyptian tombs with huacas, and features violence and
ancient vengeances in the line of Rider Haggard, Rudyard Kipling, or Emilio
Salgari.

Banditry was a ubiquitous but ill-defined crime in postcolonial Peru. Notorious but short-lived exceptions to this vagueness were the Santa-Cruz penal
codes for northern and southern Peru.[5] Otherwise, banditry does not appear
in the penal code of 1862, nor does it appear in the later one that replaced
it in 1924 (and that remained in force, heavily amended, until 1991). This
absence is even more telling if we take into account that a related offense, such
as piracy (which was nearly nonexistent at the time, but which had a heavy
presence in the collective imagination of the colonial period [Gerassi-Navarro
1999]), is abundantly defined in both codes. (For the 1862 code, see Articles
121–124; for the 1924 code see Articles 272–273.)

   During several periods of Peruvian history (in particular the 1830s, in the
wake of the War of the Pacific, and in some regions the 1910s and 1920s), banditry grew to epidemic proportions and it was experienced as such.[6] Jacob von
Tschudi, in his *Travels in Peru, during the Years 1838–1842* (1847), depicted
Lima (and most cities and villages in coastal Peru) as virtually under siege
by bandits. In a context of institutional collapse (that of the colonial imperium), Tschudi considered banditry an institution in and of itself that enjoyed
a level of organization, efficiency, and territorial reach that no other Peruvian institution had at the time.[7] "Most of the highway robbers who infest
the coast of Peru," Tschudi wrote, "belong to an extensive and systematically-
organized band, headed by formidable leaders, who maintain spies in the
towns and villages, from whom they receive regular reports" (1847, 137). This
is not unheard of. Dubois de Saligny, another foreigner also witnessing the
dire straits of a new republic (Mexico), coined the (in)famous phrase according to which Mexican banditry was "the only institution that can be taken

seriously and that functions with perfect regularity" (quoted in Vanderwood 1992, 3). The notion of bandit-into-state is an orientalist trope, amply used to depict peripheral or semiperipheral societies, be they Republican China (the proverbial "bandit country"), the steppes of Russia, fiercely anticolonial Afghanistan or India, or, of course, Spain, the Papal States (home to the legendary Luigi Vampa, friend and ally of Edmond Dantès in *The Count of Monte Cristo*), and the Balkans.

This perception of Peru as overrun by banditry precedes any real experience: on the last leg of Flora Tristán's voyage from Paris to Arequipa to reclaim her inheritance as a member of the powerful Tristán family (the trip is narrated in *Les pérégrinations d'une paria: 1833–1834*), Flora is accompanied by a less than dignified companion on the trek from Islay (where they disembark) to Arequipa. Doctor Víctor de Castellac deeply regrets having had to abandon Paris, where he could not make a living as a doctor, in order to live among the Peruvian barbarians. Upon disembarking, the doctor (whose bravery is deeply in doubt) prepares himself for the trip as if he were heading into battle. In fact, he dresses as a bandit, with pistols, knives, a saber, and saddle pistols. Tellingly, they see no bandits whatsoever.[8]

At the same time that Tschudi made his (wildly exaggerated) claim of a super-gang that had, for all practical purposes, supplanted the state, the English in India (to provide yet another example) "imagined" the thugs (and the practice of Thuggee) as a subcontinent-wide clandestine network of murderous outlaws. Thugs did exist in India, but English colonial authorities imagined Thugs as a sort of ghost state, ubiquitous and invisible, with its own religion (the cult of Khali) and distinctive social practices (Thuggee was passed on from fathers to sons throughout the centuries, it was claimed) that, ominously, ignored the most visible lines of social organization. Thugs-as-imagined (Muslim or Hindu) belonged to any caste, to any region, to any ethnicity, to any walk of life, and to any linguistic area. The suppression of Thuggee during the first part of the nineteenth century was at the same time a significant part of the (self-)legitimating narrative of English expansion in India—as it was for Egypt during the same period, and in China almost a century later—and a clear expression of the anxieties of the English before a social milieu that was not fully understood.[9] (A good example of how the image of Thuggee was impressed upon the consciousness of the English public is evident in the success of the otherwise very entertaining novel *Confessions of a Thug*, by Philip Meadows Taylor [1839]. Not by chance, this work was strictly contemporaneous with Tschudi's travel to Peru.)[10]

For Tschudi, Peruvian coastal banditry in the wake of emancipation from Spain had ceased to be a sort of unpredictable act of God, akin to a storm or an earthquake that tore at the fabric of everyday life.[11] It was more an aggravating everyday occurrence to be met with resignation. Lima was wide open to bandit raids,[12] but more ominously, one could find out, in a less than pleasant way, that every inch of Lima was under the aegis of bandits: "If they meet with resistance, [bandits] give no quarter; therefore, it is most prudent to submit to being plundered quietly, even when the parties attacked are stronger than the assailants, for the latter usually have confederates at no great distance, and can summon reinforcements in case of need. Any person who kills a robber in self-defense must ever afterwards be in fear for his own life: even in Lima the dagger of the assassin will reach him, and possibly at the moment when he thinks himself most safe" (1847, 138). Tschudi presses this point even further. He mentions that in times of war (and the first decades of the republic were times of constant strife), *montoneros* routinely filled the ranks of the warring parties. Leaders kept the outlaws in check during the campaigns (except for allowing horse stealing—the only means of obtaining mounts—and the extraction of resources from the population, since to live off the land was a common practice by most armies at the time). However, once they were discharged, they returned to a life of robbery (141–42).[13]

In 1838, Campbell Scarlett published *South America and the Pacific*. In the section of his travel memoirs aptly subtitled "Plunder and Politics," he arrives at the same conclusion as Tschudi regarding the lack of distinction between banditry and the state. Scarlett narrates the misfortunes of the Count de Sartige (a French attaché from Rio), Colonel Wilson, and Lord E. Clinton. The gentlemen were on an outing to Chorrillos when

> they encountered a band of at least fifty monteneros [*sic*], from whom they fled at a gallop, but to no purpose. A detachment from the main body was sent in pursuit of them, and their retreat was speedily cut off. They were made to dismount immediately, and were well abused for attempting to escape. "Why did you gallop from us?" said one of them to Sartige. "Because," he replied, "we took you for robbers." "Take us for robbers, indeed! We are the President's

troops. Come; give us your money and your clothes." At the same time he presented his blunderbuss. . . . In spite of all expostulation, these gentlemen were roughly stripped to the skin, and with great difficulty obtained, in exchange for their good hats, one of the shabby sombreros worn by the thieves; their trousers, one pair of shoes, and a handkerchief were restored to them. After this there was a warm debate among the brigands, whether it would not be better at once to murder them. During this very interesting discussion, the unhappy gentlemen forgot awhile their nakedness, and contrived to escape on foot. (1838, 105–7)

The episode serves as an opportunity for an unequivocal indictment of the unreal (and counterproductive) nature of the Peruvian republican order:

Events of this kind, which are not uncommon here, give rise to serious reflection. Is this liberty? Or is it only the road to it? Can civil liberty exist in the absence of such a power in the government as can afford effectual security to persons and property? What else is the object of social and political unions? Happy are those nations whose lot it is to enjoy both liberty and security. Rash and heedless must those ever be, who incur the risk of losing these where they are practically enjoyed, by seeking through change and revolution, the ideal perfection of their own fond theories. (109)[14]

However, it was not only foreigners who reached this grim conclusion. Ricardo Palma, in the *tradición* "Un negro en el sillón presidencial" ("A negro in the president's seat," circa 1908), revisits this period.[15] Palma refers to an episode from 1835, during the Orbegoso administration, in which Salaverry rebels occupied Lima. Salaverry later had to leave the city in order to defend his precarious position, leaving Lima unprotected. Taking advantage of the situation, the black bandit (montonero) León Escobar, commanding a gang of thirty men, entered Lima and reached the presidential palace, and then the very president's office, where he took a seat in the presidential chair (just as Villa would do in Mexico City eighty years later). Three Lima councilmen approached Escobar to beg him not to subject the city to the depredations that were to be expected of a black bandit. Escobar indicated that, of course, the gentlemen should not fear any misdeeds from him or his men, provided that they paid him five thousand pesos as ransom. The money, Escobar explained, would be put to good use: it would attend to the needs of his troops. After the predictable bargaining, Escobar was content with half the original sum. As promised, he left the city without harming life or property.[16] Palma met one of the councilmen of the story, who indicated that Escobar was more cordial and more reasonable in his demands than the whites who usually occupied the presidential palace.

There are two possible, noncontradictory readings of this anecdote, as told by Palma. The first one could be considered a "Cervantine" reading. The black man in the presidential chair who displays wisdom and moderation is a sort of postcolonial counterpart to the episode of Sancho Panza in the Ínsula Barataria. But there is also another interpretation. The bandit occupies the presidential chair, and lives up to his word, once given. This was precisely what Salaverry did not do, when he rebelled against the president who designated him. Escobar, like Villa, also respects the rules that regulate the moral economy of violence and protection—rules that, again, Salaverry did not respect, when he left Lima unprotected, thus failing in his first duty as a pretender to the First Office. The bandit (and a rather unimpressive bandit at that) lives by an honor system that elite appointed officials could not or would not follow.[17]

González Prada makes an analogous assertion, but it is not confined to the early republican past, nor is it expressed in Palma's amiable sarcasm. In "Nuestros beduinos" and "Nuestros tigres" (both included in *Horas de lucha*, 1908) he uses the bandit trope as part of his case against the Aristocratic Republic. In "Nuestros beduinos," González Prada expostulates: "For our public men, that is to say, for our Bedouins (since things have to be called by their names) Peru was a tent erected in the middle of the desert in a Second Arabia: they attacked and they despoiled the owners; but they don't leave yet because they still are able to exploit some leftovers of the former greatness, and they do not see another tent to assault and rob" ([1908] 1985, 293).

The image of the strongman or the corrupt statesman as robber is not that uncommon. Sarmiento, in the case of Argentina, used it with strongman Juan Manuel de Rosas in *Facundo*, and Juan Montalvo created a similar narrative regarding the Ecuadorean dictator Ignacio Ventimilla in *Las catilinarias* (1880–1882). One could also mention Vidaurre's legal and philosophical introduction to his *Proyecto de un código Penal*, in which he writes, "[When it comes to] robbery on the part of those in charge of public wealth, . . . we can say that they are the true murderers and highway robbers who sometimes sentence men that are less guilty than themselves" (1828, 18). However, González Prada is unique in the sense that he does not use the metaphor to depict the illegality (and for liberal thinkers, the concomitant illegitimacy) of personal rulers or corrupt officials. By using the Bedouin metaphor, González Prada depicts an entire class (and an entire model of crony or rentier capitalism) as a bandit organization that makes plunder its only known way of life. Additionally, this organization does not prey on a preexistent state: *it is the state*, its sole embodiment and possibility. Also, González Prada inverts the racial paradigm that turns the "inferior races" and "inferior classes" into dangerous ones. In "Nuestros tigres," he claims that

> in Peru there is a social phenomenon worthy of attention: not only murder and robbery, but also the most depraved instincts tend to be exacerbated in the decent people and the well-to-do classes. If somebody doubts this, we could ask these people if it were the Indians with sandals and ponchos who plundered the guano and the nitrates. . . . When at the Parque Inglés or at the Paseo Colón we catch a glimpse of a dandy with his Sunday best and his happy countenance, we cannot avoid murmuring *in pectore*: I bet that under the batiste dickey and the woolen frock you hide the flesh and bone of a Musolino! I bet you belong to a pride of tigers! ([1908] 1985, 297).[18]

But perhaps the most all-encompassing use of the bandit trope to embody the predicaments of postcolonial Peru occurred in the 1930s. Several "criminological" treatises dealing with banditry were written at the time: *Algunos aspectos de nuestra sociología criminal* (1930), by Víctor Modesto Villavicencio; *Los caballeros del delito* (1936), by Enrique López Albújar; and *Bandoleros en el Perú* (1937), by José Varallanos.[19] They were intended to be ample examinations of the bandit phenomenon, both in time and in space.[20] These scholars (incorrectly) point out the absence of banditry during the Inca era. Both Villavicencio and Varallanos state that the theocratic agrarian empire provided for all of the needs of the subjects, and that its well-developed state structure exerted a degree of control and social cohesion that made banditry at the same time impossible and unnecessary.[21] In fact, the affirmation of the supremacy of the state in the Inca Empire is so overwhelming that the only form of criminality that receives serious attention is that of "crimes against the state." This statement about the absence of banditry in the Inca Empire has a long history. Tschudi (1847) affirms it, and, perhaps more famously, so does William H. Prescott (1847).[22] In the twentieth century, it can be found in the highly encomiastic *La organización judicial en el imperio de los Incas*, by Horacio Urteaga, among other works.

The genetic hypothesis on Peruvian banditry that Varallanos and Villavicencio put forward is very telling. According to both, banditry in Peru began with the conquistadors, bandits themselves in the literal sense of the term. The conquistadors were the ones who brought the "germ of violence," the hybrid of criminality, empire building, and political tool that defined Peruvian banditry. Miscegenation between whites and Indians, a problem deepened by the forcible importation of the perceived crime-prone races (*razas criminógenas*), such as blacks, expanded and perpetuated outlawry as a decisive inflection in national character. This idea finds its complement in a statement made by López Albújar in *Los caballeros del delito*. López Albújar states that in Tacna, the southern region occupied by Chile after the War of the Pacific, there was no significant banditry. This was so, according to López Albújar (1936, 38), because the Chilean administration created the conditions for the development, at the regional level, of a modern and efficient state, capable of enjoying real territorial sovereignty.

It is not irrelevant to ask about the truth or falsehood of all of the aforementioned statements. But that is not the point here. What's crucial for this study is the "will for truth," in a Nietzschean sense, that these statements evidence. The history of Peru, for these intellectuals, is caught between the foundational banditry of the conquistadors and Eleodoro Benel's contemporary banditry, through the colonial and early national banditry of the runaway slaves of the coast, to the montoneros of the independence and republican eras, to the caudillos of the war against Chile and the civil wars that followed them. Banditry is for these criminologists the key to Peruvian drift between the theocratic empire and the unreachable mirage of modernity.[23]

López Albújar is largely considered a second-tier author. He was born, the reasoning goes, too late (1872) and too far away from the capitals of turn-of-the-century Latin America (Chiclayo) to really contribute something of significance to *modernista* literature. Hence, he is an epigone. At the same time, he was born too early, and his aesthetic options were too linked to the nineteenth century, for him to be a really meaningful player in the developments that defined the literature of the twentieth century. Hence he was merely a precursor to, or at best an accidental initiator of, *indigenismo* (with *Cuentos andinos*) and *negrismo* (with *Matalaché* [1928]). Indeed, *Matalaché*, a melodrama of interracial, interclass love set on the eve of Peruvian independence, and provocatively subtitled *Novela retaguardista* (rear-guard novel), embodies López Albújar's conscious assumption of belonging to the nineteenth century (since it is an ill-fated "national romance"). The gory, "naturalist" excesses in *Cuentos andinos* and *Nuevos cuentos andinos*, coupled with the use of rather conventional realist narrative techniques, seem only to confirm this line of thought.[24]

Cuentos andinos (1920) and *Nuevos cuentos andinos* (1937) are two collections of short stories largely (albeit not exclusively) devoted to outlaw violence in its myriad forms. The author was able to become familiar with this type of violence during his stint as a judge in Huánuco. The stories feature brutal forms of Indian justice ("Ushanan-jampi"), personal and decisive vengeance within the realm of Indian communal life ("El campeón de la muerte," "Cómo se hizo pishtaco Calixto") and outside of it ("Cachorro de tigre," "Juan Ravines no perdona"), bloody feuds between communities ("Cómo se hizo pishtaco Calixto," "La mula del Taita Ramún") and within communities ("El brindis de los Yayas"), cattle theft and smuggling ("Ushanan-jampi," "El licenciado Aponte"), uprisings—such as that of Eleodoro Benel—that entailed class alliances ("Juan Rabines no perdona"), and horrifying examples of how the powerful deal with outlaws ("El blanco"). All of these examples serve as emblems of the Andean culture of violence that cuts across divides of class and race.

But this presentation of outlaw violence is not intended to highlight the impossibilities of Peru as a nation-state, or to fan the flames of a supposed "Indian danger" (something in vogue at the time). López Albújar makes these stories the keystone of what I consider a rather innovative type of narrative in the Peruvian context: the Andean frontier narrative, or the Andean Western. The term Western has to be taken in a very general sense. I am referring to narratives of an epic flavor located in a frontier area. These are narratives devoted to feats of violence that are sufficiently codified within a given culture and that are carried out by larger-than-life characters. Put together, these narratives create a sort of "cultural mythology" that interacts in specific ways with the geocultural space of the nation as a whole.

Consider the example of "El campeón de la muerte." Hilario Crispín has abducted Liberato Tucto's daughter, Faustina. Prior to that, Liberato's daughter rejected Crispín as a suitor because his status within the community is ambiguous: he is considered lazy, prone to crime, a heavy drinker, a seducer of maids, and a vagrant. He is a so-called *mostrenco*, and certainly not a good catch for the daughter of a prosperous peasant such as Liberato. While Liberato sits in front of his hut chewing coca, and asking the coca (to no avail) about the fate of his daughter, Crispín appears on the premises. He is carrying a large sack, which he unloads in front of Liberato. The bloody and stinking remains of Faustina, carefully dismembered by machete blows, scatter all over the floor. To add insult to injury, Crispín tells him, "I cannot leave the sack here, because I may have to use it for you, if you dare to cross my path." Liberato, conspicuously unmoved, replies, "That's a good idea. Also, most likely the sack is stolen, and it would bring me bad luck. But since you have brought me my daughter, I think you should leave a little something to buy the candles for the wake, and some refreshments to take care of the mourners. Could you spare at least a sol?" Accommodating the brutal sarcasm, Crispín responds in kind, while evoking the origin of the whole bloody feud: "What can a mostrenco like me contribute?" Liberato goes on to look for Juan Jorge, the most celebrated murderer for hire (*illapaco*) in the area. Thanks to his profession, Juan Jorge has become a prosperous and respected member of the gentry of the area (he is listed as its richest taxpayer). Accordingly, he sets a steep price for Crispín's death. Liberato agrees. But Liberato wants Juan Jorge to shoot Crispín ten times, and to kill him only with the tenth bullet. Juan Jorge agrees, for an additional price. And he makes a point of making Liberato responsible for dispelling any doubts about his marksmanship. Juan Jorge, furthermore, does not kill at random. He makes the necessary inquiries regarding the case, and the fairness of Liberato's claim. Only when he is satisfied about the justice of the feud does he agree to kill Crispín, which he does, in a protracted execution. Once Crispín is dead, Liberato gouges out his eyes. Juan Jorge cuts out the heart, which he plans to eat to incorporate Crispín's bravery.

All of the elements of the Western as frontier narrative are present here. First, there is the feud triggered by a matter of honor (the denial of Faustina's hand). There is the initial vengeance (which, from Liberato's point of view, is the initial affront) and the challenge to the opponent to dare and seek retribution. This challenge is encoded, as it should be: It is a discussion about the sack and about the money for the wake. It is a manly challenge that, precisely because it is manly, is never explicitly uttered as such. Both parties know what they are talking about and both parties know which roles they have to play. There is a trade of barbs, but they assume the highly ritualized form of a polite exchange. There is a refusal of sentimentality even in the face of the death of a daughter. There is Juan Jorge's preoccupation with the justice of the revenge and about his oral reputation, based on his skill with the rifle. There is the "abstract" nature of the killing mechanism: all of Juan Jorge's bullets—like all of the bullets mentioned in *Cuentos andinos*—hit their target. And all enter the body cleanly. Bullets are less a lethal device—and as such, subject to the vagaries of wind, the physiology of the body they wound, and chance—than a neat form of inscription of the killer's will on the victim's body. The mechanism of vengeance is highly ritualized: the conversations and the bargaining between the avenger and the killer, the ceremonies that the killer undergoes to become a legitimate illapaco, the waiting for the victim, and so forth. These rituals engage the orientalist aspect of indigenist narratives, but go well beyond it. And finally, there is the absolute absence of the state from the scene, which in turn makes for the recognition of Juan Jorge as an informal (albeit legitimate) source of justice.

The idea of the Peruvian Western is very simple. However, the metaphysics of truth, and the moral imperative that traverses indigenism, are powerful obstacles to its currency. Any presentation of the Indian as a literary character is read from the viewpoint of its truth, and from the political standpoint of an emancipatory project.

This problem has plagued literary criticism on López Albújar's short stories from the very beginning, and it has been used to uphold as well as to condemn them. José Carlos Mariátegui, in "El proceso de la literatura" (included in *Siete ensayos*), considers López Albújar the founder of indigenism because of his ability to "capture some features of the Indian soul" ([1928] 1979, 308). Following this line of thought, Ciro Alegría, in his prologue to López Albújar's *Memorias*, credits him with depicting "Indians of flesh and blood" for the first time (Alegría 1963, 8). Escajadillo (2007), for his part, taking a cue from Mariátegui, flat-out makes López Albújar the founder of modern literary indigenism. In this case, however, the appreciation is moderated, if not nullified, by the fact that its project falls under the same interdiction that plagues all indigenist fiction: the distance between the "referent" (the "Indian world") and the representational artifact (the novel, the short story), which causes the project of representation (held as a possibility for the cancellation of socio-cultural heterogeneity) to become yet another of its symptoms.[25]

Indeed, in his short stories López Albújar creates a rather complex image of Andean outlaw violence. His stories display the panoply of forms that out-lawry can assume in the Andes whereas other authors, such as Ciro Alegría, or Manuel Scorza, or Miguel Gutiérrez, or those who are devoted to the saga of Luis Pardo, focus on the "noble bandit" image, or on a single variation of outlawry. At the same time, López Albújar counters two of the most powerful stereotypes or motifs shaping the depiction of rural violence in the Andes. According to the first one, all rural violence is ultimately linked to class and ethnic violence embodied in the struggle between *gamonal* (large landowner) and Indian communities. This is a prominent motif in *indigenista* narrative. It finds a neat expression in Alegría's *El mundo es ancho y ajeno*, but also in the short story "Ensañamiento," included in *Tempestad en los Andes* (Luis Val-cárcel, 1927). The story (whose protagonist, oddly enough—because López Albújar used this same device—is a judge) is about the cruel lynching of a gamonal by a community of local Indians. The crime confirms all the stereo-types of the barbarian Indian criminal: the gamonal is clubbed to death, his flesh torn to shreds in the craggy courtyard pavement, his eyes pierced with *tupus*. He has been broken, skinned, and scalped. The criminal investigation, however, shows that the gamonal was a murderer himself: his mistress tips off the authorities and when the floorboards of his barn are removed, the corpses of men and women, children and elderly people appear. Unable to see beyond his own prejudices, however, the judge orders the offenders to be remanded to jail, where they remain for many, many years. López Albújar, on the contrary, puts forward an image of Andean violence in which there are many different, nontotalizing lines of conflict that overlap, contradict, erase, or redraw the aforementioned class and ethnic lines (and that sometimes, but only some-times, reinforce those lines). As in the American Western, there is a political or economic conflict playing out in the background. But this conflict is super-seded by the showdown between men of courage, many times regardless of the sides.

At the same time, López Albújar contradicts the stereotype of the "passion-ate" Indian (a code word for "degenerate" and "barbarian") beset by character flaws (alcoholism, coca leaf addiction) and an atavistic penchant for irrational violence, as abundantly spelled out in the works of Oscar Miró Quesada, Víctor Pilares Polo, and José Antonio Encinas. Extreme violence occurs with unsettling profusion and naturalness in *Cuentos andinos*: eye gouging, cannibalism, mass murders, dismemberment, killings carried out in a painfully slow and sadistic fashion.[26] But these events are rarely considered "crimes"— quite the contrary—and they are never spur-of-the-moment happenings. They are regulated by a precise economy of violence, fully (albeit orally) codified, and fully legitimized (although barely, if at all, understood) by the narrator in the narration.[27] Also, there is never a mention of alcohol as a factor in the commission of acts of violence. This could not be more meaningful, especially if one takes into account that alcoholism is mentioned repeatedly as the cause of both Indian criminality and Indian degeneracy and as part of a pattern of representation of nonwhites in general. There is not a single Indian attacking a white person (something that happens abundantly in Ventura García Calderón's short stories, for example) and there is never an Indian who kills without reason. There is, in short, a carefully laid out economy of violence. Furthermore, as Castro Urioste (2006) notes (disapprovingly), it is often the leader of the community who engages in acts of violence.

Furthermore, taken as a totality, López Albújar's short stories provide an image of history that avoids two common pitfalls of indigenism. First, it avoids the idea of the Indian community as a utopia, enduring in a sort of stasis outside history, in the constant contemplation of its own cultural wholeness, until history encroaches in the form of the hacienda, as in the case of Rumi and its conflict with Amenábar's *fundo* in *El mundo es ancho y ajeno*. (This motif is analyzed in Cornejo Polar's *Escribir en el aire* [1994], as well as in Coronado's *The Andes Imagined* [2009].) Second, it avoids the concomitant idea of history as a linear (and oftentimes failed) evolution toward a certain form of modernity. Instead, López Albújar presents a social milieu shaped by diverse notions and diverse agents of historical change, and correspondingly, various images of historical conflict that are not reduced to the exclusive dynamics of the struggle between the premodern community and modern capitalism (which remains, but as one among several possible destinies). In doing this, López Albújar is able to create a literature that avoids the favorite illusion of the indigenist writer: that of the writer as the demiurge that creates the work of art as the utopian place where the heterogeneity of Peru is canceled. Instead of Ciro Alegría's pious image of the indigenist painter able to capture the soul of the Indian and be recognized by the Indian for doing so, López Albújar's narrative presents us with the image of the mix of horror and admiration that he feels for Ishaco, the son of the murdered brigand Margarino, who is able to exact bloody vengeance for his father ("Cachorro de tigre").

Does this mean that López Albújar's depiction of violence in the rural Andes is "more true" than, say, Ciro Alegría's *El mundo es ancho y ajeno*, Valcárcel's *Tempestad en los Andes*, or Icaza's *Huasipungo* (but more artificial than José María Arguedas's)? Hardly. The question of truth as adequacy to the referent is the wrong question to posit. Not unlike the American Western or kindred subgenres like the Mexican narrative of the revolution, the Argentine *gauchesca*, and its criollista spinoff, in *Cuentos andinos* the struggle for land, money, water, railroad access, political power, and prestige is ubiquitous, as are ethnic conflicts. But it is never a legitimate question to validate or reject those narratives (neither in aesthetic nor in political terms) by asking if those authors really understood their subjects. Western narratives create (or attempt to create) cultural heroes, and expand the geocultural space of the narratable. This is exactly what López Albújar accomplished. To use Juan Sasturain's (1995, 76) apt term in referring to *El eternauta* (the story of an alien invasion in 1950s Argentina), López Albújar expanded the "Peruvian verosimile." And therein rests the political/cultural value of this frontier narrative. It created a character. The ideological and epistemological contradictions are not an obstacle to López Albújar's relevance, but one of the conditions of his relevance, in the same fashion that the fundamentally paternalistic ideology vis-à-vis the gaucho of Gutiérrez and Hernández did not preclude the century-old fortune of the gaucho malo as insurgent icon.

Vargas Llosa deems *Cuentos andinos* a "shocking catalog of the sexual depravities and homicidal furors of the Indian, a subject that López Albújar . . . seems to have seen only in court, in defendants" (quoted in Castro-Urioste 2006, 56). In fact, most of López Albújar's commentators, in evaluating his literary work, give great importance to the fact that he was a judge in Huánuco, and that the cases that he narrated in his short stories were, for the most part, known to him during his stint as a judge (and as such, that he was part of the cohort of legal scholars who, from different positions, addressed the "Indian problem" mainly as one to be resolved within the realm of legislation).[28]

Ayllon, who wrote the prologue to the first edition of *Cuentos andinos*,

inaugurated this tradition. However, Ayllon's prologue is not the only para-
text that accompanies *Cuentos andinos*. In the 1920 edition, together with
the prologue, López Albújar included a dedication to his sons. (In the 1928
edition the prologue disappears but the dedication remains—as it does today.)
The dedication speaks little about his offspring, and nothing at all about his
previous literary career (by that time he had published a number of books
and was considered a mature writer, and perhaps a bit of a has-been). He
writes, instead, about the circumstances in which the book was written. He
was a lower court judge (*juez de primera instancia*) in the recently created
Huánuco judicial district. Lima's Supreme Court had suspended him because
he had issued a sentence that was in open contradiction to articles 264 and
265 of the already mentioned 1863 penal code that made adultery a crime.[29]
The case was a minor one. But its importance goes well beyond shedding light
on a biographical circumstance. It tells us something about López Albújar's
position of enunciation at the time he wrote *Cuentos andinos*. López Albújar
does not write as a judge, or from the other side of the law, but from a position
in between. He had been suspended, so he was in a yet-to-be-decided state
between judge and offender. Thus, *Cuentos andinos* can be read as a narrative
meditation on the difference between the law and the legitimate. A judge is he
who, by definition, makes the decision regarding what should happen in order
for that difference not to exist, or not to have ever existed. (A sentence is both
an interpretation of the letter of the law and the creation of a state of things in
the world—from execution to redress to absolution—that is at the same time
legal and legitimate.) But López Albújar has been (temporarily) dispossessed
of his main writing power: that of passing sentences. So literary writing is
not a complementary practice to that of passing sentences; rather, it supple-
ments the position of enunciation of the judge, a position where the Man of
the Law has a glimpse of a realm beyond himself. Thus, literature at this point
for López Albújar is not a reduplication of the epistemological privilege of the
judge, but the point of flight of said privilege.

Lauer (1997, 89) states that "the central theme of discourses on Peruvia-
ness has been that of the disjunction between past and present, and between
forms of the present." The attempt to cancel that disjunction is the defining
project of literary indigenism. López Albújar tackles the topic, but without
any attempt at synthesis. The Andean universe that López Albújar depicts
is not dominated by the overarching conflict between the hacienda and the

Indian community. Perhaps one exception is "Huayna-pishtanag," a classic
story of gamonal lust and Indian victimization. But in the only other short
story in which a hacendado appears ("El blanco"), the narrative emphasizes
the fact that the territorial order (which lives entirely outside the realm of
the state) is built upon an alliance between whites and Indians (who work as
loyal retainers of the white landlord), and the horror that an Andean (white)
gamonal causes for a *costeño* bureaucrat.

The state, when not entirely absent, is only one more of the players in the
drama of violence. And it is not as in the indigenist novel, in which the state
is an undivided ally of the landowning class (see the judge or the army in *El
mundo es ancho y ajeno*, *Huasipungo*, or *Raza de bronce*). It is not even the
dominant player, and it is not the player who seems to be on his way to dominance.[30] There is only one short story in which violence achieves a "national"
dimension: "El hombre de la bandera," where the narrator celebrates, in an
undivided fashion, the fact that the hero is able to form around him a community inspired by national ideals. In a sense, he is an ideal himself: the Indian
who becomes a citizen. It is important to note that this is a single short story,
and that it is not placed in a position of particular relevance. One can conclude
that "national violence" is not considered the superior form of violence (linked
to a superior form of consciousness) but merely an articulation among others,
in a field of forces that is at the same time multipolar and nontotalizing. This
impossibility of fully mapping violence does not bespeak barbarism or chaos,
but bears witness to economies of violence that are legitimate in their own
right. In this sense, I would argue that, more than the "psychological opening"
with which Cornejo Polar credits López Albújar, there is a cultural opening.
And the dimension in which this occurs is less political than aesthetic. Or,
better put: it is political because it is aesthetic, since it acknowledges the fundamental legitimacy (and, for a judge, the fundamental incomprehensibility)
of other economies of violence that are not those of the nation-state.

López Albújar creates, for the first time in Peruvian narrative, an epic version of the contemporary Andean subject (as opposed to the more commonplace epic version of the Inca past, contrasted with contemporary decline
or degeneracy). But it is not a national or racial epic. It is an epic that is not
inscribed in a predetermined movement of history. It is a frontier epic: the
same as that of the gauchos and orilleros of Argentina, the jagunços of Brazil,
the serranos of Mexico, the cowboys of the far West. López Albújar's Andes

are the stage in which enduring feuds, ascetic and stern characters, superb shooters, and bloody vengeances play out or perform their roles. To "create" the Andes as the setting where this frontier epic can take place provides the opportunity for some memorable scenes. And it is the place where the Indians cease to be *lo Indio* (every Indian as a metaphor of Indianness), and the mestizos cease to be *lo mestizo*.

In this respect, one of the best readers of López Albújar is Ciro Alegría—but not because of what Alegría said about him or his work. Alegría is the best commentator on López Albújar because he conceived, obviously (it seems to me), from López Albújar the character of Fiero Vásquez, a mestizo bandit who sometimes lives in the community of Rumi, and who sometimes fights on the side of the community. But he is somebody whose politics remain, in the last analysis, incomprehensible. The emblem of that incomprehensibility is Fiero's head that appears tossed in an empty ditch. The reasons remain a mystery. He has been killed, but it is not clear that he was killed while fighting for the community. He was indeed aiding the community in his struggle against Amenábar, and several *comuneros* join his ranks to exact revenge from traitors. But it is never established that the struggle between Rumi and Amenábar is the cause of Fiero's demise. Had that been the case, a more public execution would have been in order, a theater of the law *pour encourager les autres*. Thus, Alegría makes Fiero Vásquez the excessive third in the simple economy of the struggle between Rumi and the hacienda. And perhaps there is an inversion of the situation: it is not that Fiero, in social bandit fashion, helps the community to which he vicariously belongs to fend off the advances of the landowner. Perhaps (but this remains forever ambiguous) Fiero was using Rumi to fight another conflict—perhaps a conflict between landowners, perhaps another conflict of which we know little or nothing. In the mysterious character of Fiero Vásquez, clad in black, is the impossibility of fully mapping Andean violence. It is where López Albújar's original impulse survives, beyond truth, beyond morals, as the pure force of the story.

SIX

BORGES AND THE MELANCHOLIC CULTOR DEL CORAJE

There is a narrative, perhaps historical, perhaps legendary or made up of
both history and legend (which is perhaps another way to say legendary)
that bears witness to the cult of bravery. The best versions can be found in
the novels by Eduardo Gutiérrez, now unjustly forgotten, like the Hormiga
Negra or the Juan Moreira.

JORGE LUIS BORGES, "EL DESAFÍO"

His fate hovered near, unknowable but certain.
BEOWULF

How strange. This is all like a dream.
DUNCAN, DYING AFTER A DUEL, IN BORGES'S "EL ENCUENTRO"

THROUGHOUT THE YEARS, Jorge Luis Borges reiterated that epic
was "an essential need of the human soul" (2003, 41, 52, 110). He lamented
that epic had deserted poetry, which, in turn, had became synonymous with
lyric (2003, 41). And he observed that epic had taken refuge in film, particularly Westerns and gangster films (2003, 52; also quoted in Cozarinsky 1981,

15). It seems fitting, then, to begin this chapter with two films that Borges probably never saw or knew about, but that illustrate, I think, his idea of epic.[1]

The first one is Sergio Leone's spaghetti Western *Once upon a Time in the West* (*C'era una volta il West*, 1968). Its plot is rather simple: A man, the Man with the Harmonica (played by Charles Bronson), appears out of nowhere in Flagstone, a small town in the desert Southwest. Nobody knows who he is or where he comes from. But soon enough we all know that he comes to challenge Frank to a duel to the death. Frank, superbly played by Henry Fonda, is the evil railroad company henchman who clears the way for the railroad tracks at the point of his gun, either killing the landowners (as he does with Brett McBain and his children) or forcing them to sell at bargain prices. Harmonica's challenge is unequivocal. But he never tells Frank *why* he is set on fighting (and eventually killing) him. In fact, he never says much of anything, including his name. In fact, he barely speaks—he plays the harmonica most of the time, hence his sobriquet. The enigma drives Frank to distraction. But Harmonica does not impose the duel on Frank; he does not corner, publicly challenge, or shame him in order to make the duel inevitable. He just lingers, and meddles in Frank's affairs (as when he supports McBain's widow in her fight to keep Sweetwater, a nearby piece of land that holds the area's source of water). He even saves Frank from assassins. But this is not generosity. It is a statement that he does not only want Frank to die—he wants Frank to accept the challenge so that he can kill Frank himself in a fair fight. He will protect Frank's life until that is accomplished.

After a number of incidents, Frank finally accepts the duel. But he accepts the duel only in order to know why he is being challenged. Harmonica tells Frank that he will find out, but "only at the point of dying." Frank replies, resignedly, "That's what I thought." He does find out, *in articulo mortis*. Years before, when Harmonica was a child, Frank had killed Harmonica's brother. But Frank's diabolical imagination devised a refinement: Frank hanged Harmonica's brother from a stone arch, but the noose was loose. So Frank forced Harmonica to support his brother on his shoulders. The moment that Harmonica could no longer support his brother and collapsed, his brother would drop, and the noose would tighten and kill him. While Harmonica was struggling to support his brother, Frank shoved a harmonica in his mouth. "Play for your brother," he ordered. Harmonica's ragged breathing could be heard through the instrument. He eventually collapsed; his brother died.

But the revelation of the motive for the duel is not the pivotal moment of the scene. The climax includes this revelation, but lies elsewhere: it is Frank who, of his own free will, looks for Harmonica in order to accept the challenge. Harmonica does not have to chase Frank. He knows that Frank will eventually come to him because, although they are mortal enemies, they are both men of courage, bound by an ironclad code. The scene under the blazing sun in which the avenger (Harmonica) and the murderer (Frank) soberly walk and expertly assess the arena in which one of them will die momentarily is perhaps one of the greatest moments in the film. Frank dies, but he knows why he dies: Harmonica does honor his promise. He shoves the instrument in Frank's mouth, triggering the memory (which the movie does not present—we are only presented with Harmonica's flashback and not with Frank's memory of the events). Frank, eyes already glazing over, nods faintly in acknowledgment of the fairness of the challenge. He dies like a man, at the hands of a man.

The other movie is Ridley Scott's *The Duellists* (1977), based on the 1908 novella by Joseph Conrad. Lieutenant Gabriel Feraud is a quick-tempered, honor-obsessed, staunch Bonapartist young officer in the imperial army bent on European conquest in 1800. Because of a trifling matter, Feraud takes offense and challenges Lieutenant Armand d'Hubert to a duel. D'Hubert, against his better judgment but compelled by the code of honor, accepts the challenge. The first encounter is indecisive, and neither of the duelists accept it as a satisfactory conclusion. Only another duel will do. But several duels, or many instances of the same duel, all equally inconclusive, will take place throughout the years. This protracted duel creates a strange but unbreakable bond between the two men, in spite of their disparate destinies (d'Hubert thrives and marries into Restoration nobility; Feraud becomes an outcast, a ghost of the fallen Empire). This is a bond of enmity, but in Russia Feraud saves d'Hubert's life, and when Bonaparte falls, d'Hubert saves Feraud (unbeknownst to him) from the firing squad. These may be the noble actions of a worthy foe. Or they could be actions akin to Harmonica's saving Frank from the hitmen: a claim of the exclusive right of the duelist to kill his opponent himself, in a fair fight.

Both are mature men when a final and decisive showdown takes place: a running fight in a ruined château on a wooded hill, each of the men carrying two pistols. D'Hubert emerges victorious when Feraud makes a mistake and fires both of his pistols. D'Hubert pins him in position, with his pistol loaded. Finally, he has his decades-old enemy at his mercy, at the wrong end of a loaded gun. Since it is a duel, Feraud cannot try to make a run for it. He has to face his destiny. But d'Hubert does not kill Feraud. Since he owns Feraud's life, he does something much more cruel. D'Hubert does not shoot, but simply declares Feraud dead. Not defeated, but dead. From that moment on, Feraud will have to act as a dead man—that is, he has to disappear from the face of the earth forever, as far as d'Hubert is concerned. Constrained by the code of honor that has obsessively guided (or misguided) him, Feraud has no option but to obey, and to live the rest of his life as if he were dead. The movie ends with a close-up of Feraud, staring into the distance, a desperate (but understated) resignation on his face.

It is not difficult to notice the Borgesian quality of these films.[2] An oral law, different from (and opposed to) the laws of the state, rules the land (invisibly): the law of private vengeance, the law of the honor duel. The main characters are men of courage—men not necessarily virtuous, not necessarily interesting or even intelligent—who live by the prescriptions of this strict oral law, even though they know that this law will kill them (as in the case of Frank, who approaches the duel with fatalism, aware that the price of knowledge is his life) or worse (as in the case of Feraud, who lives out his remaining years with the consciousness of his defeat, a defeat so complete that it even robs him of the dignity of death). These men know that the law has to be obeyed, but not because it can punish: nothing "material" forces Frank to answer the challenge; nothing forces Feraud to obey d'Hubert's command. The law has to be obeyed because its observance defines the man of courage. Without it, he is nothing. (Tragically, he is also nothing with it, as I will show later.)

In both movies the characters' psychology is secondary; it is subordinated to (and even predicated upon) the fateful events. We know nothing about Harmonica's life prior to his brother's killing (and we know nothing about his life afterward, for that matter), nor do we know how Harmonica feels about his brother, alive or dead. We do know that his entire life—the long, long interval between childhood and adulthood, when the duel takes place—is predicated solely upon his need for vengeance (hence the name Harmonica, which is a constant reminder of the offense). In the case of *The Duellists*, we do not know how Feraud came to be so fanatical about Napoleon and duels; perhaps it was plebeian resentment, or perhaps a Sorelian (*Le rouge et le noir*) drive for advancement in an era defined by war. But this is not important: the spectacle of a man living in an uncompromising fashion, in solitude, drives the narrative. The Borgesian quality of these narratives is that they are not merely stories about brave men. They are stories about *cultores del coraje*. To this notion, as it appears in Borges, I will devote this chapter.

In his works set in the River Plate countryside or in the plebeian outskirts of the city (*orillas*), Borges would put together a minor epic populated by humble characters.[3] These characters are gauchos and *orilleros*, men of courage who inhabit a frontier world where the distinctions between lawful citizen and outlaw are fluid, and where the law of the state coexists with other, noncodified ways of regulating violence and the relationships between subjects. These men are indifferently rural or urban characters, or something in between (orilleros).[4] These men are defined by their relationship with violence. However, they do not rob, or kidnap, or extort. They are not out-and-out criminals. Borges's cultores del coraje are men who fight as a luxury (*pelear por lujo*) and predicate their identity upon their bravery and skill with the dagger (never or rarely with the gun). They can be occasional cattle rustlers, like the Nielsen brothers ("La intrusa"), or full-time cattle smugglers, like Bandeira and his men ("El muerto"). They can be on the wrong side of the state law, like the deserter and murderer Fierro ("Biografía de Tadeo Isidoro Cruz"). They can be members of rural posses like Cruz ("Biografía de Tadeo Isidoro Cruz"), electoral goons (*matón de comité*) like Rosendo Juárez ("Hombre de la esquina rosada," "Historia de Rosendo Juárez"), or bodyguards like Juan Moreira ("La noche de los dones").[5] Or they can be regular folk with a reputation for skill with the dagger, for being people not to be messed with, like Wenceslao Suárez ("El desafío"). As Borges puts it,

> We would have, then, men of very poor means, gauchos and orilleros of the riverine regions of the Paraná and the River Plate, creating, without being aware of it, a religion, with its mythology and its martyrs; the hard and blind religion of courage, of being ready to kill and to be killed. That religion is old as the world, but it was rediscovered, and lived, in these republics, by shep-

herds, cattle drivers, criminals and ruffians.... I just said that that religion is old. In a twelfth-century saga we read:

"—Tell me what's your religion—said the Count.

—I believe in my might—said Sigmund." (2005a, 178)

Borges's idea of epic during the 1930s and 1940s (the period that interests me in this chapter) was very different from the idea of epic that we found in Muñoz or Uslar Pietri (but not that distant from the notion that we find in López Albújar). But more importantly, it countered the notion of epic current at the time in Argentine culture, epitomized in the canonization of *Martín Fierro* as the foundational epic of the nation, Argentina's *Poema de Mio Cid*, and *Chanson de Roland* (this canonization was put forward most famously by Lugones [(1916) 1972]; and Rojas [(1917–1923) 1948]). Aguilar and Jelicié (2010, 17) put it clearly: "Of the three components that . . . usually define any epic genre (the organic totality of the community, the foundation of the nation, and the heroic action), Borges abandons the first two components.... The heroic actions remain, they define the epic pace of the narrative, but they are not carried out by representative warrior heroes, but by *infamous* characters.... All these characters have in common one feature: they face their destiny alone, and with undaunted courage."

This truncated or minor notion of epic is, for Borges, the true and original one. In his 1937 review of *L'Homme blanc* by Jules Romains, Borges argues that the *Iliad*, the *Odyssey, Chanson de Roland, Mío Cid*, the *Nibelungelied*, and *Beowulf* narrate local, even personal events (the *Iliad* narrates just one episode of a ten-year war, and a petty episode at that—the resentful wrath of Achilles). He goes on to say that the representation of a larger (usually national) community "is a feature that nobody fails to assign to the old epic poems, but that these epic poems never, never have" (1996b, 315). Then, for Borges, far from the epic of the Argentine nation, *Martín Fierro* has to be considered for what it is: the rather sad adventures of a paysano who, in a godforsaken corner of South America, becomes a deserter, a vagrant, a *malevo*, and a murderer in barroom brawls, as well as an occasional horse and cattle rustler. But it is Fierro's proven courage, which ignores morality and melodrama, that allows him to keep company with other quick-tempered warriors, plunderers, and outlaws: Achilles, Gettir, Roland, the Cid.

Borges derives the formula of cultor del coraje from "El Guapo," perhaps the most memorable poem by Evaristo Carriego. The first stanzas of the poem read,

> *The neighborhood reveres him. Cultor del coraje,*
> *He achieved fame as a brave man;*
> *He came out victorious from a hundred tough fights*
> *And in the prisons he endured he became a celebrity.*
>
> *He is aware of his achievements, and he is not perturbed*
> *By other men's glory, since he is feared by many,*
>
> *All the men of action in Palermo respect him*
> *And heed his fame, never contradicted.*
>
> *His face is crisscrossed by the violent marks*
> *Of deep scars, and perhaps he feels proud*
> *Of carrying those perpetual bloody ornaments:*
> *Feminine whims that the dagger had.* (Carriego [1908] 1913, 89)

Borges takes up the formula in his book *Evaristo Carriego* (1930, in Borges 2005a). There is an important difference, though. I would describe it as the migration of the word *cultor* from its primary meaning to its secondary one (but for Borges, it is a crucial meaning).[6] The word means one who tends to, who cultivates. Carriego's *guapo* and Don Segundo Sombra (in Güiraldes [1926] 2002) are cultores del coraje in this first sense.

Sombra (one of the two main characters of the eponymous novel) has killed men (Güiraldes [1926] 2002, 80) and could have been an exceptional caudillo (146), but he has chosen to abandon the life of violence. However, this does not mean (as it means for Fierro in the *Vuelta*, or for Rosendo Juárez in "Hombre de la esquina rosada") that he has to change names and abandon the places he used to live. Sombra is one with the oral law, in complete control of it. The scene in which this is most obvious is when the Tape Burgos challenges him. Sombra (like Fierro) does not accept the challenge and the scene has an anticlimactic ending: "He seems a little dumb to me," Sombra comments on Burgos (86), who has just tried to kill him (even though later on he will seek Sombra's friendship). This rejection of the challenge—Sombra can strike and win and kill, but he does not—does not cast doubt upon his reputation as a brave paysano (in the case of Fierro, declining to fight the Moreno means that he has to surrender his reputation as a fighter, leave, and change his name, if not out of shame then at least in order to avoid future challenges). In the case of Sombra, his disdain for Burgos only enhances his reputation in the eyes of Fabio (the protagonist of the novel and Sombra's disciple) and in the world of the cowboys, since, unlike what happens in Borgesian bandit narratives, his reputation is not called into question time after time after time, but rather has been established once and for all in a moment outside of the novel, outside of the dynamics and the risks of the present challenge.

But cultor is also (and, in Borges, mainly) the one who worships (*rinde culto*). We can think about characters in Borges's work who worship: the priest in "La escritura del Dios," Juan de Panonia in "Los teólogos," the unnamed magician in "Las ruinas circulares," the theologian in "Tres versiones de Judas." Taking these examples into consideration, we can suspect that *rendir culto* in Borges means to follow the law (the writing of God, the uncertain yet undefined Catholic orthodoxy of late antiquity, the commands of the God of Fire, the exegetical logic of a stern protestant) to an extreme where a truth is achieved and experienced. But this truth is the truth of the nothingness of identity, of the universe. To worship the God of Fire is, for the magician, to eventually realize that he is a dream. The priest is able to read God's writing on the jaguar. This writing is the truth of the universe, but at the same time it is a truth that voids the reality of the priest, the jaguar, and even the universe.

As the dialogue between the Count and Sigmund that Borges quoted and that is transcribed above makes clear, courage is a religion, with its rituals and worshippers. But in the Borgesian universe of violence, the cultor del coraje is not Carriego's happy guapo, or the cultivator in the sense of someone who tends to something (the local reputation), who nourishes, who lives a risky life, but rather one who is happily ensconced in the admiration of his community, and has a confident stride on the treacherous neighborhood sidewalks. The cultor del coraje for Borges is not the happy outlaw (Robin Hood, Rob Roy) who cultivates (and enjoys) an oral reputation. Rather, he is the one who lives under the brutal demand of this law, a law that simultaneously endows him with identity and dispossesses him of all identity.

The Borgesian epic is an epic in which the hero follows the oral law to the last. This is why the critical fiction "oral law" that rules the universe of the cultor del coraje should be handled with some caution. On the one hand, it should not be considered, as many literary critics do, as having (or having had) any real existence (the harsh and happy frontier days). It is, at least as far as Borges is concerned, a literary construct—which is not to say that it is culturally or politically irrelevant, but only that Borges did not pretend to be an ethnographer or a historian. On the other hand, one should not succumb to the populist fallacy that considers anything that is "oral," rural, or popular to be somehow immediately authentic and emancipatory, something that creates a transparent, unanimous sociability. The law (regardless of the modifier "oral" or "written") is, above all, a law. Its mandates are much more than those of an open and democratic challenge between heroes or would-be heroes. The oral law also has monstrous demands. Examples are the demands upon the Nielsens, who, in order to prove that they do not care about women (men should not even think about women, they say), partake in a sordid threesome, and later on share the secret of the murder of Juliana ("La intrusa"); or Manuel Cardoso and Carmen Silvera's grotesque race with their throats slit ("El otro duelo"). So the allegiance of the hero to the oral law does not make him free. It may not even make him the hero of a community. It condemns him to solitude, and to nothingness. The hero lives (and accepts) a brutal but neutral destiny.

Nobody exemplifies the melancholic nature of the man of courage so clearly as the Moreno, the character in "El fin" (a short story in *Ficciones* [1944], collected in Borges 2005a). The little we know about the Moreno, we know through Recabarren, owner of a *pulpería* (bar and general store) in an unnamed place on the plains, in the southern confines where Argentina (or, more precisely, Buenos Aires Province) ends and the so-called desert begins. Recabarren has had a stroke, and he lives paralyzed, in a forced contemplative state.[7] From his cot he imperfectly witnesses the culmination of a duel that, we realize later, had begun as a sordid drunken brawl almost a decade before. Recabarren witnesses the arrival of a stranger, who gets down from his horse and talks with the Moreno, for years a silent (almost invisible) patron of Recabarren's pulpería (the Moreno strums his guitar, never playing a song, just punctuating the long hours in the pulpería, much like Harmonica). The conversation between the two men reveals that the Moreno is not a mere loiterer, a straggler in an outpost in the middle of nowhere. The Moreno has been patiently waiting for this day. All these years have been the empty interval between a challenge to a fight (famously narrated in *La vuelta de Martín*

Fierro) and the answer to that challenge (Fierro's return in order to answer the challenge and to fight).

The ensuing knife fight is conducted in a taciturn fashion: no macho bravado, no unnecessary pathos. It culminates with Fierro's death. With this death, the Moreno avenges the murder of his brother in a different duel, in a different pulpería. Fierro's killing at the hands of the Moreno is a "labor of justice" (Borges 2005a, 502). But the scene does not strike one as the jubilant culmination of a vengeance, but more as the melancholic fulfillment of a duty. However, the Moreno and his revenge are removed from the literary codes of the social bandit. The avenger (the version of the social bandit that would define the Moreno) lives, at least in myth, in the obstinate solitude of his mission (for years in the mountains, like Memed in *Memed My Hawk*, or deep in a dungeon, like Dantès in *The Count of Monte Cristo*). But this solitude is deceiving. The avenger is not a criminal because he embodies the values of the community that he champions, or because he avenges this community after its disappearance (for example, Dantès avenges his father who died of grief because of Dantès's imprisonment). In the case of the Moreno, this community would have been his extended family (there were ten brothers, one of them killed by Fierro, as the Moreno dutifully explains in the run-up to the challenge in the *Vuelta*) and the paysanos who would understand and justify the Moreno's act. The family would embrace the long-lost son as soon as his mission was accomplished. The delivering of justice is the most emphatic proclamation of that belonging, even when it is committed in the loneliness of the plains. It is an act that will never be forgotten, and in that respect, the Moreno should be a classic epic hero.

This is what would have happened, had "El fin" been a classic epic. But in "El fin," the Moreno's revenge is accomplished in the most absolute loneliness, in the somewhat atrocious world of *El gaucho Martín Fierro* (the *Ida*), where the plain, as Martínez Estrada notes, is more akin to the nightmarish landscapes of Kafka or Conrad than to the picturesque landscapes of nationalist *criollismo* (1948, 2:173). The fight is far from being the finishing touch that would complete the neat shape of a destiny, and that would endow the long years of waiting with meaning, thus crowning a destiny and defining an identity. On the contrary, Fierro's death is the point where the Moreno loses all identity and all certainty. The narrator explains, "Once he had accomplished his work as an avenger, he became nobody. Or, to say it better, he became the other: he had no destiny on earth and he had killed a man" (Borges 2005a, 558). The Moreno fulfills his destiny—and one should remember that for Borges, the gaucho, like the compadre, "was less an ethnic type than a destiny" (2003, 129; Borges and Bullrich 1945, 8). But that destiny is a destiny not of completeness but of loss: the Moreno will not return to his family, and since Recabarren, the only witness to the duel, cannot talk, nobody can vindicate the silent courage of the fight. Like Fierro's, his life is over. The duel does not kill, it does not exalt: it makes a man into a nomad living under the weight of the law. Once the challenge is over, nobody knows how that challenge originated; there is no bragging, no congratulations to the victor. There may be a meaning to that fight, but it is a meaning that is for the Moreno and no one else to experience. It is right there, but forever lost, because it will never happen, or has already happened, or it is happening in a language that we do not understand. (Borges said, "There is an hour in the evening when the plains seem to be about to reveal something. Nothing is ever revealed. It never does, or perhaps it is revealed incessantly and we do not understand it, or we understand it but as if, like music, it is impossible to put into words" [2005a, 558].)

The desire for vengeance motivates the Moreno, of course. But melancholy is the passion that dominates even that desire. Indeed, I would argue that melancholy is a core feature of the Borgesian bandits (at least the River Plate ones). It is a melancholy that should not be confused with what Ludmer (1988) correctly identifies as the "lamentation for the loss" as one of the tones of the gaucho genre. Nor should it be confused with the nostalgia of the crepuscular writer for the luminous, open world of violence.[8] Borges's bandits, far from undivided and self-aware heroes, "live their destinies as if in a dream, without knowing who they were or what they were" ("Los gauchos," in Borges 2005b, 382). "As if in a dream," which means in the present but removed from most certainties regarding this present.

Another example of melancholic revenge is that of Azevedo Bandeira and his violent retribution against the up-and-coming young Otálora, in "El muerto" (1949, in Borges 2005a). Otálora is a rather pathetic compadrito from Balvanera, a poor neighborhood on the orillas of Buenos Aires, who lacks "any virtue other than the infatuation with courage" (Borges 2005a, 524). Having had some troubles with the law in Buenos Aires, he crosses the river, looking to become a member of the Bandeira gang (he has a letter of introduction to that effect). Azevedo Bandeira is a legendary leader of men, the chief of a gang of

rustlers and cattle smugglers who rule the ill-defined borders between Brazil
and Uruguay at the end of the nineteenth century.[9] Otálora does become one
of Bandeira's men, when chance gives him the opportunity to save Bandeira's
life from a drunken gaucho who is about to stab him (Otálora actually saves an
anonymous individual; later on, it becomes clear that he saved Bandeira, the
man he had been looking for). Otálora, incredibly, is able to become a hardy
cowboy and a leader of men, gradually and almost imperceptibly replacing the
authority of Bandeira, the nominal leader of the gang.

But Otálora embraces the trappings of leadership and possession with too
much eagerness. Only too late does he realize that these trappings are mirages
that Bandeira, the true mover of the story, has used to tempt him into treason—into usurping Bandeira's authority and stealing his woman—and into
an ambush:

> The last scene of this story takes place during the excitement of the last night
> of 1894. That night, the men of El Suspiro eat fresh-butchered lamb and drink
> hard liquor, which makes them bellicose. Somebody is infinitely and ardu-
> ously strumming a milonga. At the head of the table, Otálora, drunk, piles
> exultancy upon exultancy, jubilation upon jubilation; that vertiginous tower
> is a symbol of his inexorable fate. Bandeira, taciturn among the boisterous
> men, lets the night take its clamorous course. When the twelve strokes of the
> clock chime at last, he stands up like a man remembering an engagement. He
> stands up and knocks softly on the woman's door. She opens it immediately,
> as though she were waiting on the knock. She comes out barefoot and half
> dressed. . . . The woman tries to resist, but two men have taken her by the
> arms, and they throw her on top of Otálora. In tears, she kisses his face and
> his chest. Ulpiano Suárez has pulled his gun. Otálora realizes, before he dies,
> that he has been betrayed from the beginning, that he has been sentenced to
> death, that he has been allowed to love, to command, and win because he was
> already as good as dead, because so far as Bandeira was concerned, he was
> already a dead man. Suárez fires, almost with a sneer. (Borges 1998, 200)

Just like the killing of Fierro by the Moreno in "El fin," Bandeira's behavior
lacks, in the crucial scene of vengeance, an expected intensity. The brutal
but necessary application of the oral code of loyalty to the *primo inter pares*
should be a party within the party, full of theatrics and gloating. Perhaps he is

remorseful when he kills the man who had saved his life. Or perhaps he kills him *because* he saved his life. Otálora must die because, on the fateful night of their acquaintance, Otálora proved to be more of a man than Bandeira was. Bandeira has to kill Otálora in order to save his reputation. If he does not prove himself to be the leader, he is just an old useless man to be forgotten. But to kill Otálora, to challenge him openly, would be an act of patent ingratitude; thus he has to create the conditions in which Otálora deserves to be killed. Otálora realizes all too late that his meteoric rise to a leadership position in the gang was a trap from the very beginning. But Bandeira, like the Moreno, does not obtain any satisfaction from the triumph. It is a burden, a disgrace that, as Nietzsche claimed, "cannot be carried and cannot be cast away" (quoted in Cueto 1995, 23).

Even in *Los orilleros* (1955), the script that Borges and Bioy Casares hoped to be animated by the "the passion of adventure, and perhaps, a distant echo of epic" (Borges and Bioy Casares [1955] 1979, 200), the enduring impression that the narrative leaves us with is that of Morales, a dignified but melancholic orillero who looks for the duel with Eliseo Rojas to be his imperfect opportunity to escape from an infamous memory. Morales's statement is memorable and touching: "to look for a man of courage and of mettle, if there is any; to challenge him and then to find out who one is; that could be the solution" (211).

The culto del coraje can be taken to an extreme and become insanity. This is the case with Don Lucas, in *Los orilleros*, who realizes one night, in a duel against a gang of black men, that he is a man, and he condemns himself to repeat that scene, forever, taken over by the law (which drives him here to madness):

> Morales looks toward the ombú tree. The man [Don Lucas] is fighting by himself. He has an arm in the air, as if he were using a poncho as a shield; in the other hand he wields an imaginary dagger. Sitting by the curb there is a porter boy who does not look at him.
> EL MOZO.—Eventually, he always defeats them.
> MORALES.—He may be dreaming about something that happened.
> EL MOZO.—The Plaza de las Carretas was formerly located here. You could see people from everywhere. Once in the 1870s, some blacks from Morón appeared. They used to get drunk at the casino around the corner

from the fruit market. After that, they came to the square and bothered the passersby, until the wee hours of the morning.

MORALES.—I see. And that happened until Don Lucas quieted them down?

EL MOZO.—Indeed. He was a very polite young man, without any other ambition than that of fulfilling his obligations. But the blacks had become so arrogant that one night the man waited for them under the ombú and fought them while everybody was watching. Now he is a pitiful figure: he has a couple of drinks and he begins to relive his fight with the blacks.

MORALES.—Pitiful? He is old, he may be half-crazed, but he never forgets the day that showed that he was a man. (Borges and Bioy Casares [1955] 1979, 222–23)

I take the notion of melancholy in Borges from Sergio Cueto's essay "Sobre el humor melancólico" (1995). For Cueto (whose argument I am simplifying a bit), melancholy defines many Borgesian short stories. The emblem of this experience is perhaps the blind guardian of the books, somebody in charge of a task that is simultaneously impossible, absurd, and absolutely unavoidable, an extreme situation that cannot be resolved (like the characters in Kafka's stories). Cueto observes that "melancholy is [in Borgesian characters] the intangible distance that separates them from themselves, the resigned wonder that distances them from their own acts and makes them [protagonists and] spectators of a drama at the same time incomprehensible and indifferent. Melancholy is the manifestation of the gap that opens between man's useless power and his impossible passivity" (1995, 20).

Melancholy is, in Borgesian characters, the consciousness of inhabiting an impossible space, a space that at the same time is unavoidable. It is a universe that we accept (we cannot not accept it), but it is nightmarish. That impossibility assumes diverse forms. It is the collusion of randomness and necessity in "La lotería de Babilonia"; of reality and unreality in "Las ruinas circulares" and "Tlon, Uqbar, Orbis Tertius"; of unbounded power and utter powerlessness in "La escritura del Dios"; of total knowledge and the total impossibility of knowledge in "El Aleph" and "Funes el memorioso"; of experiencing the universe in its totality and the complete loss of the universe in "El Zahir." Melancholy is the imminence of a revelation, and the consciousness that that revelation is impossible or banal, as in "La secta del Fénix." In the stories that consider the cultores del coraje, melancholy is the mark of an equivocal relationship between the oral law from which the cultor obtains his mission and his identity, and the body that obscurely lives and dies under the weight of that law.

The cultores del coraje are melancholic because the demand that oral law places upon them is overwhelming. This is not (or not only) because death is a distinct possibility. It is overwhelming because it has no end. Borges's preferred outlaw narrative, as is well known, is that of the duel between two adversaries who do not know each other and who have no animosity toward each other. The challenge is only motivated by the zeal of maintaining or bettering a reputation (a splendid rendering or variation of this theme is the short story "Los dos," by Chilean Rafael Maluenda). Although *Martín Fierro* narrates memorable knife fights, in some cases unmotivated (such as the fights against the Moreno and the *terne* in the *Ida*), Borges found his inspiration for this motif not there, but in the unending serial novels of gauchos malos written by Eduardo Gutiérrez between 1879–1880 and 1885–1886.[10] These novels (whose plots I simplify somewhat, and whose model is *Juan Moreira*) narrate the travails of innocent paysanos turned into outlaws by the persecution of abusive state officials.[11] The abuses assume different forms: the paysano can be harassed because he has a wife or girlfriend coveted by a policeman or a landowner, or he can have a coveted horse, or a piece of land, or some cattle; he can be harassed because he would not tolerate the arrogance of the justice of the peace or the *teniente alcalde* (deputy mayor); and/or he can be harassed because he did not vote as expected. Defending his property, or his family, or his honor, the paysano kills the offender (always in a fair fight), and he is forced to become a fugitive (*gaucho matrero*). Posses relentlessly chase him. But he is also chased by his own reputation that forces him to fight other paysanos, intent on building a reputation of their own as the vanquishers of a famed gaucho malo. The novels thus become a series of armed encounters, motivated or not, fought in the open, but also in pulperías, general stores, *fondas* (cheap eateries), and voting places, and narrated in a highly stylized, highly topical fashion. About this, Laera (2004) states, "Sheer accumulation, the serial novel functions using the narrative and structural resource of the iteration: in the same novel, the succession of struggles with the police and the succession of duels between paysanos become the episodic chain of a single narrative whose condition of possibility is to be always identical to itself" (293). This "infinite seriality" (as Nicolás Rosa [1997, 158] puts it) can only be interrupted, in the tradition of bandit narratives, with the intervention of an exterior element, such as death or treason (Hobsbawm [1969] 2000, 47–48).[12]

Borges did not consider *Juan Moreira* Gutiérrez's best novel: "Moreira, as written by Gutiérrez, is a sumptuous Byronian character, who ministers with equal solemnity tears of grief and stabbings" (1996b, 277). Borges did not like the melodramatic aspects of *Moreira*, much as he did not like these aspects of Carriego's poetry either. His favorite Gutiérrez novel was *Hormiga Negra*. However, there is a feature of *Moreira* that Borges did appropriate, and turn into the cornerstone of his cultores del coraje: the overwhelming fatigue that the gaucho experiences before the challenges that are imposed upon him (what the narrator of *Moreira* calls "the embrace of fate" [Gutiérrez (1879) 1999, 297]). Moreira would like (or says that he would like) to abandon his nomadic life and the duels and fights against the posses. However, his reputation always precedes him, and there is always a paysano who, no matter what, will challenge him to fight. Perhaps Moreira does not want to fight. But his only possession, his only identity, is that of a fighter, so, willingly or unwillingly, he will have to answer the challenge and fight and kill. This degrades him morally, but above all, the realization that he is trapped in an invisible jail plunges him into a deep melancholy. His reputation, which at the same time makes him what he is, will eventually be his undoing. Unlike Fierro in *La vuelta*, on several occasions Moreira rejects offers to move to a different province where all persecutions would cease. When he leaves to hide among the Indians, he returns, apparently because he is unable to bear a life of anonymity. Moreira is condemned to repetition, until treason, an accident, or death come to liberate him from himself—this is the brutal interpellation of the law that Borges appropriated and that he used to define his stoic characters.

In Borges, the iterative principle of the challenge confirms and at the same time disarticulates the law, since it ceases to be the law of the community that fixes the subject in a position. It becomes a law that condemns the subject to an endless wandering. If the fighter of the North has to travel to the South in order to challenge the local brave (as happens in "Hombres pelearon," "Hombre de la esquina rosada," and "El desafío," among other stories), it is because the North is no longer a motherland, no longer a self-sustaining cultural community. The law ceases to rule (and hence create) a North, or it creates it only as a fleeting identity effect playing within the duel. It is only important to be from the North in order to claim the foreignness that makes the challenge possible in the South (in "Hombres pelearon," it is the opposite: the guapo from the South travels to the North with the sole purpose of challenging the local guapo). This forces the cultor del coraje to move beyond, always beyond (like the dreamers who are also dreams in "Las ruinas circulares"), toward the South, always toward another South. The law does not define a common ground, but opens an abyss through which certainty (in particular, the certainty about one's courage) falls, because there is always the possibility that there is someone braver, quicker, or more skillful somewhere else.

In "El fin," Fierro's sons can come to look for the Moreno (if word ever gets out about their father's death, which, in true Borgesian fashion, we will never know), or, for that matter, anybody who wants to make a name for himself by killing the killer of Fierro. This is not an accident; it is inscribed as the core of the law, as "Hombre en la esquina rosada," for example, proves. If the law ceases to determine the belonging to a place (the enduring reputation within a community) and condemns the body to movement that is continuous and ever-widening in scope, and to the constant loss of community, this is because the identity that this law creates is an identity always already ruined. This is melancholy: the consciousness (which can only be the consciousness of an individual) that the challenge happens outside all subjectivity and that it does not make two men meet, but rather two names (what Borges calls "la nombradía") that have been taken over by the law. (The ritual aspect of the challenge, which is always uttered indirectly, and often in a rather impersonal fashion, emphasizes this.)

The law demands a task that does not belong to the subject, but that, if not fulfilled, deprives the subject of all identity. That is why the triumph in the duel does not turn the Moreno into the champion of his family, but rather turns him into nothing, or, more precisely, it turns him into the nothing that the other was, the nothing that he already was, taken away by the unending logic of the challenge. The oral law simultaneously exalts and ruins the subject, and melancholy is the trace of that indiscernible movement. This, in the idiom of bandit narratives, is the classic Borgesian theme of "I am other" that weighs down upon many subjects of violence, from the Moreno to the title character of "Tamerlán (1336–1405)." It is also the confirmation that the end of "El fin" is not a real end: if the Moreno becomes Fierro, as the story tells us, it is possible (perhaps imperative) to think that seven years from that fate-ful afternoon another challenge and another duel will take place, either with one of Fierro's sons who comes to avenge his father or with an occasional challenger who wants to make a name for himself defeating the vanquisher of Fierro, and then the challenge would continue to infinity, in a bleak ever-growing labyrinth of steel and blood.[13] This labyrinth is bleak because it is devoid of experience (or occupied by a single experience, like the search for the book in "La biblioteca de Babel"). In "El fin," the seven wandering years that Fierro takes before heeding the challenge are equal to nothing, not worth narrating, either for Fierro or for the Moreno. There are no new roads, no adventures (or misadventures), and no love. Those years are a desert, more desolate and empty than the physical desert through which Fierro rode and in which the Moreno waited.[14]

In Borges, the challenge comes from nobody and is directed at nobody. But at the same time it is for him (the cultor del coraje) and him alone that the law is meant, and he is the one who has to carry the weight of that challenge in his own body. The law forces a performance (that of the challenge and the acceptance of a challenge), but from the point of view of this subject the per-formance is not an act; it is not different from him. It is a task that does not belong to the subject but that only he can carry out, like the man in Kafka's "Before the Law" (but the impossible interpellation of the law does not immo-bilize the cultor del coraje, as it does the petitioner in Kafka, but forces him to be always in motion—and always in the same place).

In "El Sur," the challenge of the drunken paysanos to Dahlmann happens in a dream, of course, meaning not that it is unreal (it is perhaps the most real moment of Dahlmann's entire life), but that it is governed by a secret, inscrutable causality just like the universe. That neutral entity is embodied in the old gaucho who throws him a knife. But in the Borgesian universe, all challenges happen in a dream—in a world that is at the same time immediate, undeniable, and inscrutable.

PART III

BANDITRY AND THE LATIN AMERICAN LEFT

DANGEROUS ILLUSIONS AND SHINING UTOPIAS

On *Seara Vermelha*

This is Captain Corisco facing the Dragon of Wealth.
DEUS E O DIABO NA TERRA DO SOL

JORGE AMADO (1912–2001) is arguably the Latin American fiction writer who has addressed the topic of outlaw rural violence and its role (or lack thereof) in class-based revolutionary social change with the most perseverance and coherence (and most prolifically). As a whole, his work is a sustained and totalizing exploration of northeastern Brazilian life, mainly the state of Bahia. Nearly all walks of life have found a place in his work: urban elites (large cocoa exporters, bankers, industrialists and wealthy merchants, senators and governors); urban middle classes (professional, commercial, intellectual, conservative, liberal, and radical); urban workers and urban riff-raff of all sorts (prostitutes and pimps, out-and-out criminals and borderline *malandros*, the *lumpenproletariat*, confidence men, thieves, beggars and street urchins); and larger-than-life planters and oppressed plantation workers, peasants and squatters, immigrants, popular and elite poets, sailors, fascist militants and Communist Party members, torturers and revolutionary martyrs, Roman Catholic *beatos* and Afro Bahian *pais-de-santo*. Rural outlaws play a paramount role in this rich cast of characters. Amado's literary production features all varieties of outlaw, from social bandits and avengers—cangaceiros—settling real or imagined old scores, to hired guns—jagunços—loyal to their masters, as in *Terras do sem fim* (1943), or holding more duplicitous allegiances, as in *Cacau* (1933).

This recurrence of the topic of outlaw violence is not surprising. A time-honored tradition of outlaw violence, at the same time extremely complex and tightly woven into the fabric of social life, was one of the most permanent and, for outsiders, most visible traits of the society inhabiting the arid interior of the Northeast, or *sertão*.[1] Outlaw violence gave rise to rich traditions in both popular and elite literatures, from the *literatura de cordel* to *Os sertões* (the "Bible of Brazilian nationality," as Joaquim Nabuco emphatically put it [quoted in Levine 1992, 18]), to regionalist fiction, of which Amado was one of the main pillars from the 1930s onward, culminating in *Grande Sertão: Veredas*, by João Guimarães Rosa.[2]

Amado explicitly tapped into both high and popular literary traditions. He imagined his oeuvre as a sublation of the dichotomy. During the 1930s and 1940s, he was a loyal and prominent member of the Brazilian Communist Party (Partido Comunista do Brazil, hereafter PCB), through its various transformations and Comintern-inspired strategies: Popular Front, armed revolt, narrow classism, clandestine status, collaboration with Vargas, and, at last, legal status.[3] Predictably, his literary consideration of the phenomenon of banditry revolves around the peasantry's role in class struggle and revolutionary social change. This was part of a larger political and theoretical problem—that of the revolutionary potential of the peasantry, which was at the time still a controversial issue among Communists given the rather negative assessments of the subject by Marx himself (see, for example, *The Eighteenth Brumaire of Louis Napoleon*) and the ambiguous lessons of the Russian Revolution and Stalin's own stance on the topic. Furthermore, Amado wrote the novels that I will consider in this chapter before the triumph of the Chinese Revolution, the heyday of the African Liberation struggles, the Cuban Revolution, and the wars in Vietnam.[4] Hobsbawm, a contemporary of Amado (Hobsbawm was born in 1917), wrote his seminal works on banditry *after* the triumph of the Chinese Revolution in 1949, and during the Asian and African struggles, but reached largely the same conclusions as Amado. Perhaps this is so because their ultimate interests were the same. Chandler (1987) brings this point home when he states that Hobsbawm was less interested in banditry per se than in broadening the scope of Marxist thought when it came to revolutionary activity.

Amado was, however, at least before the 1950s, quite different from other writers of the Marxist persuasion. Unlike the Mexican José Revueltas, another of the literary giants of Latin American Marxism, Amado never doubted the ability of dialectical materialism in its various versions endorsed and enforced by the PCB to provide a full understanding of the phenomenon of outlaw violence, or of the so-called laws of history. Amado was—to put it in Roland Barthes's terms—"a happy writer," and he always felt that, no matter the particular historical conjuncture, he was "on the good side of History" ([1964] 2002a, 352). Accordingly, backlands outlawry never came to embody for him, as it did for so many writers from the nineteenth century onward, the dilemmas of Latin American modernity. His novels from the 1930s to the 1950s are rife with ghastly events: treason, exploitation, abject poverty, murders, famines, rapes, epidemics, torture, and massacres. But all of these acts are only episodes, perhaps temporary setbacks in the long march of humankind toward emancipation. Hence, it is meaningful and productive violence and/or suffering. It is shocking or moving, perhaps, but never tragic, since it is part of the grand narrative of the pilgrimage toward utopia.

On the other hand, Amado's take on outlaw violence is far from an undivided celebration of the bandit hero of the third world, as is often the case with other writers on the left. The bandit is not the epic hero of a peasant struggle with cosmic overtones (as in Manuel Scorza's *Redoble por Rancas*) or an anti-imperialist icon (as in Pablo Neruda's *Fulgor y muerte de Joaquín Murieta* or Marcio Veloz Maggiolo's *La vida no tiene nombre*). Amado is sensitive to the ambiguous, even contradictory roles that banditry plays in class struggle. Thus, in spite of the fact that his value as a writer has been under siege for decades now, I would contend that his theses on banditry, which antecede by more than a decade the very similar ones proposed by Hobsbawm, should be considered among the most articulate and nuanced in Latin American literature or social science—at least until the 1970s.

An assessment of the role of outlaw violence in Amado's fiction should include at least three varieties. I would call the first one "banditry as cultural capital of the oppressed," under the form of a tradition of resistance—real or imagined—and a countermemory, alien or opposed, to that of the nation-state and the bourgeoisie.[5] It features prominently in his novels of the 1930s, such as *Cacau* (1933), *Jubiabá* (1935), and *Capitães da areia* (1937).

In *Capitães da areia* (a novel with an urban setting that depicts the life of marginal children in Salvador), there is the reality of banditry, which appears sporadically, when the professor reads the news to Volta Seca, and toward the end of the novel, when Volta Seca joins Lampião's gang. But the memory (in popular literature, oral tradition, and popular consciousness in general) and the sheer knowledge of the existence of those rebels function as a point of articulation of popular identities (showing how, to put it in Hobsbawm's terms, "the poor can also be terrible" [(1969) 2000, 63]):

> Only the caatinga belongs to everybody, because Lampião freed it. He expelled the rich and turned the caatinga into the battlefield of the cangaceiros who fight against the landowners. Lampião the hero of the entire sertão of five states. They say that he is a criminal, a heartless bandit, rapist and robber. But for Volta Seca, for the men and women and children of the sertão, he is a new Zumbi dos Palmares. He is a liberator, a leader of a new kind of army. And Lampião fights and kills and rapes and robs to further the cause of freedom. For freedom and justice for the exploited men of the immense sertão of five states: Pernambuco, Paraíba, Alagoas, Sergipe and Bahia. (Amado [1937] 1982, 183)

It is distinctive that *Capitães da areia* exhibits a more plural idea of the political. Unlike *Seara Vermelha*, in which only party activism is a legitimate form of politics (as we will see later on), in *Capitães* outlawry, art, priesthood, and criminality are, each in its unique way, forms of politics. National politics, and its institutional class expression, the Communist Party, occupy a prominent but not exclusive place in the novel. The "choral" image that closes the novel is telling in this respect:

> The voice is calling him [Pedro Bala, the leader of the youth gang, and the only one of the captains who becomes a militant, and a party stormtrooper of sorts], a voice that comes from the docks, from the bosom of the longshore-men, from João de Adão, from his father who died in a rally . . . a voice that comes from the filhas-do-santo of Don'Aninha's candomblé, the night that

the police arrested Ogum. A voice that comes from the Capitães da areia's trapiche. That comes from the Reformatory and from the Orphanage. That comes from the hatred of Sem-Pernas, throwing himself from the elevator instead of surrendering. . . . That comes through the sertão, from Lampião's gang, demanding justice for the peasants. (197)

Outlawry was still a very apparent force in backlands social life in the 1930s (Lampião would be killed in 1938, and Corisco in 1940).[6] An ongoing phenomenon, it could also act, however, as a link between past and present struggles. In *Cacau*, the old man Valentin, one of the protagonist's friends and mentors, was one of Conselheiro's *jagunzinhos* (Amado 1933, 192). In *Jubiabá*, Balduíno—the main character and revolutionary leader in the making—was an orphan who knew practically nothing about his father, except that he was one of Antônio Conselheiro's jagunços (Amado [1935] 1965, 23). His father was far from a role model (he was a womanizer and a heavy drinker), but he bequeathed a memory of rebellion that his son—whose childhood desire was to become a jagunço—later lives to honor.[7]

On the other hand, bandit stories provide the cultural framework—lacking Marxism and Marxist-inspired class struggle—in which the legitimacy of the present social order can be questioned and perceived as historical (i.e., contingent and subject to change). Consider Balduíno again. Before becoming a militant, he is an avid consumer of outlaw stories—the popular poetry sung or narrated both in the sertão and in the cities. These stories, and the tradition of insurgency on behalf of the downtrodden that they embody, are an essential point in Balduíno's character development, from happy-go-lucky lumpenproletarian to full-blown proletarian leader. This insurgent tradition, coupled with the Afro-Brazilian culture embodied in the character of Jubiabá (the pai-de-santo who takes Antônio Balduíno under his wing), constitutes a mainstay of his early socialization at a time when he does not have class consciousness, any appreciation of the historical moment in which he is immersed or the challenges he should face. Aside from Jubiabá, his childhood idol is the malandro Zé Camarão, a great singer and consummate storyteller around whom the neighbors of O Morro do Capa Negro gather to listen to lurid stories of cangaceiros. Thus, bandit narratives are essential to Balduíno's moral education, as his only childhood vision of the future was to grow up to be a jagunço. The values of independence and bravery that he puts into action later in life are taken from the stories of Lucas da Feira and Lampião. These narratives are also important to his political education; before his contact with leftist radicalism, his only understanding of class dynamics comes from the ABCs responsible for the "Robin-Hoodization" of the image of the cangaceiros. This also occurs in his "formal" education, because he only learns how to read in order to be able to read chapbooks.

Other works by Amado present a contrasting view, a second take on banditry. In these works banditry is the foundational and sustaining violence of the capitalist agrarian order. *Terras do sem fim* (1943) is perhaps not only his best novel, but also the work that most brilliantly embodies this view of the relationship between outlaw violence and the agrarian order. The novel, which has a sequel, *São Jorge dos Ilhéus* (1944), has an undoubtedly epic scope. *Terras do sem fim* tells the story of the rise and zenith of the cocoa baron class in the southern part of the state of Bahia at the beginning of the twentieth century.[8] This rise encompasses the process of primitive accumulation that allowed the transformation of nature into capital—the destruction of the Sequeiro Grande Forest, the last remnant of the Atlantic Forest in the area, and its transformation into a cocoa bean plantation. It also encompasses the dispossession of the small landowners who stood in the way of the consolidation of the large plantations, as well as the intraelite feuds for dominance in the Ilhéus-Itabuna plantation area, which pitched the Badaró clan against Colonel Horácio and his allies. All of these struggles are fought, as in Far West narratives, by small armies of jagunços under the direct command of each respective landowner.[9] This link between outlaw violence and agrarian capitalism is a well-established motif in Latin American literature, where literary works emphasize the role of outlaw violence either as the necessary condition for the process of land accumulation or as a means to fend off potential challengers to landowner rule—either other landowners or landless peasants or revolutionaries. An important example is *Shadow Country* (Peter Matthiessen, 2008), an account of the life of Edgar "Bloody" Watson (1855–1910), a real-life sugar cane plantation owner and alleged outlaw in the Ten Thousand Islands region of southwest Florida in 1910.

Latin America provides other examples. In Baldomero Lillo's "Quilapán" (collected in Lihn 1972), the motif of the private outlaw army—which, in its role as a tool of the dominant class, is indistinguishable from the official legal army—dispossessing indigenous peasants establishes a topic that will recur time and again in indigenist narrative. In Mauricio Magdaleno's *El resplandor* (Mexico, 1937), Don Gonzalo Fuentes—the conqueror and founder of the lineage of landowners that would last well into the twentieth century—fights the Otomíes occupying the lands that would become the hacienda La Brisa at the head of a gang of outlaws. Of course, this is just a later example of the centuries-old trope of the conquistadors as brigands (for this, see Hobsbawm [1969] 2000 and Dabove 2007, introduction). In Gallegos's *Doña Bárbara*, the fearsome owner of El Miedo (aptly called a "bandit captain" by her enemy Santos Luzardo) commands a small army of robbers, assassins, and cattle rustlers in charge of carrying out the manifold acts of violence necessary in the constant expansion of the limits of the *hato* and its cattle holdings. A former bandit, Ño Pernalete, acting as local political boss, ensures that an appearance of legality protects all of her maneuvering.

In Icaza's *Huasipungo* ([1934] 1994, 235), the highlands landowner Alfonso Pereira hires *chagras forajidos* (outlaws) to evict the Indians from the mountain land that they occupy—land that Pereira's American partners (or bosses) want unoccupied in order to extract timber. Finally, in Juan Rulfo's *Pedro Páramo* (Mexico, 1955), Páramo arms and maintains a large group of bandits who fashion themselves as revolutionaries under the control of his trusted retainer Damasio (also known as El Tilcuate) in order to keep the real revolutionaries in check. Before this, Tilcuate had been crucial in the dispossession of all small landowners in the Comala area that allowed Páramo to amass the large tract of land that comprised La Media Luna. (There are important differences, however. In Amado, the original accumulation is narrated as an epic, one oriented toward the future. Brutal and greedy, the colonels are still a conquering bourgeoisie. In Rulfo, the dispossession of the peasants is a criminal act, and creates a trap—the perpetual repetition of the violent past, beyond death.)[10]

In *Terras do sem fim*, the jagunço has no identity, no subjectivity separate from that of the landowner in whose service he thrives. He is a tool of the ruling class against his own class. Damião and Antônio Vítor, jagunços of the Badarós (the losing party in the conflict for dominance that is described in the novel) are two cases in point. Damião is a good-natured, naïve peasant (*camponês*), but he is also a fearsome (and fearless) murderer, with dead-on marksmanship that makes him particularly suitable for ambushes (*tocaias*). He is charged with murdering Firmo, a small landowner affiliated with Horácio's faction. But before leaving for the mission, he overhears his master, Sinhó Badaró, arguing with his brother Juca Badaró about the justice in killing another human being in the pursuit of money and power. Since Damião does not have a separate identity or an independent set of values, his master's vacillation does not engender a new consciousness, but signifies the disintegration of all consciousness, resulting in Damião's madness. The counterexample is Antonio Vítor, who remains loyal to the end, and who is so completely identified with the cause of the landowners that his ultimate dream is to become a landowner himself. He fulfills this dream when the Badarós give him a tract of land as a wedding gift and as a token of gratitude for the many killings he has committed on their behalf.

These two narrative lines represent exact opposites: banditry as an icon of resistance or insurgency against capitalism, and banditry as a shock force in the constitution and consolidation of agrarian capitalism. In the aforementioned works, there are no ambiguities, no middle ground. There is, however, a third strand in which the role of the outlaw vis-à-vis the revolution is more complex and difficult to discern. It is best presented in *Seara Vermelha*, Amado's 1946 novel, to which I will devote the rest of this chapter.

Seara Vermelha can be considered the last installment of a trilogy of novels written in the 1940s. The first two are *Terras do sem fim* (1943) and *São Jorge dos Ilhéus* (1944). This triad makes sense from a theoretical point of view: first, the formation of an agrarian capitalist economy (*Terras do sem fim*); then the development of that capitalist system into one dominated by financial capital with links to international monopolies (*São Jorge dos Ilhéus*); and finally the development of a peasant class consciousness, which enables it to tackle the challenge of capitalism in its most developed form (*Seara Vermelha*). This is advanced in the latter part of *São Jorge dos Ilhéus*, when Joaquim, a Communist militant, says, "First the land belonged to the landowners who conquered it. Then, it changed hands, and fell into the hands of the exporters who exploited it. But there will be a day in which the land will not have owners at all" ([1944] 1966, 336). In the last novel of the group, Amado chooses to change the setting, and hence the problems addressed in the novel: instead of continuing to focus on southern Bahia and the cacao culture, the novel returns to a more "classic" setting of Brazilian regionalism (the sertão) and a more classic subject (backlands culture).

Seara Vermelha is the story of the travails of a *sertanejo* family. Following a well-traveled path in Latin American fiction, the family-as-subject naturalizes larger political or cultural identities or institutions.[11] The most vulgarized example of this is the "national romance." In the case of *Seara Vermelha*, the family stands for the larger class to which it belongs: that of the peasant, sharecropper, or agrarian laborers of the *fazendas* of the sertão. This social sector was a particular target of PCB activity at the time of the publication of *Seara Vermelha*—as the novel depicts toward the end.

The family comprises three generations. Jerônimo is the eldest and the leader of the group. His wife, Jucundina, his deranged sister, Zefa, and his brother, João Pedro (who has a wife, Dinah, and a daughter, Gertrudes), belong to this same generation. Jerônimo and Jucundina have six sons and daughters. Three of them, at one point or another, abandon the home, either fascinated with the prospects of a life of adventure (Zé, who joins the gang of cangaceiro chieftain Lucas Arvoredo and becomes a noted cangaceiro himself), enmeshed in problems pertaining to the complex sertanejo honor system (João, who joins the state police), or even frustrated with the meager economic prospects of sharecropping (Juvêncio, the youngest and Jucundina's favorite, who joins the army, becomes a Communist militant, and later plays a significant part in the 1935 revolt).[12] After a long prison stay, Juvêncio becomes a leader in the newly legalized PCB, and returns to do political work in the sertão.[13] Jerônimo and Jucundina's two remaining children—Agostinho and Marta—stay with them. Nonetheless, their final destinies could not be more disparate: Agostinho makes it to São Paulo, while Marta becomes a prostitute and disappears from the narrative. There is also a daughter who had died, leaving three children for Jucundina to take care of: the rambunctious thirteen-year-old Tonho, the shy and sensitive Noca, and Ernesto, still an infant.

Jerônimo heads a family of sharecroppers (*meeiros*), eking out a meager living in the fazenda of Colonel Inácio. The fazenda is "large as a state." It is so large, according to the narrator, that some people have never left the property in their lives (Amado [1946] 1999, 31). The novel begins when Aureliano, the current owner of the fazenda, decides to sell it. As part of the agreement, all the sharecroppers have to be evicted and either must leave the fazenda or remain as day laborers. *Seara Vermelha* is thus the story of the forced transformation of sharecroppers into rural proletarians,[14] whom I will call peasants, following James Scott's (1976) use of the word, even though there is some debate regarding this terminology. The novel narrates the initial act of dispossession and the so-called "roads of hope," the various strategies of resistance or adaptation attempted by the *camponeses*: (1) southbound migration—carried out by Jerônimo and Jucundina, his remaining offspring, and his in-laws, although more than half will die or be lost in the journey; (2) banditry—Zé; (3) millenarian rebellion—Zefa and, briefly, Zé; (4) incorporation into the state apparatus—João and Nenen; and (5) last but foremost, revolutionary activism—Nenen. Some parallelisms can be found with Alegría's *El mundo es ancho y ajeno*, when the land grab by the *gamonal* Amenábar forces many *comuneros* (peasants holding land communally) to leave Rumi, and the novel traces their parallel (and failed) attempts to reestablish themselves in coca plantations and mines, as bandits, and in the city. But unlike *Seara Vermelha*, where the fazenda has to be left behind for the only successful path to be found, in *El mundo* any path other than the community proves to be a dead end.

Like *Cacau*, *Jubiabá*, and *Capitães da areia*, *Seara Vermelha* belongs to the tradition of the bildungsroman. However, instead of narrating the formation of an individual character within the coordinates of a bourgeois subject and possessive individualism, Amado narrates a process of collective learning and coming into being. Or, better yet, he narrates the individual learning of the collective—the emergence of class consciousness and the integration into the Communist Party as its vanguard. Class and party become, in this Stalinist bildungsroman, primary identity markers. When Nenen culminates his evolution from peasant to wannabe bandit to military man to elite party cadre, his identity is coeval with his class and party identity.

The novel is built upon a number of fairly commonplace metaphors and symbols. These "melodramatic exaggerations" (Assis Duarte 1996, 175) have been attributed to the popular or populist nature of Amado's literature. Without a doubt, this is consistent with his idea of literature, both in its political and in its aesthetic dimensions. Among these metaphors are (1) planting (*A seara*) and reaping (*A colheita*), which open and close the novel; (2) the journey or sacrificial pilgrimage; (3) the illumination reached at the end of the novel, as found in Jerônimo and Jucundina's southbound trail of tears, but also in Nenen's formative experiences throughout the entire territory of Brazil; (4) the sacrifice of the favorite child, when Marta offers herself to the lustful Dr. Epaminondas in order to secure her father's permit to continue south, in spite of the fact that he has tuberculosis (which would make the permit unobtainable); (5) blood—the rain of blood, the dew of blood, blood as the fertilizer of the earth, blood as a metaphor for the suffering of the downtrodden in the clutches of agrarian capitalism, the blood of virginity offered for passage, the blood of the dead as the price to pay to leave captivity, and blood as the metaphor for the upcoming revolution; (6) the cyclical or circular nature of the narrative, since the novel begins with the sertanejos leaving the sertão and ends with the sertanejos—now Communist activists—returning to the sertão; and (7) the opposition between light and darkness, wetness and dryness, as part of a larger pathetic fallacy. As is seen in the beginning of the novel, before the eviction the sertão is an idyllic rural landscape, humid and pleasant, with cows, hens, and goats. Once the sharecroppers have been evicted, the sertão becomes a hellish, dry place, populated by lizards, snakes, and the unrelenting glare of the northeastern sun.

All of the aforementioned metaphors or motifs, in one way or another, connect with economic or cultural aspects of a backlands worldview and experience: agrarian cycles, bodily functions, sertanejo ethics, and popular Catholicism. At the same time, and also following a well-beaten path in Latin American literature (which was seen at work already, in the case of *Las lanzas*), *Seara Vermelha* is a sort of archive that features most of the topics of a representational paradigm that was by then many decades old. Decades ago, at the height of Amado's prestige (his popularity remains high), these thematic preferences, as well as the aforementioned representational techniques—which were, to a significant degree, innovative at the time—helped to create the myth of the author-medium, the undivided voice of "the people." The problematic nature of this assumption, embedded in the very idea of engaged literature toward the middle of the twentieth century, is glaringly evident today, and hardly merits further commentary. It is more interesting, perhaps, to trace the ways in which Amado *creates* a literary version of the peasantry that he later claims to express in such an undivided fashion, and to reflect on the motives and effects of his doing so.

Amado introduces two distortions of the agrarian reality that he depicts. Colonel Aureliano's fazenda is extremely large (as quoted before, "large as a state"). The fazenda land is primarily devoted to agriculture: maize, manioc, and sweet potatoes are the main crops. This is not unheard of in the sertão (see for example Johnson 1971), but it is far from representative. On the one hand, in the sertão the pattern of land tenure had been gravitating for decades toward the subdivision of land to the point that many properties were not viable, given the climate constraints and the poor quality of the land that required extensive exploitation. This was one of the reasons for agrarian conflict and the rise of banditry (Pereira de Queiroz 1968). The opposite was true for the coastal strip devoted to sugar cultivation, where land monopoly was indeed a tendency. At the same time, the crops as well as the system of sharecropping that Amado presents were well known in the sertão, but they did not represent the dominant economic activity. Extensive cattle ranching was the primary occupation, and it created the "leather civilization" distinctive of the sertão (agriculture was commonly a household enterprise, as a complement to the household economy). Hence, Amado endows the fazenda and the conflict over land with a representative value that they do not actually have.

In the novel, the plight of Jerônimo's family is replicated ad infinitum, throughout the entire sertão. Amado needs this in order to (1) explain away all social developments in the sertão according to a single overriding cause—land monopoly (he was not alone in this; see, for example, Facó (1972), which explains away banditry as a direct consequence of latifundium); and (2) map the social reality following a single line of conflict (class struggle over land), and two simple opposing camps (landowners and landless peasants—or peasants on their way to being landless). (For a critique see Pernambucano de Mello 2004.) As the scholarship on backlands banditry has shown, conflicts and alliances were organized along lines that were not—or not exclusively—class lines (Lewin 1987). Simplifying and focusing on class conflict allows Amado to address his central problem without encumbrances: the revolutionary potential of the peasantry and of its traditional means of resistance, such as banditry, and the strategic means by which the PCB could unleash that potential. The problem of the transition from oppression to revolution, which in indigenist literature contemporary with *Seara Vermelha* appears impossible to solve (see Cornejo Polar 1994), is solved in *Seara Vermelha* by skirting it altogether.

But the path to the solution to this political riddle goes through the acknowledgment of a major obstacle. Unlike the "precipitate" peasantry (Yarrington 1997) of the cacao zone, the peasantry of the sertão has a cultural density that presents challenges that the Communist Party has to deal with. The sertão has a tradition of violence that has to be reinterpreted as a symptom of an exclusive class conflict, and transformed into a legitimate, albeit insufficient, protoform of revolutionary violence. This is the explicit intent of the climactic moment of the novel, the 1935 ANL (Aliança Nacional Libertadora, the PCB-inspired, Popular Front–style organization) rebellion whose leader in Natal is Nenen. As Levine (1970, 79) explains, "The ANL portrayed itself as heir to the Brazilian revolutionary tradition, claiming such precursors as Antônio Conselheiro, the martyr of the federal assault on Canudos in the early days of the Old Republic, and Lampião, the cangaceiro bandit leader, in spite of his service against the Prestes Column in the pay of northeastern *políticos*." *Seara Vermelha* is the narrative embodiment of this postulate—the exploration of a native tradition of insurgency akin to that undertaken by Engels in *The Peasant War in Germany* (1926). But in order for this tradition of insurgency to be appropriated, Amado engages in a sort of cultural ethnography that makes it malleable. This ethnography involves two operations: (1) deciding what constitutes "legitimate" peasant cultural capital, splitting it from dangerous illusions and false consciousness—the work of ideology that preserves the hegemony of the ruling class; and (2) reterritorializing those expressions deemed legitimate peasant culture in a macronarrative culminating in the party as the collective identity where all aspects of human experience—love, violence, family, knowledge—are integrated and projected toward the future. The dangerous illusions that Amado endeavors to destroy are several, creeping from right to left: interclass alliances, upward social mobility as part of the larger phenomenon of peasant differentiation, the idea of the status quo as an unmovable image of the universe, the progressive middle class as a potential ally of the peasantry, and the belief in the state as mediator in class warfare. Allow me to comment briefly on each of these illusions.

Interclass alliances, as a feature of peasant culture, are the first target of Amado's critique. At the beginning of the novel, times are relatively good: the rainy season promises to deliver, crops will be productive, and there are no conflicts in sight. Ataliba, one of the sharecroppers, is throwing a party to celebrate his daughter's marriage. By poor peasant standards, it would be an occasion to remember. Even Artur, the stern administrator of the fazenda, is considering softening his treatment of the sharecroppers. Times are not bad, but, as always, they have been better. The fazenda belongs to Colonel Aureliano, but his father, the late Colonel Inácio, is the one who built the family wealth. Inácio is a traditional, paternalistic landowner aware of and abiding by the vertical, interclass prescriptions embedded in rural culture and the gestures of protection and appreciation that peasants expect in exchange for deference and submission. This is the network of exchanges that makes the rural order workable from the standpoint of the peasants—what Scott (1976) calls "the moral economy of the peasant." But this is more than a strategy for domination. Inácio considers the fazenda his true and only capital. Agriculture is his sole activity, and hence he has no use for the excess income that the fazenda provides him—consequently leaving the money sitting idly in the bank. The fazenda is his true home, and he is a willing partner in a cultural alliance with the peasantry (albeit an unequal one).

The emblem of that cultural alliance is Inácio's patronage of sertanejo poets and musicians, such as Pedro da Restinga and Bastião. Pedro is a blind guitar player, and Inácio likes his music so much that he accords him unlimited credit in the fazenda store, as a token of appreciation for his status. As soon as Inácio dies, Artur cancels this arrangement and Pedro stops going to the fazenda. He then composes some vindictive stanzas insulting Artur and idolizing Inácio. Bastião, on the other hand, is a peasant who doubles as a musician living on the fazenda. On the occasion of Inácio's stepdaughter's marriage, Bastião is the musician, and Inácio, touched by the occasion, gives Bastião the land that he is cultivating as a sharecropper. He never actually gives Bastião the deed, but for Bastião, it is just as well—Inácio's word is his bond.[15]

From the peasants' point of view, Inácio's son Aureliano falls way short of this ideal. He does not take care of the land, relying instead on Artur's honesty to run the fazenda, which he only visits occasionally and more as a tourist than a master. And yet, he is not the classic Latin American absentee landowner. The absentee landowner still derives his money and, most importantly, his prestige and sense of worth from the fact that he belongs to the landed gentry. Aureliano focuses his energy on his financial endeavors and his social life in Rio. His landed interests in the Northeast quickly become superfluous even as a token of prestige.

This is the novel's starting point for the destruction of the cultural and economic pact between peasants and landowners. The pact is exploitative, but from the point of view of the peasants—or at least the older generation of peasants—it is tolerable. Aureliano decides to sell the fazenda to an unnamed party. As part of the sale agreement all the sharecroppers will be evicted (including

Bastião) and the fazenda will be transformed into a cattle ranch manned by salaried hands. It is most telling that Aureliano never appears, even though he is the one who sets the conflict in motion. He is only a name and a signature at the end of a letter. This disembodied quality represents the abstract nature of a market economy. Even though Amado condemns the colonels as a class, he clearly finds them more sympathetic than the aloof financiers—including Aureliano. Proof of this is Amado's obvious fascination with the Badarós and Horácio in *Terras do sem fim*, contrasted with his palpable disdain for the cocoa exporters in *São Jorge dos Ilhéus*. Aureliano in *Seara Vermelha* is not a man, but the invisible (and impersonally cruel) hand of the market. This is why the attempt to kill him, carried out by the cangaceiros, is doomed to fail from the start. It is an attempt to solve new problems by resorting to old methods. In any case, the selling of the fazenda and the eviction of the peasants who have lived there for decades is a lesson on how cultural alliances are subordinated to (and ultimately trumped by) class realities.

The novel also delegitimizes all (moral) options for upward social mobility, as part of this same breach of the oral pact. The novel presents two cases—Artur (the foreman and administrator) and Gregório (the ambitious and enterprising sharecropper)—as two variations of the phenomenon of peasant differentiation: (1) upward mobility as part of an alliance with the landowners (Artur), and (2) upward mobility in competition with the landowners (Gregório). Artur comes to the fazenda as a simple hired hand (*alugado*), but rises to the position of administrator. He professes an undivided (and for him, entirely natural) allegiance to the landowner. In spite of Aureliano's neglect of fazenda affairs (which leave a lot of room for embezzlement), Artur is scrupulously honest in his management. His honesty is a mainstay and a folkloric stereotype of sertanejo culture, in which crimes against property are considered far more serious than crimes against persons. This honesty springs from peasant culture, but it is used against the peasantry. Artur's honesty does not contradict the enforcement of the fazenda's exploitative rules. These unwritten rules prescribe that sharecroppers are not to have any commercial ties outside of the fazenda, that they have to buy all of their groceries at the fazenda store (of course at inflated prices), and that they must sell their crops to the landowner (at depressed prices). Since peasants in the fazenda are illiterate, they cannot keep accurate records of their balance at the store, and so they live in a state of perpetual indebtedness.[16]

This drives home one of Amado's points on sertanejo culture. Sertanejo morality, when divorced from clear class position and consciousness, becomes immorality, treason, and oppression. Culturally, Artur still belongs to the world of the peasants. Objectively, he does not. The perception of this gap splits the fazenda social fabric, but most importantly, it positions Artur against himself. He embodies the contradictions of his position as a classless being. He is (relatively) privileged but miserable and lonely. He exploits the sharecroppers, but is happy to be invited to their feast. Even though he never faces open defiance of his methods or of his position, he is confronted with the full panoply of "everyday forms of peasant resistance" (Scott 1985): he is the victim of silence, gossip, exclusion from the events that characterize peasant life, hate songs, and cheating. This "small arms fire in the class war" (Scott 1985, chap. 1) does not imply an open break with the rules of peasant deference (to which Artur is entitled as a representative of the landlord) and has little, if any, economic effect. Hence, they do not qualify for Amado as legitimate peasant resistance. They do wear Artur down, particularly since he is from peasant stock and knows full well the extent of the treatment to which he is being subjected. He is placed between a landlord who does not appreciate him and a peasantry that hates him. Ataliba's feast, to which he is invited, is a truce offered by the peasants (which Artur is willing to accept), and, as such, it meets the fate of all such alliances—its ruin by class-based realities.

The other example of thwarted upward mobility is Gregório. He intends to earn money by saving what he can make through sharecropping, in order to buy his own plot of land, thus ceasing to be a tenant and becoming a landowner himself. Gregório is fiercely individualistic and austere—he does not go to the party, so as not to spend money and waste time, but also because he has no relations. He accumulates money by depriving himself of any pleasures: he is celibate, he does not drink alcohol, he does not have a girlfriend or contact with his family, and he does not buy new clothing. He unwittingly follows to the letter the liberal spirit of free-market capitalism (without its Latin American bent) when he refuses to comply with the fazenda store monopoly and decides to buy seed and sell his crop outside of the fazenda. By sidestepping these time-honored practices, Gregório represents a face of modernity—market driven, individualistic, and eminently rational. He does not share in the traditional culture of the peasantry and its rituals of deference, its celebrations, and its lack of class consciousness, which allows him to defy widespread exploitative practices.

But his fierce individualism makes his path toward social mobility simultaneously heroic and impossible. He is the only peasant in the fazenda who has a degree of consciousness. However, it is not class consciousness, but rather the consciousness of a heroic bourgeois imbued with the spirit of accumulation and free competition. In this respect, he represents a superior version of capitalism. But he is stamped out by the dominant version of capitalism in the sertão—the rentier capitalism of absentee landowners, which condemns him to become a criminal when he makes a completely futile attempt on Artur's life. It is highly peculiar that, even though the news about the selling of the fazenda and the eviction is given during Ataliba's feast (at which practically all of the sharecroppers are gathered), the only one to actively react is Gregório—the only one who was not at the feast. It is not explained how Gregório knows about this unsettling piece of news (Amado avoids this problem by narrating it through another character). But in any case, it is telling that nobody organizes anything (for example, a riot), even though they are all together—a little drunk, probably—and in the heat of the moment.

One reason is that, for these peasants, oppression is part of the order of the universe. This is another of the dangerous illusions (the "illusion of inevitability" that I mentioned in chapter 4) that Amado needs to dispel. Under this illusion, exploitation is not an act of injustice, or an unacceptable break with a time-honored arrangement, but rather, as Jucundina and Jerônimo come to regard it, a part of the inscrutable order of the world—or, as Zefa prefers, incontrovertible evidence that the world is coming to an end. These two attitudes (the impassibility of Jucundina, the apocalyptic vision of Zefa) may seem antithetical to each other, but they are not—they both stem from the belief that a certain form of agrarian capitalism equals the order of the universe. Class consciousness is equated with the realization that oppression is not a natural fact, as bourgeois universalization pretends, but a historical development.

Once evicted, the family embarks on a long trek through the caatinga, in which Noca, Dinah, and Jeremías the donkey all die, Zefa disappears (later, we find out that she has joined the band of the beato Estevão), and Agostinho and Gertrudes desert the group in order to live together. The greatly reduced band arrives at Juazeiro by the São Francisco River. Even though they are not *retirantes* (forced migrants fleeing the drought), but expelled peasants, the novel treats them as such. The arrival to Juazeiro has a symbolic import: from the dry caatinga to the water margin, from the backland to the city, from nature (walking) to technology (boats and trains). It also marks their arrival at the domain of the state. The ship that will take them to Pirapora is the property of the state of Bahia. In Pirapora, they have to catch a train that will take them to São Paulo—their final destination. The train is free, and state run, as long as the retirantes can prove that they are free from infectious diseases. But their misfortunes and trials are not over. During the boat ride from Juazeiro down the São Francisco River, Jucundina's baby grandson dies from a bout of dysentery that breaks out among the boat's third-class passengers. The first-class passengers, enjoying a better diet, avoid the epidemic—if not the foul smell of the persistent diarrhea of the passengers on the lower deck. Once in Pirapora, Marta sacrifices her virginity (and her honor) by having sex with Dr. Epaminondas (the state medical examiner) in order to obtain a clean bill of health for her father, who has contracted tuberculosis due to prolonged malnutrition and hardship. Evicted from the family, she becomes a prostitute and falls victim to an unspecified venereal disease.

Even though these seem to be just two more misfortunes, they are radically different because of their context: they happen while the family is a ward of the state, so to speak. Contrary to the populist imagination of the state as mediation and, ideally, a cancellation of class conflict, here the state reproduces and enforces the class system (the poor diet on the state-owned ship kills the baby, and the requirements of the state force Marta to prostitute herself). Furthermore, even when successful, the state works, in spite of the appearance of benevolence, to ensure the supply of cheap labor for the labor market—transporting workers from a place where they are plentiful to another where they are scarce. And by doing this, the state ensures that there is a surplus in the South, thus depressing wages. In fact, this is the truth that tortures Dr. Epaminondas and that destroys his predecessor Dr. Diogenes (the latter falls from the status of respected doctor to that of barfly and town drunkard, with occasional sparks of brilliance and cynicism). It is not that they, and the state they represent, cannot solve the problems of the poor and sick, but rather that they produce the poor and the sick in the first place. They transform honest sertanejo women into sick prostitutes, and honest peasants into beggars and criminals.

Vargas, the embodiment of statist populism during this period, is never mentioned in the novel, even though it is set in the 1930s. This absence most likely has to do with the fact that the PCB and *Varguismo* (already out of power in 1946, when the novel was published) had been de facto allies in the struggle against fascism during the Second World War (see Amado's essays and chronicles collected in *Hora da guerra* [2008]). Because of this alliance, the PCB was enjoying a brief moment of legality that would end in 1948. Amado himself won a seat in the federal assembly as part of the process of the return to democracy. Vargas's absence or presence in the novel would not change the point: if classic paternalism (that of Inácio) was just a fragile mask for harsh class divisions, then modern paternalism (that of Vargas, the "father of the poor" and the Estado Novo) was, in the last analysis, no different.

The episode of Dr. Epaminondas is also a refutation of all liberal reformist attempts, when carried out in an individual fashion. Epaminondas is an image of the liberal modern intellectual: a hardworking, intelligent, compassionate doctor who rises in society through his own effort and that of his father (a tailor, devoted to his son's success). He is a humanist, interested in anthropology and epidemiology. But he becomes at the same time a victim and an executor in a class-based society. He is the enforcer of the state's mandates, the keeper of a gate that separates the modern agrarian proletariat from the human refuse that is destined to become lumpenproletariat, or worse. This task morally and psychologically destroys him. The keeper of the gate, he is slowly becoming, like his predecessor in the post, one of its victims.

In contrast to these dangerous illusions that always entail failed attempts at individual accommodation, there are means of collective resistance such as banditry and millenarian rebellion. Even though they are definitely not the conclusion of the argument that Amado puts in narrative form, cangaceiros and *fanáticos* (a pejorative term used to refer to followers of the beato) seem to have usurped the public's (and the editor's) perception of the novel (witness the covers, from the first edition on, that always—and solely—feature cangaceiros, and sometimes a beato who looks like Antônio Conselheiro). The story of the cangaceiro Lucas Arvoredo and his gang composes the first section of the part of the novel called "As estradas da esperança." Prominent in Lucas's gang is his trusted lieutenant Zé Trevoada (son of Jerônimo and Jucundina). On the other hand, there is the story of the beato Estevão and Zefa (Jerônimo's sister). When state armed forces catch up with Estevão, Lucas rushes to the aid of the *romeiros* (followers of the beato) and dies heroically in defense of a lost cause.

Lucas's saga is a compilation of episodes belonging mainly (but not exclusively) to Lampião's life and legend: (1) the almost incredible mobility on foot through the caatinga, encompassing the backland regions of six states, as well as the superb guerrilla tactics that baffled state forces for more than two decades; (2) the town invasions; (3) the branding of women; (4) the grim dancing parties that ended in gang rapes; (5) the childish weakness for perfumes, toys, and entertainments such as film, circuses, and music; (6) the unrelenting hatred of the police; (7) the collusion between banditry and millenarianism; and (8) the role of *coiteiros* (suppliers, contacts, and protectors). Crucial to Amado's argument, however, is Lucas's constant return to the "myth of origin" of his bandit career. Much like Jerônimo, Lucas's father was evicted from his land (and a worthless, arid plot of land at that). When he tried to resist, he was killed. Lucas tells this story to different interlocutors—the Senator, Zé Trevoada, the traveling salesman—at least three times throughout the novel (Amado [1946] 1999, 199, 214, 216), because this event is for him the source of his legitimacy as an outlaw.[17]

Amado takes Lucas Arvoredo's words at face value, not as an ethical shield, since they are coherent with his larger agenda. From Amado's perspective, there is a total overlap between the objective and the subjective causes of outlawry—the problem lies in the response: banditry instead of party activism. It is also important that for Amado, all violence in the sertão is class violence. *Seara Vermelha* does not emphasize (does not even acknowledge) the existence of a culture of violence in the sertão that cuts across class lines. This violence is not always and perhaps not even mainly related to land monopoly. In other words, Amado explains away this culture of violence by giving it a single origin. All of the characters who take to the caatinga do so either because they have been dispossessed of their land (as in the case of Lucas Arvoredo) or because they do not have any hope of ever acquiring it (as in Nenen's case). By acknowledging a culture of violence unrelated to class conflict, Amado would present an image of the peasantry that perhaps carries inherent contradictions.

The section on Lucas Arvoredo opens with the defeat of a military unit that recklessly decides to fight the bandit in the caatinga—his own turf. Lucas decimates the detachment and invades the unnamed (and now defenseless) town where the unit used to be stationed. Once in control, he kills his enemies within the town, loots and wrecks several stores, feasts in the hotel, exacts a significant amount of ransom money, forces everybody to attend a double feature film (Tom Mix and Charlie Chaplin), and throws a dance (in which everybody has to dance naked), which quickly degenerates into a gang rape.

This episode showcases the possibilities and limits of a "bandit politics."[18] Lucas is not a mere vandal moved by irrational lust, greed, or hatred. On the contrary, all of his acts have an internal logic. This logic is opaque and repulsive to the elite members of rural society, and Lucas himself would not be able to verbally articulate it. But it is coherent and powerful nonetheless. This logic operates through negation and inversion (Guha [1983] 1999). If Lucas does not have a class consciousness (and for Amado that is a fatal flaw), he has what Guha calls a negative consciousness, a well-developed sense of a peasant's place in rural society and of the protocols, rituals, and symbols that regulate the peasantry's relationship to social superiors. Hence, his actions are the performance of a *countertheater* that actively destroys and inverts those protocols, rituals, and symbols of the agrarian order.

Lucas occupies and disrespects spaces that, by definition, are off-limits to poor peasants—the hotel where he feasts (at the head of the table), the box in the movie theater, and the gallery in the fazenda. He extorts money from the town, but less for money's sake than in order to see the mayor of the town groveling and begging for a reduction in the amount of the ransom. He rapes and brands the town teacher, not because of her beauty (she is not particularly pretty) or due to sexual urges, but because she is blond (there is more physical pleasure for Arvoredo in touching the blond, thin hair than in the actual rape). He forces everyone to dance naked, not only to exhibit the grotesque, bloated nature of urban bodies (when compared to the wiry bodies of the cangaceiros), but also to divest the elite of all the symbols of their prestige—the highlight of the dance is the puny judge being forced to dance naked with his obese wife. As a peasant, Lucas would have been condemned to a life of deprivation and scarcity, always living on the edge of starvation. His actions in the town are, consequently, a performance of waste: throwing the feast and eating much more food than necessary, drinking heavily and breaking bottles of precious liquor, and wrecking the stores that sell the goods that peasants cannot buy.

These actions turn the world upside down. In fact Lucas literally turns the world upside down, when he forces everyone to watch the Tom Mix feature, but with the movie upside down. Lucas Arvoredo is thus sensitive to symbolism and he distinguishes how these things are related to a class reality. This subversive performance ensures his cultural prestige. For Guha ([1983] 1999), as well as for Scott (1985), these types of performances (or counterperformances) are fully political acts, even more so because they lie beyond the modern elite notion of politics. This was not the case for Amado, who fully endorsed a modern notion of politics. Lucas has a keen perception of the cultural aspects of the agrarian order, but he is incapable of casting a historical glance. In this sense, he is (for Amado) like a child or a primitive man. This comes up in the episode of the toy duck—the cangaceiros are fascinated with a self-moving toy, and they wind it up and follow its meandering through the town.[19] At another point, they mistake fiction for reality and shoot the screen where the bully harasses Charlie Chaplin (a scene similar to that in *El águila y la serpiente*, where the attendants at a showing of a documentary at the Aguascalientes Convention, incensed by Carranza's self-glorifying in the movie, shoot at the screen).

After leaving the town, Lucas and his gang take refuge in the Senator's fazenda. This episode illustrates how Lucas Arvoredo, in spite of the fact that he is respected—even admired— by his fellow camponeses, is not the champion of his class (as, for example, Coirana, the cangaceiro in Glauber Rocha's *Antônio das mortes*, pretends to be). The Senator is his main coiteiro. But that protection has a price. He uses Lucas as the muscle to either evict peasants and small landowners from their lands or to force them to sell for ridiculously low prices. From this point of view, there is no difference between these cangaceiros and the jagunços of *Terras do sem fim*. Perhaps the significant difference is that while the jagunços of *Terras do sem fim* are attached to the colonel on a permanent or semipermanent basis, Lucas is a free agent—a relatively equal partner in the alliance. This type of relationship inspired Pernambucano de Mello (2004) to coin the expression "landless colonel" when referring to professional cangaceiros (in particular the variety of professional cangaceiro dominant in the twentieth century). There are some elements of subversion in the relationship. Lucas is of peasant stock, but he demands to be treated with much more respect than a peasant. He smokes and feasts with the Senator and neglects many of the rituals of deference that the Senator believes are owed to him. Nevertheless, he remains a loyal subordinate.

The alliance breaks down when the Senator betrays Lucas, sensing that Lucas is becoming a political liability and a threat, and that he is beginning to act without due deference.[20] When Lucas realizes that he has been betrayed, he kills the Senator in cold blood. This killing adds to Lucas's cultural prestige. But the Senator is killed not because he is a class enemy, but because he proves to be a disloyal ally.[21] Later on, Lucas attacks the fazenda that used to belong to Aureliano. He and his men burn the main house, loot the fazenda store, and try to kill Aureliano—who is injured, but not killed. Again, this attack is part of the internal solidarity of the gang (Lucas does this in order to please Zé) and not a class-oriented move. And this shows how the cangaceiro, in the end, is either a traitor to his class or unaware of the glaring contradictions of his actions. The attack on Aureliano's fazenda does not contradict this, since, spectacular though it is, it has no effect on the real situation. Furthermore, Lucas is incapable of recognizing a glaring contradiction: what Aureliano has done (which deserves Lucas's punishment) is what he himself had done countless times before on behalf of the Senator. The attack on the fazenda is indeed a dramatic performance. But for Amado, politics is not a performance, but a series of tactical moves and strategies oriented toward goals of national import.

For Amado, bandit politics, steeped in peasant culture, has a flawed idea of time and space, since it extinguishes itself in this instantaneous performance. Of course, banditry implies rational calculation and the administration of time and space: timing ambushes, mapping routes of escape, and so forth. But it is not part of a long-term strategy, or a strategy that would have widespread consequences. Banditry lacks long-term economic effects. It does not introduce any durable transformation in the relations of production: the citizens of the town that Lucas plunders will recuperate and join the ranks of Lucas's most obstinate foes, the fazenda of the murdered Senator will remain within his family, and the new owner of Aureliano's fazenda will be even more severe in his treatment of the peasants.

Furthermore, Lucas Arvoredo and his gang are nomads. They are fully aware of state borders and jurisdictions, since this is crucial to successfully evading the police—state police were prevented from continuing their pursuit into a neighboring state due to a strong sense of state autonomy (Pernambucano de Mello 2004, 197). But in the novel, Lucas's gang also lacks a larger concept of territory (as does Jerônimo, who thinks that São Paulo is a country). Throughout Lucas's saga, there are no names of states, cities, or regions. This, of course, deliberately endows the narrative with a more "universal" value since it could have taken place anywhere in the sertão. But it also highlights what for Amado is a deficient historical and geographical sense, and therefore a built-in limit to the potential of banditry as a revolutionary model. Unable to conceive of a real and enduring alternative to the existing world (in this respect, Lucas is like Jucundina, minus the resignation), Lucas nevertheless dies defending another failed option of collective resistance—that of the beato Estevão. The romeiros have a much clearer understanding of class dynamics, expressed in evangelical language. The beato speaks openly against the rich, and the phenomenon has a long-lasting (if unintended) economic impact and cultural effect: it causes a labor shortage and an erosion of peasant deference. The beato has a vision, but he has not the means to carry it out or to defend his community, and hence he is crushed by the state.

Both Lucas's and Estevão's groups are harmonious and rather egalitarian communities, devoid of internal conflict. But they are unable to bring about large-scale change. In fact, they divert forces that could be used for other specific goals (as in the case of Zé, who after Lucas's death wanders aimlessly through the infinite caatinga). In this respect, the novel considers bandits and millenarian leaders objectively reactionary. Millenarianism is a pure vision without the means to carry it out. Banditry is a raw force without a vision to orient it. Communism is the place where these two limited utopian impulses are simultaneously negated and recuperated into a larger synthesis. From millenarianism, Communism recuperates the utopian vision of a just society, transformed from an otherworldly apocalyptic event into a historical and perhaps inevitable event. From banditry, Communism recuperates the collective organization of force—reterritorialized as revolutionary violence.

Nenen embodies this synthesis, this negation/recuperation of the premodern tradition of violence. Nenen is the only one among Jerônimo's sons who, from the start, has a clear consciousness of the conditions of his existence. He leaves Jerônimo's household because he does not want to eke out a living as a sharecropper. He intends to follow in Zé's footsteps, but when looking for Lucas he comes across the railroad tracks and follows them to the city and his heroic destiny. He first becomes a policeman and later a military man. He is destined first for the South, where he becomes a Communist, and later he heads toward Amazonia, where he demonstrates his qualities as a leader in the fight against the Indians. Transferred to Natal, he leads the 1935 rebellion. When it fails, he spends ten years in prison. And then, when the PCB is legalized and an amnesty is declared, he returns to the sertão to work in the short-lived peasant leagues (*ligas camponesas*) of the 1940s.

Nenen is a heroic character. But his heroism is not defined by his (undeniable) accomplishments: fighting in the jungle, storming a machine gun nest during the Natal uprising, and enduring torture and prison. These feats are all predicated on his class consciousness. Nenen is above all a hero of knowledge, and *Seara Vermelha* is, ultimately, a novel about consciousness and knowledge. Hence the relevance of the quotation from Engels that serves as one of the epigraphs to *Seara Vermelha*: "Freedom is the awareness of necessity" ("A liberdade é o conhecimento da necessidade") (Amado [1946] 1999, 6). This is why, even though the novel is full of terrible events, it is finally defined by its happiness—for example, Nenen's surprising happiness during his prison stay ([1946] 1999, 275)—because it is a novel of a sacrifice toward a revelation, a novel of the reunion between man and history, and a novel of the world as meaningful, as human.[22] *Seara Vermelha* is a political novel. But it is a political novel in which the political dimension is not really based on praxis—an effect of contingent articulation of agents—but is mainly envisioned as knowledge effect.

In a nutshell, *Seara Vermelha* is an epic of knowledge, leading from the premodern fatalism of Jucundina, to the partial, imperfect knowledge of cangaceiros and fanáticos, to the full class consciousness of Nenen. The novel's (admirable) intellectual pirouette is that this progression of knowledge happens within a single class—the peasantry. Nenen is from peasant stock, but he is not a peasant leader, although he becomes a leader of the peasantry. He becomes a leader in the army, and his ideology is perfected in prison—a modern institution par excellence. But there are no legitimate leaders of the party who do not belong to the peasantry.

The premodern answers to the land issue are symbolically refuted through family metaphors. But these metaphors are all catastrophic in nature: Marta's parents sacrifice her to the double standard of backland morality, Zé Trevoada kills his brother João in the showdown between Estevão's romeiros and the state police, and finally the family ceases to exist as such. On the other hand, the acquisition of a modern class consciousness is expressed through the parental metaphor, as Nenen becomes a sort of adoptive father to Tonho.

Tonho is the only member of Jerônimo's group for whom migration is not another link in a long line of misfortune and oppression, but rather a founding and productive experience as well as an educational event that creates an identity. That is why Tonho is the hope for the future and Nenen endows him with his legacy and his ideology through his affiliation with the PCB (Amado [1946] 1999, 277).[23]

The novel begins and ends with a meeting of sertanejos. But if in the first case the feast is an event illuminated by the false light of ideology, in the final meeting (the meeting of the ligas camponesas organized by the PCB), the true light of knowledge shines. Upon Zé Tavares's return to the sertão to proselytize, a peasant approaches him. "Mr. Tavares," he says, "you tell me, you're the one who knows, what's that thing; Communism." After receiving the explanation, he then exclaims, "Mr. Tavares, that thing, Communism, reminds me of ghosts. Don't you see, mister, that a light appears on the road and they tell us not to get closer because that thing is haunted, that it kills us just because we take a look at it. But they talk about it so much that us folks are eaten up by wanting to go and take a look. One day we won't resist, we get close and see that it's the people's father" (Amado [1946] 1999, 334).

This dialogue shows how the transformation from a passive social class into an active social class implies a dynamic link (but also an unmovable hierarchy) between local knowledge, its myths and legends, and the new materialist truths of national and international dimension. *Seara Vermelha* begins with the assumption (which it shares with the indigenist novel, its contemporary) that the peasantry has no history—no history fit for novelization, at least—and that it is the intrusion of capitalism, or of a new version of capitalism, that makes this novelization possible. This is why the peasantry in the novel has no past, no memory, and no identity separate from that of the fazenda (and the landowning class) that it inhabits. The movement of capital that sets the novel in motion (the invisible hand of the market, represented by Aureliano) starts in the South, the active pole of history. This causes the response of the sertanejos, their painful search for history: migration, banditry, and millenarian rebellion. These are traditional responses. But the culmination of the novel occurs when the peasants really begin to be contemporaries with their own history, when they understand the nature of capitalist violence as contingent and class based, and envision other worlds. This is only possible under the guiding light of the Communist Party, which also comes from the South. And from São Paulo the sertanejo goes back to the North, to the sertão—the dark lands of oppression—to shed the new light, the new *lampião* of the revolution.

EIGHT

THE HEART OF DARKNESS

On José Revueltas

To be able to withstand the truth, but also the lack of any truth.
JOSÉ REVUELTAS, *LOS DÍAS TERRENALES*

An individual who considers himself a revolutionary, but does not pose to himself the question of the place from which he is talking, is a fake revolutionary.
ROLAND BARTHES, "FATALITÉ DE LA CULTURE"

IN SPITE OF their sharing a common Communist persuasion, the biographical and literary contrast between Jorge Amado and José Revueltas (1914–1976) could not be starker. Amado followed party orthodoxy quite closely (at least during the 1940s, the period discussed in the previous chapter) and abandoned his active role within the party without much controversy (Palamartchuk 2003). Revueltas's relationship (if not affiliation) with the Mexican Communist Party (PCM) lasted his whole life, even though this relationship was tortured. He was a precocious, energetic, and faithful militant who had difficulty even conceiving of life outside of the PCM (Monsiváis 2010, 16). But he was also a harsh critic of the PCM's lack of consistency, its blind subservience to the dictates of the USSR, its rather authoritarian and bureaucratic management style, and the ethical and political implications of that management style (in his fiction, the clearest expressions of this critique are *Los días terrenales* [1949], and *Los errores* [1964]). His loyalty earned him prison stints in the Marías Islands' penal colony in 1932 and 1934.[1] His criticisms earned him expulsions from the PCM in 1943 and again in 1960, as well as scathing ad hominem attacks by former comrades, which peaked after the publication of *Los días terrenales* and the stage success of his drama *El cuadrante de la soledad* (1950). These attacks forced Revueltas to disown both works.[2] This has indeed become the trope that defines many considerations of Revueltas's life and work: Revueltas as the perennial dissident, the perennial martyr speaking truth to the powers that be (either on the left or on the right), and the perennial nomad longing for (but unable to find) a political and existential home throughout his life.[3]

Amado went on to become a best-selling author and a well-established literary figure, a household name well beyond Brazil, and the coiner of an image of Brazil for global consumption.[4] This "tropicalist" image (for lack of a better term: Brazil, and by extension Latin America, as a violent but vibrant and sensual land, an image later exploited by the Boom's lesser practitioners or imitators—Isabel Allende, Laura Esquivel, Antonio Skármeta, Ángeles Mastretta, et al.) was much reviled among many and conspired decisively toward Amado's later critical prestige. Revueltas, on the other hand, never became a mainstream writer. He won a number of literary awards, such as the Farrar & Rinehart Award for *El luto humano*, as well as the 1967 Xavier Villaurrutia Award for his life's work. He had a devoted following among writers as well as within the 1960s youth movement, and he saw, relatively early in his life (1967, when he was in his early fifties), his fictional work compiled in a two-volume hardcover edition, which Revueltas uneasily recognized as a career landmark (1967, 1:8).[5] But he remained a controversial writer and public figure, whose literature is hard to grasp when considered apart from the political commitments and intellectual dilemmas that marked (and marred) his life.[6] This would fulfill, to a large extent, Revueltas's own wish. He did not want his literary works to be considered in isolation from his political commitments and views (Crespi 1979, 94), even though, as Sánchez Prado (2007) has noted (and this is the point of view adopted in this chapter), his literature cannot always be read as a mere illustration of those commitments and views (expressed both in his political actions and in his theoretical and political writings). As I will discuss later, on many occasions his novels exceed or modify those views.

Amado wrote riveting melodramas with ease. In those melodramas, the romantic and the political comfortably intertwine (Bush 2008). He also wrote adventure novels with an epic flavor. This ease emanated from his gift for narrative, but also (and perhaps decisively) from a core conviction: historical materialism, as spelled out by the Brazilian Communist Party, provided an eminently intelligible and even optimistic image of the world. Revueltas's literature also has a melodramatic imprint. It is melodrama à la Dostoyevsky, with the emotional and ethical pitch of his brooding murderers and self-sacrificing prostitutes, or à la Dickens, with his reveling in urban material and human decay.[7]

But unlike Amado, Revueltas is an arduous read.[8] His prose is not "efficient," and sometimes it is jarringly tortured. Monsiváis (1975, 178) rightly alludes to Revueltas's "feverish and excessively analogical prose, whose main aim is the creation of verbal atmospheres." Revueltas, in fact, seems to subordinate (with varying success) the overall economy of his narration to the single-minded purpose of making each paragraph, and even each phrase, the locus of a situation that triggers a distinctive emotion or intuition.[9] In Revueltas, any action or interaction has multiple repercussions. It becomes a chasm of desperation, of surprise, of wonder, of anguish. Each human exchange is a complex web of misunderstandings, of passions, of silent challenges, of memories (expressed in excessive and often unfortunate adjectives or metaphors). This is particularly baffling in the case of Revueltas's peasants, who seem to have more in common with Raskolnikov (Dostoyevsky was, indeed, one of the decisive influences on Revueltas),[10] with Hamlet, or with Erdosain (the main character of *Los siete locos*) than with the more laconic Mexican peasants of, say, Juan Rulfo, or the more colorful characters of the novels of the Mexican Revolution.

Both Amado and Revueltas infuse their narratives with Christian tropes and motifs. One example is the motif of the pilgrimage as expiation. This pilgrimage can be either through the desert (the scorched caatinga in *Seara Vermelha*) or through water (the flooded plain in *El luto humano*). While in Amado the characters do reach the promised land (and so the death of those left behind becomes a meaningful sacrifice for the good of the community), in *El luto humano* the pilgrims move in circles, in an empty, open labyrinth of water that has neither entry nor exit—the pilgrims end their failed attempt at escape in the exact same spot where they began. In *Seara Vermelha* the arrival in the South, with its double meaning of modern agrarian capitalism and modern peasant consciousness, bespeaks the future. In *El luto humano* (conflating the spatial and temporal dimensions) the impossibility of leaving the flooded plain is the impossibility of escaping a condemned past. In Amado the use of Christian tropes strikes the reader as strategic, part of a deliberate conflation of popular and literate cultures, intended to give maximum intelligibility and efficacy to the political message, in a fashion reminiscent of Mexican muralists, e.g., Diego Rivera's *Entrada a la mina* (1923), *El pan nuestro* (1923–1928), *La liberación del peón* (1931), and *El abrazo* (1923).[11]

As Paz (1997) and Sánchez Prado (2007), among others, have shown, Revueltas's relationship with a Christian worldview is much more complex. Ruiz Abreu ([1992] 1993), for example, frames significant parts of his biography around Christian tropes (martyrdom, sainthood, asceticism, guilt). For now, suffice it to say that Christianity—a particular brand of Christianity—is not considered merely a pernicious or misleading ideology, or a language intended to make a political message more palatable or intelligible. It is a worldview crucial to Revueltas's perception of both the human and the Mexican condition that coexist uneasily with his Marxist persuasion.

As I examined in the previous chapter, Amado embraced the character of the northeastern peasant insurgent (the cangaceiro and the jagunço) from the rich tradition of both popular and elite northeastern regional writing, and he successfully territorialized this figure within a modern revolutionary narrative (and within a modern aesthetics: that of socialist realism). This territorialization allowed Amado to reach (at the fictional level, at least) a synthesis between cultural nationalism and internationalist class-based politics, one of the main challenges of Latin American Communism at the time. The dramatic emblem of this synthesis is, perhaps, a scene in *Vida de Luiz Carlos Prestes* (1942), which consists of a nocturnal conversation by a campfire, somewhere in the sertão, between the narrator of *Prestes* and a cangaceiro named Zé Bahiano. Zé Bahiano was the darkest figure in Lampião's gang; he was the one with the penchant for branding "indecent" females with a hot iron bearing his initials. However, his interlocutor, an intellectual and an activist, convinces him that Prestes's fight and his own are parallel and compatible, if not one and the same. (This seems counterintuitive, since Lampião had received a government commission, as well as a military rank and modern arms, in order to fight the so-called "Prestes column." He never did it, though.) Zé Bahiano, a person who lives by an exacting code of bravery, is also persuaded by the narrator that Prestes's mother's bravery, crisscrossing Europe in a campaign to rescue her granddaughter from the Nazis, is equal, if not superior, to Lampião's (Amado 1942, 60–63). The encounter is marked by a conversation, and in this conversation the active one is the intellectual, who brings the outlaw, through the pure force of argumentation, to "his" side.

Even if it goes beyond its intellectual parameters, Revueltas's literature, like that of Amado, is born of deeply ingrained concerns within Mexican Marxism. In Mexico in the 1930s and 1940s, the issue of the peasantry's revolutionary potential (or lack thereof) was at the same time urgent and intractable for the Left. Mexico was still an overwhelmingly rural country—the census conducted in 1930 showed that more than 70 percent of the labor force was devoted to rural activities (Ruiz Abreu [1992] 1993, 79). In addition, it was challenging to define the nature of the Mexican Revolution. Although the peasant elements had been defeated or co-opted, and the revolution became a revolution "from above," as Alan Knight ([1986] 1990, 2:517–27) puts it, the Mexican Revolution was indeed a peasant revolution, the first "successful" one of the twentieth century, and the official revolutionary narrative (as well as opposition elements on both the left and the right) kept the peasant at the forefront of its mythology.

Revueltas tended to think of the Mexican Revolution as a nationalistic and modernizing bourgeois revolution, whereas the PCM had varied positions regarding the nature of the revolution throughout the years. Once the thorny issue of the definition was at least provisionally solved, it was imperative to establish a coherent relationship (either cooperative or adversarial) with the state that emanated from that revolution (and reined in the demands from below), and with the vast sectors of a Mexican peasantry that seemed to oscillate between support for the status quo (in particular after Cárdenas engaged in large-scale land redistribution and the organization of *ejidos*—communal land devoted to agriculture) and ferocious opposition, either in the form of the Cristero Rebellion or in more "modern" forms, such as strikes like the one in Nuevo León in which Revueltas participated and that formed the anecdotal basis for *El luto humano*. This relationship was subjected to changing (even contradictory) political and intellectual pressures from internal and external sources. The task of consolidating the Soviet state, the rise of fascism in Europe, the Second World War, and then the onset of the Cold War were global priorities that trumped the specific needs and priorities of the Mexican Communists (Carr 1992; Ruiz Abreu [1992] 1993). On the other hand, Revueltas's work is contemporary with the reflection on *lo mexicano* that would define a sector of Mexican literature, arts, and humanities for years to come (e.g., José Vasconcelos, Edmundo O'Gorman, Octavio Paz, Alfonso Reyes, Manuel Gamio). This line of inquiry was not indifferent to Revueltas, and he would visit it in his fiction as well as in his theoretical and historical writings.

The novels by Revueltas that I will examine in this chapter, *El luto humano* (1943) and *Los días terrenales* (1949), are also, in the last analysis, about knowledge, just like Amado's. But unlike Amado's they stage the loss of knowledge by the *letrado* (party militant or priest) confronted with the rural outlaw, as well as the militant's access to another sphere, a sphere that we could call "the ethical experience of the Other." To a degree, it is the same experience that Muñoz presents in *Vámonos-2* (which I examined in chapter 4). But Muñoz focuses on the character of the outlaw himself, and on the conditions and consequences of his denial of any compromise with the modern regime of violence and subjectivation. The letrado in *¡Vámonos con Pancho Villa!* is a somehow "flat" character, a stereotypical, almost parodic version of an American serviceman who is not intrigued by Tiburcio's refusal: his inability to understand makes him indignant and vengeful. In Revueltas, both of the novels center on men of letters who interact with the outlaw. The novels narrate the catastrophic consequences of this interaction, not for the outlaw, but for the letrado.

Revueltas disliked and rejected the expression "man of letters" (*hombre de letras, literato*), in favor of the term "writer" (*escritor*) (Revueltas 1967, 1:8). This distinction is the one between an institutional position and an ethical and political commitment. But this rejection is not unequivocal. To cease to be a man of letters and to become a writer is not a decision that can be made once and for all. The challenge is precisely that a writer is not a condition in society, a civil identity, something that you can "be," but rather a constant state of risk, something that you are always becoming: man of letters is what one fatally is, but a condition that one constantly struggles to exceed—and this excess is called, precisely, literature. It is, *mutatis mutandis*, the distinction that Barthes posits between *ecrivains* and *écrivants* ([1964] 2002b). And in both novels to be examined here, what is dramatized is that scene of risk (and ultimately of loss) from man of letters to writer—although the paradox of this transition is that its happening precludes the possibility of any work ever being carried out.

As I mentioned, in both novels there is an encounter between a peasant outlaw and a man of letters (embodied as a priest, a militant, an artist, a professor). This is the case with the priest and Adán in *El luto humano*, and with Gregorio and the Tuerto Ventura in *Los días terrenales*. These encounters are, in both cases, catastrophic for the men of letters involved—but not because the outlaw kills any of them (although both wind up dead). In fact, both encounters assume, on the surface, the form of collaborations. But for a priest, or a militant, death is never the worst danger. It is the meaning of that death that is always at stake (martyrdom *ad maiorem gloriam dei*, or Judas's abject suicide). The encounter between outlaw and man of letters is an ethical and political collapse that destroys what the letrados believe in, that is, it destroys what they are (or what they think they are). The priest and Gregorio do not immediately die as a result of their encounter, but they become murderers. The priest murders Adán, a former revolutionary, outlaw, government henchman, and assassin; Gregorio becomes an accessory after the fact to the murder of Macario Mendoza, chief of the *guardias blancas* (landowners' forces intended to intimidate and kill agrarian activists [*agraristas*], and in general to maintain the rural status quo). Both the priest and the militant are men of the Book, men of the Law (the eternal laws of Creation, the inexorable laws of History). Their fateful encounters with (and pollution by) the universe of violence embodied by the outlaws entails a loss of their privileged relationship with the law and an unavoidable slipping into a universe of violence. In *El luto humano*, the priest's life ends as a direct result of that pollution. Gregorio, on the other hand, embraces it fully, and finds a truth at the other end. But he is going to die all the same.

Las lanzas coloradas and *¡Vámonos con Pancho Villa!* also feature a conflict between men of letters and outlaws, with catastrophic or at least unsettling consequences for the former (or for all involved, since the outlaws also die). There is a crucial difference, though, between these novels and those of Revueltas: *Las lanzas* and *Vámonos* are intent on creating, out of the respective civil wars depicted in the novel, a popular subject coeval with the nation. The experience of the radically heterogeneous, refractory outlaw (Presentación, Tiburcio) is supplementary, as opposed to complementary, to the nationalistic reading, and partially ruins it (or at least exceeds it). By contrast, in the two novels I will examine here, the excess vis-à-vis the national or revolutionary narrative is front and center.

Studying these novels side by side is justified for many reasons. They share a number of other traits, such as the dilemmas of the militant and the relationship between dead ones (Natividad, Pérez) and live ones (Úrsulo, Fidel, Gregorio), and the subject of a dead girl (Chonita, Bandera). This death is received with indifference by the militant father (Úrsulo, Fidel), and destroys the marriage that had produced the offspring (with Cecilia, with Julia). Both marriages, however, are doomed from the beginning, since the husbands, with their rather "primitive" masculinity, cannot get over the fact that the wives had lost their virginity to other men (in fact, both husbands suspect their daughters are not actually theirs). Also, in both novels a person not normally associated with violence (the priest, Epifania the prostitute) murders a goon (Adán, Macario Mendoza) as revenge. In both novels the murder is discovered when the corpse appears floating in the water. (Water, in fact, is in both novels the condition of possibility of life—the irrigation system, the communal fishing—but it is also associated with death, as water carries the dead to the presence of the living.) In both novels the revolution is the school of violence (Adán, Ventura, Calixto, and Natividad are all revolutionary fighters), but that violence can be traced to either a historical tradition or an existential trait (a "Mexican" trait, the novels argue) that goes well into the past. And finally, in both novels there is a historical defeat (the defeat of the strike to improve the conditions at the irrigation system, the repression of the march from Puebla to Mexico City), but that defeat is the condition of possibility for the experience of something else, a "truth" of sorts.

In these novels, neither of the two outlaws commits dazzling feats of violence. There is no Villa or Maisanta or Presentación or Lucas Arvoredo. It is the mere presence of the outlaw as the embodiment of an incomprehensible universe of violence that defines the novel. Even if the priest is sensitive to the universe to which Adán exposes him, he is unable to endure this experience, and suicide is the only answer to this "disaster." Gregorio, on the other hand, fully embraces this experience, and makes it the condition of possibility of a new ethical experience (if for the PCM politics determines ethics, for Gregorio ethics determines politics).

El luto humano takes place in a dilapidated, almost deserted village in the north of Mexico one night during the 1930s.[12] Chonita—Úrsulo and Cecilia's only daughter—has just died. Úrsulo is a ferocious anticlerical agrarist, but he grudgingly consents to humor his wife and go look for the local priest to administer, postmortem, the last rites to the little girl. In order to reach the priest's house he has to cross a river, swollen by a copious rain (with obvious apocalyptic overtones) that has been falling and flooding the barren landscape. Úrsulo has to ask Adán, the owner of the only available boat around, for help. Adán and Úrsulo are sworn enemies, because Adán had murdered Natividad, the leader of the striking peasants working in the irrigation system, a government initiative for rural development that brought fleeting prosperity to the area through cotton cultivation. Úrsulo was a small landholder, persuaded by Natividad to join the laborers' strike. By the time the novel begins, the strike has failed, as has the irrigation system (its construction, it seems, was rife with poor planning and corruption, which accounted for a flawed design and shoddy materials), and the area has reverted to its prior condition but is now haunted by memories of violence and defeat. Everybody has left, except for the priest, Adán, Úrsulo, and some agrarist loyalists. It is not clear why anybody would stay, since there is nothing to do (and certainly nothing to fight for), aside from eking out a meager living.

Adán agrees to cross Úrsulo over the river. They look for the priest, who, in turn, agrees to minister the postmortem rites to Chonita. The priest is a character overwhelmed by guilt, and deeply unsure of both his mission and his calling.[13] The reader does not know it until later on, but while en route to Úrsulo's, the priest murders Adán, as a long-overdue revenge for Adán's role in the killing of Cristeros. Chonita's wake proceeds, now with the priest, until it has to be interrupted and the hut evacuated because the waters keep rising. The group (enlarged by Jerónimo, his wife Marcela, Calixto, and his wife Calixta) tries to make a run for it, fully knowing that there is no real escape. They wade in the water for hours, losing Jerónimo, Calixta, and the priest. The latter commits suicide, drowning himself, overwhelmed by guilt for having murdered Adán. After hours of miserable struggling, they realize that they have been wandering in circles, and that they are back at their starting point, standing in front of Úrsulo's house. Hopeless, the band climbs to the roof of the house, to wait for the inevitable. While they are there, Adán's corpse appears, floating by the house, as a posthumous accusation and an advance warning of the imminent fate that awaits all: becoming fodder for the waiting buzzards. Adán disappears when a buzzard, more daring (or hungrier) than the rest, start to feast on his eyes (Revueltas [1943] 2003, 181), a fate that they will all share in a moment.

All of the characters are obsessed with their pasts. In fact, a significant portion of the novel is made up of recollections—through indirect discourse, or directly through the voice of the narrator—of the characters' previous lives. This obsession with the past can take the form of their lives flashing before their eyes at the moment of death, perhaps, although this is questionable since some of the characters, such as Adán and Natividad, are already dead when the flashbacks occur. But inversely, it can be argued that death is not what triggers the recollections; rather, death is *caused* by the impossibility of overcoming the past. Adán is the visible emblem of this past, the ghost that returns from the depths to haunt the living. But what does Adán's corpse mean? Roger Bartra ([1987] 2003, 45) argues that Adán's "return," carrying the secret of his murder, is an allegorical example of the "primordial mourning" for the peasant hero, inhabiting the "subverted premodern Eden." Adán's corpse would be "the corpse of the peasant that lingers in the national consciousness." And, he adds, this is "why this consciousness frequently appears as a feeling of both nostalgia and anxiety, both defining features of the melancholy syndrome. This reaches the point where it is firmly believed that beneath the turmoil of modernity there is a mythic substratum, a flooded Eden with which we can only have a melancholic relationship: only by way of a profound nostalgia can we have contact with him and to communicate with the beings that populate it. It is impossible to materially communicate with them, but they are, however, the *raison d'être* of the Mexican" (44).

Bartra's symbolic reading is justified. "Adán," muses the narrator, "father of Cain, father of the human race. This body inhabited by Death meant a lot. It was not an occasional body, but a deep one: a somber process" (Revueltas [1943] 2003, 111). In another instance Adán's corpse is called a "messenger." Aside from this, the novel ends by openly positing an allegorical reading that is optimistic and forward looking, thus contradicting the pathos of the rest of the novel (much like what happens in the indigenist novel).[14] Interestingly enough, there is no place for Adán in that allegorical scheme. Bartra cleverly positions Adán as the focus of the novel, and not Natividad, the irreproachable revolutionary peasant, whose presentation is highly stereotypical and commands little credibility,[15] or Úrsulo, his flawed successor. And he also identifies the conflict that energizes the novel: the impossibility of relating to the peasant, but the (melancholic) certainty that something like a truth, even a horrifying truth, lies therein. In this respect, Bartra's reading is irreproachable, and informs my own. However, I depart from Bartra's reading in the characterization of Adán. Adán is supplementary to any possible allegorical reading, because he is not the hero of a subverted Eden, but a bandit, a *sicario* or paramilitary, a traitor, a murderous enemy of the peasantry. In fact, he is the one who makes collective redemption impossible—either the return to an Edenic, theocratic past, in the form of the Cristiada, or the possibility of any utopian future, in the form of a Communist-inspired strike.

Adán is not a social bandit. He is not even a character like Lucas Arvoredo. He is a hired gun with a long history of violence: a revolutionary in the 1910s, a Cristero chaser in the 1920s (173–75), and a killer of agraristas in the 1930s. Adán inhabits Cain's solitude. But the "reasons of Cain" are not translatable to the language of the man of letters. He kills for the government, but he does not seem to care for the government. He is paid for his services, but he does not seem to care for money either (his lifestyle is similar to that of the dirt-poor peasants around him). He kills and dominates, but he does not seem to be particularly cruel or enamored of the trappings of power. Just like in Tiburcio's case, the only predicate that seems to be appropriate is "denial." But as Revueltas puts it, it is an "empowering denial" ([1943] 2003, 154), because, unlike the dialectic denial that points to a synthesis, Adán's negation has no synthesis. It is a nonsynthetic negation whose emblem is the destruction of the crops, like a sheer offense against the productive, rational order. Adán finds his destiny at the hands of the Cristero priest. The priest is a "priest of Rome" (i.e., a rebellious priest), but he is painfully aware that none of what is happening around him has to do either with Rome, or with Mexico as a modern nation-state. Therefore, his position in the Cristero War is entirely false, since his leadership is based upon misrecognition.

The appearance of Adán at his doorstep is a turning point in his life. Even though Adán had killed the Cristero leaders Guadalupe and Valentín in a most

gruesome fashion, the priest had never met Adán personally. On this particular night, Adán is helping out people he does not care much about. But it is
what he is, what he represents, that profoundly impacts the priest. Adán fascinates the priest, and this fascination crosses a line that does not allow for a
return. It fascinates him the way the eye of the old man, veiled by a cataract,
fascinates the narrator in Edgar Allan Poe's "The Tell-Tale Heart" (1843). Not
by chance, Adán's eyes, made of "frozen shadow," are repeatedly mentioned
in the novel, and they are the first thing that the buzzard eats. Just like the
old man in Poe's story, Adán fascinates, and that triggers in the beholder dark
(and heretofore unknown) impulses and desires. Just like the old man, Adán
fascinates like something that has to be destroyed, and is destroyed. But just
like in Poe's story, that destruction is an illusory liberation, since the fascination is a trap from which there is no escape. When they destroy the object of
their fascination, both the narrator in Poe and the priest destroy themselves.
When they want to move away from the horror, they (tragically) surrender
more entirely to its impersonal domination. Unlike in "The Tell-Tale Heart,"
however, the priest's fascination is not explained away as the delusion of a
deranged mind, but as a deep cultural necessity: his horrified recognition that
he belongs to the same universe he has been trying to escape all of his adult
life. The priest, indeed, has spent his life running away from violence. He has
participated in it, but always reluctantly. He has always recoiled with disgust
and horror from the acts of violence carried out by his partisans or by his enemies. The revelation he cannot endure is that he also belongs to this world of
violence. To a certain extent he could endure (at great cost) being next to it,
validating it. But being a full participant puts him in the same place that he
detests.

The priest kills Adán by stabbing him in the back. The murder is not pre-
meditated. But it is not by chance that a knife is the murder weapon. Where
does the knife come from? The sudden appearance of a knife in the hands of
the priest might be a narrative misstep (or neglect), or it could enhance the
symbolic value of this manner of killing. The knife is the synecdoche of Mexican violence par excellence, as Úrsulo makes us aware early on.[16] The narrator
does not call the priest *cura*, or *padre*, names exclusive to Catholic clergy, but
sacerdote, which can refer to a Catholic or a pre-Columbian priest, that is, the
priest of the Aztec sacrifice.

If Adán represents Mexican violence, or violence so primordial that even the name "Mexican" is an excessive attribution (as the priest muses repeatedly), by killing Adán, as a priest, with a knife, he is not avenging the cause of Christ the King ("Viva Cristo Rey" was the rallying cry of the Cristeros), or the cause of his peasant community destroyed by Adán. He is not avenging Natividad, or Guadalupe. He is surrendering to the dark, alien powers that he fearfully recognized in Adán. Once the corpse of Adán is given to the waters, the priest becomes Adán (a traitor, a murderer—the same crimes that Adán, the murderer of his brother, was guilty of) and he ends like him: at the mercy of the furious waters that will not afford him forgetting or forgiveness (the same subject, as we saw earlier, appears in Borges). Consider the scene of the death of the priest:

> The stone was nearing the heart, and the body was dying.
> A gust of wind made him swallow a lot of water.
> It was imperative to cry out an expiatory word, the same one that he tried to cry out next to Úrsulo and his companions.
> "Adán," he thought of saying.
> But he lay down softly, to disappear in the water. (Revueltas [1943] 2003, 80)

Days later, Adán returns (110). His body refuses to disappear in the river of oblivion, because he is the conveyor of a message: that of perpetual war, of unending violence, of a past that refuses to pass, because it is forever present as the very secret of the present. Like Januario in *El periquillo sarniento*, this is another bloated corpse that has a message. But in *El periquillo* it is a warning: "Repent, it is not too late." In *El luto humano*, the corpse's appearance means that it is already too late, that it has always been too late.

Los días terrenales is, among other things, a scathing critique of the PCM (this is the way in which it was initially received, and the sticking point around which polemics raged at the time). Specifically, it is a critique of the Stalinist ethos that dominated the ideology, the political style, and the public and private sociability within the party (Escalante 1991, 195; Koui 1991; Crespi 1979, 93–94). Gregorio, the protagonist of the novel, is an activist, an intellectual, and a visual artist, a member in good standing of the PCM. He does not partake, however, in the ultraorthodox attitude demanded of him. Gregorio's

counterpart is Fidel, the militant firmly entrenched in (and the enforcer of)
the party dogma. As a hyperbolic demonstration of the dehumanizing power
of this dogma, Fidel stubbornly ignores the agony and death of his own daughter, Bandera, even though he is in the same room with the dying child. (Most
readings of the novel deal with the opposition between Gregorio and Fidel.
This is an entirely legitimate option, but it will not be my focus here.)

Gregorio has been sent by the party to organize peasants in Acayucán, a
rural area in Veracruz. He is the liaison with the local community leaders, and
in particular with *el tuerto* (one-eyed) Ventura. (As in the case of Adán, there
is the motif of the eyes—or the eye—as the memory of a violent past. Ventura
lost his eye during his years as a guerrilla.) Ventura is a most capable leader.
His prestige is undeniable and has various sources: his lineage as a peasant
insurgent (from a time prior to the revolution), the marks of which he carries
on his body (he lacks an eye, as already mentioned, but also an arm, and his
body is badly scarred and weathered); his ability to mix modern and traditional community organization tools (more on this later); and a good dose of
mystification (he acts as if he had "double vision").

Gregorio falls early and completely, albeit reluctantly, under his influence.
The novel begins with Gregorio, who looks at (and falls under the spell of)
Ventura, who is directing the fishing operation in the river that belongs to
the community and the subsequent distribution of the catch (an operation
with obvious evangelical overtones) (Revueltas [1949] 1991, 8–16). Gregorio
admires Ventura, a natural-born, legitimate leader. But beyond that, Ventura
fascinates Gregorio. This fascination does not exclude repulsion (Ventura is
ugly and his breath smells strongly of fermented corn), nor does it exclude
fear. Fascination implies the casting of a spell. And there is a spell in the fact
that it is impossible for Gregorio "to stop looking at Ventura, the man that represented such a live parcel of the people: sardonic, crafty, sensual and cruel"
(12). Fascination excludes understanding, and it is centered on the marks that
Ventura's violent life has left on his body: the facial scars, the arm stump, the
places where Ventura's vast energy seems to concentrate:

> Gregorio started to understand that portion of Ventura's mystery that had
> not revealed itself to him, the portion of mystery that was impossible to dis-
> cover even in the crushing previous moment, when that man's solitary eye

seemed to drench him inside with a corrosive liquid. That stump was a contradiction [*contrasentido*] of sorts, but at the same time it was as if the contradiction, the denial, were the only true thing.

This was so because Ventura seemed to obey, from his very essence, from
the foundation of his soul, a congenital and thick sense of denial. Hence that
live piece of flesh, also intelligent, small and infranatural, in which the fore-
arm was interrupted, that dirty and blind eye. (14)

Gregorio tries to capture (and exorcise) Ventura's singularity by territorializing it in a series of tropes taken from his own cultural capital. First, Gregorio
"sees" Ventura as part and parcel of a long historical genealogy:

By the light of the bonfires, the face of the Tuerto Ventura was visible in all
its unexpected and extraordinary magnitude. Men with that face had ruled
the country [*país*] since time immemorial, indeed from the times of Tenoch.
Ventura's features showed something impersonal and at the same time
something that belonged to him alone, and of which he was aware. As if it
was inherited from all former leaders and caciques, but even more from the
trees and the stones. This is how, from up close, the faces of Acamapichtli or
Maxtla, of Morelos or Juárez may have been, faces that were not completely
human, not completely alive, not totally coming from the womb of a female.
They were faces like leather, like earth, like History. (12)

Tenoch, Acamapichtli, Maxtla, Morelos, Juárez. This series places insurgents alongside sovereigns and founders of states, a very common procedure
(as I examined in the case of Chávez and Maisanta). But in this case, there is
a crucial displacement and an elision. The displacement initiates the historical (or mythical) series with Tenoch, the founder of Tenochtitlán. But the
novel does not occur in the Valley of Mexico, and there is no reason given in
the novel to assume that the people of the area have a historical or mythical
memory linked to that of the Aztec Empire (unless that memory was imposed
through the mediation of nationalist mythology, pre- or postrevolutionary,
as happened for example in Chiapas with *Zapatismo*). Gregorio is assigning
Ventura's violence and leadership a dimension that it does not have, a *Mexican* dimension. Ventura does not need this genealogy—he never refers to himself as Mexican, and he never speaks about Mexico. Mexico can be for him an

entity with the same reality or lack of reality as the Virgen de Catemaco, or Rosa Luxemburgo. Ventura is not at all an ignorant man. But he does not abide by the same distinctions as Gregorio: those between local, national, and global, between religious and secular, between lawful citizen and outlaw. Gregorio, on the other hand, needs this genealogy (and the distinctions it implies) in order to give meaning to his work, and to be able to understand the alliance that he wants to forge with Ventura. That is why he proposes it.

There is also an elision: the series ends with Juárez, and it does not reach the present. Two more leaders should be included: Madero (as leader of the bourgeois revolution, which for Revueltas is the Mexican Revolution's nature), and the hypothetical leader of the future peasant-proletarian revolution—let's call him (it is obviously a he), for the sake of convenience, Gregorio (or somebody who inhabits the same world as Gregorio). This is, with the addition of Marxism, the old liberal narrative. Gregorio needs that series in order to link the bandit's violence to a Western tradition of violence. He thus makes Ventura a "precursor," that is, valuable but historically relegated to the past. Gregorio thinks (even though his voice is oftentimes impossible to discern from that of the narrator), "Thus it was not difficult to imagine when in his mysterious escapades of fifteen or twenty days he devoted himself to cattle rustling in Oaxaca and Chiapas, and to see then like an equestrian lightning bolt, from one place to the next, holding the reins with his teeth while his only arm cracked the lasso; it was not difficult either to picture his youthful image in 1907, when he fought in the guerrillas of Hilario C. Salas, a kind of somber spark, a kind of unrelenting black burst" (Revueltas [1949] 1991, 12–13). This tradition would culminate in Gregorio himself. The series, then, is a procedure aiming at intersecting (at least at a symbolic level) the sociocultural abyss that separates the "two" (the many) Mexicos. This intersection did happen, but in a direction opposite that which Gregorio would have liked.

At the same time that Gregorio territorializes the scene in classical art, in his own and exclusive knowledge of classical art, he "reads" the scene of the corpse that appears floating on the river as a quotation of el Greco's painting *El entierro del Conde de Orgaz* (floating corpses are another leitmotif in Revueltas's narrative). But the scene ceases to have biblical or artistic resonance and becomes the abjection of violence outside the law when the Conde de Orgaz becomes the putrid corpse of Macario Mendoza.

Without ever exercising violence, without ever arguing, just with the mere exertion of his charisma, Ventura forces Gregorio to accept (even to embrace) heterodox decisions, decisions that contradict his Marxist identity. The catch is to be offered to the Virgen de Catemaco, the true owner of the river according to the peasants of the community (Revueltas [1949] 1991, 15), even though this community is affiliated with the PCM. Gregorio even agrees to restore the image of the Virgin, fully knowing that he is not restoring an artistic object, but a devotional icon (20). The gender relations in the community follow very different patterns than those sanctioned by party standards. Ventura speaks to Gregorio about the struggle for women's rights that the organizations are carrying out. Immediately thereafter, Ventura commands his wife to come and snatch, with her teeth, the chigoe that is stuck between his toes (19).

Negativity (the attribute that Gregorio identifies in Ventura) could be the active force in a more or less happy transculturation, where Marxism (as the password for modernity) and tradition would coexist and reinforce each other. The emblem of this harmony would be the division of the fish carried out simultaneously as Communism, a communitarian indigenous moral economy, and Catholic fraternity. This harmony is surprising, since it seems to embody different conceptions of identity and collective affiliation that at first sight would seem to be in conflict. The catch is distributed to each of the villages, represented by their respective caciques (Sotoepan, Santa Rita, Comején, Jáltipan, Acayucan, Chinameca, Ixhuapan), but also to the "organizations" (the Centro Rosa Luxemburgo and the Juventud Comunista) (Revueltas [1949] 1991, 18).

But the happy transculturation (with its evolutionary or dialectic logic that moves from premodern to modern) becomes all of a sudden the threatening "reverse transculturation" (Beverley 1997, 280), whose logic is imposed from below by the bandit. Ventura forces Gregorio (again with the sheer force of his legitimacy as leader) to become an accomplice (after the fact) in the murder of Macario Mendoza. This situation implies a complete reversion of epistemological privilege. Ventura has Macario killed by Epifania, the pitiful local prostitute. Ventura carries out an act of violence outside the law for Gregorio's benefit, but without Gregorio's knowledge or approval, and against Gregorio's beliefs. Gregorio is put in the impossible situation of not being able to either accept or condemn the killing.

After this, Gregorio will never be the same. He surrenders to the world of the outlaw when he has sex with Epifania (epiphany: the name could not be more telling). Openly out of gratitude (she saved his life, after all), but really for darker reasons, he has sexual relations with her, fully knowing that it is likely she will give him gonorrhea, a disease that, in the world before the popularization of penicillin, is sure to live with him for a long time, if not forever: "It was an act of love, of gratitude, or desperation. But maybe, however, it was something close to suicide too.... By contracting the disease in that conscious and deliberate fashion, Gregorio cleansed himself, he made a sacrifice of his sex, an affirmative act of renunciation, with which he recuperated the sense of purity, of isolation, of essential loneliness that would help him to understand the signs, experimenting in his own body, of the destiny of his brethren" (Revueltas [1949] 1991, 156). That surrendering is indeed an epiphany. It makes him capable of enduring "the truth, but also the lack of any truth" (170). This is not an ennobling sacrifice, like the hunger, excess of work, lack of sleep, or lack of human contact that Fidel endures. These are the sufferings of a monk, an ascetic, a saint. He is secretly (or not so secretly) proud of them, and they are the pillars of his sense of self. But this sense of self is firmly anchored (at least, so Fidel likes to believe) in an image of the world, and of history. Gonorrhea, on the other hand, strips Gregorio of all the imaginary shortcuts by which he sustained any kind of sense of preeminence. His calvary is not suffering, but abjection, in the long, painful scene in the dispensary where Gregorio goes to treat his ailment. Gregorio and other unfortunates are humiliated and abused before, during, and after the painful draining of the urethra.

Gregorio's becoming Other is at the same time abject and an unheard-of purity. It is a horror that puts him, for the first time, close to (but never in touch with) his brethren (Revueltas [1949] 1991, 152–54). His brethren were not the comrades of the party, but the scum of society, his companions in suffering. Gregorio's suffering puts him in an impossible place between abjection and purity, an excessive place. Gregorio is simultaneously completely alone and in the company of millions.[17] The experience of abjection does not mean abandoning the party. On the contrary: it is then that he becomes a worthy revolutionary. Although before, he aspired to be a leader, he now becomes one of them.

The novel begins at night (in the countryside) and ends at night (the asphyxiating night of the jail). It begins with the melancholic reflection on loss and ends with the jubilant acceptance of that loss. The revelation that happens

to Gregorio is "empty"—that is why it happens in the dark. This emptiness
is not the Poe-like horror of the man buried alive (the relation between the
last scene of the novel and "The Pit and the Pendulum" is telling). Or, to put it
differently, it is the horror, but it is a horror that is also the experience of a radical freedom. It is freedom from history, from the pursuit of happiness, from
love, from hate, from redemption. The revelation is the "great acceptance" of
death (the novel does not say so unequivocally, but it strongly suggests that
Gregorio is going to die), but not as a desperate escape (like the priest's) or as
a crowning sacrifice (like Fidel's), but as the true human condition. It is the
joyful embrace of the tragic condition of humankind. The redemption that
Marxism has to look for is not to achieve the stasis of the satisfied need, which
for Gregorio would turn humans into happy pigs. It would be the freedom that
would allow humankind to see the horror, its being for death, to stare at the
void in the eye, or to let the eye of the void stare at you.

PART IV

BANDITRY AND THE DILEMMAS OF LITERATURE

NINE

BORGES AND MOREIRA

Inglorious Bastards

It is a broken and sacred thing that our idle imagination
can enrich irresponsibly.
JORGE LUIS BORGES, "LA DIOSA GÁLICA"

I have asked: What's Gutiérrez's distinct contribution to the gaucho myth?
Perhaps I can answer: to refute it.
JORGE LUIS BORGES, "EDUARDO GUTIÉRREZ, ESCRITOR REALISTA"

IN SEPTEMBER OF 1957, Francisco Petrone, an actor best known for his performances in gaucho films such as *La guerra gaucha* (1942) and *Pampa Bárbara* (1945), offered Borges and Bioy Casares the opportunity to adapt *Martín Fierro* as a film script. This would seem like a golden opportunity. Borges and Bioy Casares had just tried their hand at scripts on the *culto del coraje* with *Los orilleros* and *El paraíso de los creyentes* (published together in book form in 1955). The scripts were never produced—part of the long and generally frustrating relationship between the two friends and the film industry. *Martín Fierro* would have provided the chance to do for a different medium, and hopefully for a mass audience, what Borges had successfully done in "El fin" and "Tadeo Isidoro Cruz": to dislodge Fierro from the nationalist epic and to recuperate the poem's dimension as a narrative of adventure, destiny, and courage. The script would have afforded the opportunity to make *Martín Fierro* into a Western, away from the pious nationalist narrative, full of exempla and moralizing passages. In an ideal world, it would have been a major cultural intervention.

During several nights in September and October, Borges and Bioy Casares (and occasionally Bioy Casares's father, a frequent and esteemed interlocutor in their conversations) discussed, half in earnest, half in jest, different aspects of an adaptation: how to present the idyllic portion of Fierro's life prior to his draft (they considered representing this as an animated feature), how to depict (or not) the Indians and frontier life, and what actor would be best to play each character. But they concluded that, in the political context of the time, the project would be impossible to carry out: 1957 was still the heyday of the Revolución Libertadora, the military coup that put an end to Juan Domingo Perón's presidency (1946–1955), and the coup enjoyed significant civilian support, including that of Borges and Bioy Casares. Borges would be named director of the National Library in 1955, the same year as the coup. The predicament of a poor paysano at the hands of an abusive and corrupt state would be read, Borges correctly feared, as an all-too-transparent allegory of the present. Fierro would stand for the Descamisados (a nickname for Peronists) and the nineteenth-century army for the anti-Peronist armed forces of the mid-twentieth century (Bioy Casares 2006, 369).

Borges and Bioy Casares agreed that the possibility of a populist reading is indeed present in the book. In fact, in their conversations (faithfully recorded by Bioy Casares) there are many derisive mentions of the perceived similarities between Peronist ideology and Hernández's poem. They even speculate that had Hernández lived in the 1940s, he would have been a Peronist (Bioy Casares 2006, 379, 382). Chances were, Borges speculated, that Perón wanted to make a movie as a secret homage to Peronism (the choice of writers seemed odd, in that case, since Borges and Bioy Casares's anti-Peronism was very well known). Therefore, the project did not come to fruition. Borges's prediction, however, was to come true. Years later, Fernando "Pino" Solanas directed *Los hijos de Fierro*, a continuation of sorts of *La vuelta de Martín Fierro*, in which Fierro (a transparent allegory for Perón) leaves, and his sons (the Peronist people and militants of the Resistencia) have to deal with the realities of an oppressive anti-Peronist, anti–workers' rights Argentina.[1]

Borges's prediction, in fact, would become even more relevant than he could have imagined in 1957. With the triumph of the Cuban Revolution in 1959, and the wave of revolutionary movements in Latin America, the gaucho insurgent (in its varieties as gaucho malo fighting the police posse, or as montonero fighting the army) was appropriated by the leftist insurgency (either Peronist or more orthodox Marxist). The gaucho insurgent provided, much like the cangaceiro for Amado or the llanero for Chávez had, a powerful icon that made it possible to inscribe current struggles in a long tradition of popular struggles.[2] The Montoneros logo (or coat of arms) is a powerful illustration of this: it features a *tacuara* (the nineteenth-century montoneros' weapon of choice) intersecting an automatic rifle in the shape of an X.[3] The upper quarter of the intersection is designed to represent the V in "victory" (or, more to the point in the Peronist lexicon, *Venceremos*). Nested inside the V was the P of "Perón." The logo, then, intersects premodern struggles (those of the historical montoneros) with modern anti-imperialist, anticapitalist ones (the automatic weapon of the modern guerrilla). That intersection is Perón himself, linking the old montoneros (a "lineage of bandits" in liberal thought, as Sarmiento [(1845) 1977, 174] put it, from Artigas to Peñaloza to the modern ones—who, ironically enough, would be denounced by Perón himself, after the fallout, as bandits.[4]

In the 1930s and 1940s the outlaw was in Borges's narratives the protagonist of a minor epic, which had an ethical value ("Bravery is one of the few virtues of which men are capable" [Borges 1996a, 500]) as well as a cultural one (to debunk the aspirations of state-sponsored nationalism). But these were, to a significant degree, polemics within the liberal establishment, instantiations of the liberal state. From the late 1940s on, that cultural dispute assumed new, much more ominous meanings, and the factions (at least in Borges's mind) were irreconcilable. Borges would embrace his identity as a liberal intellectual and as one of the preeminent figures in Argentine culture (director of the National Library, professor at the National University of Buenos Aires, prestigious speaker at universities in the Americas and Europe), and would fight the cultural fights of his time.[5] This would entail, among other things, revisiting his prior exaltation of the outlaw. In 1961, in the pages of *La Nación*, Borges reflected upon the urgent relevance of Sarmiento: "During our childhood, *Facundo* afforded us the same thrills as Verne's inventions or Stevenson's pirate adventures. The second dictatorship [Peron's, the first one being that of Rosas] has taught us that violence and barbarism are not a lost paradise, but an imminent danger. Since the 1940s we are contemporaries of Sarmiento and of the historical process examined and condemned by him; before that time we were already his contemporaries, but we did not know it" ("Sarmiento," collected in Borges 2003, 68).[6]

There are many other examples of this same idea. Allow me to present one more: "A curious convention demands that each country in which history has randomly and fleetingly divided the earth should have its classic book. England has chosen Shakespeare, the least English of all English writers; Germany, perhaps to counter its own defects, has chosen Goethe. . . . When it comes to us Argentines I think that our history would be different, and it would be better, had we chosen the *Facundo* and not the *Martín Fierro*" (Borges 1970, vii). Curiously, this lamentation about the place of the gaucho malo in Argentine culture (*Martín Fierro* justifies and exalts the outlaw, while *Facundo* condemns it) prefaces *El matrero*, an anthology of literary instances of the rural outlaw. The anthology does not shy away from showing the complex nature of the character, and if it is not a lionization, it is equally far from being an indictment. And it is equally far from being an outlier.

In 1965 Borges would publish *Para las seis cuerdas*, a book of poems intended as milongas (for guitar only) that celebrated the exploits of old-time compadres (Juan Muraña, Nicanor Paredes, Calandria). In 1970, *El informe de Brodie* would feature a majority of short stories dealing with gauchos and compadres. And the topic would be present in all of his later books, from *El libro de arena* ("La noche de los dones") to *La cifra* ("Milonga de Juan Muraña") to *Atlas* ("Milonga del puñal," "La cortada de Bollini").

In fact, in 1974, he interpreted his own historical position (and relevance) through the lens of the culto del coraje. At the end of the one-volume edition of Borges's *Obras completas* (1974) there is an apocryphal, tongue-in-cheek "Biographical notice."[7] It claims to be a reproduction of the entry on Borges from the *Enciclopedia Sudamericana* published in Chile in 2074. The biographer states that to understand the fame that Borges enjoyed during his life,

we should not forget, first of all, that Borges lived in a country in decline. He belonged to a warrior lineage and he always felt the nostalgia for the epic destiny of his ancestors. He thought that bravery was one of the few virtues of which men are capable. But this led him, like so many others, to the irresponsible veneration of criminals. Thus, his most famous short story was "Hombre de la esquina rosada," whose narrator is a murderer. . . . His secret and unconscious desire was to weave a mythology of a Buenos Aires that never existed. Throughout the years, he unknowingly contributed to the exaltation of barbarism, which culminated in the cult of the gaucho, of Artigas, and of Rosas. (1996a, 500)

Strangely for 2074 (but prudently for 1974), the biographer does not add the obvious name that (for Borges) would complete this series: Perón, who the previous year had won in a landslide election a third presidential term, only to die shortly afterward, leaving behind a country mired in a growing spiral of violence and a deepening economic crisis.

This chapter will, then, address this ambiguity. Borges critically revisited gaucho and orillero literature—including, prominently, his own—in order to rewrite, and sometimes to destroy, the gaucho and orillero myth as he himself had erected it, and in order to intervene in the cultural conflicts of the 1950s onward. Annick Louis (2009) shows how, in his later prose, Borges conducts a "critical rereading" of his own aesthetic of the 1930s and 1940s, not only by adopting a particular form of realism, but by revisiting the problem of the relation between personal political positions and aesthetics. My reading of Borges is heavily indebted to hers.

In some short stories of this period, Borges flatly renounces the culto del coraje. This is the case, for example, in "Historia de Rosendo Juárez" (collected in *El informe de Brodie*), which is a rewriting—in a literal sense—of "Hombre de la esquina rosada" (collected in *Historia universal de la infamia*). Like many of the stories in *El informe de Brodie*, Borges appears in the narrative as a mature writer, with a well-known oeuvre, who receives the story from somebody else, either as a confidence ("El indigno"), as an interesting story ("La intrusa"), or—and this is what interests us here—as a correction of a prior story ("Historia de Rosendo Juárez," "Juan Muraña") (Louis 2009). In "Historia" Borges revisits his most famous short story, in order to completely alter its premises.

In "Hombre," Rosendo's rejection of the challenge posed by Real is still a mysterious act—the short story is narrated to Borges by Real's killer, who remains unnamed, and who imperfectly sees and hears what's happening in the center of the action, where Real is challenging Rosendo. In "Historia" the secret has disappeared: Rosendo (who narrates his version of the events to Borges) is just disgusted with the life that he is living, and with the demands of the oral law that have forced him to kill, to become an electoral goon, and to allow his best friend's death. The short story (or Rosendo's memory of the fateful night on the pink corner) gives biographical and psychological density to the nonsubjective play of the challenge. In "Hombre," it does not matter who Rosendo or Real or the narrator are—the short story does not make any attempt to present the characters, but only states that they are from the North or the South, and that they live up to the expectations and prescriptions of the oral law. In "Historia," Rosendo arrives at the climatic moment of the challenge with some serious baggage: experiences, disappointments, and regrets (such as the death of his friend) distance him, not in a melancholic way but in a critical one, from the logic of the challenge. He sees himself in Real, and he does not like what he sees.

Even the challenges are deprived of the neatness that they had in prior short stories. Rosendo's first killing is less than an unequivocal victory: he charges his enemy without warning, without announcing that the duel has begun, and he cuts his enemy's face in a rather treacherous fashion, thus obtaining an unfair advantage. *Primerear, madrugar* (to attack without warning, without giving one's opponent the opportunity to defend himself) are not legitimate ways to fight: as the examples of "El desafío" and "El fin" show us, there is a ritual or courtesy between duelists, which states that the duel does not begin until both fighters are ready to begin, and have stated so (in "El desafío," they even eat together prior to the duel, thus showing that the duel will be conducted in good faith). Therefore, Rosendo (whose transgression is not witnessed by anybody) is, from the beginning, an impostor. From the beginning, unbeknownst to everybody, the champion of the oral law is he who has run afoul of the oral law.

The same goes for Real. In the duels narrated by Borges in the 1930s and 1940s, the challenge is always elegant, even when understated. "Hombres pelearon" (an otherwise rather imperfect narrative) is an excellent example: the Chileno walks from the southern orillas all the way to Palermo to challenge and fight another guapo, Pedro el Mentao (Pedro the Famous). After hours of walking, he arrives at his destination (a general store at a corner in Palermo) and goes directly to El Mentao. He tells him, respectfully (an exaggeration of deference is one of the rules of the challenge), that he is looking for a man who is supposed to be a brave and skilled fighter and that the man is called El Mentao. He wants to see what all the fuss is about. El Mentao, without acknowledging that he is the man the Chileno is looking for, calmly stands up and says to him, "If you want, we can both go and look for him in the street." In this story, verbal and emotional sobriety, deference (real or pretended), the absence of insults, and an indirect style all remind us of the best challenges in *Martín Fierro*, such as the superb challenge by the Moreno to Fierro. They are men facing their destiny, ready to kill or to die (the two forms of the *desgracia*—to kill a man in a fair fight is called a "misfortune," not a murder). Real, in "Hombre," is the same way: collected, sober, a man among men, who verbalizes his challenge according to its prescriptions, who does not waste his bravery on opponents whom he does not consider worthy.[8] In "Historia" he is just the opposite: drunk, dubitative (he takes a long time to come around and finally challenge Rosendo), and showy (he insults Rosendo and does not show the necessary restraint and deference). Rosendo does not despise him. He sees in Real a poor guy, like himself (or like Francisco Ferrari in "El indigno"), trying to live by a brutal and demanding code. That, Rosendo realizes, is the true desgracia.

But "Historia" is an extreme example. Rosendo rejects his prior life and leaves and reinvents himself as an honest, hardworking old Argentine (*criollo*). This is an ending similar to that of *La vuelta de Martín Fierro*: Fierro rejects the Moreno's challenge and leaves the area, after changing his name in order to become a decent paysano. (The two short stories replicate somewhat the two-part structure of *Martín Fierro*, and the two different ethics of the poem.) In other cases, the oral law is obeyed to a grotesque end ("La intrusa," "El duelo"), or it is renounced, but with more complex, long-lasting consequences. An example of this is "El indigno," in which the narrator again receives the story from a man who has refused to enter into the universe of the cultores del coraje. But his decision is more complicated than mere denial. Santiago (Jacobo) Fischbein, a young Jewish teenager (*un rusito*) from the orillas, is taken as a protégé by Francisco Ferrari, a barroom malevo and occasional criminal whom Santiago initially idolizes but later, for reasons not clearly articulated, betrays to the police. He does not betray Ferrari for money, to redress a grievance, or to do the right thing. In fact, Ferrari is his friend; he trusts Santiago, and is the only male figure whom Santiago can look up to. The betrayal is an undignified act (it is Santiago's best-kept secret, which he only tells to Borges decades after the fact, so that he can write about it, once he furnishes the story with daggers and fights). It is, however, the point that marks his transition from a despised Jew of the orillas into a well-read, respectable citizen of modern Argentina. It is a betrayal of the universe of violence of his youth, but unlike the case of Rosendo Juárez, in which this betrayal allows the possibility of a reinvention, Santiago turns his betrayal into the problematic foundation of his new identity: an identity that will forever bear the mark of Judas. The fact that many, many years after the event, he chooses to tell it to a friend, so that his friend can make it into a short story, says all that we need to know. (Santiago sells books as an adult. He tells the story to Borges so that his life can become a book: this equivocal episode of his youth encompasses the entirety of his life, his chance at surviving as a memory.)

In both stories, the allure of the culto del coraje has a name: Juan Moreira. Rosendo remembers his career as a bodyguard, electoral goon, and barroom malevo: "There was not a soul who would not respect me. I got a woman, the Lujanera, and a nice-looking golden sorrel. For years I pretended to be Moreira who, most likely, in his time pretended to be some other circus gaucho" (Borges 2005b, 442). Regarding Ferrari and his gang, Santiago says, "In spite of the last names, the majority of them Italian, he considered himself (and was considered by the others) a criollo, and even a gaucho. One of them would be a teamster or a cart driver; another may even be a butcher; the familiarity with the animals would make them feel close to the country folk. I suspect that their deepest wish would have been to be Juan Moreira" (437).

Borges would use Moreira again, in this later rewriting of the gaucho malo. This is not an accidental choice by Borges. Moreira is, and has been, a powerful cultural signifier in Argentina. As Ludmer puts it, "The recurrent depictions of Moreira (the genealogy of the Moreiras) make up a literary history of Argentine violence, from the end of the nineteenth century up to now. The different Moreiras are, in each instance, the cultural artifacts . . . of a violence that delineate physical and symbolic spaces that change with history" (1999, 244). She adds, "As a cultural artifact, as a 'real' fiction of a criminal hero, Moreira defines each time some kind of territory, of frontier, of struggle or debate, and he unleashes wars around meaning and interpretations, wars that define the main lines within Argentine culture" (245).

"La noche de los dones" is one of the last great pieces (if not the last) of the gauchesco/orillero cycle (Piglia 1986, 55). The short story was published in 1971 in *La Prensa*, a conservative Buenos Aires daily, and collected in 1975 in *El libro de arena* (included in Borges 1996a). The plot has the sobriety (the "direct style," Borges called it) that is typical of Borges's later works.[9] The setting is a friendly gathering of men. Don Jorge Borges (Jorge Luis's father) participates in the conversation. Most of them are educated, so they engage in a discussion on the problem of knowledge. They argue the merits or flaws of the thesis on knowledge as a form of memory. Predictably, the names of Plato and Francis Bacon make an appearance. An elderly man, not equal to the topic or the tone of the conversation, decides to intervene all the same. But unable to drop illustrious names, he offers the gathering the personal memory of a night in 1874 in Lobos, Buenos Aires Province. The narrator, at the time a teenager, is initiated by a friend (the hired hand Rufino) into the travails of nightlife in the bar, hotel, and brothel La Estrella. There, completely by chance, he witnesses the death of Juan Moreira at the hands of the police. That very same night the teenager experiences the generous (although somewhat distant) love of the *cautiva*, one of the establishment's girls.

Moreira dying against a wall is one of the limited number of events that Argentines will not completely resign themselves to forgetting. Other scenes include Facundo Quiroga directing his wagon, with fatalism and temerity, toward Barranca Yaco (Borges himself narrates this event in "El general Quiroga va en coche a la muerte," in *Luna de enfrente* [1925, collected in Borges 2005a], and, many decades later, in "La tentación," in *El oro de los tigres* [1972, collected in Borges 1996a]); the young Sarmiento, beaten up but still undeterred, crossing the border pass toward Chile, in *Facundo, o civilización y barbarie* (Sarmiento [1845] 1979, 4–5); the haughty unitarist who insults his torturers, fully knowing that the provocation means his death, in *El matadero* (Echeverría [1871] 1993, 111–13); Fierro and Cruz contemplating with desolation and stoicism the last dwellings before crossing to the desert, in *El gaucho Martín Fierro* (Hernández [1872] 2001, 190); and Don Segundo Sombra vanishing in the uncertain twilight—of the day, and of his historical cycle (Güiraldes [1926] 2002, 314–15). Like the story of Fierro, the story of Moreira "can be everything for everybody, because it is capable of almost endless repetitions, versions, perversions" (Borges 2005a, 600). "La noche" revisits the well-known Borgesian formula of the partially distorted rewriting or cultural translation of a crucial scene from a classic (as we already saw in "El fin" and "Biografía de Tadeo Isidoro Cruz") or of his own literature (as we saw in "Historia de Rosendo Juárez"). In "La noche," Borges rewrites the chapter "Check Mate" ("Jaque mate") from *Juan Moreira*, by Eduardo Gutiérrez. This is perhaps one of the better-known episodes in Argentine literature (to the point that it is not necessary to have read the novel to know the scene).

There are, I would propose, two types of modifications. There are those that, it seems to me, do not decisively affect the nature of the conflict or the characters. In *Juan Moreira*, the bandit dies in the afternoon: Andrade and Moreira are ambushed while taking a nap with their usual sexual partners. In "La noche," the struggle takes place very late at night, perhaps in the wee hours of the morning. In *Juan Moreira*, with the bayonet of his carbine Chirino pins Moreira to the wall that he is trying to climb up. Moreira's inability to cross the line between the built environment and the open pampa is one of the cores of signification in the novel (because it equals the end of the open pampa, and the frontier society that it created). Perhaps the best moment in Leonardo Favio's 1973 film version of *Juan Moreira* is the one in which Moreira, just about to cross to the other side, is able to catch a glimpse of the open pampa that would give him refuge. Just at that moment, he feels the pain of Chirino's bayonet (the camera captures the scene from the outer side of the wall, so we can only see Moreira's face). In "La noche," Moreira's death occurs outside La Estrella. But in this case, Moreira has already climbed over the brothel's last courtyard and is climbing down the other side of the wall when Chirino catches up to him.

In the novel, the horses are in the back, as a justified precaution (Gutiérrez [1879] 1999, 279). It is precisely in order to reach his horse that Moreira wants to climb the wall where Chirino finishes him. In "La noche," the bandits' horses are in the front, tied to the hitching post of the brothel, so they are out of reach from the start: Moreira's escape is perhaps doomed from the very beginning, precluding dramatic getaways, like the all-too-frequent ones in the novel. These are differences that, as far as I can assess, do not go to the core of the story, but that perhaps illustrate Borges's belief that we only have versions of versions of versions, variations without an original. In Borges's version, even the fact that the old man was an actual witness is not decisive in this respect, because, as he himself confesses, he cannot fully distinguish the memory of that night from the fictional versions with which he is also familiar: "After so much time, I do not know if I remember the man that I saw that night or the one that I would see so many times in the circus arena. I remember Podestá's full black beard. But I also remember a fairish complexion, dotted by marks of the pox" (1996a, 43).[10]

But other differences between the novel and the short story are more important, and may help us define Borges's intent in rewriting, almost a century later, the death of Argentina's most important outlaw. On the one hand, there is the different (and antagonistic) place that Moreira has in the rural community. On the other, there is the difference between the journalist/researcher/advocate who narrates *Juan Moreira* and the framed narration by the old man in "La noche." I will examine each one separately.

In Gutiérrez's novel, Moreira and Andrade are gauchos. They are gauchos in the somewhat vague sense that Gutiérrez understood the term—Juan Moreira is not a gaucho *stricto sensu*, but, as Prieto (1988) has noted, an entrepreneur who links, culturally and economically, the urban and the rural realms. "Gaucho" for Gutiérrez has more of a cultural and even a moral meaning than a strictly economical-legal one. In the novel, Moreira and Andrade are regular guests (or paying customers) of La Estrella, where they always seem to be welcome. In "La noche," they are just "drunken orilleros," feared, despised, and avoided by both men and women (Borges 1996a, 43), and metonymically associated with Indians (the din of the *malón* [Indian raid] in the cautiva's narrative coincides with the din of the drunken orilleros entering La Estrella). In the novel, Moreira is not a robber, but (like Martín Fierro) an avenger. Moreira lives—or says that he lives—in order to avenge the offenses committed against him, the first one being that by the teniente alcalde Don Francisco, who humiliated him by putting him in the stocks when Moreira claimed the money that Sardetti, the owner of the local general store, owed him but refused to repay. In "La noche," by contrast, the attitude of the people at La Estrella bespeaks the fact that they do not consider Moreira a social bandit, but a bully and a goon.

Nowhere is this more prominent than in the episode regarding the puppy. In the novel, Moreira has a dog, Cacique. Cacique is loyal and vigilant, providing early warning when enemies are approaching. Moreira values his dog as much as his horse, and whenever he stops at a pulpería, he takes care of his horse and his dog first (he calls them "his people"). His dog is also the only one to visit his grave. (This is, of course, a well-known romantic motif: witness Efraín's dog in *María*.) In "La noche," Moreira is a vicious sociopath, and this is evidenced in his treatment of animals. When he enters La Estrella, a little dog wants to play with him. Moreira, for no reason, hits it in the head with his *rebenque* (whip), killing it instantly. It is this act of gratuitous cruelty that prompts the cautiva to take the young man to his room.

In *Juan Moreira*, the last fight is a long and carefully choreographed encounter, like all fights in Gutiérrez's novels (unlike what happens in Hernández's poem, where the fights are caused by alcohol or chance, and are rather clumsy affairs—with the notable exception of the fight against the Indian in *La vuelta*, whose noble purpose is to save the cautiva from further abuse). Drawing an anachronistic comparison, the martial scenes in Gutiérrez remind us less of the gaucho literature than, *mutatis mutandis*, films by John Woo (*A Better Tomorrow* [1986]; *A Bullet in the Head* [1990]), the Wachowski Brothers (*The Matrix* [1999]), or Quentin Tarantino (*Kill Bill: Vol 1* [2003] and *Vol. 2* [2004]; *Django Unchained* [2012]). Moreira has two short blunderbusses (*trabucos*),[11] and he repeatedly charges the posse while shooting simultaneously in opposite directions, with equally deadly aim (the blunderbuss, granted, did not require great aiming skills) (Gutiérrez [1879] 1999, 283). Later on, with the dagger as his only remaining weapon, Moreira defeats a large posse armed with sabers, daggers, and carbines (285–88). He only dies when the coward Chirino (who hides during the entire encounter) attacks him from behind (289). The action repeats the classic motif of social bandit narratives: the bandit is invulnerable and can only die by treason. Famous examples include Pat Garrett shooting Billy the Kid in the dark, without warning; Robert Ford shooting Jesse James in the back; and Pancho Villa riddled with bullets in Parral, years after he had peacefully rejoined civilian life. (In the case of Moreira, the treason is double: Cuerudo's revelation of Moreira's whereabouts, and Chirino's cowardly ambush.)

In "La noche," only one shot is heard, the fight is confusing, and it does not seem memorable. Gutiérrez narrates a battle, a climactic showdown destined to begin one of the most enduring myths in Argentine culture; Borges narrates a rather commonplace police operation, only memorable to the impressionable mind of a child. In Gutiérrez, Moreira dies like a hero. Even when mortally wounded, he dies charging, admired even by those who are responsible for his death (except Chirino, of course), since victims and killers expose their bodies, according to the prescriptions of the oral law of courage:

> Moreira's aspect was awe-inspiring. A stream of blood running from his chest drenched his clothes, all the way down to the spurs; his eyes glared and pain had contracted that arrogant and disdainful smile that was always playing on his lips.
>
> —Here I am, motherfuckers!—he continued—. Here I am!—And he thrust his dagger so powerfully that he stopped in their tracks the advance of those who were seeking to finish him off....
>
> Moreira took his dagger out and looked at Varela [who had just saved Larsen, another member of the posse, from Moreira's attack], with something resembling admiration; he wanted to charge again, but a vomit of blood completely drenched the front of his shirt. He fell to his knees, utterly debilitated by the copious loss of blood....
>
> Then everybody charged him at the same time; Moreira's head was lying in the pool of blood he had just thrown up, the last of his blood that gushed forward when he fell to the ground.
>
> Even in this situation, that exceptional man raised his arm, still wielding the dagger, and he attempted a last thrust against his attackers. But that arm that only death could weaken, that for the first time was lowered without having wounded an enemy, fell to never raise again. Moreira slowly and painfully raised his head, and he gazed, still full of arrogance, upon Chirino's body, which was close nearby. He gradually lowered his head, with his forehead soaked in blood, and he remained still as a corpse. (Gutiérrez [1879] 1999, 291)

In "La noche," on the other hand, Moreira dies at Chirino's feet, between moans that exclude both words and heroic gestures *in articulo mortis*: "The sergeant jumped forward and stabbed him. The man fell down, where he remained lying on his back, moaning and bleeding to death. Suddenly, I [the old man, then a boy] remembered the dog. The sergeant, to finish him off once and for all, stabbed him with the bayonet again" (Borges 1996a, 44). Moreira "dies like a dog" ("muere como un perro," as the Spanish saying goes), the most undignified of deaths. (Contrast this, for example, with the death of Real in "Hombre de la esquina rosada," who dies with his face covered by his hat, to hide the undignified spectacle of his agony). And there is a strong suggestion that the boy is quite happy that the bully has met an undignified end (the fact that the boy remembers, at this moment, an act of unnecessary cruelty committed by Moreira). And finally, in the battle scene in the novel, Chirino is a coward who hides behind the curb of the water well and only strikes when he can do so without exposing himself (the epitome of the cowardly act). The novel despises him, and forgets him immediately. In "La noche," Chirino is the hero of the day, congratulated and most surely envied by his comrades in arms.[12]

Borges's rewriting of the episode in this fashion has a very clear goal: to divorce Moreira from the populist narrative that was dominant in the 1960s and 1970s. This narrative was composed of political as well as moral features. We can imagine a counterpoint. "La noche" shares the distinction as the better-known retelling of Moreira with the 1973 movie directed by Leonardo Favio, which was both a box-office and a critical success legendary in the annals of the Argentine film industry (King 2000, 89).[13] *Juan Moreira* premiered the day before Cámpora took office (Cámpora was the left-leaning president elected with Perón's blessing, and with the exclusive goal of securing Perón's return to Argentina after eighteen years of exile). It isn't clear if Borges knew Favio's *Juan Moreira* or had any idea about Favio's existence. But Borges was aware of the cultural universe of 1960s and 1970s populism, from which *Juan Moreira* (the movie) emerges. Until quite recently, the only one who had mentioned the relationship between "La noche" and Favio was film critic Alberto Farina (1993, 34).[14]

The movie makes a political and a moral point in order to advance its populist agenda. The political one has to do with the fact that the body and the story of Moreira are the point around which a popular identity coalesces. The movie begins with Moreira's funeral, during which an off-camera voice details the state case against him. But the funeral triggers an uprising, in which there is a dispute around (and for) Moreira's corpse, with the rallying cry of "Viva Juan Moreira, mierda!" (Long live Juan Moreira, motherfuckers!). This scene is completely absent from the novel, where the opposite happens: Moreira's killers, in fact, are in awe of his bravery, but his funeral is not narrated and his grave is lonely and neglected. In any case the movie's intention is clear: to create a popular subject as the keeper of Moreira's memory and legacy of violence from below. This point is further brought home when later in the movie the paysanos sing and praise Moreira's violent feats around the campfire.

The movie's second scene cements this political case with a moral one. It features a long close-up of Moreira's face (a very good-looking Moreira), patiently waiting at the offices of the teniente alcalde for a meeting in order to make his case against Sardetti. During the meeting, Francisco is rude and dismissive and abuses the meek and respectful paysano. Moreira is a victim, and all of his murders and moral shortcomings are consequences of this initial offense.

"La noche" argues against this by morally separating the bandit from the paysanos, who look at him with fear and disgust (hence interdicting any possibility of the bandit becoming a representative or a champion), and by divorcing him from the trope of victim (hence putting his acts of violence beyond the pale of the rural community). But destroying the populist reading of the novel—a reading that the novel itself promotes—does not mean that Borges gets rid of Moreira. In "La noche" Borges attempts a heterodox reading of the novel—so heterodox, in fact, that most critical approaches to rewritings of Moreira, or of the relationship between Borges and Gutiérrez, leave "La noche" aside (see Balderston 2000; Ludmer 1999; Villanueva 2005). "La noche" can be considered a radical return to Gutiérrez, a particular version of Gutiérrez and his writing of the gaucho malo. I would call this return "the adoption of the perspective of Hormiga Negra."

Borges wrote a short note on Gutiérrez, published in *El hogar* on April 9, 1937. He considered *Hormiga Negra* a novel superior to *Juan Moreira*, which is to say, superior to all of Gutiérrez's novels, since it is the one—the only one—through which Gutiérrez survives in Argentine cultural memory. "It is, of course, an arduous read," Borges wrote, adding, "Its prose is of an unsurpassable triviality" (1996b, 278). It has a few memorable scenes (like the duel with the guapo from Santa Fé, Filemón Albornoz), but Hoyos, the novel's title character, has few redemptive virtues: he is evil (in a petty way), he is treacherous (and treachery and disloyalty are the ultimate sins in bandit narratives), he is abusive (he not only beats women—a taboo for social bandits—but he beats old women, and he does not just beat them: he beats them with enthusiasm and gusto), and he is mentally unbalanced. Like the young son in *Taras Bulba* (Nikolay Gogol, 1835) or the title character of *O Cabeleira*

(Franklin Távora, 1874), he is incited by his father to go deeper into a life of violence. He robs from the weak without discrimination and he kills without reason and without provocation. In Borges's eyes, he has a single virtue that redeems him: courage.

In "La noche" it is difficult to recognize in the figure of Moreira the story of the bejeweled, seductive, and artistic rider, the Byronian character conscious of his place in society, and the hero of former sorties against the Indians that inhabits the Argentine imagination. Borges endows Moreira with the features of his evil brother in arms, Hormiga Negra. Thus, he rewrites the story of the social bandit (the Hobsbawmian avenger) from the viewpoint of the story of the unpopular bandit. Critics of nineteenth-century *moreirismo* read *Juan Moreira* as a moral fall when compared to *Martín Fierro* or *Santos Vega* (for this debate see Prieto 1988). In the twentieth century, those who refute Fierro's transactions with the liberal-oligarchic state (as posited in *La vuelta*) read *Juan Moreira* as the fulfillment of the insurgent possibilities that Fierro did not dare to carry out. Borges proposes reading all of the series in reverse, starting with its later and less illustrious ending, *Hormiga Negra*. Borges affirms (and contemporary scholarship proves) that in the last quarter of the nineteenth century, Fierro was not the culmination, either in political or in literary terms, of the series of the gauchos malos, but merely another one (and perhaps not even the most prominent one).[15]

This perspective allows us to see, in Gutiérrez's novel, the perspective of the paysanos, those whose dignity Moreira infringes upon as a matter of fact, with total ease and complacency. This allows us also to see that Moreira's commitments with the state are not accidental, but the core of his identity. Before the scene in which the teniente alcalde insults him and throws him into a life of crime, Moreira is already a goon and the enforcer of the liberal-oligarchic state. In Favio's movie, on the other hand, the alliance with conservative politicians happens *after* his fall, making it an accidental (and perhaps unavoidable) compromise. When Moreira's career is examined, his relationship with his political bosses is always emphasized. As part of this, it is (correctly) remarked that Moreira establishes alliances that are political as well as affective, based upon a common oral code of bravery and honor. The paramount examples of these alliances are the ones with Alsina, which is formed before Moreira becomes a bandit, and with Marañon, which is formed after he becomes an outlaw. The symbols of these alliances are the dagger and the horse given to him by Alsina, both of which become an essential part of his identity.

When Moreira is working for a given political party (he changes loyalties in the novel), he never seeks to win the hearts and minds of the poor paysanos, but to terrorize them into voting for the party for which he is working. These are not precisely the ways of a popular hero. The novel indicates, "The paysanos were so subdued that they declared . . . that they had decided to abstain from voting in the election, rather than be on bad terms with Juan Moreira, who, after all, was more powerful than the police. If they were to be stabbed by Moreira nobody could undo that" (Gutiérrez [1879] 1999, 245). Predictably, "election day arrived and it was a unanimous win by the nationalists, since no one dared to vote against don Juan Moreira" (245). Note the "don" that goes along with the name of Moreira. It is not, in this case, just a courtesy to Moreira's age or family status. For the paysanos, Moreira is not just another paysano, but one of the group above the regular paysanos.

Ludmer (1988), in her groundbreaking reading of the gaucho genre, maintains that *Juan Moreira* is the true continuation of the *Ida*. While this statement is completely true, it may be true in two different ways. The one proposed by Ludmer rests upon the identification of both the Fierro of the *Ida* and Moreira as fighters against the modernizing state. The other interpretation also returns to the *Ida*—not to the flight to the desert as a radical gesture of resistance, but to the initial scene in which Fierro, while singing at a pulpería, is forcibly drafted to the frontier's military forts, since he is not voting according to the desires of the judge (Hernández [1872] 2001, 114–15). We can well imagine Moreira in the scene, not in Fierro's group (that of the victims), but as one of the merciless goons who carries Fierro to the frontier. Had Fierro voted as the judge would have liked him to do, the election would have been unanimous (*canónica*), as the obedient Moreira was capable of achieving for his own political bosses. Or we can allow our imagination to go in a different direction, and imagine Fierro as one of the fearful paysanos driven like cattle to the voting places (voting was not secret back in the day).

As in "La noche," in Gutiérrez's novel Moreira is not liked by the paysanos. It is true that the novel registers scenes in which he is flattered and even cheered in the pulperías, where he lives surrounded by adulation and deference. But as Scott (1985) and Guha ([1983] 1999) have explained, adulation and deference in the presence of a superior do not equal true friendship or an enduring alliance. Adulation and deference belong to the public transcript; they are performances of the weak in front of the powerful, of the unarmed paysanos in front of the one who carries daggers, pistols, and blunderbusses, and who counts on the support of the caudillos. This performance does not show a real appreciation, but an acute perception of a situation of unequal power. The hidden transcript is accessible, at least in this case, by paying attention to what the paysanos do not do or do not say. And in *Moreira*, as "La noche" teaches us to read it, there is a lot that the paysanos do not do or do not say. After many years as an outlaw and a "popular hero," Moreira has only two allies: Julián (also caught by the police in La Estrella) and his brother Inocencio (who, far from avenging the death of his brother, ends up a cop [Gutiérrez [1879] 1999, 258]). The paysanos are only spectators who never actively help Moreira, and who never join his purported emancipatory crusade against the police posse.

When Moreira leaves Matanzas because he has killed Sardetti, nobody lends a hand to his wife Vicenta. This would be inconceivable in the case of a noble robber or an avenger à la Robin Hood, whose community would be proud of its steadfast support. The many paysanos who supposedly are Moreira's friends, who ate beef and drank liquor when partaking of the wedding feast, abandon Vicenta to die of hunger. Not only do they not help her, but they also let her believe that Moreira is dead, which means they do not pay even an occasional visit to the woman. And this is not the desolated (or isolated) world of *Martín Fierro*. In *Juan Moreira* there are neighbors and cities and railroads and telegraph lines. The paysanos actively but silently refrain from helping him; they refuse to be part of his community.

Even his bosom friend, the compadre Giménez, sees in Vicenta's situation not an opportunity to exert mythical peasant solidarity, but an occasion to rob Moreira of his wife (Gutiérrez [1879] 1999, 157). Giménez is not censored for taking advantage so basely of Moreira's misfortunes, even though his treason happens in front of the community's eyes. This lack of punishment for the infringement of the oral law speaks volumes about where the community's true sympathies reside. Finally, when Moreira dies, nobody visits his tomb, with the exception of Julián (294–97).

Giménez and Cuerudo, false friends of Moreira, are traitors. But "traitor," in this case, is only a trope for what exceeds the nationalist-populist identity articulations. In Borges, from "La forma de la espada" and "El indigno" we know that the identity of the traitor is a complex one. In fact, "La noche" invites us to read *Juan Moreira* from the perspective of the traitor, from the perspective of Giménez, of the Cuerudo or of Chirino, bringing to light what the criollista interpellation, later statist, later populist, silenced. If in the past there have been splendid readings that strive to understand and justify the motives of the equivocal actions of the gaucho (what Ludmer [1999, 238] aptly calls "the double politics of the gaucho malo"), why not reason the same in the cases of the traitors Jiménez and the Cuerudo? For them, as for the cautiva or the narrator of "La noche," Moreira is, in the best of cases, a drunken goon and a showoff (an *orillero borracho*) whose weapons and appearance tie him more closely to a gangsta rapper (a criminal variation of the Byronian character) than to the ascetic Martín Fierro or Don Segundo Sombra. In the worst of cases, Moreira is a terrible enemy, but never a communal hero. In Borges's story, the true hero (to the degree to which the term "hero" is applicable in this context) is Chirino, and the true heroine, the cautiva.

The case of Cuerudo, who betrays Moreira to the police (and this is the condition of possibility of the events of "La noche"), is perhaps clearer. In the novel, Cuerudo, during a night of gambling and alcohol indulgence, challenges Moreira, but later recants, convinced of Moreira's superiority. He offers Moreira his friendship, but Moreira chooses to treat him as a servant and doormat, with fatal consequences. Cuerudo is the Judas of the novel (Gutiérrez [1879] 1999, 267). But as Borges himself taught us (in "Tres versiones de Judas," from *Ficciones* [1944], and in "La Secta de los Treinta," from *El libro de arena* [1975]), Judas is a more complex character and the drama of the Passion can be read differently. From the perspective of "La noche," Cuerudo is not Moreira's nemesis, but rather his secret mirror, since he is as much a traitor as Moreira is; he is also as much a warrior and a singer, and just like Moreira he is able to enter into alliances with the state and its representatives in order to defeat his enemies. Cuerudo is not Moreira's Judas but rather his secret truth. He is the living proof that Moreira is not a popular hero, not because he cannot live up to the standards of the popular hero, but because there is no "popular" in the novel. Rather, there is a complex network of alliances instead of totalizing subject positions; there is a web of nonhierarchical passions, of resentments, and of fragile and fugitive alliances that do not coalesce into an enduring, all-encompassing identity playing out its political possibilities in an all-encompassing conflict. There is no "popular" because the space of the novel, and thus the space of Borges's short story, is that of the equivocal passions of the multitude. "La noche de los dones" invites us to return to the scene, simultaneously cruel and moving, of very flawed men fighting because of the pure temptation of danger. These men are brutal, and more often than not evil, and their political options can be random, whimsical, and incomprehensible.

By "returning" to the moment when Moreira was not the larger-than-life myth, but just another brutal gaucho, "La noche" wants, impossibly, to return to the elusive moment before the myth of the gaucho malo as national subject. Borges wants to make *Juan Moreira* a work that does not talk about Argentina, about its people or its oppressors (the landowning bourgeoisie and American imperialism), but about the exclusive passion for courage, of courage without reason (like art), of courage divorced from its equivocal commitments and transactions, of courage and its dubious relationship with the powers that be. It is this courage without morality (or which is a morality in itself) that the old man cannot forget, the moment of sheer experience before all narratives that transformed his life forever. This is the most precious memory the old man has. He owes Moreira his transformation from a boy into a man (in the same way that Santiago owes Ferrari his transformation into a man in "El indigno"). The memory of the outlaw is not, for Borges, the key to Argentina's history. It is not even the key to the old man's complex history, but an enigma that comes time and again and that will come in the uncertain future not as an epic, or as a gift that he does not deserve, and not even as a memory for the old man to relish, but as impoverished and worn-out words.

TEN

LANGUAGE, THE DEVIL, AND THE (OUT)LAW

On *Grande Sertão: Veredas*

Why darkness & obscurity
In all thy words & laws
That none dare eat the fruit but from
The wily serpent's jaws

WILLIAM BLAKE, "TO NOBODADDY"

Destroy, O Lord, and divide their tongues:
for I have seen violence and strife in the city.

PSALM 55

LIKE THE AGED man of action in "Hombre de la esquina rosada," Riobaldo Tatarana is both the narrator and the protagonist of *Grande Sertão: Veredas* (1956). Riobaldo is an aged, respectable landowner. He recounts (for a listener who remains silent and anonymous: we only know that he is an urban, educated man) his adventures as an irregular fighter at the beginning of the twentieth century.[1] He went from being part of a force chasing outlaws (jagunços), to becoming an outlaw himself, and finally to becoming an outlaw chief, crowning his career as vanquisher of all other outlaw chiefs of the region and avenger of Joca Ramiro. Riobaldo's youthful exploits take place in an area comprising northwestern Minas Gerais, southwestern Bahia, and eastern Goiás, in central Brazil (Viggiano [1974] 2007). At the time, this area was a cattle frontier, where the reach of the state or federal governments was tenuous at best. Any authority that the state exerted depended upon the mediation (either aid or resistance) of the colonels, who were local landowners who doubled as military and civil authorities. The narrative is meandering, digressive, and does not respect a chronology of events. But (as suggested above) it is possible to reconstruct three distinct periods in Riobaldo's life. The first period comprises his early life with his mother, his education under the care of his godfather Selorico Mendes,[2] and (after he leaves his godfather's society) the period that he spends in the service of the landowner, military leader, and political aspirant Zé Bebelo. Riobaldo is his teacher at first, and later he becomes his secretary. In this capacity, he accompanies him in the campaign that Zé Bebelo launches against the jagunços roaming the area.

By bringing law and order (as defined by the state) to the sertão, Zé Bebelo intends to burnish his credentials as a politician vying for state or national office (Guimarães Rosa [1956] 1986, 110), and to set the conditions for his vast plans for the development and modernization of the area (111). Zé Bebelo wins two battles and proves to be an adept leader, with certain incurable limitations. Riobaldo, however, deserts after a while (as the novel explains later, a jagunço can leave his band at any time, provided that it was not during an armed engagement and that he returns whatever the chief gave him [429]). It seems to him that war is not his calling (115).

On the road, he crosses paths with a group of jagunços. In this group, he reencounters a very young man named Diadorim (although he goes by the name Reinaldo) (133). Several years earlier, Riobaldo had had a brief but intense encounter with him, of obvious erotic overtones (84). Drawn by nothing else but his attraction to Diadorim, he decides to join the roving band of outlaws. This overwhelming attraction, and the difficulties and ambiguities that Riobaldo experiences in order to come to terms with it (homosexuality is a powerful taboo in this otherwise all-male society), are two of the major topics of the narrative. (The relationship between Riobaldo and Diadorim is very close, but it is rife with tensions and misunderstandings that stem from the ambiguous and potentially forbidden nature of their attraction, and also from the fact that Riobaldo sees in Diadorim a force that can draw him onto a bad path—or a good one, alternatively.)

The decision to follow Diadorim inaugurates the second period of Riobaldo's life. He becomes a jagunço rising star, aided by his greater-than-average intelligence and his remarkable marksmanship. He serves under different chiefs: first under Hermógenes, then later under Joca Ramiro, supreme leader of the jagunços. Much like feudal lords and their *mesnadas* (armed retinues), jagunço hierarchies are layered: each leader commands his men, and puts himself under the leadership of a more powerful leader, who is *primus inter pares* (of course, the medieval subtext is present throughout the novel). Leadership depends primarily on social class: chiefs are commonly landowners (with the exception of Riobaldo), although landowners are not necessarily jagunço chiefs. But leadership depends also on charisma, organizational skills, prestige, and martial prowess. Under Joca Ramiro's leadership they defeat Zé Bebelo; later on, Riobaldo serves under João Ganhá until Joca Ramiro is betrayed and assassinated by Hermógenes; later still, Riobaldo serves under Medeiro Vaz, who unites Joca Ramiro's loyalists in a failed attempt to bring vengeance to the traitors Hermógenes and Ricardão, the so-called Judases (throughout the novel, the followers of a particular chief are known, as a collective, by their chief's name; hence the Mederiro Vazes, the Joca Ramiros, and so forth). Riobaldo then serves again under Zé Bebelo after Medeiro Vaz's death.[3] But in spite of Zé Bebelo's organizational skills and superior mind, the war is not going well. Zé Bebelo seems incapable of devising an effective strategy that will allow his forces to engage the Judases on their own terms. Riobaldo thus grows tired of Zé Bebelo's lack of effectiveness, his diversions and delays, and his affinity with landowners (such as Seó Habão) rather than with his own jagunços. Riobaldo eventually overthrows Zé Bebelo, with the presumptive help of the devil, with whom he may or may not have sealed a pact (this will be discussed later on).

This opens the third part of the novel: Riobaldo as the jagunço chief Urutú Branco (Urutú is the Portuguese name for a kind of poisonous snake). After some initial hesitation, Riobaldo carries out a brilliant tactical move: the crossing of the forbidding Liso do Suçuarão. Medeiro Vaz had already tried to cross this patch of badlands between Minas Gerais and Bahia in a previous stage of the war. It was a catastrophic failure that presumably cost him his life. The second time around, things go surprisingly well (with the help of the devil, it seems). This surprise feat allows Riobaldo to arrive undetected at Hermógenes's fazenda and to capture his wife. This forces Hermógenes to stop dodging Riobaldo's forces and engage (unlike the surprise the loyalist suffers in the Fazenda dos Tucanos) on Riobaldo's terms. Riobaldo defeats and personally executes Ricardão at the battle of Cererê Velho. This is the prelude to the climatic showdown, in which Riobaldo vanquishes Hermógenes at the battle of Paredão. But victory comes at a high price. During the knife fight that decides the struggle, Hermógenes and Diadorim kill each other. (After Diadorim's death Riobaldo discovers that Diadorim was, in fact, a woman.) Overwhelmed by pain at the death of his true (but never entirely acknowledged) love, Riobaldo quits his position as chief on the spot.

Upon the death of Selorico Mendes (which happens shortly afterward), he becomes the heir and the owner of two productive fazendas. He marries Otacilia (his girlfriend and fiancée throughout the novel), and remains a peaceful landowner for the rest of his life. It is in the twilight of this life, in a setting never completely elucidated (we have only glimpses of the conversation: why it happens, where it happens, what the relationship is between the interlocutors), that Riobaldo provides the *racconto* that composes *Grande Sertão*.

Grande Sertão is the culmination and reinvention of the Brazilian regionalist narrative. *Pedro Páramo*, published just a year before Guimarães Rosa's novel, did the same for the novel of the Mexican Revolution (itself a kind of regionalist novel), and Borges's short stories did something similar for the gaucho genre. As we examined previously in this book, outlaw violence is a defining topic in Brazilian (and Latin American) regionalist narrative, since the alternative space of sovereignty that the outlaw emblematizes is, from different political perspectives, the focal point of cultural preoccupations centered on the topic of the viability and legitimacy of the nation-state. In fact, as Antônio Candido (1970) has amply documented, the literary presence of backlands outlaw violence can be traced back to the very origins of postcolonial Brazilian narrative.

Even though it is part of the São Francisco river basin, the sertão of Guimarães Rosa is not the arid sertão of Euclides da Cunha's *Os sertões*, or of Amado's *Seara Vermelha*. In fact, it is not a desert in the literal sense of the term. "Sertão" here (as in many other regions of Latin America with the word *desierto*) does not refer necessarily to an area with low or extremely low amounts of annual precipitation. "Sertão" is shorthand for either a rural (usually, but not exclusively, cattle) frontier or for the land beyond the frontier.[4] In the frontier depicted in *Grande Sertão: Veredas* cities are irrelevant: no part of the action takes place in a city, or even in a village of any significance. In fact, the only villages that play any role in the narrative are Sucruiú, blighted by an epidemic of smallpox, and Paredão, scene of the last battle. There are no reliable means of communication in the novel (a letter sent by Nhorinhá, one of Riobaldo's lovers, takes eight years to reach its destination [Guimarães Rosa (1956) 1986, 82]), and human-built transportation infrastructure practically does not exist: there are no roads or railroads until late in Riobaldo's life. The river is the only significant means of transportation, but there are no large steamships—the only river crossing, that in which Riobaldo and Diadorim meet at the beginning of the novel, is in a canoe (87), and the central state has a very weak presence, if any at all.

In the novel there are also no judges or lawyers, no established police forces, no hospitals, jails, or public schools. There are military forces that fight the jagunços, but it is clear that they come from somewhere else, from outside the area. And they do not enjoy or aspire to a monopoly on violence. In fact, throughout the nineteenth and early twentieth centuries, police and military forces were often pawns in local and state conflicts; in that respect, they were not that different from jagunço bands. In the novel, police forces are allies of Zé Bebelo's irregulars or they act in coordination with them, so they are not a force acting independently from the colonels. On the other hand, the jagunço leaders are not outcasts, but prominent landowners.

In Guimarães Rosa's sertão the culture (material and otherwise) of the area is defined by cattle ranching, a veritable "leather culture" whose image is the Fazenda dos Tucanos, where everything, notes Riobaldo, is made out of leather or cattle by-products (Guimarães Rosa [1956] 1986, 291). The political, economic, and military life is centered on the fazenda. In fact, the landmarks in the territory are not cities, but fazendas: the bands of jagunços, in their marauding, either in pursuit of another band or in flight from other bands, go from fazenda to fazenda, where they enjoy a hospitality reminiscent of medieval or Homeric narratives. This itinerary is significant not only because fazenda landowners are the owners of the means of production (and hence the only ones able to provide resources in a region of extreme poverty), but also because the fazendas are the tissue of the social fabric in the area. The fazendeiros are the military chiefs (Joca Ramiro and Hermógenes are the most telling examples), but also the godfathers in charge of the welfare of their subordinates and their families, the judicial authorities, and the moral directors. They are also the economic and political link between the frontier and the central state (throughout the first century after independence, the central state and its party politics learned to coexist with this status quo, and not to fight it, since, informal as it was, it provided a degree of social stability to the area). The novel depicts (as is analyzed by Nogueira Galvão [1972]) the internecine struggles between these landowners/military leaders (the jagunço chiefs) and their retinues (the jagunços or *cabras*), and, above all, the demise of this order with the victory of Riobaldo, the only jagunço chief who reaches that position without being a landowner (he will become one, but, as explained above, through an inheritance, and not as a result of his martial feats).

The term "jagunço" in the novel is similar to that in Amado: the jagunço is an armed retainer of a landowner (to call the supporters of Conselheiro and Canudos jagunços was intended to portray them within known parameters, and the whole Canudos phenomenon as an attempt at a power grab). In Amado, however, the jagunços are the muscle that furthers the landowners' class interests (land accumulation), whereas in *Grande Sertão* the conflict is usually around revenge, honor, and supremacy. It is not primarily economic or political in nature. The fazendas are not a prize, and consequently they are not usually attacked, and the families are not party to the conflicts. (One prominent exception is Hermógenes's fazenda, but his is attacked because he is a traitor, so the rules of war do not apply to him.)

This brief summary and contextualization, while necessary, does not highlight those aspects of the novel that make it unique. The formal complexity, the linguistic experimentation, the rich intertext, the self-reflexive nature of the narrative, and the complexity of its worldview are what stand out first and foremost. And, not surprisingly, these are also the features that have received the greatest amount of critical attention. Building upon these rich contributions (in particular Idelber Avelar's [1994] brilliant Deleuzian reading of the novel, which moves away from the readings that posit it as a mere synthesis of different strains within Brazilian culture), I would like to examine a particular aspect of the novel that I consider key. I will argue here that the novel's self-referential bent is, to a significant degree, directed to the exploration of the paradoxes of violence. And the paradoxes of violence in the novel are, above all, the paradoxes of meaning in language.

The question of language, its meaning, and its uses revolves around the scene (or the lack thereof) of the pact with the devil. Riobaldo becomes a jagunço chief. In that capacity, he defeats Hermógenes (who also has the reputation of having made a pact, and who embodies the terrifying powers of unleashed entropic violence) and establishes law and order in the area. But if this triumph is due, as it seems, to the pact, then law is not what it seems. It is not the end of the entropic violence, but just another face of it.[5] Evil is not what is suppressed, or at least put at a distance from the new law (that of the nation-state), but it is the unacknowledged foundation of the law. And Riobaldo is not Hermógenes's nemesis, as he fancies himself to be, but his secret equal, as, more than once, he fears himself to be. Riobaldo's leadership, Riobaldo's violence, is what carries out the transition from one "legal" (albeit oral) order (the law of the sertão, represented by Joca Ramiro) to another legal (now written) order (the law of the nation-state). It is in this respect that we call Riobaldo's violence "sovereign." As such, as I will explain in more detail later, he is outside the law, since he does not fully belong to either of these two orders. Riobaldo can live with that. He cannot live, however, with the suspicion that he is acting on behalf of a darker sovereign, who in the novel is called by many, many names, as if the devil were the unleashed proliferating power of language itself. He is o demo, o capeta, o satanazim, o Que-Diga, o Tal, o Arrenegado, o Cão, o Cramulhão, o Indivíduo, o Galhardo, o Pé-de-Pato, o Cão, o Sujo, o Homem, o Tisnado, o Coxo, o Temba, o Azarape, o Coisa-Ruim, o Mafarro, o Pé-Preto, o Canho, o Duba-Dubá, o Rapaz, o Tristonho, o Não-sei-1e-diga, o que-nunca-se-ri, o Sem-Gracejos, o Outro, o diá, o Que-Não Há, o Capiroto, o Rabudo, o figura, o morcegão, o Careca, o tunes, o cramulhão, o debo, o carocho, o mal encarado, O-que-não-existe, o Sem-olho, O-que-Não-Fala, O-que-Não-Ri, o Muito-Sério, o cão extremo, o Coisa-Má, o Maligno, o Pai do Mal, o Tendeiro, o Manfarro, o Solto-Eu, o Ele, o Sempre-Sério, o Pai da Mentira, Lúcifer, Satanás, o Dos-Fins, o Austero, o Severo-Mor, o Tentador, o Anhangão, and o Arrenegado.

Allow me to frame, in a different manner, how the topic of language in the novel invokes the problem of the pact. Critics have frequently (and correctly) highlighted the creative aspect of Guimarães Rosa's language: Riobaldo

creates new words by substituting suffixes (e.g., *abominoso* instead of *abom-
inável*). Or he derives a nonexistent adjective from a noun, or creates a verb
from the enumeration of vowels ("o vento aeiouava"). He also coins words
by joining words from different languages, as if he were speaking in tongues.
(Nogueira Galvão [1972] provides the example of the name of a character, Moi-
meichego, made out of "Moi," "me," "ich," and "ego.") Speaking in tongues can
be a sovereignly bestowed gift of the Holy Spirit, as with the apostles at Pen-
tecost: "All of them were filled with the Holy Spirit, and they began to speak in
other languages as the Spirit enabled them" (Acts 2:4). This gift is bestowed
to the apostles to spread the new law, and it is given together with the power
to cast out devils from people. But speaking in tongues can also be a sign of
demonic possession. Who is to decide, in Riobaldo's particular case, if this is
a gift from God or from the devil? Nobody can, and even Riobaldo himself is
incapable of understanding the source (divine or demonic) of his power (if he
really has any, linguistic or otherwise).

The very beginning of *Grande Sertão: Veredas* provides a powerful indication that the relationship between language and violence will be a guiding
thread of the novel. The narrative, in fact, starts with a bang. A shot is heard,
and Riobaldo begins his monologue (and the novel) by explaining to his listener that there is no reason for alarm. The bang is a shot, but it is only target
practice. This explanation of the meaning of violence (or of the source of violence) moves immediately to the topic of the devil (Riobaldo's rifle has been
borrowed to kill a deformed calf that the locals have deemed to be the devil),
and from there to the topic that will occupy the entire novel: the existence
of the devil, and the possibility of making a pact with him. These are no idle
musings, of the kind that nostalgic old men who have seen better days like to
indulge in. Riobaldo returns obsessively to the topic of the pact with the devil,
because he needs to know if he made a pact with him or not: his soul and the
meaning of his entire life are at stake.

The novel is thus a long, tortuous attempt at interpretation (the narrative
aspect is, in fact, secondary to the interpretative one). The pact, indeed, may
or may not have been made. Riobaldo went to the proverbial crossroads, at a
location called Veredas Mortas. There he called for the devil, asking him to
appear. He had pictured the scene more than once. He waited. But the devil
never came. After a long and tiring night, during which nothing seemed to
have happened, Riobaldo returned to camp. But is it true that the devil never

appeared? Perhaps he did. Riobaldo provides plenty of indications that something may have happened there—not because he witnessed anything, but because things changed after that fateful night. This was not just a failed appointment in the middle of nowhere. The horses start to obey his will (Guimarães Rosa [1956] 1986, 378); he becomes more outspoken and assertive (373); he projects a forceful image that makes Seó Habão recognize him as a leader. Because of that, Seó Habão gives his own horse to Riobaldo as a present (379). As a leader of the group, Riobaldo is able to do what Medeiro Vaz could not: cross the Liso. And it is clear that somebody is helping him, since it is surprisingly easy for him to do. (Previously, it is mentioned that the Liso has hellish, demonic resonances [29, 37, 40, 41].) He also hears voices. And when after the bittersweet victory over Hermógenes he tries to go back to Veredas Mortas to renege on the pact, he discovers that the place does not exist (532).

So, the pact was made. But how did it happen? Riobaldo never saw or listened to the devil. He never signed the mythical document, and he never shed the necessary blood. This uncertainty is what moves the problem of the pact from a mere moral problem, regarding means and ends (although this problem will never disappear), to a problem regarding language, the dark powers or risks of human language, and the demonic potencies that inhabit it. Because if the pact was made but Riobaldo was unaware of it, it is not a moral problem, and not even a problem regarding the meaning of words, but it calls into question the very nature of language. Perhaps the pact was made but it was conducted in a language that Riobaldo was not able to grasp. But if he was not able to grasp the language in which the pact was made (even though he may have been speaking it), perhaps the pact was made before the trip to Veredas Mortas. Perhaps Riobaldo did not go to Veredas Mortas to seal the pact, since he may have sealed it at any time, anywhere, and not necessarily by invocations and rituals, but in everyday conversation. Perhaps he went to Veredas Mortas to try and frame the pact as an understandable human exchange, something that could be either accepted or rejected (whereas if he did not control the language in which the pact was sealed, he could not be sure of whether he was entering into the pact or not—this, as we will see, is the condition of human language, according to the novel).

Riobaldo suggests early on that becoming a jagunço entails some degree of complicity with the devil (Guimarães Rosa [1956] 1986, 3). So perhaps the pact was made when he became a jagunço. But he decided to become a jagunço out of love for the angelic (and unambiguously good) Diadorim. So it may be that, when one thinks one is doing good, speaking the language of love and virtue, in fact one is sealing the deal with the Other (*o Outro*). This opens up a somber perspective for Riobaldo. Perhaps going to the crossroads was not the sealing of the pact, but only the confirmation of the pact, and when one decides to sell one's soul to the devil, it's because, without knowing it, it has already been sold (30). But then, if this is the case, the pact is not a decision that humans can make, because, as Riobaldo states, "Everything is the pact" (273). Speaking is (or may be) an exposure to the possibility of the pact. If Riobaldo did make a pact with the devil, can he renounce it? How, and in which language? Since he does not recall making the pact, there is no traceable origin, no specific speech act that can be identified as the pact, so there is no way to renounce it. Or, to put it differently: to try to renounce the pact is to acknowledge that there is a pact, that the pact was made and that it is in force (this is what Riobaldo means when he says, "If you avoid something too much, you end up living with it" [2]).

And even more problematic still: even if it is possible, *should* he renounce the pact? As I mentioned, Riobaldo does not want to be a jagunço. He becomes one because of his attachment to Diadorim. At first he is in the gang only to be with him, and then because once he knows that Diadorim is Joca Ramiro's son, he wants vengeance for his death as much as Diadorim does. To a degree, Diadorim inspires the pact, since Riobaldo would not be a jagunço without him, let alone a jagunço chief. (We should remember that it is Diadorim who first tries to make Riobaldo a chief, when Medeiro Vaz dies. Riobaldo sternly and decisively refuses, and there is a standoff between the two [Guimarães Rosa (1956) 1986, 67], which is only resolved when a compromise candidate, Marcelino Pampa, is made chief [68].) But as Candido (1970, 63) rightly notes, Diadorim is an angelic figure (a warrior angel, "delicate and terrible in battle"). So the pact may have been God's work. By summoning the devil, Riobaldo may have enlisted the devil as an aide in a godly cause (killing Hermógenes, the son of the devil): "When one does not want to do something when God orders it, one does it when the devil asks for it" (Guimarães Rosa [1956] 1986, 35). The pact may have been a pact with God. Or it may have been a pact with the devil, who works for God. Or it may be that there is no difference between God and the devil. Perhaps the devil is another name for God, the lesser image that God needs to interact with humans. Riobaldo, indeed, suggests that humans

are creatures so debased that God can only work in them through the devil
(30). Conversely, humans can only see God under the guise of the devil (30).
God may be hidden or he may be ubiquitous, but he operates in invisible ways
(as is shown in the parable of the acid that acts unnoticed, but that dissolves
metal [15]).

This is perhaps the only way to understand some passages of the novel,
in which Riobaldo sees clearly that Hermógenes is a traitor. He warns Diadorim about this, but Diadorim dismisses his concerns (Guimarães Rosa
[1956] 1986, 153). Perhaps this is so because Diadorim knows that Hermógenes is ultimately doing God's work—like Judas in the drama of the Passion,
in Borges's "Tres versiones de Judas." (Candido [1970, 65] hints at this when he
mentions "A hora e vez de Augusto Matraga" as a precursor to *Grande Sertão:
Veredas*.) On the other hand, the idea that while you think you are doing God's
work you are in fact working for the devil is present in the anecdote of Valtei
and his parents (Guimarães Rosa [1956] 1986, 6). Riobaldo suspects this: to
long for good in an excessive fashion can be to long for evil (9). The opposite
may also be true, as the anecdote of Aleixo shows (5).

What then is the relationship between the pact and the novel? The novel is not
a consequence of the pact. It may be an extension of the pact. The novel has
a leitmotif: "To live is very dangerous." It is dangerous indeed, but not (or not
only) because in the sertão you are liable to get yourself killed by "a hot bullet
or a cold dagger" ("bala quente ou faca fria"), as the expression goes. There
is another risk. It is the risk that with every word there is the possibility (or
not) of a pact with the devil. This is shown in the parable of the squash. The
squash is there, but it is impossible to know whether it is the good one, which
nurtures, or the bad one, which kills. And it is not that a keen eye would be
able to decide whether it is one or the other. In fact, any species of squash can
change into the other, for no reason, and there is no way to know it (Guimarães
Rosa [1956] 1986, 4). There is no sign to distinguish good from evil. Or, to be
more precise, the signs collapse into indistinction: they may be signs or not.
And since "the sertão is as big as the world" (60), but at the same time "without
a place" (500), this is a risk that inhabits human language. Or, to put it differently, it is a ubiquitous fact that human language is potentially inhabited by
the devil. This potentiality *is* the devil.

If nobody knows what is being said when something is said (or even whether something is said at all, since even when nothing seems to be said, silence can be a form of assent, as evidenced by the fact that the pact may have been made without any words being uttered), then nobody knows who he or she is. Quelemén, a firm believer in Kardec's theories (Guimarães Rosa [1956] 1986, 9), convinces Riobaldo of the truth of reincarnation and notes that your son, your best friend, could have been (and in a way, still is) the reincarnation of your worst enemy in a previous life (5).

Riobaldo's monologue returns time and again to the question of the existence of the devil (as a precondition for the possibility of the pact). And he would like to find an answer to this problem in the law. He longs for all the powers that be to convene and declare that the devil, in fact, does not exist (Guimarães Rosa [1956] 1986, 8). But this will never happen. Even if it were to happen, human law (and the medium of human law is human language) does not apply to the devil. The devil is precisely what ruins human language (at the same time that he makes it possible). This is one of the ways in which we could understand the enunciation that the devil is the reverse of man (3), and that by himself, the devil has no existence. The devil is the "other side" of language. Riobaldo goes back to this on several occasions, but nowhere is it expressed better than when he says that the devil "does not have to be to exist. Since people know that he does not exist, it is precisely then that he is able to control everything" (48).[6]

Guimarães Rosa once said that the language he was looking for was the language that humankind spoke before the Tower of Babel (quoted in Reis 1997, 295). Indeed. But of course, this quest only prolongs post-Babelic confusion. Like speaking in tongues, the biblical reference should be invoked. Babel has less to do with language than with power (or with language as the locus or medium or tool of power). Babel is the scene of a challenge to God, and of a punishment that becomes the act of sovereign law, God's act of confusing languages. The law of God punished men's hubris, and the punishment confirmed the power of that law. But the punishment is also what makes God's law forever impossible for men to understand. From then on, any discussion among men about the law is futile, as well as urgent and essential. (Babel, one should remember, was not only a tower, but a city: the emblem of the human community.) "Babelic" does not refer to the many ways in which something can be (or cannot be) said, but to the emptiness (the disconnection between word and the law, a disconnection in which the law is forever affirmed) that lurks behind every single human word. It refers to the hollowing out of meaning that makes languages possible (and failed). So the law exists and it exists as the origin of human language. But it cannot be translated into human language. So there is no transcendent law (but, as in Kafka, there is a Law) that will reassure humankind, Riobaldo, of his transactions with the world.

Riobaldo would like us to believe (would like himself to believe) that he is talking about the past. He emphasizes time and again that now it is a different time, not only for him (youth is a time to be denied later on [Guimarães Rosa (1956) 1986, 15]), but also for the sertão in general, and that violence is a thing of the past. Banditry has ceased. Former jagunços beg for alms. People are ashamed to go to the cities dressed in leather. Even cattle have lost some of their former mettle (17). People are mellower, and soon killing will be unheard of (14). Now there are highways for cars, like the one the government is building (18), and railroads (10–11). Now Riobaldo reads hagiographies (7). (He used to read outlaw novels [333], or novels about power, sovereignty, and God-sanctioned violence.) He has women who pray for him (9). He would like an unequivocal conversion, a sign, like the apparition of the Holy Virgin in the sky, the way it happened to Joé Cazuzo (12–13). He conceives the idea of a City of God (like Canudos) (41). Indeed, Riobaldo is currently a landowner, a respectable person, not violent at all. But he became a landowner with the death of Selorico Mendes. This death occurs, suspiciously, very close to the time in which Riobaldo defeats Hermógenes. It leads us to think that Riobaldo becomes worthy of that inheritance when he becomes a jagunço chief. Thus, indirectly, the inheritance is achieved as a result of the pact.

As we saw, it is not clear that the pact was ever made. And if it was, it was made outside the language that Riobaldo speaks. Therefore, Riobaldo, even though he unendingly speaks about the pact, cannot really speak *about* the pact. On the contrary, the pact speaks through him. Since it was never signed (in a way that Riobaldo is aware of), it cannot be renounced, and hence it may still be valid and operating. Riobaldo seems to be consumed by the effort to deny that the pact was made (or, in contradictory fashion, that the devil even exists, like those, quoted by Freud, who said that Marco Polo had never been in China, and that there, he had desecrated the cross). But in that passion, the pact is still operating. That's one reason why Riobaldo's narrative is not a "life" (in which events are ordered according to a teleology, i.e., a meaning as a final cause) but flowing matter (*materia vertente*).

Riobaldo speaks. But is he speaking? Or is the devil speaking through him? Is what is being said the truth? I would argue that no good answer can be given. Riobaldo is in the same position as the narrator of Borges's story "La lotería de Babilonia," who tells of how the lottery in Babylon evolved from a trivial pursuit into the force that regulated the universe. Each human action was subjected to a growing (in fact an infinite) number of drawings. In fact, it was the result (unbeknownst to the agent of the action) of the lottery. The problem for us readers, or one of the problems, is the following: when we are reading the short story, and in spite of the fact that the narrator seems to be an exile, we never know if the story is about the lottery, or if the narration was decided *by* the lottery. We do not know if the lottery is the topic of the narration, told by a narrator worthy of our trust, or if the lottery is trying to hide (or to exaggerate) its own role in the life of the Babylonians. Or perhaps the lottery does not even exist.

In the same fashion, in "La Biblioteca de Babel" (and the use of the Babelic metaphor is significant here), we read a narrative by an anonymous librarian who speaks about his theories on the Library, his hopes, and his unshakable melancholy. But the librarian himself says that everything that can be said in the twenty-four orthographic symbols is already printed in the unending volumes of the Library. So two uncertainties (horrible certainties) arise: first, the librarian is not writing about the Library. The Library (nobody) is writing the librarian. It has written the librarian into existence eons before the actual librarian came to being. And second, we are not sure whether the language that the librarian speaks is our language, rather than an imperceptible (infinite) variation in which "library" means, as the librarian suspects it does, "whale" (and what would that mean, in the closed space of a Library?). Like the man of Babylon, and like the librarian, Riobaldo is speaking in and from a space that lacks any certainty regarding language. And nowhere is this space of neutrality better represented than in the scene in which Riobaldo becomes chief.

Riobaldo says of himself that he is different from everybody else (Guimarães Rosa [1956] 1986, 8). He also says that there were only two possible destinies for him: to become a jagunço chief or a priest—that is, to become a giver of the law or a reader of the Law (we already saw this option in Revueltas in the dyad Adán/Cristero priest). When he becomes chief, he acts like a true sovereign: like Moses, he climbs a mountain (Itabé de Pedra), while the other jagunços remain behind (387). Like Moses, he is the foundation of a new law. Like Moses, he leads an entire people with him toward a promised land (the inhabitants of Sucuiú [391]). But the sovereign moment, the moment of the covenant in which he becomes Moses, is an event that happens beyond the law; it is embedded in language, but beyond language. This event is the scene of his assumption of leadership. At the beginning of the novel, when we do not know much about the novel, he mentions (before we know that he is talking about himself) that Urutú Branco is a victim of destiny (10).

Let's recapitulate: Riobaldo's distrust and dislike of Zé Bebelo grows gradually. It starts with the initial fatigue with his "prose mentality" (Guimarães Rosa [1956] 1986, 276), and with Zé Bebelo's devotion to organizational minutiae, which sometimes renders him unable to see the big picture. This increases when Hermógenes's forces unexpectedly surround them in the Fazenda dos Tucanos. They have no way of escaping the siege through military might alone, so Zé Bebelo conceives the idea of sending letters to government officials. In these letters, he lets them know that were they to descend upon the fazenda they would get the catch of a lifetime. Riobaldo is not sure (in spite of Zé Bebelo's assurances) that this scheme is just a clever strategy to entrap the Judases and use the ensuing confusion to escape (289). Riobaldo fears that Zé Bebelo is betraying the gang. Although he does not use that opportunity to desert Zé Bebelo, a little while later Riobaldo loses faith when they end up wandering aimlessly through the sertão. In fact, they are lost (377), with no prospects of even catching Hermógenes. While resting at Seô Habão's fazenda, he fears not only that the forced idleness is bad for morale (377), but that they may quit the war entirely.

João Goanhá's arrival precipitates things. João Goanhá is of the same rank as Zé Bebelo, so theoretically he can dispute Zé Bebelo's leadership. Still groggy from sleep (João Goanhá and his party arrived unexpectedly, very early in the morning), Riobaldo asks, "Well, who is the chief now?" Everyone remains silent. Riobaldo realizes why: he himself has become, unexpectedly, the chief (Guimarães Rosa [1956] 1986, 384). The transfer of power (later explicitly acknowledged by Zé Bebelo) happens in an interval outside of time, and during which nobody is present (even though everybody is physically there). Riobaldo, whose question has (or is intended to have) a different meaning, is not present (even though he is there), since something is said without his intent. This is an emblematic scene, I would argue, since the problem of language is indeed the problem of the sovereign and the law (Agamben [1995] 1998, 21). The pact is what remains outside the law, outside language (the void of the misunderstanding), because it is what incessantly ruins language and law (but at the same time, it is what defines language and law). The devil inhabits language in the power of misunderstanding.

The devil inhabits the infinite (but invisible) distance between interlocutors, because he destroys, or makes precarious, and even dangerous, the illusion of mutual understanding. Thus the devil simultaneously destroys the human community (because the illusion of understanding is essential to dialogue and to interaction) and creates it (the reposition of the illusion of understanding recreates a community). But the scene of Riobaldo's ascent into leadership shows that the community is based on a demonic misunderstanding.

Riobaldo's question is interpreted as a challenge. But nobody utters that challenge, since it is not Riobaldo's will that poses the challenge. The devil does. It remains an enigma why Riobaldo does not clarify what he was "saying." Not only that, but once he realizes that his question was a challenge, he kills the two men who opposed his bid for power. This is more than just a quick mind at work, or an uncanny ability to read and grasp an opportunity. Language has, neutrally (or diabolically), operated a distribution of bodies, of hierarchies, and it is up to everyone to play the part. When he asks who the chief is now, he is not yet chief. But between the question and the lack of an answer an event occurs in which he has already become chief. His becoming-chief is a neutral event, an event at which nobody is present, but whose consequences everybody experiences. Nobody is present, I said. The paradox would be to give this Nobody an impossible density, in the same way that at the beginning of "Las ruinas circulares" it is said that "Nobody [*Nadie*] saw him." Later on we become aware that this Nobody is the god of fire. In the novel, Nobody is the devil. But not as a "citizen"—as "o Que-Não Há," or, as William Blake put it, as "Nobodaddy": the origin that ruins the very idea of an origin.

ELEVEN

AN ABUNDANCE OF HATS AND A SCARCITY OF HEADS

On *La guerra del fin del mundo*

*The laws of a city can never function well where no one is afraid, nor can
an army be sensibly controlled, when it has not the protection of fear and
respect. . . . Know that when a man feels fear and shame, then he is safe. . . .
Let some terror be established where it is needed, and let us not suppose that
if we act according to our pleasure we shall not in time pay for our actions
with our pain.*

SOPHOCLES, *AJAX*

"I FORESEE THAT mankind will resign itself more and more fully to
more and more horrendous undertakings; soon there will be nothing but
warriors and brigands" (Borges 2005a, 121). So reflects Dr. Yu Tsun in the
deposition (dictated, reread, and signed by him) that composes the body of
Borges's short story "El jardín de los senderos que se bifurcan." Tsun is a man
of both classical and modern education. He is an educated Chinese man, the
last scion of an ancient family, stained by an ancestor of disreputable memory; he is a former professor of German at the Hochschule in Tsingtao. The
dark pessimism of the phrase that I just quoted is not the idle posturing of a
scholar from a family in decline. By "horrendous undertakings," he is referring
to his own actions as a German spy in wartime England and the murderer of

the Sinologist Stephen Albert, the man for whom he could not feel anything but gratitude.

For Yu Tsun, then, the future has two exclusive emblems: warriors and bandits (*guerreros* or *bandoleros*). Spies and murderers (and treacherous ones, shooting when the victim's back is turned) like Yu Tsun will be the forerunners of that future, or one of the shapes that that future will take. One can understand the first of those emblems (the warriors) since Borges is writing about a minor episode in a total war (the First World War), in 1941, that is to say, during the darkest days of another total war: the vastest, the bloodiest, the most traumatic of all total wars in the history of the world (not the bloodiest war *tout court*—only the bloodiest in its class). The mention of the other emblem (the bandits) is perhaps more difficult to understand. At least on the Western front, the one that Yu Tsun knows and is concerned about, the First World War seemed very distant from any kind of banditry. Unlike the factions in the (strictly contemporary) Mexican Revolution, the Russian Revolution, or the civil war in Republican China, the First World War appeared to be the climax of the best and worst of the scientific bureaucratic rationality that animated the ascent of Western modernity (of course, we had to wait until the Second World War to really witness that climax).

In the canonical works that narrate the First World War, such as *Le feu: Journal d'une escouade* (Henri Barbusse, 1916), *Stahlgewittern* (*Storm of Steel*, Ernst Jünger, 1920), and *Im Westen nichts Neues* (*All Quiet on the Western Front*, Erich Maria Remarque, 1929), the impact of the narrative is usually predicated upon the contrast between shining, cold steel, and suffering (if not rotten) flesh; the contrast between the glare of the explosions and the dullness of the trenches' mud; the contrast between the overwhelming, impersonal, and oftentimes inscrutable bureaucratic machine that directs the war and the ill-used body of the foot soldier. In contrast to the open space of bandit narratives, First World War narratives tend to be defined by the enclosed (or labyrinthine, or under siege) space of the trenches. Futurism and expressionism celebrated the war but, again, the aesthetic aspects worth celebrating tended to be linked to the technical or organizational aspects (the speed of planes, the unstoppable advance of tanks, explosions that lit the sky). Furthermore, the modern total war was (or could be) horrendous, but it was understandable, at least for us, since total war was the climax and the *reductio ad absurdum* of modern reason, and of the nation-state as the modern political and cultural synthesis par excellence.

"Banditry," on the other hand, does not signal to the present or the future as a nightmare of reason, but to what escapes reason: a present or a future that has ceased to be recognized as essentially linked to the peculiar (and fleeting) human avatar that the nation-state and its subjects represent.[1] The banditry that Yu Tsun alludes to does not seem to define, necessarily, a future mode of waging war (even though the Islamic State, the Taliban, the goons of the "Donetsk Popular Republic," and the pirates of the Horn of Africa seem to fulfill that prophecy). Banditry seems to allude to a paradoxical relationship between violence and identity, a relationship in which violence is not the barbarian past of a race, ritualized under the form of tyrants, criminals, and psychopaths; nor the future, under the form of terrorists, paramilitary gangs, and gangs of inconceivable or shameful objectives. "Banditry" is the name for that somber memento where the links between identity and violence are (and always have been) intimate, but at the same time become, for us, impossible to understand.

That is, strictly, the case of Yu Tsun. Treason and murder are the acts through which he loses his own identity: he kills Albert, a man whom he recognizes as his better, the man who revealed to him the secret of his lineage, and who in some way returned his lineage to him, since it removed the badge of infamy that weighed upon it. By killing Albert, he becomes an abject being: he is not only a murderer, but mainly an ungrateful man. However, without the ingratitude and the betrayal, that revelation would never have happened, since he would not have gone looking for Albert in the first place. Embracing the role of traitor to the last (not running away from Madden, but going to Albert's house, killing him, and thus faithfully transmitting the message to his bosses in Berlin) is what allows him to reconcile himself both with his past (it is in the run-up to the murder, and somewhat by chance, that Albert reveals the secret of the labyrinth to Yu Tsun) and with Germany (for a moment, Albert is Goethe). Writing—the deposition before the law—is born of that act in which Yu Tsun loses himself, at the same time that he finds himself. Writing is the trace of that paradox, where Yu Tsun narrates his most abject moment, and the most exalted moment of his life. It is not the world of horse cavalcades in the plain or in the mountains, of open-air bravery, but an undecidable position before the law, where the individual comes into being and loses itself.[2] This is, as we analyzed in chapter 6, the experience of the melancholic outlaw.

This duplicity reappears in Borges in the most unexpected of places: "La Biblioteca de Babel." There, the librarian's despair before the evidence that the knowledge that the Library houses is total, but that it is impossible to access that knowledge, degenerates into acts of violence that hint at the imminent extinction of the librarian's race: "Epidemics, heretical discords, pilgrimages that inevitably degenerate into banditry, have decimated the population. . . . Perhaps superstition and fear mislead me, but I suspect that the human race—the only one—is about to become extinct" (Borges 2005a, 505).[3] Banditry, again. But in the Library there are no king's highways, or anything to rob. Robbing or destroying books is a futile exercise, as the librarian notes, in a Library that is presumably infinite. "Banditry" (if we pass over the inherent uncertainty about the meaning of any given word in the Library) can only be a metaphor for entropy, a symptom of a form of the end that denies the Library, or that perhaps brings about the coming of its secret destiny. Since the Library is utterly indifferent to human destiny (which it predates, and which it will survive), the extinction of the human race is the true coming into being of the Library, where the neutrality of language will shine (although it will shine for no one, since none will be left to witness it) in its neutral splendor. And is precisely in this melancholic statement (humankind is degenerating into suicides or bandits) that the short story finds its condition of possibility, or at least its need: "The methodical act of writing distracts me from the present condition of humankind" (505): to narrate the end of humankind is a way to keep it at bay—understanding, of course, that that end is already narrated in one (or, in fact, in many) volumes in the Library. In one of them, it is narrated in the exact same fashion as in "La Biblioteca de Babel."

In a very different format (that of a vast war-and-adventure novel),[4] Mario Vargas Llosa's *La guerra del fin del mundo* (1981) visits the same problems. Vargas Llosa's fictional retelling of the story of Canudos remains for many his most ambitious and accomplished literary enterprise. It was an instant classic and an enduring best-seller.[5] *La guerra del fin del mundo* tells the story of Canudos.[6] But as one of the characters in the novel observes, "Canudos" does not name a story, but an infinite, ever-expanding, ever-bifurcating tree of stories (Vargas Llosa 1981, 433).[7] We can group these stories, or the novel's characters, into two categories, noting that they seem to be a fulfillment of sorts of Yu Tsun's prophecy: warriors and bandits, on the one hand, and intellectuals on the other. Warriors are the peasants who join Canudos's pious cause before or during the fight to die for the true faith, among the faithful; they are the cangaceiros who find God (Pajeú, João Abade, João Grande, Pedrão, Joaquim Macambira); they are the bandits affiliated with the landowners, and the ones who can be considered the "real" jagunços even though the novel— and history—calls all of Conselheiro's followers jagunços, in order to delegitimize the movement. They are the soldiers and officers (of the state police, the state militia, and the federal army) who fight under Lieutenant Pires Ferreira, Major Febronio do Brito, Colonel Moreira César, and finally under General Ártur Oscar, the one who will finally win the war for the republic.

On the other hand, there are the intellectuals, whose destinies Canudos impacts in vastly different ways. There are sertanejo intellectuals, like the Dwarf, a consummate storyteller whose repertoire includes stories that date back to the Middle Ages (like the *História do Imperador Carlos Magno e dos doze pares de França*, a story that also figures prominently in *Grande Sertão: Veredas*). There is Father Joaquim, the conduit between Canudos and the outside world during the bitter siege that ends with the fall of Canudos, and the León de Natuba, the misshapen creature who faithfully records Conselheiro's every word and every act, in order to add a "fifth Gospel to the Bible." There are also urban intellectuals, with different formations and diverging political beliefs: the anarchist activist and amateur phrenologist Galileo Gall, who dreams of reaching Canudos because he fancies that Canudos is the spearhead of world revolution; the Baron of Cañabrava, the embodiment of the very idea of the nineteenth-century politician and intellectual, an aristocrat whose political career and personal life Canudos damages beyond repair; Nina Rodrigues and Honorato Nepomuceno de Albuquerque, criminologists of the Bahian school commissioned to examine Conselheiro's exhumed head; and the nearsighted journalist, a talented pen for hire and wannabe decadentist writer who becomes the improbable center of this constellation of characters.

The notion that the novel is a meditation on literature and the destiny of the modern intellectual has been examined (see, for example, Elmore 1997). My reading is consistent with this perspective, but with a very specific emphasis. I will dwell on three or four characters and on three specific episodes in which these characters are involved. I propose that these episodes enact possible (and divergent) destinies of the modern intellectual when faced with outlaw violence. By "outlaw violence" I am referring to that of the Conselheiro's jagunços, to that of the cangaceiros who lead the jagunços in the battlefield, and that of the landowners' *capangas* (armed men), who, even though they are fighting against Conselheiro, following their patrons (the colonels), nevertheless belong to the same cultural universe as their enemies, and understand violence in the same fashion. The "face-to-face" is not an accident, an anomaly, or the random intersection of two parallel universes; rather, this contact defines the intellectual's social mission and relevance. The medium of this contact is, in all three cases, a head, a living or decapitated head. It is the head of Conselheiro, separated postmortem from his body, examined by the Bahian scientists and then sunk into the sea. It is the heads of Barbadura, a cangaceiro, and of Tiburcio, a capanga, erroneously read by Galileo Gall. And finally, it is the head of Moreira César, decapitated by the jagunços. In this last head the nearsighted journalist finds the fatal call of destiny.[8]

The first head that occupies my analysis is that of Conselheiro, and its destiny as narrated in the novel. The triumphant leaders of the fourth expedition are not satisfied with taking Canudos, with destroying the "Troy of mud" (da Cunha [1902] 1995) and setting it ablaze, or with slaughtering the few survivors with daggers (thus denying them salvation in the afterlife).[9] They need more. They want more. With dogs (known embodiments of Satan) they torture the Beatito, Conselheiro's closest aide, in order to find out where the dead leader is buried. They exhume the corpse and take some body measurements. The photographer Flávio de Barros captures the now universally known picture. They then cut off his head and send it to Salvador, so that it can be studied (Vargas Llosa 1981, 432). But the report by Nina Rodrigues is irritatingly brief, and it tersely states that the cranium shows no evident abnormality.[10] However, things cannot stand like this. Honorato Nepomuceno de Albuquerque writes a dissenting report, in which he concludes that "that skull was typically brachycephalic according to the classification by Retzius, the Swedish naturalist, with tendencies to short-mindedness and to extreme single-mindedness (for example, fanaticism). And, on the other hand, the cranial curvature was exactly the same as that mentioned by the wise Benedikt in epileptics that, according to Samt, had the missal in their hands, the name of God on their lips, and the stigmata of crime and brigandage in their hearts" (433). Once the exams are finalized, and the disagreement between these two verdicts established, the authorities sink the head in the Atlantic, at the exact midpoint between the San Marcelo Fort and Itaparica Island.

The state (under the guise of its lettered staff) carries out two crucial procedures on Conselheiro's head: first it reads it, and then it writes on it. In the morphology of the skull, Albuquerque reads the deleterious influence of both environment and heritage. By doing this, he is able to territorialize the entire Canudos phenomenon, a territorialization that is a spectacular way to reinstate the epistemological privilege accorded to the state as the place where all instances of the social are symbolically totalized and resumed. In the novel (in the path of da Cunha's *Os sertões*), Canudos is not only the military scandal of the defeat of urban modernity and of a modern military armed with European weaponry at the hands of dispossessed peasants led by rural bandits. It is an epistemological scandal, for which there is no adequate narrative.[11] More than necessary, this scandal makes all of the versions of monarchist or British conspiracies imperative. (Proving these versions correct would make Canudos a war between equals, which, regardless of which side won, would keep the prestige of modern institutions—and of modernity itself—intact.) In fact, the Jacobin plot to produce a box of British rifles headed for Canudos, as part of the foreign aid to the fanatics—a plot that costs Gall (conveniently framed as a British agent) his life—is barely fictional, if at all. Many stories like this, involving boxes or bottles with suspicious substances, were reported in the newspapers of the time.

To read the head of Conselheiro, and then to rewrite it by stating beyond doubt that Canudos was born fully armed out of that head, like Pallas Athena out of Zeus's (or like the son from the magician in Borges's "Las ruinas circulares"), reinstates a dominant narrative that revolves around the degeneracy of the inhabitant of the backlands. It takes Canudos away from history and politics, reducing it to an event of criminal psychiatry, a "natural" anomaly (the contradiction is glaring, but still reassuring), and a formless residue of history. The divergence between the reports by Nina Rodrigues and Albuquerque, and the fact that the verdict of banditry has to be confirmed at all costs, shows the state's will to truth (Nietzsche), which is far more powerful and enduring in imposing a version of reality than Epaminondas's still-crude concoction of a British agent by using the red hair of Gall, or the willful self-deception of those who "saw" the redcoats prowling the sertão, and the supposed ravages of advanced weaponry (when in fact it was exactly the opposite).

The other procedure performed on Conselheiro's head is more complex, and involves the manner of its disposal. Vargas Llosa's account (the sinking of the head in the sea) differs from the historical record. In reality, after the head was severed, "it was displayed on a pike and subsequently taken to the coast, where it was held high at the front of a military parade for all to see and finally given to Nina Rodrigues to be examined for congenital abnormalities, with the results that we know. The head remained a curiosity on display at the Medical Faculty until the building burned down at the beginning of the twentieth century" (Levine 1992, 184). The novel is rife with these divergences, condensations, and expansions (see Bernucci 1989). It is highly significant, however, that such a crucial event, such a well-known fact involving the most important character in the Canudos drama, should be rewritten. This is especially striking since what really happened already provides a wide array of symbols: the forces of civilization parading a head on a pike, the "real" city (Salvador, as opposed to the monstrous city, Canudos) as the stage for such a ghastly spectacle, and a modern army parading in front of the decomposed head of a "bandit chief." Vargas Llosa chose to omit these events entirely from his account.

In the novel, the head is thrown into the sea with the purpose of making it unreachable, thus consigning it to oblivion (in reality, the head was given to Nina Rodrigues for precisely that reason [Nina Rodrigues 1939, 131]).[12] But the location seems to be no secret. The last appearance of the Baron in the novel shows him witnessing, in awe and disbelief, how pilgrims row or sail to the place where the head was sunk, and then throw flowers as funereal offerings (Vargas Llosa 1981, 508). And what is more important, the head is not sunk in an undetermined, random location in the open sea (unlike the corpse of Osama bin Laden, for example, making it effectively impossible to locate). Rather, it is placed within constant view of the city, at a point exactly halfway between the fort and the island, at the entrance to the bay, and thus practically in the path of all ships entering or leaving the port.

A suspicion arises: perhaps the head of Conselheiro was not hidden at all. Perhaps the purpose was for it to endure the same fate as other famous outlaw corpses. Bandits are not merely executed. They are quartered, their body parts hanged, nailed to trees in crossroads, in squares, in markets, at the entrances of towns, and, very prominently in the Brazilian case, photographed or made part of traveling exhibits to ensure maximum publicity.[13] The head of Conselheiro is not merely thrown into the sea. It certainly has to be unreachable, but it has to remain right there, invisible but always in plain sight, in order to be a constant reminder of what must always be remembered-as-already-forgotten (to use Anderson's [(1983) 1996, 204] expression): the material and epistemological violence that originates and sustains the nation-state. It is hidden, because "civilization" at the dawn of the twentieth century is supposed to have confined these spectacles to the past (or to the limits of the penitentiary).[14] It is always in plain sight, because civilization is animated by the same lust for revenge as its imaginary foe, banditry.

I would call this (in this case perpetual) display of the body of the vanquished enemy a reassertion of elite hegemony, the theater of the law. In this theater, the head of Conselheiro is deprived of his own voice, his irrecoverable voice that set the backlands ablaze. And it becomes a silently talking corpse, the enduring memory of violent state retribution, and the warning, the promise, of more violence to come. The military massacre, and the burning and razing of Canudos, are only part of the preliminary violence necessary to exorcise the "real" threat of Canudos, the symbolic menace of a violence whose origin and regime are incomprehensible (like the threat of ISIL, an organization that does not threaten the territorial integrity of the United States or its economic might, but rather threatens what the United States and the West represent—it is in this sense that ISIL is an "existential threat").[15] To direct (or to participate in) that theater of the law, as a form of exorcism of outlaw violence, is one of the destinies of the modern intellectual, and one of its meanings: the intellectual as the reluctant yet willing instrument of the definition and suppression of the enemies of the state.

A contrasting destiny of the modern intellectual is embodied in Galileo Gall. Gall is an anarchist, a writer, and a professional revolutionary, a sworn enemy of the state. And he shares his profession as a reader of skulls with the criminal anthropologists of Bahia. Galileo Gall is not his real name. He adopted the last name as an alias, taken from Franz Joseph Gall, one of the creators of phrenology. (The political statement behind the adoption of "Galileo" as his first name hardly needs to be explained.) The novel contains two scenes of Gall's head reading. Both of the heads that Gall reads belong to subjects of outlaw violence: the guide and capanga Rufino, who is hired to guide Gall and the weapons given by Epaminondas to Canudos (Vargas Llosa 1981, 62), and the cangaceiro Barbadura, whom Gall encounters en route to Canudos (198).

Unlike the criminologists of Bahia, Gall operates without the material and symbolic guarantees provided by the state. That is, he reads heads while his own head is on the line. (This is more than a mere play on words: Epaminondas needs his head—his head of fiery red hair, something as rare in Bahia as anarchists—to present as proof that the English, in collusion with the supporters of the deposed Braganza, are sending weapons to Canudos.) Furthermore, he is a staunch supporter of Canudos and he dies trying to support Canudos's cause. But his problem is, to a point, the same as that of the Bahian criminologists: how to interpret outlaw violence from the viewpoint of modern knowledge. As an anarchist, Gall has a different idea of modernity, and he does not want to suppress premodern violence altogether; rather, like Amado (*Seara Vermelha*), Neruda (*Joaquín Murieta*), and the poet friend of Naún Briones (*Polvo y ceniza*), he wants to transform it into modern revolutionary violence. He is an apostle of modernity and, like the Bahian criminologists, he cannot relate to Canudos or to backlands violence in general without exerting some kind of epistemological violence. In his case, he has to interpret Canudos as a case of "primitive rebellion" (I borrow the term from Hobsbawm [(1959) 1965], but I consider it apt in Gall's case), and as a revolutionary movement that has no self-awareness of its true nature and of its place in history. Of course, the jagunços are firmly placed in a different history, one of divine trial and posthumous redemption, the final test before the impending Second Coming. Gall is not like Father Joaquim, formerly an amiable man with readings and virtues as well as vices, who hearkens to the call to Canudos and becomes a convert, a warrior, and a martyr. In all cases, he is a follower of that man who showed him the light. Gall fancies himself the likely leader of the movement, who knows about his prospective followers what they do not know about themselves.

But Gall never delivers the weapons that he sought to deliver. He never mobilizes the masses in support of Canudos. He does not even reach Canudos. His actual role is that of a mere commentator and interpreter of what he never really sees, writing letters to a French radical publication (*l'Étincelle de la révolte*) that, unbeknownst to him, ceased to exist years before. This ghostly dialogue with nonexistent readers via a defunct outlet is a fitting and melancholic emblem of his destiny. But Gall's problem goes beyond failure. For a true revolutionary, failure, defeat, is one of the conceivable destinies (and not necessarily the worst one). The problem is that he who wanted to be a guide for the sertanejos dies lost in the sertão. Without Rufino, he loses his bearings in the myriad tracks of the caatinga, alternately bone dry and impassably muddy. But above all, he is lost in the web of backlands violence, a violence that he tried and failed to reduce to "class" violence. After killing two assassins sent by Epaminondas to kill him (at this point, Gall realizes that he has been used by Epaminondas as a disposable pawn, as he is to be killed in possession of the weapons to show how the British and monarchical conspirators are aiding Canudos), Gall rapes Jurema (Rufino's wife) and thus breaks his vows of revolutionary chastity. From this point on, his pilgrimage to Canudos (without the weapons) becomes an escape from Rufino's vengeance. Gall, who thought that he had understood Rufino sufficiently when he read his skull (Vargas Llosa 1981, 62) and that he was able to establish a distance between the rational being—himself—and one dominated by "Marvelousness" (62), ends his life as Rufino's equal, in a fight to the death inscribed in the oral code of honor and vengeance that carries both away.[16] His is not a march toward the future, but an uncertain escape from the past. And we must remember that Gall has been, up to that moment, the man with no concerns about the past, and not contaminated by the past.

Gall represents the second possibility of the modern intellectual: the man who speaks truth to power, who opposes the state, and who fancies a relationship of knowledge and solidarity with the world of peasant violence, about which, in reality, he knows very little. This ignorance costs him his life. Gall is not a caricature (none of the intellectuals in the novel are): he is brave, incorruptible; he has devoted his life to a cause that has condemned him to live without a land, without a home, without love. And he loses his life in a brave (but fruitless) effort to reach the place where he thinks his life (made up of failed attempts, approximations, partial or fleeting successes) will achieve its climax. It is not difficult to imagine why, in 1981, this depiction of the revolutionary intellectual (which is, to a certain extent, also an homage) met with almost unanimous rejection by the Left.[17]

The third destiny is embodied in the shortsighted journalist. As a field correspondent for the republican *Journal de noticias* (edited by the unscrupulous

Epaminondas Gonçalves), he is embedded with the third military force sent to quash Canudos. He becomes Moreira César's shadow even though the colonel openly despises him, and has many reasons (in his mind) to do so. Above all, he is despised due to the fact that he is an intellectual, a dangerous but necessary species, according to the colonel.[18] He has many physical and moral handicaps: he is ungainly, he is weak, he wears extremely thick glasses, and he is impaired by allergies that make him sneeze constantly.[19] The two men, however, establish a strange bond. And this happens not only because of the journalist's endurance of the forbidding trek and his determination to reach Canudos, which surprises Moreira César. It is also perhaps because he recognizes that both men represent certain ideals related to modernity: the autonomy of literature, and the national-statist rationality as the exclusive affiliation (and pathway for social organization), respectively.[20]

The journalist follows the expedition, not as a convinced republican, but as an artist: he wants to be close to Moreira César because of the thrill of being close to a celebrity of mythological stature (Vargas Llosa 1981, 140). He dreams of being Brazil's Oscar Wilde, and like Wilde (or better yet, like Dorian Gray), he lives chasing new experiences outside of his comfort zone: drugs, *candomblé*, the bohemian life. Military life and the thrills of war and gore are thought of as another edgy experience. By doing this, he intends to embody the ideal of a decadentist. And he seems to be fulfilling this desire to his heart's content. When Moreira César has an epileptic seizure, the journalist is there (194). He is also there when the colonel—forced by epilepsy to accept the hospitality of the Baron in Calumbí—clashes with his host, and the journalist obviously enjoys the symbolism of the moment (the twentieth century facing the nineteenth) (209). The failed assault on Canudos is narrated from his perspective (and as I will explain shortly, the visual metaphor is crucial). And when Moreira César is mortally wounded, the journalist not only witnesses the event, but is in charge of helping during the surgery that tries to save the colonel's life (305). He is even in charge of putting the colonel's last will on paper (307).

Let's go back to part 3, chapter 7, of the novel. The inconceivable has happened. The third expedition sent to quash Canudos has been shamefully defeated, and Moreira César has died, along with many other officers. The expedition, organized with European discipline and technology (in which Moreira César was a fanatical believer), has become a terrorized, amorphous mass in flight (Vargas Llosa 1981, 323–24). And the jagunços will give no quarter to the military during its long retreat back to its rearguard base. At a particular moment in the novel (which constantly alternates among different viewpoints) we learn the fate of the shortsighted journalist. With the defeat of the army, he is lost in the no-man's-land between the army in flight and the circle of fire and piety of Canudos. This risk to his physical integrity is more than compensated for by the privileged opportunity to see the battle (or, rather, the flight) as nobody else can see it (323–24).[21] In fact, he experiences the entire scene of the defeat as an opium dream: he remains lucid, distant, and almost totally in control (327). While walking with Father Joaquim, just snatched from the jaws of Moreira César's revenge, he contemplates, without much emotion, a horrid spectacle: the jagunços decapitating the dead, collecting the heads in bags, and later displaying them on pikes (326).

Unexpectedly, he sees something that will change his life: he takes a close look at one of the heads that is crawling with flies. There is no doubt: it is the head of Moreira César (327). Distracted and startled by this discovery, destiny catches up to him in the rather humble form of an allergic sneeze. The convulsion of the sneeze makes his glasses fall and break (327). Until the end of the war, he will be almost blind, and he will be in Canudos, living off charity, overwhelmed by fear and uncertainty. The simultaneity of a horrible sight (that of the head) and horrible sight (his extreme nearsightedness) is not mere chance. The two events are causally related (although it is a symbolic causality that operates outside of time). The sight of Moreira César's head is a negative illumination that robs the journalist of all the guarantees upon which he has based his identity.

The journalist, blinded, has to be taken to Canudos. He will be one of the few survivors of the subsequent massacre. Furthermore, he will be at the very center of the events. He is lodged in the arms depot of the jagunços, and because of this, he is close to all of the important characters at the very center of a defining event in Brazilian history: the Vilanova brothers, João Abade, Pajeú, João Grande, the León de Natuba, the Beatito, and Pedrão. For some inexplicable reason, he even commands the attention of Conselheiro himself. Had the papers of the León de Natuba survived, or had he been able to keep writing until the very end, the nearsighted journalist would have been a secondary, although memorable, character in the New Gospel. He is the undeserving recipient of a huge, albeit enigmatic, favor: the authorization to leave Canudos before its fall, granted by Conselheiro himself almost *in articulo mortis* (it is not quite clear how Conselheiro even knows about him).

But unlike his experience with Moreira César, he can no longer see or understand anything. Canudos is for him only an amorphous fog pervaded by terror (of the soldiers as well as the jagunços), and, later, by the unexpected happiness of desperate love.[22] The journalist went to Canudos in search of experiences, which were to be attributes that would legitimize his becoming a superior man of letters: Canudos was supposed to be a raw experience transformed into narrative material, according to preexisting aesthetic and ideological codes. (This is significant: had he not lost himself in Canudos, the only "authorized" testimony of the campaign would have been military dispatches and reports, and, above all, his articles and chronicles written prior to his arrival at Canudos, which sported a cavalier ignorance.) The journalist goes from one form of ignorance to another: the ignorance of one who has not seen, to the ignorance of one who has been blinded by what he has seen.

He does have experiences: he finds love, he finds history, he finds terror (in its double meaning: as uncontrollable fear of death, and as avenging republican fury), he finds passion (religious as well as intellectual), and he finds sacrifice. He has, in fact, many more experiences than he would have cared to. But one of these experiences (the one that defines the others) is the opaque realization that the whole event of Canudos is, for him, impossible to understand or depict. The codes that have sustained his practice as a writer (and "writer" is his entire identity, as shown by the fact that he does not have a name, but is referred to only as "the journalist") are now irrelevant.

Why is the decapitated head the portal to this experience? The desecration of the corpse and the spectacular display of the head on top of a pike is a form of writing. The thrust of the state is to make that writing "natural," or at least legitimate. But Moreira César's head has an impure origin. It is the ominous writing of those who do not write. It is the performance of the ominous law of a society without a state. But the head of Moreira César is also terrifying because of what it says about the journalist himself, about the civilization that underwrites him. The corpse of Moreira César is decapitated and its head displayed. The corpse of Conselheiro is decapitated and its head displayed, although the theater of the law is carried out in a more inconspicuous fashion. It is clear that the destinies of both heads mirror or echo each other. This is not unheard of, since the countertheater of the poor responded to the theater of the law, as E. P. Thompson (1975) first, and Anton Blok (1998) and Ranajit Guha ([1983] 1999) later, documented and analyzed. In this dynamic, insurgents (bandits, urban mobs, etc.) deliberately mirror (in an inverted or transgressive fashion) the practices of the state (the contemporary decapitations in Mexico and Syria are telling examples).[23]

But in *La guerra del fin del mundo* things are more complicated, because the "original" theater belongs to the jagunços. They are the ones who display the head of Moreira César. State retribution comes second, and therefore, the state's theater of the law is a grim mimic of the jagunço law, and the dynamic ceases to be that between law and outlaw and becomes a dynamic between two forms of vengeance, of outlaw retribution, that is intended to purge the social body of the threat but that makes the threat more permanent by installing it at the center of state actions. This dynamic also appears in the act of burning: the mirrored events of the burning of Calumbí and the later burning of Canudos (Vargas Llosa 1981, 184).

In the scene of the examination of Conselheiro's death, the body of the bandit is written by the state as a kind of pedagogy of terror (and in order to punctuate a self-legitimating narrative). In the episode with Moreira César's head, the body of the state representative is written by the bandit. This writing pollutes and destroys the identity of those associated with the state. But if this is really the case, the jagunços claim an epistemological privilege, and the journalist, whose practice has always been put under the economic and cultural guarantees of the state, has always been at the service of a form of barbarism that does not speak its name. This is why, even though Canudos and Bahia are supposedly contrasted as premodernity versus modernity, or civilization versus barbarism, things are not really quite so. Canudos is sustained by a dedicated millenarian fervor. But it is an eminently rational community: well organized, self-sustaining, and measured in its appetites and in its expressions. The bandits in the novel have truculent, bloody pasts, and they are fearsome warriors. But in Canudos they are not represented as bloodthirsty monsters, but rather as meek people (albeit resolute in the defense of Conselheiro, like Pajeú), able organizers (like Vilanova), compassionate leaders (like the Beatito), and humble companions (like João Abade).[24] The same cannot be said of the city of Salvador, where fanaticism, deceit, greed, bloodlust, treason, and sadness reign.

So in the head of Moreira César there is a message: the affirmation not of a rebellion, but of a superior (or at least alternative) form of sovereignty. Canudos is, in both the novel and the written tradition that precedes the novel, compared or identified with the Vendée, the counterrevolutionary peasant revolt in western France at the end of the eighteenth century. To cut off Moreira César's head is a sovereign act that shows that the jagunços are not like Vendée, not a counterrevolutionary movement, but, in a heterodox form, the revolution itself.[25]

The journalist knows that César's head speaks *to* him and *about* him, but the very nature of the message makes it all but unreadable, because it speaks of powers that are not the powers of the letter associated with modernity, but rather those that define his identity and his practice as irrelevant.[26] The journalist acknowledges this when he says that he has become a monster and that he has always been one: "He was also a monster, crippled, invalid, abnormal. It was no accident that he ended up where all the crippled, unfortunates, abnormals and sufferers of the world had come to congregate. It was inevitable, because he was one of them" (Vargas Llosa 1981, 451).

Gall erroneously thinks that he can interpret premodern outlaw violence, but that he can keep his distance from it. The journalist, to the contrary, understands the message cyphered in Moreira César's head for what it is: something absolutely present and something absolutely incomprehensible that destroys any aesthetic of epistemological distance. We cannot say that the journalist happily embraces that collapse (since it is forced upon him). But when he goes back to Bahia, that collapse continues living within him. He does not try, using the blessing of the temporal, geographical, and cultural distance, to recuperate the certainties that he has lost. It is in that lack of certainty that he finds, however, the possibility of literature.

The destiny of the journalist can, finally, be contrasted with that of the Baron. The Baron, a former employer of the journalist at the newspaper that was a rival of Epaminodas's, has lived in Bahia his entire life and has directed or influenced the state's destiny for the better part of his life. He is the owner of the land in which the community of Canudos was established. He knows (or thinks he knows) inside out (as is clearly shown in the case of Rufino) the codes regulating violence, honor, and deference in the backlands. But the Baron fails catastrophically in his attempt to understand Canudos, and he pays dearly for this failure: he loses his fortune, his wife, and his political clout.[27] He who wanted not to be a politician and a landowner, but an intellectual and a scientist, is painfully aware of all of these losses, and of the reason behind them. He resigns himself to surviving as a relic of what he considers a gentler past; he abandons all work and becomes a private citizen, embracing dubious erotic and aesthetic pleasures. This is not the case with the short-sighted journalist. He has lived for months in darkness. He never emerges from it, because he discovers that he has always lived in it. But that darkness and uncertainty are his call to produce a work (Vargas Llosa 1981, 341): a work about what he did not see, about what he did not understand, a future and conjectural work that, far from clarifying Canudos, will take us into that fog of near blindness and horror that is his life, a paradoxical "in between," more deserted than the sertão.

From this perspective, *La guerra del fin del mundo*, in addition to being a war novel, a bandit novel, a historical novel, a political novel, is a novel about "becoming a writer." It is a novel that narrates the transition (infinitely postponed, perhaps) from the *écrivant* (the salaried journalist, master of the modest tools of a subaltern but firmly established craft) to the *écrivain*, completely invested in a calling in which, at the end of the day, he will not find justification or satisfaction. The condition of possibility of that "becoming a writer" is the polluting contact with the body written by the bandit, and the immersion in the outlaw world. But that contact is not a plus, a richness that will endow the narrative with the edge of the witness's account. It is the destruction of all he assumed that a writer was that transforms him into a writer. We never read a single line of his projected work on Canudos. But we can guess that it will be neither an apology for Canudos (he was terrified of being there) nor a denunciation of the military (after all, the character to whom he feels most closely related is Moreira César). It will not be the work of a convert, or of an analyst, or of a witness. That paradox justifies Rama's (1982, 600; 1988, 104) epithet, coined to salute the release of the novel: the "masterpiece of a fanatic of literature." This is of course a play on words, since "fanatic" (together with "bandits") was the derogatory term used to describe the followers of Conselheiro.

La guerra del fin del mundo enacts, under different conditions, a fanaticism that implies a double certainty: the absolute need for literature and the impossibility of literature as a privileged locus of enunciation. Perhaps the shortsighted journalist will become the Brazilian Oscar Wilde, as he dreamed of before going to Canudos. But he will not be the Wilde of *The Picture of*

Dorian Gray or "The Sphinx," but the outcast who called himself Sebastian Melmoth. And, as such, his work will fulfill the destiny that Borges (2005a, 217) conceived for literature in "La supersticiosa ética del lector": "I do not know whether music can despair of music or marble of marble. I do know that literature is an art that can foresee the time when it will be silenced, an art that can become inflamed with its own virtue, fall in love with its own decline, and court its own demise."

TWELVE

BANDITRY, NEOLIBERALISM, AND THE DILEMMAS OF LITERATURE

On *Plata quemada*

PLATA QUEMADA **WAS** one of the most anticipated, controversial, and successful Argentine novels of the 1990s.[1] It is the account of the short and brutal saga (from September 26 to November 6, 1965) of a gang of Argentine urban bandits, comprising Marcos Dorda (also known as "El Gaucho rubio"), Brignone ("El nene"), Mereles ("El cuervo"), and Mario Malito, the brains of the group. With the support of a vast (and never completely elucidated) network of politicians, policemen, and army personnel, the gang holds up an armored truck transporting cash belonging to the municipality of San Fernando, in the Buenos Aires metropolitan area—it amounts to at least seven million pesos, or half a million dollars. Disregarding the implicit code of conduct between criminals (*la pesada*) and the police (*la taquería*) that calls for no unnecessary killings, the robbers recklessly murder two guards, the treasurer of San Fernando Municipality, and a bystander, while also wounding or maiming others. This puts the police in pursuit of the bandits, who decide to betray their unnamed associates, to not divide the haul with the police and the informers, and to escape to Montevideo en route to Brazil. This decision violates yet another prescription of the outlaw code: to never betray a loyal— or useful—accomplice.

While hiding in Montevideo, the outlaws act in a careless and fatalistic fashion, jeopardizing their situation by exposing themselves too much. They further compromise their situation when they abandon and try to kill one of their Uruguayan associates. The gang ends up cornered in the apartment where they have futilely sought refuge from a police force several hundred strong. Unwilling to surrender, they resist in a desperate, defiant, and awe-inspiring way, reminiscent of both *Scarface* and the movies of Quentin Tarantino.[2] Uruguayan Radio Carve and Monte Carlo TV broadcast the long siege live. After a bloody gunfight that lasts hours, the gang members, fully aware of the impossibility of any escape, decide (I will come back to the topic of who, if anybody, "decides") to burn, bill by bill, what remained of the half a million dollars they had stolen. They send the flaming money floating down to the street, to the astonishment and anger of the crowd and the police. When the police launch their final assault, Mereles and Brignone perish, while Dorda, badly wounded, survives (some of the gang members—in particular Malito—escape, and their destinies are the subject of conjecture). Emilio Renzi, a reporter commissioned by the Argentine journal *El Mundo*, writes the uncertain chronicle of the event. That chronicle forms one of the novel's main narrative voices.[3]

Ricardo Piglia does not particularly appreciate the narrative work of Vargas Llosa. However, *Plata quemada* shares a number of traits—and, I dare say, the same overarching concern—with *La guerra*. Both narratives pivot around journalists, who find the ambiguous call of their writing vocation in the events that they witness. Both journalists are embedded within military or police operations whose ranking officers despise them (or at least have an ambivalent relationship with them). Both journalists have a revelation of their lack of understanding of the events that they are witnessing; that experience seals their destiny as literary men. Both novels narrate a siege that is carried out to the bitter end. Both events are surrounded by conspiracy theories (in the case of Canudos, that of the English monarchist support; in the case of the bank robbers, that of the Peronists). In both cases, those theories cannot be proved or disproved by the characters. In both cases, there is a relationship between criminality and a faction out of power (monarchists and Peronists, respectively), and thus a questioning of the boundary between political and criminal. In both cases, the "criminals" are considered to be "out of their minds," either prey to fanatical beliefs or deranged by the effects of drugs. And finally, in both cases, this is explained (or attempted to be explained) by the use of positivistic criminological knowledge. (The name of the psychiatrist in *Plata quemada*—Dr. Bunge—is significant, since it brings to mind Carlos Octavio Bunge [1875–1918], one of the intellectuals who in turn-of-the-century Argentina promoted a societal vision infused with positivistic, social Darwinist ideas.)

Even though it is set in the 1960s, this is a novel that works with (and reflects upon) the raw materials of its own present. *Plata quemada* is, indirectly, a novel about the 1990s, the demise of modern Argentina, the triumph of neoliberalism (a triumph that seemed so irreversible at the time), the wholesale commodification of social life, and, as a consequence, the enthronement of the market as the regulator of said social life.[4] The novel provides an emblem for this whole process: money. The ownership of money, its acquisition by legal or illegal, dignified or undignified means, its contemplation, its imagining, its counterfeiting, and its destruction are the key element around which the novel revolves.[5] I thus consider *Plata quemada* a social novel, in the same problematic sense that Piglia regards novels by Roberto Arlt, or the American crime novel, as social literature. According to Piglia, both move beyond the standard terms that define social literature (i.e., the Sartrean theory of engagement, the aesthetic of socialist realism, or Lukács's theory of reflection) and address the social realm as complot, narrative web, and enigma whose core is the relationship between power (and the law) and fiction (as narrative) ([1986] 2006, 22, 62, 176). Money, Piglia argues, is oftentimes the defining medium in that relationship.[6] Just like in Piglia's masterpiece *Respiración artificial* (1980), in *Plata quemada* the historical issue is entangled with that of writing.[7]

Also like its predecessor, in *Plata quemada* the political and aesthetic dilemma of literature (now at the end of the twentieth century) is embodied in the character of Emilio Renzi. Renzi is present in Piglia's fiction at least since *La invasión* (1967), and he reappears as the main character in his latest novel, *El camino de Ida* (2013). Laden with autobiographical features, Renzi is a dramatization (sometimes serious, sometimes ironic) of a certain totalizing way of relating to literature. More than once, Piglia has laid claim to his own convictions regarding the ethical and political preeminence of literature in the world. In Arltian fashion, Piglia dubs this preeminence "intensity."[8] But unlike *Respiración artificial*, in *Plata quemada* the certainties that support this totalizing way of relating to literature are profoundly questioned (although, by necessity, never discarded). It is possible, therefore, to put forward the hypothesis that in *Plata quemada*, through Renzi, Piglia revisits the assumptions that defined his practice as a "modern" writer, one of the eminent writers of the second half of the twentieth century.

Not by accident, the events narrated in the novel take place in 1965, and in the novel's Borgesian epilogue, Piglia explains that "the first contact with the story narrated in this book" happened in April 1966 (1997, 249). Piglia published his first book of short stories (*La invasión*) in 1967. Therefore, one could think of *Plata quemada* as a sort of fictional return to the original scene of Piglia's literature, a reflection on his entire literary production from the standpoint of the nineties, where Renzi, as the embodiment of the modern intellectual, is trapped between two logics that exceed him, two universes alien to him: that of triumphant capitalism and that of outlaw violence. It is in this inhabitable in-between that Renzi finds the conditions of possibility—which are identical to the conditions of impossibility—for his now uncertain practice. It is not an accident that *Plata quemada* appeared between two major works written by members of Piglia's generation: *Escenas de la vida posmoderna* (1994), in which Beatriz Sarlo provides an analysis of the transformations of cultural life in Argentina in the 1990s, and *El cuerpo del delito: Un manual* (1999), by Josefina Ludmer, which traces a cultural and literary history of Argentina and which convincingly argues for the nature of crime in fiction as a cultural limit (*frontera cultural*), a tool to "differentiate and exclude" (14).

Modern Argentine literature was, in many ways, born of the impure alliance between bandits and men of letters (Ludmer 1988, 1999; Prieto 1988; Dabove 2007). I would like to show that *Plata quemada* is another link in this series and, just like Borges's work, is in close dialogue with the *novelas populares con gauchos* (Laera 2004) written by Eduardo Gutiérrez in the 1880s. In *Respiración artificial*, written and published during the military dictatorship called Proceso de Reorganización Nacional (Process of National Reorganization), Piglia explores a powerful parallelism: the one between his own generation and the liberals who were exiled, marginalized, or murdered by the Rosas regime ("Who amongst us will write *Facundo*?" famously asks one of the novel's characters). In *Plata quemada* Piglia positions himself as continuing the work of the heterodox writers of the 1880s. The story of the gang of bank robbers rewrites the stories of gauchos malos of the gauchesco/criollista cycle, since the novel explores another powerful parallelism: the one between the modernizing leap of the last quarter of the nineteenth century, and the neoliberal, postmodern transformation of the last quarter of the twentieth century.

This urban rewriting of a rural myth can be traced (like many things in Piglia) to Arlt.[9] In *El juguete rabioso* (1926), the young Silvio voraciously reads serial novels about Spanish bandits (in particular those on Diego Corrientes), lent to him by the neighborhood shoemaker. These stories provide the framework for his stint as a small-time robber, when he and his buddies form a gang that, significantly, steals books—and Silvio keeps one of them for himself, a biography and anthology of Baudelaire. His criminal education and his literary education are one and the same, and both happen outside the law. But they have long projections. At the end of the novel, Silvio has the opportunity to actually meet a social bandit, or a degraded, urban version of a social bandit. Instead of the commanding appearance, instead of being "beautiful as a rose," as the shoemaker says of Diego Corrientes ([1926] 1999, 88), he is ugly and filthy. Instead of the equestrian feats that are attributed to rural bandits, he drives a ruinous cart. Instead of the valleys, plains, or mountains of the legends, his realm is the colorful but grotesque and pestilent produce and meat market. But he is a petty thief who is popular, well liked, and loyal. He also has a superb knowledge of his community. Silvio (for reasons that are not fully elucidated) betrays him (his only friend), telling the authorities about the bandit's plans for a home invasion and robbery.

For progressive intellectuals, the 1990s were a decade ushered in and seared by a double defeat: the defeat of the revolutionary project of the 1960s and 1970s and the defeat of the center-left democratic project of the 1980s. The hyperinflation that ravaged Argentina during 1989–1990 paved the way for the imposition of the neoliberal reconversion model in Argentina (a model that would itself be dismantled during the following decade by Néstor Kirchner, president from 2003 to 2007, and his wife and successor, Cristina Fernández de Kirchner, president from 2007 to 2015). Carlos Saúl Menem, president from 1989 to 1999, dismantled the welfare state and liberalized the economy, thus enthroning the market as the decisive agent in the social scene. In addition, he aligned Argentina closely with U.S. foreign policy (the so-called "carnal relations" between the two countries, as the Argentine foreign minister at the time put it); imposed the politics of "forgetting and reconciliation" in relation to the immediate past (the Dirty War and the dictatorship) and the rifts that had torn society apart since 1945; and canonized a peripheral version of postmodern cultural populism (from Xuxa to Ricky Maravilla and Marcelo Tinelli) that was enthusiastically embraced by an exhausted (and shrinking) middle class.

In spite of the recent and forceful comeback of populist rhetoric and politics during the Kirchners' administrations, and in spite of the recuperation of the role of the state and the revisiting of the past through the reopening of the trials for the 1970s genocides, in some respects the neoliberal project has triumphed in Argentina (witness the victory of Mauricio Macri in the 2015 elections). Once again, the model of export-led growth has been embraced as the main source of foreign currency and tax receipts. However, this time, it is an even more radical version of the nineteenth-century one, since twenty-first-century Argentina is well on its way to becoming an economy based on the monoculture of soy. This is accompanied by a fast and in many cases violent concentration of land and an increasing dependence on the cycles of commodity prices in the international market. It is easy to imagine a twenty-first-century Argentina as a simpler and at the same time more complex version of the nineteenth-century one (for good and for bad).

Plata quemada runs counter to the two dominant narratives of its time: that of the end of history (made famous by Francis Fukuyama's *The End of History and the Last Man*, 1992), and that of the end of the nation-state as the primary locus for identity affiliations. In these narratives, both history and the nation-state were to be replaced by global markets, since national conflict, as the engine of history, and citizenship, as the main subject position, were to wane in the face of consumption as the all-powerful identity-making system (see, for example, the theses by Néstor García Canclini, in particular those posited in *Culturas híbridas* [1990] and *Consumidores y ciudadanos* [1995]. Now largely out of fashion, they were intensely discussed at the time).

Piglia's novel, far from embracing this post-utopian utopia, returns to the 1960s. Against the postmodern commodification of the historical memory of the 1960s, and even of its most conflictive figures, such as Che Guevara,[10] Piglia sees the decade through the prism of one of its most confusing and refractory aspects, the politics of the outlawed Peronismo de la Resistencia (the Peronism of the Resistance movement), exploring but deliberately not explaining its links with the extreme Right and the extreme Left as well as with organized crime. Also, unlike the narrative of the demise of the nation-state (sponsored not only by neoliberal ideologues, but also by other Latin American novels of the time dealing with criminal violence),[11] Piglia delib-erately works within the nationalist imaginary and, more specifically, within the tradition of national literature, thus tapping into the powerful Argentine tradition of the rural bandit.

Like Eduardo Gutiérrez, Piglia finds criminal stories in police archives that help him think critically about contemporary reality.[12] Like Gutiérrez, Piglia tries to lay the foundations for a new kind of popular novel. (In Piglia's case, we can refer to what Rama [1988, 89], talking about Vargas Llosa's *La guerra del fin del mundo*, dubbed the *novela culta popular* [highbrow-popular novel]). Like Gutiérrez, Piglia contrasts the legal (state-centered) perspective on outlaw violence with the oral law of the male challenge (a defining feature, as Josefina Ludmer [1988] reminds us, of the gaucho genre). Like Gutiérrez, Piglia positions his outlaws at an uncertain intersection between crime and politics, between horizontal alliances and vertical ones.

Dorda, the main character in *Plata quemada*, is a "Gaucho rubio," a "blond gaucho," like the real Juan Moreira, even though Gutiérrez invented a char-acter whose main attribute was his pitch-black hair and thick beard. (Also like the real Juan Moreira, Dorda is not a "real" gaucho, but rather more of a rural-urban character.) But the similarities go well beyond mere nickname or physical appearance. Dorda is described in the same fashion as Gutiér-rez's gauchos malos. As far as the narrator is concerned, Dorda is "an outlaw, a rebel [*retobao*], a murderer, a gutsy and feared man in the Province of Santa Fe, in the frontier general stores" (Piglia 1997, 224). There are two important points worth noting here. The first is the use of the form "retobao" instead of the standard form "retobado" by the third-person narrator (and not by one of the characters who also narrates), a usage typical of gaucho pronunciation, as it has been handed down from the gaucho genre. The word "retobao" is a staple of the genre as well as of Gutiérrez's novels, as uttered by the rural police officers (*los justicias*) and the rural justices of the peace, both of whom are the ubiquitous nemeses of the outlaw in the genre ("gaucho retobao" is synonymous with "gaucho malo").

Second, the reference to the "frontier general stores" in Santa Fe is signif-icant. Toward the middle of the twentieth century in Santa Fe Province (at least in the area where Dorda lives), there was no longer any "frontier proper" in the classic sense of an area of weak, sporadic, or nonexistent sovereignty of the nation-state.[13] So on the one hand, the voice of the narrator is intersected by the voice of the gaucho genre. On the other, a realist novel changes to a sort of crossroads of temporalities where Dorda is simultaneously a modern criminal (he sports a machine gun, not a dagger), living in a modern society (Santa Fe was the success story in agrarian Argentina, where a class of white farmers to which the Dordas belong established and achieved a significant degree of prosperity), and sometimes a nineteenth-century *matrero*, living in frontiers beyond the reach of the law, carrying on the "traditional" forms of sociability (such as the *pulpería* [bar] fight). This is evident in the following passage:

> This lasted until that afternoon in which they were playing sapo at the general store, all of them quite drunk, and they began to make fun of him [Dorda] and they laughed and they kept making jokes at his expense. The Gaucho could not speak and defend himself. He only smiled, with empty eyes. Old man Soto made him the butt of all his jokes that evening: they provoked and provoked him until the Gaucho murdered him treacherously. He did him in when Soto was drunkenly trying to climb onto his horse, trying to reach the stirrup with his leg and the Gaucho, as if he were trying to stop that ridiculous dance, produced a weapon and killed him. His was the first death in a series that had no end (according to Bunge, quoting the Gaucho). All his misfortunes [*desgracias*] started that day. (Piglia 1997, 224)

This was a drunken fight with fatal results motivated only by the prescriptions of male honor, like the ones in *Martín Fierro* or *Juan Moreira*. Also, just like in the gaucho genre (read through Borges), the killing is not a murder but a *desgracia*, an unfortunate but unavoidable shedding of blood.[14] And just like in Borges's orillero fights, or Gutiérrez's serial novels, this desgracia opens up an "infinite series,"[15] one in which the gaucho malo/Gaucho rubio becomes at the same time a fierce, cool, and supremely elegant fighter,[16] possessed of a martial elegance that contrasts with a cheap and showy sense of personal elegance, and someone intent on the humiliation and suppression of the hated police.[17] This uphill battle, this infinite fight, pervades Guitérrez's gauchos malos with a distinct sense of fatalism, to the point where Moreira's death is, to an extent, "suicide by police." Malito's gang is pervaded by the same fatalism (98) that prompts them to take unnecessary risks, such as Nene's sexual escapades in

Plaza Zavala (reminiscent of Moreira's sexual escapades in the brothel La Estrella), where he meets Margarita Taibo (also known as Giselle, also known as "la morochita del norte de Río Negro" [99]), and the whole gang's orgies that bring them into contact with a taxi boy who will later inform on them to the police (134).

Just like in classic bandit narratives, Dorda's identity oscillates between monstrosity, abjection, and epic. And he appears, like the Rob Roy of William Wordsworth, in open disjunction with his own time: "He came an age too late; / Or shall we say an age too soon?" ponders Wordsworth in his superb poem "Rob Roy's Grave" (1803–1807). As Brignone puts it, "Let's assume that there is a war, or that he would have been born in the era of General San Martín, the Gaucho, Nene used to say; he would have a statue erected in his honor. He would be, I don't know, a hero. But he was born at the wrong time" (Piglia 1997, 79). This affirmation echoes some of Sarmiento's classic statements on the two "bandits" who, together with Rosas, epitomize the River Plate predicament: José Gervasio de Artigas and Facundo Quiroga.[18]

Much like in classic bandit narratives, in *Plata quemada* the demise of the bandit is brought about by female treason. Indeed, females are twice traitors. Under duress, Blanca Galeano, Mereles's lover, reveals what she knows about the gang's escape to Uruguay (Piglia 1997, 89). Margarita Taibo, on the other hand, disowns her relationship with Nene, accuses him of rape, and most likely provides information that leads the police to the gang's hideout (201).

Dorda and Nene are a couple. But the issue of homosexuality in the novel has less to do with gay culture (in its liberal, American-inspired meaning) than with the gaucho couples archetypal of the gaucho genre (perhaps with a passing nod to Osvaldo Lamborghini).[19] Such is the case with Fierro and Cruz (Cruz dies sweetly in the arms of Fierro, who is devastated by his death), Moreira and Andrade (who kiss each other on the mouth, and who embrace each other like two tender lovers), and Santos Vega and Carmona (who profess to each other a love beyond death, such that when Carmona dies, Vega is unable to survive him much longer). This has less to do with gay culture than with a circulation of desire among men in certain social spaces such as jail, bars, boxing, and certain professions—including, notably, literature (Piglia [1986] 2006, 206).

And finally, the drawn-out siege of the gang could be understood as a rewriting of Moreira's last fight. Completely surrounded in confined spaces (an apartment, a room in a brothel), Moreira (and Malito's gang) put up a fight in which bravery, martial skills, and manly bravado, in the face of vastly superior police forces, amount to "the most formidable siege ever recorded by the River Plate police" (Piglia 1997, 133).

But this analogy has a limit, since *Plata quemada* has, vis-à-vis its precedents, both a deficit and a surplus. On the one hand, the novel does not harbor populist or leftist illusions about the idea of the gang as a metaphor for "the people." Piglia deliberately departs from the well-established tradition that presents criminality as prepolitical popular (or class) rebellion. In the tradition of the gaucho as an icon of resistance, the constitution of a popular subject is decisive. In *Plata quemada* the people is entirely absent. This absence can be doubly specified: in the novel there are no proletarians or real activists, only criminals, policemen, and the elements that revolve around them (such as male and female prostitutes, psychiatrists, etc.), a journalist (to whom I will return), and the derided middle class (the bank treasurer, the shop owner whose vehicle is stolen during the getaway, the bakery owner who calls the police, the owner of the deli, Blanca's parents, the witnesses to the siege), all of whom lack a story and for all of whom money is the principle of reality. The urban bandits are institutionalized subjects who become hardened criminals in jail, in the reformatory, or in the psychiatric ward. Therefore, in their criminal careers they do not resort to a previous cultural or human capital—in terms of knowledge or social reciprocity—as an asset. The criminals have no allies, real or virtual, only accomplices or paid associates. Nor do they have a community that they can rejoin. That is why their only option is exile, and why they constantly betray everybody. (They refuse to share their haul and flee, killing the Chueco Bazán as a warning and leaving Mereles's girlfriend behind. While in Uruguay, they even try to kill the Uruguayan in charge of helping them.)

However, connected to this deficit, there is a surplus, an event that makes the gang's isolation and incomprehensibility radical and eliminates the possibility of its being reversed: the burning of the money. This is pure performance (hence, entirely at place in the 1960s), like Olivera's installation made of thread and water pails in *Rayuela*, but much more shocking and threatening. It is an entirely public act since the entire country can watch it. But at the same time, it is a completely secret act. It just happens, unexplained, inexplicable. The novel dwells extensively on the perspective of the characters inside the apartment, which is under constant audio surveillance. (The operator of the listening device, Roque Pérez, is one of the significant "voices" that narrate the novel's events [Piglia 1997, 179, 188].) But in spite of this, the novel never relates the decision-making process that leads to the act. Suddenly, from a viewpoint outside the apartment, we see (along with everybody else) a column of white smoke. And then, when the viewpoint shifts indoors, we realize that even those who are burning the money seem to be horrified by their actions ("To burn money is a sin," states Dorda, who is in charge of burning it [189]).

This is not a simple oversight: the burning of the money is an act without a subject (that is what makes it an event), or, to be more precise, an act for which the Western imagination cannot imagine a subject: "Money was the only thing that could possibly justify the deaths; if they did this, they did it for money. But if now they are burning it, that means that they have no morals, nor motives, and that they act and kill gratuitously only because of their taste for evil, pure evil" (190). The burning of the money is a "gratuitous" act (the reference to Roberto Arlt, as read by Oscar Masotta [1982], is unavoidable),[20] an occurrence of "pure evil." Dorda indeed reflects on the nature of evil. Significantly, he does not make it a personal attribute or a personal failure: "Evil—said Dorda, very high because of the mixture of speed and cocaine—is not something that you do voluntarily. It is a light that comes and carries you away" (Piglia 1997, 73). There is no "evil will," since evil will is, for Western thought, an epistemological impossibility. (The will, the argument goes since Plato, may want things that society regards as evil, but the very act of volition considers them good, since they satisfy the will. Hence, the will only wills the good. Therefore, evil does not exist as the object of volition, or it exists only negatively.) The gang is close to this paradox of pure evil, of the evil will, when they burn the money without a purpose (not even a purpose of defiance), and they do it without manifesting a will: "una luz que viene y te lleva" (a light that comes and carries you away).

The burning of the money breaks all social pacts, even those that include criminals. But it does this not with the goal (stated or unstated, conscious or unconscious) of founding a new social pact, nor of returning to a previous one (Nene, Cuervo, and Dorda are not Luddites or peasant rebels). They do not seek a "world upside down": "Everybody understood that the act was a declaration of total war, a direct and methodical war against society in its entirety" (Piglia 1997, 192). In essence, it is a war not only against the entire society (*toda la sociedad*) but also against any society (*toda sociedad*), including their own "criminal society."

In society money is not only the means of exchange of goods. Exchange has become the rationale for all human interactions. The burning of the money is, on the one hand, a repudiation of that logic, but it is also, as the novel expresses, an act for which there is no possible exchange in the form of punishment or retribution. Killed, maimed, or tortured, the criminals ultimately win, because they put themselves beyond winning or losing. The mob that abuses Dorda, already half dead (Piglia 1997, 242), is certainly letting loose a "primal instinct" of revenge. But revenge is a form of exchange and communication destined (in this case) to exorcise an act that does not belong to the orbit of exchange or communication. And it fails to do so.

"Somebody does something that nobody understands, an act that exceeds everybody's experience. That act does not last, it has the fleeting quality of life itself, it is not narrative, but it is the only act that is worth narrating" (Piglia [1988] 1998, 35). The burning of the money is such an event. It has a foundational character, since it makes Renzi's evolution from a journalist to a writer possible. The burning of the money has, indeed, an aesthetic dimension that the novel emphasizes:

> The way in which they burnt the money is proof of their genius as well as of their evil, because they burnt the money making the hundred-peso bills that they were incinerating very visible, one after another, the hundreds burnt like butterflies whose wings are touched by a candle's flame and they flutter for a second still, already on fire and they fly through the air for an infinite instant before burning down to the ground, consumed by the flame.
>
> And after all those unending minutes in which they saw the bills burn like birds of fire, there remained only a pile of ashes, a funerary tribute to society's values (as one of the witnesses declared on TV), a most beautiful column of blue ashes that glided down from the window, like the drizzle of the burnt remains of the dead that are spread on the ocean or the meadows or the forests, but never over the filth of the city streets; never should the ashes float over the stones of the concrete jungle. (Piglia 1997, 193)

But this is not what is decisive here—quite the contrary. This aesthetic translation (burning bills as butterflies or firebirds) is really a way of territorializing the event (and by doing this, it suppresses its power to produce commotion), making the burning of the money a kind of *memento mori* or, perhaps, an illustration of "Vanitas vanitatum omnia vanitas." In fact, there is a powerful collective impulse to provide a narrative that incorporates what just happened into the order of things. The novel affirms that the act "paralyzed the city and the entire country with horror" (Piglia 1997, 190), but the reterritorialization occurs simultaneously with the event itself, in the form of the TV and radio broadcasts. They amplify the horror by giving it maximum exposure. At the same time, however, they distance it as spectacle (and horrifying spectacles are a privileged mass media commodity, in particular in the 1990s mass media). In this way, a "Medieval Sabbath" or an "act of cannibalism," as the TV host Jorge Foister puts it (191), inevitably becomes a "reality show" where horror is edited and suppressed, while exposed, because of its exposure, for mass consumption. (This transformation of a horrifying reality into a mass media spectacle appears for the first time in the novel when Lucía Passero, the bakery owner, witnesses—and causes—a death. But for her, watching from behind the window "was like watching a movie that was played for her alone" [124].)

There is another attempt in the novel to understand (or tame) the event, this time from an "empathetic" point of view, by incorporating it into the flow of academic discourse: "In an interview with the journal *Marcha*, the Uruguayan philosopher Washington Andrada pointed out that he considered the terrible act a kind of innocent *potlatch* carried out in the context of a society that had forgotten that ritual, an absolutely and completely gratuitous act, a gesture of sheer expense and sheer waste that in other societies has been considered a sacrifice offered to the gods, because only the most valuable deserves to be sacrificed, and there is nothing more valuable among us than money" (Piglia 1997, 192–93). However, the philosopher is mistaken. A potlatch is never a gratuitous act. It is an act of destruction, of course, that has no discernible economic motivation or rationale. But it is still an act of exchange, since it earns the performer prestige and preeminence, and it is above all an act of community building, quite the opposite of the event discussed here.

Renzi is the only character who tries to understand the act on its own terms, even though he is not free from assigning a transcendental (sacrificial or tragic) meaning to the event. This occurs when he calls Dorda "a Christ . . . a scapegoat, the idiot who suffers everybody's pain" (Piglia 1997, 240). But for the most part, Renzi is acutely aware of his lack of epistemological or ethical privilege. One should recall that in *Respiración artificial*, Renzi appears comfortably installed in all of the intellectual, political, and ethical guarantees that define the modern writer. Renzi is on the good side of history, on the good side of the cultural wars of his time. And he knows it. The novel is firmly (and subtly) installed in the horror of the dictatorship, but that horror is not intensified by self-doubt. In *Plata quemada*, Renzi is dispossessed of all those assurances. First and foremost, his knowledge of the fact that he is narrating is imperfect. In addition to this, Renzi's position in structural as well as ethical terms is rather precarious. The novel is a critique of the role of money in society. But Renzi, its chronicler, writes for money, and not even for a lot of money. And unlike the great nonfiction writer of the 1960s, Rodolfo Walsh, who engaged in arduous and problematic investigations in which crime and politics intersected, Renzi writes with fear, and he writes what he is allowed to write, as he himself confesses to Police Chief Silva.

Many facts crucial to a complete or even sufficient understanding of the story remain obscured. For example, the degree of involvement (if any) of the gang with the Peronismo de la Resistencia is never clear. Sometimes it seems that this involvement is just a claim by the police, made out of paranoia or to legitimize extreme measures taken against the gang. Sometimes it seems to be a claim by the bandits themselves, made out of either delusional fantasies or sarcastic attempts at legitimation (Piglia 1997, 132, 162). Similarly, the degree of involvement of the police and/or the army with the gang is never clear (140). These uncertainties, in turn, make the novel's main scene (the siege and the burning of the money) completely obscure, in spite of its enormous visibility. Something is happening—criminals are fighting the police. But is this a law enforcement operation? Is it a monumental cover-up? Is it a bloody revenge that a criminal faction (in police uniform) is exacting from former allies, on a spectacular scale? "We had the experience but missed the meaning; an approach to the meaning restores the experience": T. S. Eliot's quote serves as an epigraph to *Prisión perpetua*. In *Plata quemada* we have (or we think we have) some of the facts (the experience), but we do not have the meaning. Therefore we have nothing. (Renzi, the one supposedly in charge of providing that meaning, leaves us completely in the dark, because he is in the dark.) Or, to put it another way: Renzi inhabits, in a conscious fashion, that lack of meaning that defines the space of literature.

In *Respiración artificial* Renzi is a rather overbearing and pedantic *porteño*. But he is the undeniable main character of the novel. *Plata quemada*'s Renzi is a secondary character, full of doubts and misgivings. He is full of doubts, except one: he understands that the one who is closest to the meaning of the event that defines the novel (and his future career as a writer) is the one who is incapable (and unwilling) to explain it to him: Dorda, the true artist of the novel. Dorda is the novel's artist in two ways. First, he possesses all of the mythic features of the avant-garde or 1960s artist: he is deranged, he is a multiple addict, he is suicidal and nurtures his own demise, he has mystical tendencies, he is misunderstood (Piglia 1997, 243), he does not care about money (69), he does not have an oeuvre (his "art" is pure performance), he is unaware of the fact that he is an artist, and he is, in effect, in touch with evil.

But he is an artist in a more decisive, profound way. Renzi, much like a dedicated student, looks for words in a dictionary, and asks for his supervisor's permission to use big words (such as *hybris*, or *muthos*) in his chronicles (Piglia 1997, 91, 106). Dorda, on the other hand, has a tortured relationship with language. He is aphasic (79) and he does not know how to express himself, and therefore he goes weeks and months without talking. But precisely because of this, "he knows how to transform words into living things, needles that poke your flesh and destroy your soul like an egg broken by the edge of the frying pan" (186). For Dorda, words have personal resonances, as in the case of *pusilánime* (pusillanimous) (160) or *pupilo* (pupil) (221). For Dorda, language does not translate reality; language is reality: "Dorda watched the serial movies and he always translated the movie as if he were inside it, as if he lived all the events in the movie: 'Once he was expelled from the movie theater run by the local parish because he put his dick out and he started to pee: he was watching a kid in the movie who was urinating, his back to the camera, in the middle of the night, in the middle of the countryside . . . ' verbatim from the sacristan to Dr. Bunge in the psychiatric report" (81). This is why he is also the one who is constantly reading the world as a system or as prose made up of obscure signs, with an invariably ominous meaning of which he is the interpreter (12).

Dorda is an artist, and radically so, because the burning of the money is a radical experience with signs (that is what money is, after all: a sign) that goes far beyond mere experimentation or mere scandal. The burning is a performance that is, by definition, intransitive, immanent, incommunicable (although emphatically communicated), that escapes all translation, all foundation, all sharing, with a power to produce commotion that can only be imperfectly exorcised: a truly artistic act. It is artistic as well as political, since it intervenes in the symbolic economy of the polis, but it intervenes only as an irrecoverable interruption.

Renzi moves toward that ideal of art and is forever excluded from it. He is condemned to move in between this ideal and the mundane realities of twentieth-century Argentina. But in his failure to reach it, he finds his condition of possibility as a writer. *Plata quemada* narrates the experience of the beginning of writing, and in that beginning, it narrates the clear consciousness of the end. As I noted earlier, modern Argentine literature was born in the nineteenth century of the impure alliance of bandits and men of letters. At the other end of the historical cycle, in *Plata quemada* Piglia adds another impure alliance: that between Renzi and the Gaucho rubio. The bandit allows Renzi to imperfectly access the experience from which he will become a man of letters, and at the same time divests him of all the certainties about that condition.[21]

THIRTEEN

WHAT IS A BANDIT?

I PREFER NOT TO close this book with a usual "Conclusion" chapter, as I find conclusions a rather artificial portion of books like this one, a remnant of a positivistic ideal that tied our disciplines to the nineteenth-century scientific method, with hypotheses and proofs. Rather, I would like to finish with some reflections that, hopefully, will help reinforce what this book (and the one preceding it) has tried to do.

Banditry, as a lurid emblem for nonstate rural violence, speaks to some of the core dilemmas of Latin American modernity and its two pillars: the nation-state as its exclusive politico-cultural synthesis and a coherent capitalist economy as its dominant economic system. At least three reasons account for banditry's centrality in Latin American culture. First, the existence of a national state, as an institutional cluster exerting territorial sovereignty, as opposed to segmentarity (i.e., the low reach of the administrative political center that resulted in internal frontiers) and heteronomy (i.e., discontinuous control over the territory and its population) was, in many countries, until well into the twentieth century, less a reality than an aspiration, and it was the locus of fierce struggles. Mexico, Colombia, Venezuela, Brazil, and Peru come to mind as the most extreme cases of this phenomenon.

Second, in many countries, the state's acquisition of the monopoly on violence did not entail the outright suppression of private, nonstate violence, but rather its co-optation, through a protracted process of negotiation (which did not exclude conflict) and coexistence. Witness the existence of hacendados' and planters' private retinues (many times composed of current or former outlaws, as in the case of Peruvian Eleodoro Benel's or the Brazilian *coronéis* forces) as enforcers of the agrarian status quo that combined integration into global markets with premodern institutions of domination or control.

Finally, as Centeno (2002) observes, Latin America's process of nation-state formation was very different from its European counterpart, where, as Tilly (1975) has demonstrated, international war played a crucial role. Latin American nations lacked the identification of an external enemy as the stimulus for the development of a national identity. For the elites vying for national dominance, the greatest threat was not from competing elites across the border, but from the masses below. Thus the bandit became the dual embodiment of challenges from "outside" (but claimed by the state as "inside") and from "below." Because of this, the rural outlaw was at the same time the paramount Other of Latin American modernity, and its secret, hidden but undeniable truth.

Although banditry is primarily associated with highway robbery (*robo en despoblado*), cattle rustling (*abigeos, cuatreros*), or an attempt against private property (kidnapping for ransom, blackmailing, protection rackets, jacquerie), brigandage is much more. It may comprise such diverse offenses as resisting authority, smuggling, and homicide, conspiracy to commit a crime, possession of prohibited weaponry, vagrancy, desertion, rebellion, and poaching. In fact, any challenge to state rule could be, and frequently was, at one point or another, labeled "banditry": from the runaway slave who took to highway robbery as a means of subsistence, to the mighty Pancho Villa, leader of thousands of men and ruler of a vast territory in northern Mexico; from the greedy character bent on profit (such as Tomás Urbina) or the ultraviolent one bent on butchery and rape (such as Inés Chávez García or Rodolfo Fierro) to the restrained insurgent with lofty aims (such as Maisanta or Emiliano Zapata) or the nationalistic guerrilla leader of hemispheric relevance (such as Augusto César Sandino); from the millenarian partisan (the jagunços of Canudos) to the professional fighter and electoral goon (Juan Moreira).

This protean nature of the bandit, historical or fictional, is yet another reason for its continual political relevance and cultural productivity. Banditry is dazzlingly ubiquitous in Latin American culture, from popular ballads (i.e., corridos) to high modernist novels, from political essay to art-house film, from mass-produced crafts (many Chinese made) to avant-garde painting. But this ubiquity is one of the reasons for the difficulty of coming up with a simple, all-encompassing definition of banditry. Latin American penal codes are less than useful in providing more clarification, since they don't usually define banditry as an offense. The words *bandolerismo, bandidismo,* and *bandidaje* (codes define actions considered crimes or misdemeanors, not the subjects of those actions) are mostly or totally absent from penal codes, even if specific offenses commonly related to banditry, such as the ones enumerated above, are present. Still, it is striking that a word so commonly used and recognized as "banditry" has not translated into an action verb (*bandidear*), as so happened in Catalan, with the verb *bandulejar.*

Simplifying a bit, it is possible to speak of two options when studying banditry. We could call these (for reasons that will be apparent later on) the realist option and the nominalist option. These are not mutually exclusive, and most authors who study banditry make use of both. The realist would try to identify a certain cluster of behaviors (e.g., robbery), certain motivations (e.g., profit, vengeance), a certain context for such behavior (e.g., wars and their aftermath, foreign invasions, revolutions, social transformations), certain collective dispositions (e.g., legitimacy crises), and certain agents (e.g., violent entrepreneurs) that can unify and homogenize the multiple manifestations of banditry and anchor a possible definition of more or less universal validity, or ground a number of conceptual distinctions. The discursive dimensions are considered secondary, except for those discursive manifestations endowed (in the eyes of the researcher) with a certain epistemological privilege (e.g., police and judicial sources, as opposed to folk tales or fictional accounts). This current of thought has produced some of the best case studies to date. Paul Vanderwood (1992), Richard Slatta (1983, 1987, 1991, 1994), Linda Lewin (1979, 1987), Rosalie Schwartz (1989), Miguel Izard (1981, 1982, 1983, 1984, 1987, 1988), and Peter Singelmann (1975) are some of the representatives of this line of thought. Others include Maria Isaura Pereira de Queiroz (1968), Billy Jaynes Chandler (1978, 1987), Frederico Pernambucano de Mello ([1985]

2004, 1993), Louis A. Perez Jr. (1989), Gonzalo Sánchez and Donny Meertens ([1983] 1984), Alan Knight ([1986] 1990), Ana María Contador (1998), and Hugo Chumbita (2000). Many other examples could be offered, of course.

The distillation of this critical current could be the deliberately terse definition provided by Richard Slatta: "Banditry is the taking of property by force or by the threat of force" (1994, 76). This definition has the virtue of simplicity, and it covers diverse manifestations of banditry. But it leaves several factors that are crucial to the understanding of banditry unexplored. Up until the twentieth century, "property," in the Latin American context, was not an obvious and unequivocal concept. Indeed, the concept was suffering profound transformations. The bloody struggles between liberals and conservatives in core zones of the region were an expression of this phenomenon, whereas the ancestral corporative rights of the peasant communities and of the church were being challenged by the new liberal concept of private property. Even less clear was the concept of property in frontier zones, such as both coasts of the River Plate or the Venezuelan plains. In these regions, the claim to property was not the precondition of the struggle, but its ultimate goal, since stray or wild cattle often did not have a clear proprietor, and the idea of landed property linked to a state system was a novelty and one that was hotly contested. Therefore, "crime against property" was not a crime that was easily defined.

Furthermore, as Miguel Centeno (2002, chap. 1) notes, Latin America, with the exception of the income related to foreign commerce, did not have a fully functioning central tax system for most of its postcolonial history. This lack of a revenue base made state support for the army and the police forces onerous during the first postcolonial century. Due to this fact, "the taking of property by force or by the threat of force" was one of the main activities of all armies and state armed forces well into the twentieth century. The only differences between banditry and army expropriations (euphemistically called "contributions" or "warranties") were the scale of plundering and the inherently dubious state sanction of the army's actions. Therefore, unless one agrees with the fact that Slatta's definition applies to most armed forces throughout the long nineteenth century, for example (something that would not be completely far-fetched, as the War of Reform and the Mexican Revolution show), we cannot make this an unequivocal criterion for defining banditry.

Finally, this simple definition leaves out a more "philosophical" problem: the taking of property by force or the threat of force is what states usually do.

The legitimacy (or the perception of legitimacy) of the agents conducting the taking is perhaps the only difference (as Levi 1988 notes), since it is difficult or impossible for most of humankind to "opt out" of the nation-state system and its tax imperatives, without running afoul of the law. This legitimacy is based upon the claim that taxes are intended for the common good, so they are not robbery, or protection money, but everyone's contribution to that common good.

For most of humankind, this has been true, or at least believable. But allow me to present an example that is a sort of *reductio ad absurdum* of this claim. Until 2016, whenever a U.S. citizen arrived in Argentina, he had to pay a tax, amounting to around one hundred dollars. The tax, called the "reciprocity fee" by the federal authorities, was indeed reciprocal, but of the negative kind. It was retaliation for the fact that the United States requires a visa (and charges a fee to obtain it) for all Argentine citizens entering the country. But U.S. citizens were not required to have a visa to enter Argentina. They just had to pay, without a pretense of a service rendered, or a need addressed. If you refused to pay, you were denied entry. Customs and the Military Aeronautical Police enforced compliance. Was this not a literal act of banditry? Money was exacted from travelers, for no good reason other than because armed personnel could force them to pay. The fact that these armed personnel claimed state sanction (and in fact, they are part of the state) did not change the fact that the reciprocity fee was "the taking of property by force or by the threat of force." That the cosmopolitan flair of the international airport had replaced the lonely king's highway did not change the fact that this was a scene more reminiscent of Michael Kohlhaas being shaken down by the feudal lord than of the bourgeois-democratic vision of a social contract and a common good.

Nominalists, on the other hand, focus precisely on an analysis of the discursive dimension, which encompasses at least three areas: (1) letters, interviews, *anónimos* (anonymous threatening or libelous messages), and in general all semiotic production (including performances of violence with a secondary meaning, such as burnings, brandings, beheadings, vandalism, codified modes of torture, and execution, like the *corte de corbata* or the *corte de chaleco*) by historical bandits themselves, their allies, or their supporters; (2) laws, codes, news, official reports, and state acts (including performances of violence with a secondary meaning: public executions, public display of the outlaw's corpse) produced at the time that a given historical bandit acted, and that were relevant to "framing" his actions as acts of banditry (or to disputing that label); (3) the way a particular historical bandit entered into the cultural memory of a given community (local, national, international), and how this memory was rearticulated in new and changing conflicts. In this case, the same can be said about fictional bandits, or bandits whose historical status is dubious (such as the Gauchito Gil in Argentina or Jesús Malverde in Mexico).

The basic assumption of scholars studying from this perspective is that the act of nomination (or self-nomination) of a given rural subject of violence as a "bandit" should not be subjected to a "truth test" (i.e., is this subject of violence really a bandit, or is he a revolutionary, or just a criminal, or something else?). The nomination is a social fact worthy of study by itself, indeed a material fact with material consequences that we ignore at our own risk. So instead of contrasting this act of nomination with a supposed essence that would allow one to dictate whether a given outlaw was in fact a bandit (or not), one should engage in a study of the conditions of the emergence of this particular act of nomination in order to recover the conflict from which this particular instance of the bandit label (or trope) emerges. Thus, instead of dismissing (or confirming) the act, one should investigate the "politics of naming" (Bhatia 2005) of which banditry is a product (or the arena of the political conflict).

Moss, in his seminal work on banditry on Sardinia, distinguishes between "banditry as an offence in its own right" (the realist option) and "banditry as a classification of offences" (the nominalist option) (1979, 480). In regard to this second meaning, he adds that, just like the notion of "terrorism," the term belongs to the metalanguage of crime, rather than being a crime itself—a term that "classifies a set of offences, generally in terms of some underlying characteristic of the geographical area or social category in which they are concentrated" (480). In this latter sense (the most important one, as it turns out), the term is no longer a legal one but rather becomes the focus of an extremely variegated literature (criminology, travelogues, historical and political essays) conceived and put to use, first, to divide one set of communities—the Barbagia—from the rest of Sardinia, and, during the Risorgimento and afterward, to distinguish Sardinia and the southern communities from the hegemonic northern Italian identity.

Following Moss's (1979) line of thought, we can argue that "banditry" is an act of language (a speech act, in a very broad sense) that relates to another speech act, not to a "thing" (except, of course, that a speech act is a thing). Therefore, each articulation of the bandit trope is always the singular effect of a singular conflict of forces, and should be questioned not from the standpoint of its truth, but from the standpoint of its uses and its effects (in the genealogical sense developed by Foucault, reading Nietzsche). The defining feature is not what the bandit does (this is usually rather clear), but rather the conflict over the representation (hence the value, political or otherwise) of what the bandit does. This conflict could occur not only between peasant and landowner, but also between sectors of the elite, or between sectors of the peasantry.

But the uses of the bandit trope can go well beyond the mere gesture of exclusion. Stephanie Barczewski (2000) analyzes how during the long nineteenth century, various intellectuals appropriated and "used" the legendary characters King Arthur and Robin Hood (of whose historical existence there is little, if any, archival evidence). Such appropriations had different political agendas and encompassed varied debates: the debate on the existence and the nature of a British identity; conflicts between English, Irish, Welsh, French, and German; the rise of English studies; the formation of an Anglocentric racial ideology (both the justification for and the critique of the imperial enterprise); the promotion of English exceptionalism; and the justification of either conservative or radical politics. Barczewski restricts her examination mainly to literature (in a wide sense). But her narrative rightfully belongs to the history of the British Empire, since what she traces is the constitution of an ideological framework for empire (or a criticism of it) and its evolution through time.

Barczewski's task is made easier by the fact that Robin Hood is an unambiguous figure: model of all noble robbers, his belonging to any study in the field does not have to be justified, since Robin Hood defines the field. Barczewski examines the uses of the bandit figure, but the identification of the outlaw qua outlaw is unnecessary, since it is obvious. But the question of what exactly is a bandit (or who exactly is a bandit, as opposed to a rebel, a revolutionary, or an insurgent) is usually far more complex.

Thomas Grünewald ([1999] 2004) faces the task in an illuminating way. The book examines banditry as seen through the lens of Roman historians. Unlike Robin Hood or King Arthur, who because they were not real did not hamper those who wrote about them, the bandits considered by Roman historians were historical insurgents of various stripes dubbed *latros*, who were contrasted with legitimate enemies, or *hostes* (usually from other states, or forces large enough or organized enough to be granted status compatible with that of the Roman State). Grünewald notes how run-of-the-mill highway robbers, common pirates, and farm and villa plunderers are mentioned scantily and cursorily by Roman historians and literary men. The words *latro* and *latrocinium* are used mainly metaphorically, to frame particular political and military struggles such as slave rebellions, resistance against Roman expansion, conflicts between pretenders to the imperial throne or political factions, and avengers in dynastic conflicts. This labeling was double-edged: it could serve the purpose of delegitimizing any threat to the security of the Roman State, but some authors crafted these bandit narratives in order to criticize the Roman order (e.g., to contrast an emperor with a bandit, and exalt the bandit as a model of how the emperor should act).[1]

Explicit in Moss and Grünewald, and implicit in Barczewski, is the assumption that there are *mainly* metaphorical uses of banditry, or at least that the metaphorical uses have a wider and deeper relevance outside the local level or particular conflicts. Indeed, if a trope is to have a life outside of its original context of emergence, it cannot be defined in its entirety by said context. It has to be an empty signifier, open to articulation (Laclau 1996). Grünewald ([1999] 2004), coherent with the consequences of this theoretical postulate, follows a prosopographical approach: he traces *any* use of the word "latro," and reconstructs a genealogy of the emergence of the word in the Roman context without appealing to a "reality principle." He thus cancels the opposition between reality and discourse. He never questions whether the so-called "latros" were "real" bandits. If they were called bandits, and treated and remembered as such, the texts in which that act of nomination is carried out are legitimate subjects of study. Banditry is indeed, above all, a trope articulated in a narrative framework, and its interest and its productivity have less to do with its truth (in terms of adequacy) than with its efficacy as an intervention, as a figure of discourse in a given field of forces of which that discourse is the arena. This approach does not provide us with a blueprint for research, but it is a necessary precaution that allows us to address the problem in the potentially correct way.

In the field of Latin American studies, Gilbert Joseph, Michael Schroeder,

Chris Frazier, Max Parra, and Amy Robinson are some of the representatives of this line of thought. (For a presentation of this line of research, see Robinson [2006, 2009] and Dabove [2007].)

Another point of contention surrounding bandits, inside academia, is the debate regarding the social or political nature of banditry, as opposed to its merely criminal nature (i.e., profiteering, murder, sociopathic acts). The first modern definition of banditry, as crafted by Eric Hobsbawm, steps squarely into this fray. Social bandits, he explains, "are peasant outlaws whom the lord and state regard as criminals, but who remain within peasant society, and are considered by their people as heroes, champions, avengers, fighters for justice, perhaps even leaders for liberation, and in any case men to be admired, helped and supported. This relation between the ordinary peasant and the rebel, outlaw and robber is what makes social banditry interesting and significant. It also distinguishes it from other kinds of rural crime" ([1969] 1981, 17). This definition (amply criticized, when not flatly rejected) has been very influential; if anything, it has been used as a useful counterpoint. It presents all of the terms that would inform the debate on banditry for the half century that followed, namely: (1) robbery is crucial, but it does not exhaust the definition of banditry; (2) the very notion of banditry emerges out of a conflict over who has the power to define a certain behavior (either the local or national elite, or local communities), and the locus of this conflict is discursive; and (3) there is a changing, ill-defined, but live relation of either affiliation or representation between the bandit and a larger community.

Hobsbawm defined social bandits as prepolitical: representatives (in different ways, conscious or not, clearly articulated or not) of a larger community, but not reaching what for him was the true definition of politics (i.e., class politics). For his critics, the whole idea of bandit politics, as a politics that advances the interests of a group larger than the gang and its supporters and beneficiaries, is erroneous. Bandits are, at best, profiteering or violent entrepreneurs (i.e., merchants of violence as a commodity). If they have any politics, it is contrary to the interests of peasants since bandits tend to side with the rural elites (those capable of providing money and protection). On the other hand, historians specializing in Latin America who have incorporated Guha's ([1983] 1999) and Scott's (1985) understanding of banditry into their perspectives do not examine banditry as mere criminality or as a

rudimentary form of peasant resistance, but rather as a form of peasant politics fully articulated into a peasant consciousness. In this approach, banditry
belongs to a continuum of resistance that runs from gossip to open rebellion.
Furthermore, these scholars focus their epistemological and ethical concerns on the impossibility of translating peasant conceptions of politics into
a nationalist-statist notion of politics. Both can negotiate and even collude,
but they remain essentially heterogeneous.

For the nominalists, then, banditry (either the actions of the bandit or the
memories of the bandit, as a historical or fictional figure) is always political.
This is so not—or not necessarily—because the bandit has a conscious political agenda (based on class, ethnicity, or national affiliation, although in many
cases the bandit may have or may ally with those who have or pretend to have
one), but rather because his very actions, when they collide with the law of the
state, bring the conflictive founding nature of any social order to the fore. This
is the case, as Foucault mentions, with "popular illegalities" that are made into
crimes (1975, 299–342). Thus, the peasant who cuts wood, makes charcoal,
or hunts game in a forest formerly public but recently claimed by a landlord
becomes an outlaw who has to be ready to violently defend his livelihood. The
same goes for the peasant who uses pastures that used to belong to a community, or that used to be public land, and who now becomes a trespasser; or for
the peasant who kills a cow eating his crops, and who becomes a rustler.

But these very acts enact a notion of ownership, of land use, and of citizenship that puts the social edifice that the state law upholds into question.
Banditry may also not be easily translated into modern ethical values (or values with which we are comfortable). The Plateados who exacted protection
money from hacendados and the well-to-do in central Mexico in the nineteenth century, and who kidnapped those reluctant to pay and subjected
them to horrible tortures *pour encourager les autres*, may have been cruel
psychopaths who enjoyed torturing their fellow man. But the fact remains
that the Plateados became a para-state that collected money in exchange for
protection, just like a state (and, in mid-nineteenth-century Mexico, perhaps
more efficiently than the state). That collusion (of which Charles Tilly [1975]
has written brilliantly) between war making, criminality, and state making is
a political phenomenon, if nothing else, because it challenges the perceived
notions of what politics is.

It is imperative for historical actors to distinguish between outlaw and lawful violence and to make a value judgment. The decision on value is essential to any kind of organized life, as Nietzsche emphatically stated. By the same token, it is imperative for analysts of discourse (who can go by any disciplinary rubric) to suspend that decision, and to show how the distinction between lawful and outlaw came to be in each particular instance. But one thing is certain: while the facts are usually clear (cattle or money changed hands, a crop was burned, a person was threatened or tortured or killed), the meaning of the act (its position before the law) is, in and of itself, impossible to determine. The decision on the meaning of the act is a foundational political act that "creates reality" (since it creates identities and functions as a cause for other acts). And political, in this case, does not mean "distorted by particular interests." There is no option between political and nonpolitical when it comes to a judgment regarding meaning—any decision is political since the grounds for the decision lie not in the nature of the act, but in the interplay of forces that produce truth, as the condition of the social visibility (as lawful or outlaw) for that act. In other words: how the bandit trope was articulated in this particular conflict at a discursive level is just as essential as (and to a degree impossible to distinguish from) the actual act.

I would like to close these pages with one example. Its controversial nature (since it deals with a national, and indeed a Latin American, hero) may help illuminate what I am trying to convey. In 1927 the U.S. Marines staged one of many interventions in Nicaragua. In the wake of that intervention, the United States brokered an agreement between the Conservatives and the Liberals to pursue an electoral solution and to put an end to the ongoing civil war. Only Augusto César Sandino, at the time a minor Liberal leader in northwestern Nicaragua, objected to this solution. He rose in arms to oppose the accord, thus leading a major insurgency that made him into a hemispheric and indeed an international icon. Schroeder (1996, 2005) and Macaulay ([1967] 1998) superbly record how official Marine reports, semiofficial Marine publications, personal letters by privates as well as officers, and the Nicaraguan and American press and politicians dubbed Sandino a brigand (*bandolero, bandido, ladrón, latrofaccioso*).

Deeming banditry any form of irregular resistance to a foreign army, or using banditry as a legitimation for a foreign occupation, was (and is) a tried-and-true discursive technique. It was used in Cuba in the wake of the 1898 invasion (Perez 1986, 1989), in Haiti with the *cacos* after the 1916 intervention (Schmidt 1995), in the Philippines after 1898 (Linn 2000), and in the Dominican Republic after the first American intervention (Calder 2006; Franks 1995). Of course, this rhetorical strategy was not only crucial to the dynamics between imperial powers and antioccupation partisans. It was also part of a usually quite effective "politics of naming" (in Bhatia's term) carried out by political powers on their way to becoming a power consolidated against its challengers.

It is for this reason that the Franco regime labeled (and persecuted) as bandits the Spanish Republican guerrillas in the post–Civil War period (and passed a law against "banditry" to that effect). It is also for this reason that the Cuban government dubbed the fight against Cuban counterrevolutionaries in the Escambray region in the first half of the 1960s a *lucha contra bandidos* (González de Cascorro 1975). It is for this reason that the Soviet regime dubbed the 1920–1921 anti-Bolshevik peasant rebels centered in Tambov (the so-called Greens, led by Aleksandr Antonov) bandits (Landis 2008). It is for this reason that the French revolutionaries dubbed the royalist and Catholic insurgence in western France (the Vendée, a movement that went on to become a kind of eponym for backward-looking, counterrevolutionary peasant uprisings, from Canudos to la Cristiada) banditry. And perhaps the most bloody and systematically conducted of all of these examples of labeling is the vast—but ultimately failed—Nazi campaign of extermination of partisans and "enemies of the Reich" conducted by the SS in the Eastern Front, from 1942 to 1945. The so-called *Bandenbekämpfung* ("combating banditry," as opposed to *Partisanenbekämpfung*, "combating partisans") became the third component of the Nazi regime's three-part strategy for German national security, together with genocide (*Endlösung der Judenfrage*, "the Final Solution to the Jewish Question") and slave labor (*Erfassung*, "Registration of Persons to Hard Labor") (Blood 2008).

Returning to the particular case of Nicaragua and Sandino: from a critical perspective, it is not a matter of judging whether Sandino was indeed a bandit, or of insisting, with righteous indignation, that of course he was not. It is not a matter of siding with the Marines (and their later minions, Somoza and the National Guard), or with historical or contemporary Sandinistas. Both choices would imply a renunciation of analysis and a belated and irrelevant engagement in the conflict (of course, one may choose to engage in the conflict, but at a cost). The bandit label, much like the terrorist label, was not (it was never) a mere blunt or cynical act. Sandino's insurgency, as Schroeder (1996) traces very well, did not spring from a vacuum, but rather was deeply rooted in a long tradition of nonstate rural violence in the Segovias that long preceded the American intervention.[2]

Indeed, "Sandino's rebels . . . refashioned for their own purposes . . . the idioms and practices of gang warfare, gang violence, and ritual terror in pursuit of political power" (Schroeder 1996, 389). Sandino's demand of contributions from friends and foes was called *garantías*, a designation used by local armed parties to refer to the extortion of rural landowners. He also engaged in arms smuggling (crucial to the war effort) from Honduras in the North, a border area with a long preexisting tradition of smuggling of all kinds, and he employed professional smugglers to do so; he recruited highway robbers in his ranks, among them some of his most loyal and effective warriors, such as the bandit/general Pedro Altamirano, also known as Pedrón; and he borrowed tactics (ambush, permanent mobility, extortion) and practices pertaining to brigand warfare—among them the infamous mutilations *corte de chaleco* and *corte de corbata*, whose most renowned practitioner was Pedrón (see, for example, Lizandro Chávez Alfaro's short story "Corte de chaleco," in Chávez Alfaro [1963]). Sandino and his followers ransacked villages, haciendas, and mines (when they belonged to Conservatives, Americans, or enemies of the cause), and sustained their troops with extensive cattle rustling.

It is nonetheless obvious that Sandino far exceeded the common definition of banditry: he successfully framed his struggle within a hemispheric and global context (and obtained hemispheric and global fame). Sandino's brigand practices were a means to an end, focused on achieving control of the state or at least a favorable balance of power vis-à-vis said state (witness the terms of the final armistice, signed before his assassination) as well as vis-à-vis the United States. So it could be argued that "bandit" in Sandino's case was not (or not only) a derogatory analogy to an out-and-out robber, rustler, and racketeer, but the name of a serious threat (of contested but increasing legitimacy) to the security of the state. For the sake of argument, one might toy with the idea that Sandino was a latro in the Roman tradition, but more in the vein of the noble Viriatus (the Lusitanian leader who fought off the Romans until he was treacherously murdered) than that of the criminal Bulla Felix. The same can be said of Mao Tse-tung's popular army (Mao was inspired by *The Water Margin*, a celebrated medieval bandit novel, and by the tactics of contemporary bandits [Hobsbawm (1969) 2000, 115]), and of the anarchists in Argentine's Patagonia during the famous 1921 rural strike (which ended in a wholesale massacre), or the anarchist and Bolshevik bank robbers (the expropriators) in the early twentieth century (Hobsbawm [1969] 1981; Bayer [1972] 1992).

But in these cases, as in Sandino's, the labeling itself was a fact with significant consequences, much like the current "war on terror," which allows U.S. drones to bomb targets in countries with which it is nominally at peace and whose sovereignty it nominally respects (e.g., Pakistan, Yemen), or allows the labeling of insurgents as "enemy combatants," making them potentially subject to "enhanced interrogation techniques" (i.e., torture) and years of imprisonment without due process (see Yoo 2003; Yoo was the Bush-era architect of this policy). In the Nicaraguan case, the labeling determined how participants at all levels experienced the war, since it gave them their sense of purpose and identity. As Schroeder (2005) shows, many of the Marines on the field, risking their lives with little to expect in terms of political power, economic gain, or career advancement, lived through the protracted conflict, believing in good faith that they were chasing bandits—something that, in many cases, they resented doing, since it was a brutal, tiring, and mostly inglorious business. The labeling of Sandino's irregulars as bandits determined how the conflict was legitimized and financed by the United States. Since it was not acknowledged as a war proper, the budget appropriations process worked differently.[3]

The labeling also determined how the war played out in relation to other conflicts in other areas of the world: Japan invaded Manchuria with the avowed intention of "protecting Japanese lives and property," the same excuse the Americans had used in Nicaragua—even though prior to the intervention no American lives or property had been harmed. Henry Lewis Stimson, the U.S. secretary of state—and former envoy to Nicaragua—reacted to the Japanese invasion, but Japanese diplomats lectured him on the fact that in the invasion of Manchuria the empire was only taking a page from the American foreign policy playbook, "protecting the lives and properties of its nationals" (MacAulay [1967] 1998, 201). Also, the labeling of Sandino as a bandit determined how the coercive capabilities of the Nicaraguan state developed (i.e., the creation and mission of the Guardia Nacional as a security—not a defense—force, and many of its extralegal protocols). Finally, it determined the way in which Sandino's murder was planned and justified, and how Somoza himself legitimized his own historical necessity—which he did in, among other venues, his book, *El verdadero Sandino; o, El calvario de las Segovias* (1936), where the image of Sandino-as-bandit is pervasive. In other words, the task (or one of the possible tasks) is not to decide, sorting fact from fiction, whether Sandino was a bandit or the unblemished hero of the Latin American emancipation (or any of the more ethically opaque variety of middle options). The task in this case and throughout this book is, in the presence of a defined corpus of texts, to analyze how (and why) the bandit trope was articulated; how it confirms, challenges, or ignores other articulations of the trope in this or in other conflicts; and what role it came to play in such conflicts.

Bandits thrive at elusive crossroads: the crossroads of languages, of domains, of sovereignties. Tracking down the bandit is impossible because his name is legion. It is only possible to trace the myriad conflict scenarios in which the bandit appears, and how his role has played out in each of these. As the ultimate Other that defines Us, outlaw violence has been one of the most prominent dramatis personae in the dreams and nightmares of Latin American culture.

NOTES

PREAMBLE: PORFIRIO DÍAZ'S PARADOX

1. Just a few days earlier, both the storming of the city and Díaz's precipitous resignation were far from foregone conclusions. Although revolutionary forces had the city under siege, Madero, always the cautious leader, did not want to risk a military intervention by the United States by attacking the border town and accidentally harming American citizens or property. Also, Madero was wary of the other revolutionary movements, nominally under his leadership but effectively out of his control, that seemed to be cropping up across the federation. So he was willing to negotiate an armistice with the government and hash out a political compromise. Pascual Orozco and Francisco "Pancho" Villa, Madero's ascendant military leaders (who later became bitter enemies), were dissatisfied with Madero's prudence and willingness to compromise. So they conspired behind Madero's back to create an incident that would unleash the battle, thus forcing Madero's hand into allowing them to attack and defeat Juárez's garrison. The plan went well, and Juárez was taken. The occupation by the revolutionaries was not a decisive action in strictly military terms. But Juárez gave the revolutionaries control of a major rail and border-crossing hub, essential to the rebels' supply of arms and provisions. It also gave them access to American and international media—the battle occurred literally under the eyes of the American public and media (see Romo 2005). Juárez provided a

makeshift "seat of government" that would legitimize their revolutionary identity and their claim to power. Contrary to expectations, the revolutionary forces
did not indulge in any of the barbaric excesses that the Porfirian press assigned
to them, a potentially decisive factor vis-à-vis American recognition (Katz
1998, 103). Furthermore, the occupation dealt a public relations blow to the
Porfirian regime. It belied the notion that the revolutionaries were only a minor
challenge, brigand-like in nature. It gave even more momentum to uprisings
throughout the federation, and it highlighted the regime's military and political
weaknesses. The aging (and ailing) Díaz was left with no other option but to
grudgingly agree to a lopsided bargain: exile for himself, and the establishment
of an interim government that would oversee free and open elections.

2. The Mexican Revolution was the first Latin American revolution, and one of
the world's first successful revolutions of the twentieth century. John Mason
Hart ([1987] 1997) and Eric Wolf ([1969] 1999) place the Mexican Revolution
in a global context, in order to argue its place in the twentieth-century revolutionary movements. Both authors draw illuminating comparisons between the
Mexican Revolution and other movements around the world, although with different emphases. Hart compares the Mexican Revolution with late nineteenth-
century/early twentieth-century developments in other semiperipheral traditional societies largely based upon agrarian economies (i.e., Russia's revolution
of 1905, China's revolution of 1911, and Iran's revolution of 1906). He highlights
what he calls "global causation": the shock to traditional peasantry of the introduction of agrarian capitalism, as well as the interplay between revolution,
nationalist ideology, and the middle classes. Wolf's book, on the other hand,
is more concerned about the role of the peasantry in modern (i.e., Marxist or
anticolonial) revolutions, a concern that he shares with Eric Hobsbawm. (Not
by chance, Wolf's book and Hobsbawm's *Bandits* are both from 1969.) Thus he
compares the Mexican Revolution with other "peasant wars of the twentieth
century" whose ideological content was much more influenced (or determined)
by Marxist ideology: Russia's revolution of 1917, China's revolution of 1949, and
Cuba's revolution of 1959, as well as anticolonial wars in Vietnam and Algeria.

Tutino (1989) takes a different approach. He argues that the Mexican Revolution was the culminating (although not the last) act of a long century of peasant unrest that began in the late colonial period (the mid-eighteenth century
onward). Instead of focusing on the last part of the nineteenth century (as Hart
does) or the twentieth century (as Wolf does), he sees a continuum between

early nineteenth-century independence wars, mid-nineteenth-century civil wars, late nineteenth-century widespread rural unrest (from Sonora to Yucatán), the revolution, and the Cristero War.

3. Knight ([1986] 1990), on the other hand, highlights the continuities between the triumphant revolution and the decades-old liberal process of state consolidation.

4. All translations in the book are my own, unless otherwise noted in the list of works cited. Sometimes I use (and modify) an existing translation. Proper attribution is given in such cases.

5. In the original typewritten text, a capital letter for "People" is used only in the first instance of the noun. However, all instances of the word throughout the message are consistent with this reverential usage, as in, for example, "the will of the people." This same oscillation occurs in the use of the word "Nation."

6. For a discussion of three prerevolutionary brands of liberalism and a placement of Porfirian rule in the tradition of liberal thought and political practice, see Knight (1985). Knight distinguishes "Constitutional liberalism," "Institutional liberalism," and "Developmental liberalism" and broadly places Porfirio Díaz's regime within the latter one. For a more in-depth examination of Porfirian liberalism, see Hale (1990, 2008).

7. According to Bell (1914, 2), elites from all over the world heaped praise upon Díaz: "He was 'the Moses and Joshua of his people' by the phrase of Andrew Carnegie, 'the prodigy of nature' according to Tolstoy, a personage 'to be held up to the hero worship of mankind,' as Elihu Root explained."

8. *Encargo* can be a dignity that is bestowed upon someone (*cargo*) or a task that can be given to someone ("encomendar, poner al cuidado de alguien" or "imponer una obligación"). In any case, the active subject is the one that makes the encargo, while the person "in charge" is only the passive recipient or follower of somebody else's will.

9. History has its ironies: When Díaz was riding the train that was to take him to Veracruz and to exile, it was attacked by an "armed gang" led by a chieftain named Caloca. The person in charge of the armed escort was none other than Victoriano Huerta, later to play an infamous role as Madero's murderer and the leader of the counterrevolutionary coup of 1913 (Huerta 1975, 19).

10. Some of the most notorious names in the Mexican gallery of outlaws belong to this period: the Plateados (a gang or cluster of gangs active in central Mexico at mid-century, in particular during the Reform Wars and the Intervention);

Heraclio Bernal (1855–1888, active in Sinaloa, and perhaps the most important and intriguing Mexican outlaw after Pancho Villa); Manuel Lozada (1828–1873, active in Tepic and Nayarit); Chucho el Roto (1858–1894, active in Veracruz); and Santana Rodríguez Palafox, also known as Santanón (1910, bandit and early revolutionary, affiliated with the Magonismo). For specific accounts of Porfirian Mexican bandits, see Girón (1976), Meyer (1984, 1989), Vanderwood (1992), Frazer (2006), and Robinson (2006, 2009).

11. This is the case, to provide just a few examples, with the Valencian *fueros* and its relationship with baroque banditry (Ruff 2001, 222); the phenomenon of *cangaceirismo* in the Brazilian Northeast nineteenth century, linked to local elites' fierce defense of state autonomy vis-à-vis the national government; and the intangibility of landed property and the power of political landowners (*coronéis*) (Pernambucano de Mello 2004).

12. This is the reason that, for example, eighteenth-century English landowners, while passing draconian and ever more numerous capital statutes in Parliament, resisted both the creation of a constabulary and the institution of the office of state prosecutor. They were afraid that these would "lead to despotism, a political police serving the Crown" (Hay 1975, 41).

13. See Grünewald ([1999] 2004) for several fictitious morality tales taken from Roman sources about encounters between outlaws and sovereigns where the similarities between (or even identities of) each group are the focus of the narrative. The character Jonathan Wild, in Henry Fielding's *The History of the Life of the Late Mr. Jonathan Wild the Great*, states, "In Civil Life, doubtless, the same Genius, the same inducements have often composed the Statesman and the Prig, for so we call what the Vulgar name a Thief. The same Parts, the same Actions often promote Men to the Head of superior Societies, which raise them to the Head of lower and where is the essential Difference if the one ends on Tower-Hill, and the other at Tyhurn? Hath the Block any Preference to the Gallows, or the Ax to the Halter, but what is given them by the ill-guided Judgment of Men?" ([1743] 2010, 29).

14. The Battle of Rellano was won, to a large degree, through the use, for the first time, of the *máquina loca*, a locomotive loaded with explosives and sent down the railroad tracks to smash into the enemy's trains. The máquina loca went on to become one of the icons of the revolution.

15. In his *Retrato autobiográfico* (which I will discuss later), Villa states in unequivocal terms that Governor Aurelio González, as well as Abraham González (at

the time a member of Madero's cabinet), had given him authorization to exact resources from Parral (Villa 225).

16. Huerta was one of the few senior officers of the Federal Army who adamantly insisted on seeking a purely military solution to the uprising, and he never ceased to consider the revolutionaries as bandits.

17. In "Truth and Juridical Forms," Michel Foucault ([1974] 1994) shows how the divorce of power (politics) from truth is one of the founding myths of the Western episteme, and how that myth emerges at a precise moment (classical Greece) and has a well-defined history.

INTRODUCTION

1. I delve into this more extensively in the last chapter of this book ("What Is a Bandit?").

2. *Bandido* and *bandolero* are the two main portmanteau terms in Spanish for rural banditry. In Brazilian Portuguese, *cangaceiro* and *jagunço* are the main terms, but not *bandido*, which in Portuguese can refer to any criminal (rural or urban) and mainly to a robber. In both languages there are, however, dozens of other terms that are more specific to some practices, regional, idiosyncratic, or outdated. For an examination of the parallel lexical development of the terms "bandido" and "bandolero," see Álvarez Barrientos and García Moutón (1986). (The parallelism did not preclude many semantic overlaps. In fact, the authors' thesis is precisely that over time, "bandido" assumed the noble connotations of "bandolero," whereas "bandolero" became synonymous with "robber.") For the Portuguese case, see Pernambucano de Mello (2004). Shaw (1984) also provides an illuminating explanation of how the terms *lestes* (Greek) and *latro* (Latin, from Greek) evolved from their more ancient meanings (plunderer as a way of life, and mercenary, respectively) to their later derogative connotation of outlaw.

3. I analyze this in greater detail in the introduction to *Nightmares of the Lettered City* (2007). In any case, this is why many bandits took great pains to prevent law enforcement from obtaining the corpses of fallen comrades. When Lampião's older brother Levino was killed, it is said that Lampião cut off his brother's head, in order to prevent his identification and subsequent abuse (Pernambucano de Mello 1993, 58). In eighteenth-century England, rioting was common to prevent the authorities from displaying the bodies of hanged crim-

inals, or the Royal College of Surgeons from using the corpses as material for dissection and teaching. The most celebrated case was the riots that followed Dick Turpin's hanging in 1739 (Sharpe [2004] 2005).

4. According to Claudio Lomnitz, Fernández de Lizardi enacts a change in the attitude vis-à-vis death. Fernández de Lizardi's *Diccionario burlesco y formalesco* contrasts the popular attitude toward death and the newly executed (ironic and flirtatious) with the "proper" attitude (i.e., heroic or martyr-like). Perico's horror (and reflection) when faced with the spectacle of Januario's death bears witness to the removal of Perico from a "popular subject position" to a new model of bourgeois identity (Lomnitz 2008, 38).

5. In "Alturas del Machu Picchu," Neruda ([1950] 2006, 116) expresses the same conviction about the poet's ability to speak for the dead (in this case, the pre-Columbian or indigenous past):

   I come to speak through your dead mouth.
   All through the earth join all
   the silent wasted lips
   and speak from the depths to me all this long night

6. Janes mentions that "human cultures have elaborated five principal types of traditional, authorized beheadings: the ancestral head, removed after death, not taken by violence; the trophy head, taken in warfare or raid; the sacrificial head, taken from a living person by decapitation in the performance of a religious rite; the presentation head, taken in a political struggle to remove a contender or a rival; the public execution, proceeding from a legal decision" (2005, 14).

7. We can also mention *The Water Margin* (also translated as *Outlaws of the Marsh*), the classic Chinese medieval novel, in which Wang Lung, "the White Clad Scholar," the supreme leader (ruler of Fraternity Hall) of the Liangshang Marsh gang, turns to a life of banditry after failing his exam to enter the imperial civil service.

8. This possibility of drawing wide-ranging comparisons was one of the initial stimuli for Hobsbawm's *Bandits* (1969), the official founding text of the field—but not the first, by any means. It remains to be seen, however, if this universality bespeaks the universality of the phenomenon—somehow related to the existence of some universals in peasant or rural culture, itself a debatable topic—or if it is just a consequence of the fact that the lingua franca of "bandit studies"

is English, and the field remains, sometimes involuntarily, heavily Anglocentric. In this case the purported universality would be mostly an effect of a (mis) translation.

CHAPTER 1: *SPECULUM LATRONIS*

1. Prior to the current association of terrorism with the global jihad and ethnic nationalism, the labels were overlapping (they still are, to a degree). See also the examples of the anarchists (both terrorists and "expropriators") who led the Patagonian rural strikes at the beginning of the twentieth century (Bayer [1972] 1992), or those who carried out bank robberies to finance their cause (Bayer [1972] 1992); or of the nationalists in Chechnya prior the Chechen Wars (Russell 2005). Another excellent example (related somewhat to the "expropriators") is the double label of terrorists and robbers (*asaltantes*) that Juan Domingo Perón applied to the Montoneros in 1974, when he opted for the right wing of his party and broke with the left (the Montoneros were the leftist armed organization within the Peronist movement whom Perón had sponsored and goaded into armed action as well as political agitation, in order to destabilize the military dictatorship known as Revolución Argentina and propitiate his return to power) (Vezzetti [2009] 2013). A splendid literary example of this overlapping is that of *Michael Kohlhaas*, by Heinrich Kleist (1808), and its contemporary rewriting by E. L. Doctorow in *Ragtime* (1975).

2. The effort to fend off the bandit label was undertaken by other rebels of the same period. Sometimes this happened through the means of spectacular or misguided actions. The Dominican *gavilleros*, for example, took the risky action (militarily and politically) of kidnapping the American administrator of a sugar mill only to release him later, unharmed, but committing him to deliver the message that the gavilleros were nationalist fighters, not common bandits (Calder 2006, 203). In another context, avoiding the bandit label may have been one of the factors that persuaded the Filipino nationalist Emilio Aguinaldo to downplay guerrilla warfare and engage the Americans in conventional battles, as corresponded to an aspirational national government—a strategy that carried disastrous consequences (Linn 2000).

3. Villa says in his *Retrato autobiográfico* that he chose this name because it was also the name of his grandfather (who sired Villa's father out of wedlock). The name change would have been intended to restore his affiliation with an hon-

orable lineage. His enemies, on the other hand, argued that he chose the name because it was that of a nineteenth-century bandit who, like Villa, roamed Durango, Sinaloa, and Chihuahua. Herrera ([1939] 1964, 12) even said that Villa was part of the "original" Villa gang, and that Arango took the name after the death of the older bandit. The evidence for either case seems to be inconclusive.

4. José Vasconcelos's multivolume memoir, and in particular *La tormenta* ([1937] 2000), written and published after his turn to right-wing politics, consistently talks about Villa as a bandit, although Vasconcelos does not refer to him as Arango. Vasconcelos compares Villa to a "beast in heat" (70) and clearly states that "Villa's lack of education [*incultura*] prevented him from going beyond the condition of a mere highway robber [*salteador*]" (73) and an "outlaw" [*forajido*] and a criminal (183) who turned his back on Eulalio Gutiérrez, the leader Vasconcelos preferred (154, 175), who was responsible for bringing Mexico back to the era of the South American montonera and the Santanista *caudillo* rule (145). He does not mince words, however, when it comes to Carranza and his faction. He considers Carranza "not a statesman, but the leader of a bandit gang [*banda latrofacciosa*]" (72), whose followers were even worse than the Villistas when plundering and raping (136). He considered the revolution in its Carranzista-Obregonista-Callista outcome a "cannibal orgy" (123), "confusion and piracy" (229).

5. In fact, Villa's reputation as a bandit has harmed him to this day. In his massive and purportedly comprehensive *Invisible Armies: An Epic History of Guerrilla Warfare from Ancient Times to the Present*, military historian Max Boot mentions Villa, an undisputed master of guerrilla warfare, only once, and only as part of a broader discussion of Hobsbawm's book on banditry (Boot 2013, 51).

6. Herrera ([1939] 1964), whose tenacity when it comes to libel is noteworthy, maintains that Villa enlisted in the revolutionary ranks entirely by chance, and as a kind of sanctuary for the persecutions that he was suffering (15). She denies Villa any participation in the actions that led to the fall of Díaz (15–16).

7. Villa's ideological legacy is also questionable. The Dorados, a fascist group led by a former Villa officer, active in the 1930s, attempted to equate the former guerrillas with the new European paramilitary organizations (the German brownshirts or the Italian blackshirts) (O'Malley 1986, 171). On the other hand, Villa was also hailed in the 1960s as the father of leftist revolutionaries and guerrillas (Blanco Moheno 1969).

8. The *Retrato* is one of the two first-person narratives produced during Villa's

lifetime that were considered autobiographies. The other is *Vida de Francisco Villa contada por él mismo*, written by Ramón Puente (1919).

9. Guadalupe Villa and Rosa Helia Villa offer a brief biographical account of Bauche Alcalde in the introduction to the *Retrato*, and Taibo ([2006] 2010), in his biography, has a chapter partially devoted to Bauche Alcalde ("Las autobiografías y los autobiógrafos"). The most detailed biographical account that I know of, however, is the (largely favorable) one penned by Gálvez Cancino (2004). Pérez Rul, in the biography of Villa that he wrote (under an alias) in the United States, after the dissolution of the División del Norte, sheds an unflattering light on the character of Bauche Alcalde. He considers him a bombastic adulator, a careerist, and a traitor at heart, in the vein of that other literary con man associated with Villa, José Santos Chocano (1916, 35).

10. The editors argue that Manuel Trillo—Villa's longtime secretary, killed alongside him in 1923—took the dictation. Bauche Alcalde would have transcribed the stenographic notes taken by Trillo, polished and adorned Villa's oral style, and interspersed his own opinions freely in order to put together the manuscript as we know it today (Guadalupe Villa 2004, 31). It seems that Trillo's notes survive (the editors do not mention who has them, and Katz was unaware of their existence), and they seem to have been examined by Guadalupe Villa (who reproduces one page). The notes have not been deciphered since it seems that Trillo used a personal stenographic style whose key he did not share. Guadalupe Villa maintains that dates, numbers, and places can be identified in Trillo's manuscript and these seem to correspond to Bauche Alcalde's notebooks. The problem that is not resolved is that of how Bauche Alcalde was able to transcribe them (Trillo's assistance, perhaps?).

11. There is some dispute about this. The date in the manuscript reads "February, 1914." The context suggests that the manuscript by Bauche Alcalde was finished on that date. The editors, on the contrary, consider this date as marking the beginning of the dictation.

12. The notebooks had a circuitous history. Katz mentions that "when Manuel Bauche Alcalde left Chihuahua, he turned the memoirs over to Villa's personal physician, a Dr. Raschbaum, and when the latter left Villa's service in October 1914, he gave the memoirs to Luz Corral, Villa's wife. For unknown reasons, she was unable to keep them, and they came into the possession of Villa's last wife, Austreberta Rentería" (1998, 831). The manuscript then passed to Hipólito Villa Rentería, son of Austreberta and Pancho Villa. He gave them to Guadalupe

Villa, who made photographic reproductions of them. Hipólito asked to have the manuscript back (purportedly only for a short time), and at the time of his death, the manuscript seems to have been lost (Guadalupe Villa 2004, 37–38).

It remains unclear why the manuscript was not published in 1914. Katz (1998) offers several plausible (but unverified) hypotheses: Villa did not recognize himself in Bauche Alcalde's heavily edited account; Villa had begun to distrust Bauche Alcalde's loyalty, therefore dissolving the association upon which the text was predicated; or the murder of Benton (an English subject whose death, in very equivocal circumstances, created an international scandal) made the publication unadvisable. Taibo ([2006] 2010) agrees with Katz, but adds that Bauche Alcalde may have taken a more active role in preventing the publication, since he had distanced himself from Villa after his brother Joaquín had been deposed as chief of staff of the Chao Brigade after a dishonorable defeat (370). Manuel would switch alliances and become Pablo González's secretary, while Joaquín would remain loyal to Villa. Joaquín would be executed by the Carrancistas after the battle of Celaya.

13. In this respect, my analysis complements such works as Parra (2005), Anderson (2001, 2007), and Katz (1998). In particular Anderson (2001, 2007) shows how Villa and his agents during 1913–1914 were able to manipulate American public opinion to avoid presenting Villa as the "Mexican Other," but also played to the themes of quintessential Americana: "His publicity message championed democracy (versus authoritarianism), formal education (versus illiteracy), self-reliance (versus craven dependence), egalitarianism (versus aristocracy), and social justice for the poor (versus elitism).... Further, the propaganda highlighted Villa's singular individualism, homespun honesty, earnest preparedness, personal bravery, and indefatigability" (Anderson 2001, 174). Far from the stereotype of the greaser, Anderson (2007) adds, Villa presented himself as a south-of-the-border embodiment of Frederick Jackson Turner's frontier thesis.

14. One example: the narrative of some military actions is interrupted in order to transcribe the reports that the federal officers gave of these same actions (146, 149). A footnote by Bauche Alcalde states that these texts come from archives (something that seems to contradict the idea that the text is only the record of Villa's dictation). In the facsimile, these "federal versions" seem to be handwritten (not authored) by Bauche Alcalde himself. Perhaps a comparison between Bauche Alcalde and Trillo would resolve this problem.

15. There is no mention of the time that Villa spent in the Federal Army as a forced recruit, or of his links to foreign capitalists (for whom he seems to have worked on several occasions), or of how exactly he became an acquaintance of Abraham González, the man who recruited him to fight for the Maderista uprising.

16. There are words and tropes that Villa (or any rural folk, for that matter) would have never used; there is also a knowledge of science and history that appears (even in watered-down versions) quite out of place, such as anthropological theories of heritage (Francisco Villa 2004, 75), historical explanations centered on the "degeneracy" of the popular classes caused by the oppression of the Spanish conquerors and their descendants (76), and the tracing of a historical arc of Spanish ruthlessness toward other cultures from the Middle Ages to the present, including the extermination of the Muslims and Aztecs (76). There are numerous mythological references and analogies, and political commentary (in particular when criticizing the Porfirian era) on matters that Villa clearly could have had no knowledge of or interest in, such as the financial dealings of Limantour or the politics of the Mexican drama stage under Justo Sierra (recall that Bauche Alcalde was a drama and music critic). For comparison's sake, the reader can contrast this with the anecdote about his time as a bandit that Villa tells Martín Luis Guzmán, reproduced in *El águila y la serpiente* ([1928] 1961, 439). This anecdote's lack of adornment and moralizing, and its attention to seemingly useless (but telling) details, bespeak more about its authenticity than the more grandiose style of the *Retrato*.

17. This concept was productively taken up by Brazilian anthropologist Frederico Pernambucano de Mello in order to coin another notion, that of the "ethical shield." The ethical shield is the deliberate attempt to "socialize" (and thus justify) the actions of Brazilian *cangaceiros* (in particular Lampião), distancing their public image from what they really were (professional bandits) and creating an image of "avengers" or "outlaws" (2004, 120).

18. Villa and Salvatore Giuliano were both contemporaries of the emergence of the new mass media. They were featured in films and they gave interviews for journals and newspapers. They also exploited the medium of photography and the popular press to further their legends (Chandler 1978, 1988). Both Giuliano and Villa were also aware of the basic tenets of the romantic bandit legend: Giuliano was extremely good looking and used that to further his legend. Villa's equestrian images are, on the other hand, his signature ones.

19. "Entrevista de Lampião em Juazeiro do Norte," accessed July 29, 2016, http://forums.tibiabr.com/printthread.php?t=103926.

20. I refer to this as a strategic use of truth because, even though the feud was, to a degree, the original factor that thrust Lampião into banditry, his career became focused on profit soon afterward. As such, Lampião's narrative was the prime example of his concept of an "ethical shield" that allowed him to downplay his identity as a professional cangaceiro (*cangaço meio de vida*) and highlight his identity as an avenger (*cangaço refúgio*). Pernambucano de Mello (2004, 140), who coined the aforementioned distinctions, also notes how Lampião changed his "ethical shield" according to place and circumstance. In Pernambuco, Lampião's home state, his image was more easily linked with that of the avenger. But when in Bahia—where he spent a significant portion of his career, and where he, as an avenger, had no business—he acted in such a way as to change his image to that of a "redistributionist" Robin Hood, unmooring his legitimacy from his biography (209).

21. In 1892 the story was actually edited and translated into English as an adventure story by Elizabeth M. Edmonds: *Kolokotrones, the Klepht and the Warrior, Sixty Years of Peril and Daring*.

22. *Blood Meridian*'s Mexican portions occur in some of the same areas (tinged by McCarthy with hellish overtones) as those prowled by Villa.

23. Some of his "tricks" include his escape from prison disguised as a lawyer; his infiltration of enemy-held cities disguised as a charcoal merchant; and his deception of the enemy, both in humorous episodes (as when he leaves hats behind, to make the Federales think he is leaving a fully manned rearguard, thus covering his retreat) and in war-changing feats (as when and his troops enter Juárez in a coal train).

24. There is no mention of his official wife, Luz Corral, to whom he was already married by 1914.

25. López Negrete was the owner or (more likely) the renter of the hacienda Santa Isabel, in Durango. Villa refers to him as "the master" and compares his tyranny to that of a feudal lord, thus implying that López Negrete was the owner of the hacienda. The editors of the *Retrato*, however, mention that the hacienda belonged to a third party and that López Negrete was only renting it (Francisco Villa 2004, 79n4).

26. See Shaw (1984, 48) for the notion of the Roman bandit as an emperor *manqué*.

27. In *Outlaws of the Marsh*, Liu Chong, instructor of arms in the Imperial Guard,

joins the band of outlaws because of the persecution of his wife by Marshall Chao. The avenging of a female family member's honor is prominent in the story of another outlaw who became a national hero, the Australian Ned Kelly, whose mother was sentenced to three years of jail time for attacking a lawman, solely on the shaky evidence of the lawman's testimony (Seal 1996, 152).

28. In most cases (including Villa's narrative) the original offense is a defining event, but not a driving one. The career of the bandit moves forward, and is not focused upon avenging the assault upon honor (although the event may be remembered time and again, as so happens in *Juan Moreira* for example, but only to claim the aforementioned "ethical shield"). One of the few novels almost entirely focused on the dispute around the female body is the Turkish classic *Memed, My Hawk* (Kemal [1955] 1961). Memed's sweetheart is brutally courted by the village's boss and largest landowner. The rest of the novel is a long feud between these two, and the female figure never loses its central role in the narrative.

29. There are some other versions: Pérez Rul mentions that López Negrete raped Villa's sister (as opposed to just attempting it), and that Villa killed the attacker (as opposed to just wounding him) (1916, 42–43). Puente relates a version largely consistent with the one in Bauche Alcalde, but the victim is the other sister, and the gun is a different gun (1919, 45). Villa told Flores Urbina, in an interview, that he entered the revolution to avenge his sister, seduced and abandoned (*burlada*) by a captain in the Mexican army (Flores Urbina in Taibo [2006] 2010, 54). John Reed writes that Villa had to take to the hills because, while working as a milk delivery boy in Chihuahua, he killed the government official who had violated his sister ([1914] 1999, 122). *The Life of General Villa* (1914), the movie made by Mutual Studios whose script, it seems, Villa approved, depicts the Arangos as well-to-do ranchers, not as poor sharecroppers or day laborers. In it, two federal officers chase *both* of Villa's sisters. The younger one is kidnapped, raped, and left to die. Villa kills one officer and vows revenge against the surviving one, whom he finally finds (and kills) in the midst of (where else?) the battle of Torreón. Colonel John Biddle, a member of the U.S. general staff in Mexico, provided yet another version that was even more colorful. "One story has it that the sheriff of the county eloped with Villa's sister and fled to the mountains. Villa pursued him with some ardent men, caught the couple, forced the man to go through the marriage ceremony, made him dig his own grave, and Villa shot him and rolled his body to the grave" (Katz 1998, 6).

The versions go on and on. Of course, Villa's enemies deny any heroic trait in Villa's taking to the hills. John Kenneth Turner creates a truly infamous account of an event that is not informed by any virtue: "He was the go-between in the love affairs of an officer of the Rurales. But true to nature, Villa was playing an angle, also helping the officer's rival. When the officer became aware of this, he gave Villa a beating, to which Villa retaliated by killing him in a treacherous fashion" (1915, 9). Celia Herrera claims that when he was seventeen years old Villa became a criminal after stabbing a friend with whom he had fought ([1939] 1964, 11).

30. There seems to be no official record in Durango of the attack or of the ensuing persecution. Villa, however, affirms in the *Retrato*, "The persecutions against me were unleashed with formidable strength. In all districts of the state I was identified as a dangerous criminal and to all of them the order arrived that I should be apprehended, wherever I was found, alive or dead" (Francisco Villa 2004, 82). Villa was in custody on three different opportunities—he mentions only two, on pages 82 and 86—but it seems that he was not questioned (or punished) for this, even though he blames all his misfortunes on López Negrete's relentless persecution. Katz (1998, 56) hypothesizes that Villa may have left his home to avoid conscription or the drudgery of a peasant's life.

31. These terms are not absent. But they are subordinated to the dominant one (conflict as moral melodrama).

32. See Bowman (2005) for a discussion of other historical cases (Palestine, former Yugoslavian republics) in which the memory (i.e., the identity) of the nation as imagined community is constructed around the trope of victimization.

33. Hobsbawm ([1969] 1981) proposed the "bandit-peasant" link as the cornerstone of the social bandit identity. Revisionists heavily criticized this, highlighting the "peasant-landlord" link and maintaining that, on the contrary, bandits are opposed to the objective interests of rural communities. In fact, that notion and Hobsbawm's use of sources are two of the main criticisms directed at the social bandit thesis. Other scholars have analyzed cases that bypass the discussion. For example, Blok (1998), himself a harsh critic of Hobsbawm, examines how the Dutch "Goat Riders" of the seventeenth century belonged to a tight-knit occupational group (skinners, butchers, and other "unclean" occupations), which, on the one hand, placed them on the margins of society, but on the other created a strong sense of group identity, which proved ideal for a successful criminal enterprise. Ruff (2001, 236–38) mentions religious or national

affiliations as identity-creating markers for bandit gangs and their supporters. So banditry can have wide support, though it is not necessarily class based, but rather based on other affiliations that may or may not include the peasant.

34. These three denominations do not correspond to our current nomenclature: as in northeastern Brazil, "friend" conveys an affective bond as well as a military relationship, the same as "compadre," which means "relative by choice" as well as "accomplice" and "trusted business partner."

35. This inversion can be found in many examples of Mexican literature. See, for example, the discussion between Agüilita and Perico in *El periquillo sarniento*, by José Joaquín Fernández de Lizardi (1816); the contentious exchange between Astucia and the judge, and the related conflict between the tobacco smugglers and the state tobacco monopoly, in *Astucia*, by Luis Inclán (1865); and the parallel criminal state mounted by Relumbrón (aide-de-camp of the fictional version of Santa Ana) in *Los bandidos de Río Frío*, by Manuel Payno ([1891] 2000). A text strictly contemporary with Villa's, Bell's *The Political Shame of Mexico* (1914), uses this inversion repeatedly to refer to the Porfirian regime (8–9).

36. The establishment of a genealogy complements this inversion. The state-as-criminal-organization has its roots in Spanish banditry—not that of Diego Corrientes, Tempranillo, or Los Siete Niños de Écija, but that of the conquistadors. The conquistadors-as-bandits is a motif fully articulated around the time of the Spanish American Independence (and even posited by Hobsbawm [1969] 1981), but it can be traced to Bartolomé de las Casas's *Brevísima historia*, a text that also makes another identification used in the *Retrato*: that of exploitation as anthropophagy (Francisco Villa 2004, 81, 89, 125). For the cannibal trope in Latin American culture, see Jáuregui (2008).

37. The trickster is a figure with an illustrious lineage, from Robin Hood and Hereward (Keen [1961] 1987, 18) to Chucho el Roto. Although it does not define Villa, it is also present in the text (Francisco Villa 2004, 151, 166, 189, 267, 269, 271, 279). Other instances of tricksters are Estache the Monk (demon and trickster), Fouke (trickster and avenger), and, of course, Zorro.

38. This motif of the outlaw turned loyal law enforcer also appears in the case of the Spaniard José María, "El Tempranillo," who obtained a pardon and became a guard at the royal service in the mail coaches of Andalucía. He was, in fact, killed defending a convoy against an assault led by his one-time lieutenant (Pitt-Rivers [1954] 1971, 180).

39. In his one-sided correspondence with Madero, Villa insists that his imprisonment was caused by slander and misunderstanding. That is why he repeatedly
asks for an opportunity to talk to Madero face to face, an opportunity that was
never granted.

40. This is a motif that appears in many outlaw narratives, such as "The Outlawry of
Earl Godwin" (Jones 1998), where Godwin is separated from Edward the Con-
fessor by Robert (a priest, and a Norman). Godwin is outlawed because Robert
convinces Edward that Godwin is guilty of the death of his brother, and that
he was plotting against him. Godwin flees, puts together an army, and comes
back. All the Englishmen go out to receive him, since he is a popular leader. And
Godwin, instead of attacking the king, falls to his knees in front of the king and
demands, not forgiveness, but the opportunity to prove his innocence. The king
agrees, and all is settled in a satisfactory fashion.

CHAPTER 2: HUGO CHÁVEZ, MAISANTA, AND THE CONSTRUCTION OF AN INSURGENT LINEAGE

1. According to his equally colorful (albeit far less successful) successor, Nicolás
Maduro, Chávez (like the Holy Ghost) embodied himself in a bird that followed
and inspired Maduro. In 2014, a version of the Roman Catholic Our Father, but
with Chávez substituting for God, was unveiled as the "Prayer of the Delegate"
(Oración del delegado) in the Third Congress of the United Socialist Party of
Venezuela (III Congreso del Partido Socialista Unido de Venezuela). This is not
altogether a new phenomenon. After the 1992 coup attempt, an early version
of the paternoster surfaced (Guerrero 2013, 17). It was titled *Chávez nuestro*.
There was also a *Credo Chavista*, a version of the Roman Catholic Credo (Elizalde and Báez 2007). In interviews with peasants in Barinas, Guerrero found
the strong conviction that Chávez was sent as a Chosen One, either by divine
providence or by Bolívar (Guerrero 2013, 17). Of course, this intersection of
popular religion and politics is not unique to Chavismo, or even to Venezuela
(much to the chagrin of Chávez's opponents, who would like to think—or pretend to think—that Chávez is just an aberration). For a longer lineage of this
intersection in Venezuela, see Coronil (1997) and Taussig (1997).

2. A cursory web search reveals many images and videos of Chávez depicted as a

monkey, or as a "red gorilla," a depiction obviously linked to his Afro Venezuelan heritage.

3. In the classic praetorian coup (and, as I have mentioned, Chávez's was far from
this), the alleged source of legitimacy was usually (but not always) *la patria*
(the fatherland), which the military does not represent, but rather rescues from
a foreign or corrupt force. The military in twentieth-century Latin America
fashioned itself ideologically as the protector of last resort, not of subjects or
institutions, but of "values" crucial to the definition of nationhood. That is why,
in right-wing military parlance, the patria is usually different from (or even
opposed to) "the people." I have already explained how this was not the case for
Villa, for whom "la patria" was "the people."

4. The locus of that poietic potency is his voice (understanding voice as a complex
of words, intonation, body, and context of performance). I adapted the term
"poietic potency" from Domingo Faustino Sarmiento ([1845] 1979). Sarmiento
is perhaps emblematic of the political and epistemological dilemmas of the
liberal intellectual confronted with a ruler who is at the same time authoritarian, undoubtedly popular, and endowed with a rare political talent. As is well
known, there was no love lost between Sarmiento and Juan Manuel de Rosas.
Sarmiento considered Rosas a monster, a bandit, a tyrant, a murderer, and a
cannibal. But at the same time, he considered him a political genius, worthy of
hyperbolic praise. Consider, for example, the paean that he devoted to Rosas
and his cynical (but accurate) understanding of human nature: "Rosas! Rosas!
I fall to my knees; I prostrate myself before your all-powerful mind! You are as
great as the River Plate, as great as the Andes! You and you only have understood how despicable is human nature, its liberties, its science, its pride! Tread
upon it! All the rules in the civilized world will follow your lead; the more inso-
lent you become, the more obedient they will be" ([1845] 1979, 179).

This is not sarcastic (or if it is, the sarcasm is directed against himself and
his faction as well as against Rosas). Sarmiento considers Rosas a sort of (per-
verted) Plato. He comments on Rosas's taking office in 1835, "The State is a
tabula rasa upon which he will write a new and original thing. He is a poet, a
Plato. He will bring his ideal Republic to fruition, following his own design"
(Sarmiento [1845] 1979, 206). The epithet might sound surprising, but it is not.
In Rosas, Sarmiento identifies poietic potency, the talent to create a myth (in
the sense of Georges Sorel) that is expressed in the battle cry "Long live the

Federation, death to the savages, disgusting, traitor Unitarists!" That myth articulates, without rest, all of the instances of the social realm. This myth creates the social as the scene of a conflict of indefinite duration that happens in a time of exception. For almost two decades, this legitimated a state that was organized as a warrior machine, and it legitimated Rosas as a ruler with the "Sum of All Public Powers."

5. In this chapter, I follow broadly the brilliant analysis that Ana Teresa Torres carries out in *La herencia de la tribu* (2009), when it comes to the analysis of Chavez's legitimating narrative. I introduce an additional element to Torres's analysis: I focus on the centrality of Maisanta, and the presentation of Maisanta in Chávez's oral performances. Emilio Modesto Guerrero (2012, 2013) puts forward some theses about the relationship between Chávez and Maisanta that largely confirm my own. At the time I began presenting and publishing on this topic, around 2010, I was unaware of Guerrero's work—his two books in which he examines this topic were still years away. However, in this chapter I quote him extensively, since his work is complementary to mine.

6. Studies and estimations have been conducted on the massive amounts of hours that Chávez devoted to talk as part of his functions as president. All the estimations (all partial, to my knowledge) render staggering numbers. Chávez has an illustrious precedent in the young Fidel Castro, whose epic discourses and lectures were famous for never ending, and a continuator in Cristina Fernández de Kirchner, Argentine's president until late 2015, whose communication strategy seemed to be predicated upon oversaturation. Guerrero (2013, 19) states that Chávez far surpassed prolific communicators such as Winston Churchill during the Second World War, and Franklin D. Roosevelt during the Great Depression. He surpassed even Juan Domingo Perón, Benito Mussolini, and Hitler. Guerrero notes, however, accurately in my view, that unlike the aforementioned charismatic leaders, Chávez had a penchant and a knack for the pedagogical register, as opposed to the commanding or prophetic, or preachy (19).

7. The original version was delivered as follows:

Te metiste conmigo, pajarito. Te metiste conmigo, pajarito, ¿no? Tú no sabes mucho de historia. Tú no sabes mucho de nada ¿sabes? Una gran ignorancia es la que tú tienes. Eres un ignorante, Mr. Danger. Eres un ignorante. Eres un burro, Mr. Danger. Eres un burro, Mr. Danger. O para decírtelo más bien ... para decírtelo en mi mal inglés, en mi bad English, you are a donkey, Mr.

Danger. You are a donkey. Me refiero, Uds. saben, para decirlo con todas sus letras a Mr. George W. Bush. You are a donkey, Mr. Bush. . . . Te voy a decir algo, Mr. Danger. Tú eres un cobarde, ¿sabes? Tú eres un cobarde. ¿Por qué no te vas a Irak a comandar tus fuerzas armadas? Es muy fácil comandarlas desde lejos. Si algún día se te va a ocurrir la locura de invadir Venezuela, te espero en esta sabana, Mr. Danger. Come on here, Mr. Danger. Come on here. [Applause] Come on here, Mr. Danger. Cobarde, asesino, genocida, genocida, genocida. Eres un genocida. Eres un alcoholic, Mr. Danger. Es decir eres un borracho. Eres un borracho, Mr. Danger. Eres un inmoral, Mr. Danger. Eres de lo peor, Mr. Danger. [Addressing the audience] ¿Cómo se dice 'de lo peor' en inglés? [Inaudible response from the audience] The last! You are the last!

8. "Chavez te Metiste conmigo Pajarito.avi," YouTube video, 3:32, posted by "MartesNegro1," December 4, 2010, https://www.youtube.com/watch?v=MzacoTiyVG8.

9. Chávez ordered Guaicaipuro's remains to be symbolically moved (since his remains are lost) to the National Pantheon on December 8, 2001. Chávez often mentioned Guaicaipuro as well as other indigenous leaders in his speeches, in contrast to what he termed American imperialists and interventionists and their policies directed toward Venezuela. The Venezuelan government gave the name Misión Guaicaipuro to the program that aimed to restore communal land titles and rights to Venezuelan-remaining indigenous peoples.

10. Of course, I do not say that Chávez created this narrative ex nihilo, or that he did it by himself. I do think that he was very aware of it, and of how to place himself as its culmination, and that he "performed" this narrative often, deliberately, and effectively.

11. As I will show in my examination of *Las lanzas coloradas*, there are other versions of Venezuela's national struggles that emphasize the dialectical synthesis between enemies. Chávez poses nothing of this sort.

12. Izard and Slatta (1987, 35–36) explain, "The llanos early on became an area of refuge for a wide variety of persons. Fugitives from authorities in the settled coastal areas found sanctuary in the vastness and anonymity of the llanos. Black slaves escaped to the plains from coastal sugar plantations. In addition, Arawak Indians had already moved to the remote llanos after being driven out of the Caribbean in the early decades of the Spanish Conquest."

13. Disguised as a royalist reaction, the main character in this civil war was the "Legion from Hell," the fearsome llanero lancers under the leadership of the Asturian-turned-llanero José Tomás Boves. Boves and his montoneros soundly defeated the white Creole (*mantuano*) armies led by Bolívar in 1813–1814; they destroyed the Second Republic, and terrorized whites to the point of causing the exodus of most of Caracas's whites to the east, away from Boves's advancing hordes (a memorable literary rendition of this exodus is presented in *Boves, el urogallo* [1972], by Francisco Herrera Luque). Years later, in a singular reversal of allegiances, the llaneros became the fighting force that defeated the royalist armies when they deserted and flocked to the armies of another llanero, José Antonio Páez, the founding father of Venezuela. I will discuss this kind of change in allegiances by the llaneros in more detail in the next chapter.

14. Tapia mentions a number of people to whom he is indebted. Perhaps the most significant of these oral sources (from the standpoint of the present) is José Esteban Ruiz-Guevara, who had extensive knowledge about Maisanta (Guerrero [2012, 52] mentions that he even penned a novel—so far unpublished—about him: *Maisanta: El último filibustero*). Tapia acknowledges this by dedicating his work to him. But Ruiz-Guevara was also Chávez's intellectual mentor during his crucial teenage years in Barinas (53).

15. Some examples of published testimonies are *El libro de mis luchas* (1936), by Emilio Arévalo Cedeño, stubborn anti-Gómez fighter, and *Motivos llaneros* (1957), by Antonio Paiva. Both devote several pages to profiles of Maisanta.

16. The many documents (the majority of them from the archive in Miraflores) that Botello would use for his 2005 biography, which included letters from Maisanta and his sister Petra, would not be widely known until much later (and they provide an image of Maisanta that is much less epic than that put forward by Tapia).

17. The mission consists of a series of antipoverty and social welfare programs. Its name, Vuelvan Caras ("turn around") comes directly from patriotic llanero mythology: it is said to have been the order that Páez gave to his llaneros during the battle of Las Queseras del Medio, in 1819. The sudden turnaround of the llaneros and their charge against the advancing royalists surprised the royalist infantry, which fled in disarray. This turnaround decided the patriot victory against a numerically superior enemy.

18. The entire event can be watched on YouTube: "(2006) Hugo Chávez preside

Graduación de Misión Vuelvan Caras, habla sobre Maisanta," YouTube video, 58:34, posted by "Luigino Bracci Roa," October 9, 2013, https://www.youtube.com/watch?v=jYWxAj6BTvw. Emilio Guerrero mentions a similar event, in the same venue, that developed in a very similar fashion. But Guerrero mentions that it happened in 2004, right after the defeat of the recall effort against Chávez (Guerrero 2013, 130). Although I have not had access to the video of this event (if indeed there is a one), it is a fact that in order to defeat that effort, Chávez created the "Comando Maisanta," and the recall signatures are at the origin of the "Programa Maisanta" fiasco—a program to track members of the opposition, in particular those who signed the recall petition.

19. Chávez seems to have had (or have been favored with) a sense of historical correspondences. In the 1970s, as a young officer, he was destined for Barinas, where there were Marxist guerrillas at the time. The troop was quartered in La Marqueseña, Maisanta's hato. It seems that Zamora had also camped there during the Federal wars (Blanco-Muñoz 1998, 48–49). In the hacienda there was an abandoned car that used to belong to the guerrillas. In the trunk there were books, and in particular one book: Federico Brito's *Tiempo de Ezequiel Zamora*.

20. Botello provides numerous examples. Perhaps the most significant are the exchanges between Gómez and local officials (as in the case of Porfirio Díaz, local officials were required to inform often and in surprising detail about developments in their areas), and between foreign officials and their superiors or Venezuelan representatives. See Botello (2005, 49, 54, 55, 58, 67, 70, 71, 74, 76, 80, 81, 83, 94, 103, 104, 118, 119, 153, 155, 157, 185).

21. This is an important difference from Villa's account. The mother has a decisive role in Maisanta's becoming an insurgent. And the memory of this role is perpetuated by the fact that she gives him the scapular that eventually gives him his name.

22. In his interview with Blanco-Muñoz, Chávez mentions something that Tapia does not: that when Maisanta entered the property of a well-to-do citizen (a hacendado or business owner), he allowed the people to plunder at will, as an impromptu wealth redistribution act (Blanco-Muñoz 1998, 650).

23. "Chávez y Víctor Hugo (Los Miserables)," YouTube video, 1:53, posted by "peritolir," February 14, 2008, https://www.youtube.com/watch?v=Ul7JE_mKlXw.

CHAPTER 3: THE BURNING PLAINS

1. The novel belongs to the avant-garde movements throughout Latin America that attempted a synthesis between avant-garde aesthetics and various strains of cultural nationalism, such as Argentine avant-garde *criollismo*, Caribbean *negrismo*, strands within Peruvian and Ecuadorean *indigenismo*, and Brazilian *modernismo* (Videla de Rivero 1994; Verani 1986). For a specific treatment of the Venezuelan avant-garde, see Osorio (1985).

2. Indeed, Uslar Pietri's public persona was more akin to a nineteenth-century man of letters than to a twentieth-century professional writer. He was a politician, a diplomat, and academic, an exile, a corporate executive, and a media figure (in newspapers and TV) as much as he was a writer (or, to put it differently, these were all aspects of the same impulse). From his early youth, he occupied rather prominent political positions, founded political parties, and was a presidential candidate who obtained significant support in the 1963 elections. Very few twentieth-century Latin American writers (aside from Rómulo Gallegos, president of Venezuela in 1948) can boast of the degree of public influence or name recognition that Uslar Pietri enjoyed in Venezuela. Although his prestige endures because of his literary production, at the time he was best known by the public at large as the author of a long-running column of political and cultural commentary, significantly titled *Pizarrón* (blackboard), published from 1948 to 1998, as well as from his TV program *Valores humanos*. (The titles bespeak the humanistic liberal tradition in which Uslar Pietri placed himself.)

3. Two well-known instances of "literature as national healing" in the Latin American context are the indigenist novel, as studied by Antonio Cornejo Polar (1994) and the nineteenth-century national romance, as studied by Doris Sommer (1991). The "classic" indigenist writer (i.e., Ciro Alegría) tried to accurately (and sympathetically) depict the Indian community and its plight as part and parcel of the national realm. This was intended, in Cornejo Polar's (1994) reading, as a symbolic "suture" (*sutura homogeneizadora*) of the radical cultural differences ("sociocultural heterogeneity," as he puts it) within Andean nation-states. In national romances, as studied by Sommer, there is a metaphoric relationship between the legitimacy and generative power of the heterosexual romantic relation depicted in the novel (i.e., the ability of the lovers to consummate the relationship—within wedlock—and bear children) and the legitimacy and feasibility of a given national project, and its capacity to harmoniously

integrate seemingly irreconcilable differences. See also Elías Palti (1994), who studied the formulation and enactment of the ideology of the novel as social synthesis in the case of the Mexican Ignacio Manuel Altamirano.

4. The death of Fernando is (or may be) a *literal* fratricide, since, as I will explain later on, Fernando may be Presentación's half-brother. Fernando dies speared and run over by some unidentified royalist lancers (Uslar Pietri [1931] 1993, 201). These lancers may or may not have been part of the force that Presentación led against La Victoria. However, in the melodramatic framework of the novel, this lack of identification only emphasizes the plausibility of the fratricidal hypothesis. In fact, Fernando dies just after Presentación joins the charge against La Victoria, so the likelihood of them crossing paths was high.

5. Simón Bolívar issued the decree on June 15, 1813. The Cartagena Agreements by Antonio Nicolás Briceño inspired it, and it drew on the lessons of the successful Haitian independence war and of the blunders and eventual fall of the first Venezuelan republican experiment (1810–1812). The decree promised death to any Spaniard or Canarian who would not actively support the republican cause. It was proclaimed and put into effect during the Campaña Admirable that ended the royalist restoration led by the Canarian officer Domingo Monteverde. The intensification of the hostilities by the patriots backfired when Boves led a successful counterattack from the llanos, displaying an equal or greater degree of ruthlessness.

6. *Cesarismo democrático* (1919), the pathbreaking and highly controversial essay by Laureano Vallenilla Lanz, was among the first to posit the thesis that the 1810–1820 war in Venezuela was a civil war as much as it was a colonial war. *Las lanzas coloradas* seems to follow this thesis closely. In fact, Uslar Pietri was Vallenilla Lanz's secretary when the latter was ambassador in Paris, and Vallenilla Lanz was a friend of the Uslar Pietri family, so the relationship (personal and intellectual) predates the Parisian period when Uslar Pietri wrote the novel (Arráiz Lucca 2005, 23–24). A classic account of the Boves uprising is that of Arturo Uslar Pietri's brother Juan (1962).

7. The novel calls El Altar a hacienda, but it belongs more to the Caribbean plantation model: it produces sugar, a cash crop for export, and it is worked exclusively by slaves. No free peasants (either laborers or sharecroppers) appear in the novel. In fact, the only free person aside from the masters is Presentación himself.

8. Presentación's origin is unknown. He just appeared one day, as a complete

stranger, and Don Santiago (Fernando's father) immediately gave him the position of foreman, perhaps the most important position in the plantation after the owner himself (Uslar Pietri [1931] 1993, 62). The fact that this act of trust is never explained suggests that there was a previous relationship of an obscure origin. The novel also mentions that Don Santiago had a penchant for sexual intercourse with female slaves (26), so an illegitimate child would not have been anything out of the ordinary. Presentación says about himself, "He did not know how to obey. He had the flesh of a master" (89). Unlike Fernando, both Presentación and Don Santiago are imposing figures, with violent personalities. They are both impulsive and lacking in reflection (for Don Santiago, see 26).

Sab, hero of the eponymous novel by Gertrudis Gómez de Avellaneda (1841), is also an illegitimate descendant (nephew) of the hacienda owner, born of the extramarital relationship between the brother of the landowner and a slave (Sab's mother). Sab also rises to the position of foreman. Sab and Presentación, however, are the exact moral (and political) opposites. Sab could have been a leader of men, just like Presentación, but he explicitly refuses the possibility of leading a slave uprising to further his goals (eminently, to obtain the love of Carlota), and he is never capable of disentangling himself of the predicament posed by his split identity as a mulatto. In fact, this irresolution kills him, since he is unable to either openly aspire to Carlota's hand or to abandon all hope. Presentación, on the other hand, is not conflicted by his identity (or at least, not crippled by it), and he does not think twice about burning the hacienda or raping Inés.

9. Uslar Pietri said, "It is the reference to which we go more easily. The independence [war] is the most important cultural and moral common good that we Venezuelans have" (quoted in López Ortega 1994, 409). In another interview, he readdresses the topic: "I did not take the path of the historical novel because I had an archeological bent or a reconstructive obsession. I thought that in order to express the national being, outside of mere landscape painting one should start by looking for it in the hours in which it reached its highest and most revealing level of intensity. I felt that in the creative and destructive impulse of the war of Independence our creole condition has revealed itself more fully" (quoted in Parra 1993, 46).

10. It is not entirely clear if the novel replaced the failed film project, or if they were parallel projects. Two letters (from January and December of 1930, respec-

tively) to Josefina Vallenilla Lanz mention that the novel predates the film project. Uslar Pietri's conversations with Arráiz Lucca (2001), on the other hand, indicate that the novel was initially a movie script. This incompatibility doesn't affect the interpretation that I offer in this chapter.

11. Arráiz Lucca (2005) partially transcribed the letter in his book. I am grateful for the facsimile of the original that the late Domingo Miliani generously shared with me.

12. Even the tall tales (*consejas*) that appear in the novel have a clear political meaning. Prime examples are the one that Espíritu Santo tells his fellow slaves (which I will discuss later) and the one that a female slave tells Fernando as a boy: a folk version of the birth of Jesus, but one that is also a clear political allegory.

13. The depth of this pious nationalistic intention can be gauged in a letter dated right after the publication of *Las lanzas,* in which Uslar Pietri complains about his novel's not having made an impact (after only three weeks!). He goes on to add that his book "has laid bare the soul of an entire people," and that it is a "work of infinite understanding" (Arráiz Lucca 2001, 479–80).

14. Barthes notes in "Tacite et le baroque funèbre" ([1964] 2002c) that for Tacitus's patricians, death was an event full of meaning. In fact, death was an act in which the soon-to-be-dead man acquired an agency that provided the guarantee of a life properly concluded (and thus, properly lived). The mark of the fitting closing of a cycle was the "maxim," or memorable phrase, put on the lips of the man about to die. In Eduardo Blanco's *Venezuela heroica* (1881), for example (as in most pious nationalistic narratives), the characters always die with a word—an appropriate word—in their mouths. These words link them to a project (the future Venezuela) and to a genealogy. Ribas is thus heroic like Leonidas—of Thermopylae fame—and like all desperately heroic leaders of antiquity.

15. A word about David's life and death: David imagines his own death while flirting with Inés and trying to impress her with romantic credentials. ("I am a cursed man. I love freedom and I roam the world fighting for it. Someday I will die alone, in a forgotten corner of the world, and I will not have anybody to close my eyes" [Uslar Pietri (1931) 1993, 80].) He likes to talk about bandits and the danger they pose. But he talks about a highly stereotypical (romantic) version of Spanish bandits. Instead of the dubious and fearsome guerrillas of the Spanish independence war (like El Empecinado), in which he presumably participated, his bandits are touches of quaint local color who add a thrill to the land-

scape of the sierras and who are invoked to impress the gullible Inés. Ironically, David dies as he predicted he would: alone in a remote corner of the earth. But he dies at the hands of real bandits (172), not gentle romantic ones. And since he has not contributed to the cause of independence, his death is as futile as that of Fernando. David conceives of himself as a Byronian character (*avant la lettre*, of course: Byron would die fighting for Greek independence years later), and he does indeed die in a Byronian fashion. Perhaps he dies even more "Byronically" than Byron did: Byron died in his bed, after all, disillusioned with the factionalism rife among the Greek insurgents.

But in another sense, Byron, as a romantic character, was able to ally himself with other romantic characters: the bandits of the Balkans. Byron exalted Ali Pasha, a bandit lord infamous for his army of ruffians and their exploits throughout Albania. Byron commemorated him in *Childe Harold's Pilgrimage* (1812–1818), wherein he describes the man's charisma and positive leadership qualities along with his savagery and instability. Ali Pasha was in many ways a role model for Byron himself, who idealized his banditry as a form of struggle against oppressive forces. David, on the other hand, dies at the hands of the llanero version of Ali Pasha (Boves). But he is fighting on the wrong side, and there is no mutual recognition (to Boves, he is just another *catire* [blonde]).

16. The only hint of something close to a romance is the flirtation between Inés and Captain David. However, this romance never develops.

17. The novel uses the repetition of phrases as a device: "Have a good morning, don Presentación"; "Seven thousand riders charging through the plains!"; "Bolívar is coming"; "Long live the Liberator!" These phrases never have a clear subject of enunciation, and they oscillate between the individual and the collective utterance. But they exemplify three clearly different stages: the colonial caste order (the greeting based on the relationship of bondage) in the first example, the war situation in the second, the civic situation and the exaltation of the national hero in the third and fourth.

18. Ironically enough, Uslar Pietri detested Chávez, who was for him the embodiment of the failure of any hope for a liberal, democratic Venezuela. In the interviews with Arráiz Lucca (2001) published the year of his death, his opinion is unequivocal: Chávez, he said, is "a raving madman, supremely ignorant. He talks utter nonsense. What a shame that the country cannot find the right path.... This man speaks with unbelievable arrogance and self-importance. He

has heard some phrases somewhere and they have stuck with him, like that one about 'savage liberalism,' he is happy to repeat that one" (39).

19. The novel is somewhat cyclical, in an ironic way. It begins with Presentación walking majestically in the sun (the novel compares his promenade in the hacienda as that of a foreman in a parade under the sun [Uslar Pietri (1931) 1993, 9, 11]), while the frightened slaves peer out from the dark stinking barracks (9–10) that Presentación considers the embodiment of the weakness that he hates and despises (85). It ends with Presentación in a dank cellar reminiscent of the barracks in El Altar (207) while there is a parade going on outside, glorious and jubilant under the blazing tropical sun that Presentación tries to grasp with a last effort of his dying hand (212).

20. The novel says, "He is coming. The man who has obsessed Venezuela. He is arriving. He is going to pass right by him. He will be able to see him riding along. Making an effort he will be able to see his face, from between the bars of the window of his prison cell" (Uslar Pietri [1931] 1993, 211). However, unlike other instances in the same free indirect discourse, it is deliberately unclear here whose words these are (they could be the narrator's, or Presentación's). To collapse both voices, to "occupy" Presentación's stream of consciousness with the narrator's voice, plays to the ideological goal of the scene: to invest his death with a meaning congruent with the nationalist purpose of the novel.

21. In Rulfo's "El llano en llamas" (collected in the volume of the same title), Pichón experiences the same awe in front of the fire consuming the fields of ripe corn: "It was very nice to see the fire move forward in the fields, to watch the entire plain turning into cinders; and that huge burn, with the smoke swirling above, that smoke that smelled of wild grass and honey, because the flames had already reached the cane fields" ([1953] 2001, 98).

22. Boves was among the few Latin American caudillos who did not have a specific region to be loyal to—even though his base was from the llanos, he was not a landowner. He was not even Venezuelan. So, in addition to dying without accumulated riches, he is an exception to the classic caudillo paradigm, since caudillos are usually linked (through ownership or solidarity) to a particular region. In fact, after the king failed to name him captain general (a slight that wounded his pride), Boves did not want to remain in Caracas and preferred to keep fighting (Uslar Pietri 1962).

23. This idea of space disregards the distinction between interior and exterior

(horses enter buildings, either houses or churches), the distinction between sacred and profane (massacres are carried out in churches, balls are carried out in order to desecrate the performance of sociability), and the distinction between center and periphery (the slaves from El Altar, who have just rebelled, take the central square as their headquarters).

24. The war with spears is semantically opposed to the war with firearms. In Sarmiento ([1845] 1979), this opposition was the opposition between civilization and barbarism. In Venezuela, historically, as García Ponce (1965) reminds us, modern war implied costs, foreign loans, transactions, and concessions to foreign capital, as well as commitments that would later on prove difficult (or impossible) to fulfill. The firearms became less a symbol of the national war than a predictor of the unfortunate destiny of a dependent nation-state in the making.

CHAPTER 4: "BODIES FOR THE GALLOWS"

1. For an examination of the place that political assassination (and the memory of the dead) had in revolutionary and postrevolutionary Mexico, see Sánchez (2010).

2. O'Malley (1986, 88), quoting Monsiváis, argues that the fascination with Villa was merely a fascination with an exotic and despised Other. The middle class, avidly consuming stories about Villa, was enjoying just a cheap (and culturally distanced) thrill. This may be true, but only to a point. No character of such an enduring power of fascination is just a cheap thrill (although he can also be that).

3. Both of Muñoz's novels are devoted to losing factions in the revolution (Orozco's Colorados, and the Villistas). The same is true of one of the most important filmmakers at the time, Fernando de Fuentes. The movies of his "revolutionary trilogy" (*El prisionero 13* [1933], *El compadre Mendoza* [1934], and *¡Vámonos con Pancho Villa!* [1936]) are devoted to Huertismo, Zapatismo, and Villismo, respectively.

4. In an interview with Carballo (1965, 273), Muñoz mentions (with a certain degree of resentment) that he did not fully enjoy his early role as the scribe of Villa's story. Villa does not appear in *Se llevaron el cañón*, but he is mentioned repeatedly as the presence that haunts and harasses Orozco's Colorados. The biography was written and initially published as a short text in 1923, right after

Villa's assassination. Muñoz published a much longer version of his biography of Villa in 1955 as *Pancho Villa, rayo y azote*. The same interview makes evident that, even though he appreciates Martín Luis Guzmán (he considers him—in 1965!—the greatest Latin American stylist alive), he somewhat resents the fact that Guzmán's accounts of Villa completely overshadowed his own text, and he denounces the implicit truth claims that Guzmán makes. The theory of Pancho Villa's murder in the script is that it was not at all a political murder, but merely (well-deserved) personal vengeance. Villa wanted to take land away from a man named Melitón, in order to give it to one of his officers. This injustice started the chain of events that ended with Villa's death. The script features a series of flashbacks in which many episodes of *¡Vámonos con Pancho Villa!* are revisited, such as Villa's wound in Guerrero and his hiding in the cave (although there is no character who would be Tiburcio's equivalent).

5. Other short stories by Muñoz on revolutionary themes are not related to any particular faction in the struggle (e.g., "El saqueo" or "El feroz cabecilla," the latter of which is a parody of federal officers' self-aggrandizement, much in the style of similar scenes in *Los de abajo*), or they are devoted to a favorable depiction of the Federales or the federal *soldaderas* ("El Niño," "Es usted muy hombre," "El enemigo," "Dos muertos," "Servicio de patrulla"). In most of these cases, the Villistas appear as the enemy.

6. Torres was one of the negotiators of Villa's surrender in 1920. It seems that he also had contact with Villa during his retirement years in the Canutillo hacienda. His works, most of the time, are focused on the lurid, quaint, or bizarre aspects of the Villa legend, and they are good examples of texts that try to profit from the public interest on Villa and that try to highlight (and aggrandize) the author's role in the narrated events. A testimony to this is that throughout Torres's life, the same works were published under different titles, or in somewhat different arrangements, perhaps in an effort to give an illusion of novelty to the same material.

7. This scene, in which the explosions and the federal searchlights create dramatic contrasts of light and darkness, reminds the reader of the major (but unacknowledged) influence that *L'Feu*, by Henri Barbusse (1916), had on Muñoz.

8. The opposite occurs in *Se llevaron el cañón para Bachimba*, which is a revolutionary bildungsroman. The protagonist-narrator of the novel, Abasolo, is a youngster of urban background, with no previous experience of the world. He

follows Marcos Ruiz, the Orosquizta leader who introduces him to the ways of the world. Marcos himself was not a fighter by vocation: he was a teacher, and a "true" revolutionary.

9. And it is an army whose homogeneity, cohesion, and singleness of purpose Tiburcio remembers with pangs of nostalgia in *Vámonos-2*, when the División has devolved into a roving band of riders, united only by desperation and mistrust of strangers and of each other.

10. *El verdadero Pancho Villa* (1936), by Silvestre Terrazas, is a coherent attempt to analyze the Villista phenomenon in its political and social aspects. It was written by one of the few intellectuals who was influential in Villa's entourage and who was loyal to Villa to the very end of his rule in Chihuahua. (Unlike other intellectuals, Terrazas did not desert Villa. He obtained Villa's permission to leave, when Villa's administration was crumbling, at the end of 1915.) However, Terrazas's work would not be published in book form until 1984.

11. Ángeles does appear (fleetingly) alongside Villa in the chapter "El vagón 7121," which narrates Tiburcio's despondency and eventual desertion after the death of Máximo while the battle of Zacatecas rages around him (he is assigned duties carrying and caring for the many wounded men). Tiburcio catches a glimpse of Ángeles discussing the plan of attack with Villa. Ángeles is credited as the mastermind behind the successful attack strategy. In fact, he penned an account of the battle, promptly published by the state of Chihuahua (see Ángeles 1914).

12. Katz (1998) comments that Villa's loyalty was the cause of some fateful military and political decisions. We have seen already some unfortunate consequences of this, in his loyalty to Madero that was not reciprocated. His loyalty to Maytorena would launch him into the disastrous Sonoran campaign in late 1915 that sealed the destiny of the División. His loyalty to De la Huerta (and De la Huerta's political ambitions) led him to make some ill-advised statements to the journalist Hernández Llergo (such as the statement that he could have forty thousand men under his command at a moment's notice), which are considered to be an indirect cause of his assassination.

CHAPTER 5: THE ANDEAN WESTERN

1   In Andean Peru, as well as elsewhere in Latin America and the world, conflicts over land found their expression as conflicts over stray cattle. Claimants to property would impound an opponent's cattle, claiming that it was

making illegal use of pastures and waters, or trampling crops. Those whose cattle were impounded could counter with an accusation of cattle rustling by the impounder. However, if the original owner of the cattle tried to repossess it through extralegal means, the accusation of cattle rustling could be turned against him. See literary expressions of this in *El mundo es ancho y ajeno*, by Ciro Alegría ([1941] 1963), where this conflict lands Rosendo Maqui in jail, and is at the origin of Fiero Vásquez's stint as a bandit, as well as in *Redoble por Rancas*, by Manuel Scorza ([1970] 2002). For a similar conflict in another context (southeastern Australia), see Seal (1996), 151.

2. "El campeón de la muerte," "Ushanan-jampi," "El hombre de la bandera," "Cachorro de tigre" (*Cuentos andinos*); "El brindis de los yayas," "Huayna-pishtanag," "El blanco," "Cómo se hio pishtaco Calixto," "Juan Rabines no perdona" (*Nuevos cuentos andinos*).

3. Mariátegui argues his case: "In the forbidding mountains, in the faraway gorges [*quebradas*], where the law of the white man has not yet arrived, the Indian still keeps his ancestral law alive. *Cuentos andinos*, the book by Enrique López Albújar, a writer pertaining to our radical generation, is the first one which in our times explores these paths. These short stories capture, in their dry and hard strokes, the crucial emotion of life in the mountains, and they present some features of the Indian soul." One of the main virtues of *Cuentos andinos*, for Mariátegui, was that it presented the much-exalted Andean communism in a positive light: "'Ushanan-jampi' . . . is a vigorous, well-written short story. Additionally, 'Ushanan-jampi' is a precious document of Indian communism. This short story informs us about how popular justice works in small Indian villages, where the law of the republic almost never reaches" ([1928] 1979, 287).

4. Like those of López Albújar, Maupassant's stories deal with bloody revenge carried out in a matter-of-fact fashion, and narrated with a degree of condescending good humor—for instance, in "Historie corse," an otherwise charming female asks for a gun when the narrator asks her what she would like to receive as a present. This mixture of childish innocence and a penchant for extreme violence defines several short stories in *Cuentos andinos*, such as "Cachorro de tigre," in which Ishaco carries out a gruesome revenge against Valerio, his father's killer (he plucks Valerio's eyes out, and keeps them either as a trophy or to magically prevent persecution), but remains docile, good-natured, and as candid as a child to the narrator (who had taken him in when he was just a young orphan).

5. The Código Penal Santa-Cruz del Estado Nor-Peruano, for example, displays a precision that most Latin American codes lack. Articles 237–239 define the nature of bandit gangs (*cuadrillas de malhechores*) and the penalties for their members, while Article 153 identifies specific penalties for "robbery in public highways or outside populated areas." On the other hand, Article 497 exempts the killer of a highway robber (*salteador*) from any penalty whatsoever. There was also legislation as well as executive orders that dealt with banditry. Examples are the executive orders—*decretos*—from 1836 and 1838, signed by Santa Cruz and by Orbegoso, respectively. These decretos were clearly directed toward curbing the epidemic of banditry in the first decades after independence. Interestingly, they simultaneously acknowledge and deny the phenomenon: they deny it, in that they do not mention it, and they include it in the larger—and better-defined—category of robbery. But they acknowledge its existence in that they turn robbery into a crime that should be dealt with by military tribunals. In the previous *Proyecto de un código penal*, by Vidaurre (1828), the author indicates that the "murderous highway robber" (*ladrón de caminos asesino*) should be condemned to forced labor for life. The Santa Cruz code does not prescribe the death penalty to highway robbers, but Tschudi (1847, 140) tells us that "robbers, when captured and brought to Lima, undergo a very summary trial, and are then sentenced to be shot. The culprits have the privilege of choosing their place of execution, and they generally fix on the market-place. They are allowed the assistance of a priest for twelve hours prior to their death, and they are conducted from the chapel to the place of execution, carrying a bench, on which they sit to undergo the punishment. Four soldiers fire at the distance of three paces from the culprit; two aiming at his head, and two at his breast." On the illegal execution of highwaymen during the independent decades, see Aguirre (2005, 11).

6. Banditry remained endemic in certain areas of the Andes. See, for example, Poole (1988) and her study of cattle rustling in Chumbivilcas. Poole notes that during the years of Sendero Luminoso, Chumbivilcas became a sort of "Liberated zone" and that Sendero allowed the activity of bandits since it was crucial to the terrorist organization's acquisition of weaponry (Poole 1988, 392). A little more distant in time, see Orlove (1990) and his study of cattle rustling in Cusco on the eve of the agrarian reform. Also, until recently banditry was endemic in the north, in particular in the border areas between Peru and Ecuador.

7. In Peru, as in the other former centers of the Spanish colonial power, "order" and "disorder," or "order" and "chaos," were highly relative terms. Peter Klarén ([2000] 2005, 185) points out that the political and economic disarray of the early republic provided the opportunity for a reinvigoration of a traditional Andean economy and its communal organization. In a similar fashion, Florencia Mallon (1995) has shown how in Mexico, the disruptions brought about by civil war and foreign intervention allowed for the emergence of a popular brand of liberalism that empowered peasant communities.

8. This motif is not new: at the beginning of Dickens's *A Tale of Two Cities*, one of the main characters is traveling in a coach, toward Dover. The threat of being held up adds terror (and excitement) to the trip. And it figures prominently in the nineteenth century in the travelogues of foreigners traveling in Mexico.

9. For India, see Wagner (2007). For Egypt, see Brown (1990). For China, see Billingsley (1988), as well as Harvey Howard's memoir *Ten Weeks with Chinese Bandits* (1927), which was very popular at the time and is still very entertaining.

10. In a different colonial context (Australia, in particular New South Wales), the "respectable" classes of urban dwellers, confronted with the bushranger outbreaks of the 1850s and 1860s, in addition to pressing for the passing of the so-called "Bushranging Act" (the official title of this legislation was "An Act to Suppress Robbery and Housebreaking and the Harboring of Robbers and Housebreakers"), complained about the perceived existence of a "robber union [that] embraces a very large proportion of the inhabitants of a certain condition and occupation in life. Many are connected by family relations. They have hereditary traditions of violence and outrage" (*Sidney Morning Herald*, 1864, quoted in Seal 1996, 131).

11. Banditry was considered in this fashion (as an unpredictable act) in much of ancient Roman legislation (see Shaw 1984, 15).

12. "A universal panic pervades the city of Lima whenever a detachment of Montoneros enters within the gates. On every side are heard cries of 'Cierra puertas!' (Close the doors!) 'Los Montoneros!' Every person passing along the streets runs into the first house he comes to, and closes the door after him. In a few moments the streets are cleared, and no sound is heard but the galloping of the Montoneros' horses" (Tschudi 1847, 142).

13. For an examination of the relationship between montoneros and politics (in particular liberal politics), see Walker (1990).

14. In fact when the time came to tear down the walls of Lima, in the mid-

nineteenth century, the objections were related to the fact that bandits would have unfettered access to the city (Aguirre 2005). Thus, the wall, constructed against pirates in the context of an imperial struggle for dominance, ended up serving a much more modest purpose.

15. He does so, dealing with banditry, in other *tradiciones* as well, such as "El sombrero del Padre Abregú" and "La proeza de Benites."

16. Tschudi also narrates (presumably) the saga of Escobar, though he speaks of two bandits, "Leon" and "Escobar":

> Within the last few years, two negroes, named Escobar and Leon, were daring leaders of banditti. Leon, who was originally a slave, commenced his career of crime by the murder of his master. He eluded the pursuit of justice, became a highway robber, and for many years was the terror of the whole province of Lima. The police vainly endeavored to secure him. Leon knew the country so well, that he constantly evaded his pursuers. When the price of 2000 dollars was set upon his head, he boldly entered Lima every evening and slept in the city. At length placards were pasted about, calling on Leon's comrades to kill him, and offering to any one who might deliver him up dead into the hands of the police the reward of 1000 dollars and a pardon. This measure had the desired result, and Leon was strangled, whilst asleep, by a zambo, who was his godfather. The body was, during three days, exposed to public view in front of the cathedral. (Tschudi 1847, 139–40)

17. Walker (1990, 110) analyzes the political role that montoneros played in the civil strife between conservatives and liberals, stating that montoneros were far more than mere bandits. Their presence, in the environs of the very center of conservative power (the axis Lima–Callao) "constituted a crucial obstacle to the consolidation of power by the conservatives" (135).

18. Giuseppe Musolino, also known as the "King of Aspromonte" (1876–1956), was an Italian brigand and folk hero. His exploits, as well as his capture and trial, were famous in the Hispanic world at the beginning of the twentieth century. Not only were his career and trial amply covered in the press at the time, but novels were written and translated about him while he was still alive. An example is *Musolino: Su vida y su proceso* (purportedly only translated, compiled, and annotated by the Spaniard Francisco Javier Cobo). The work is from 1902, a year after Musolino was apprehended.

19. These texts were written as part of a new interest in the "criminal question" (in

particular the "Indian criminal"). This interest was spurred not only by developments in European criminology, and its racist appropriation in Latin America, but also by the wave of unrest of the early twentieth century (Flores Galindo 1990), coupled with the anxiety motivated by regional and international events (the Mexican Revolution and the Russian Revolution, for example).

20. They posited a number of still-relevant distinctions, such as that between bandits of the coast and bandits of the sierra (Varallanos), or the relationship between banditry and the existence (or lack thereof) of communal forms of organization (López Albújar).

21. In Poma de Ayala's *Nueva Corónica* (1980), in the chapter "Hordenanzas del Inga," there is a particular mention of highway robbers and the penalties they would incur (five hundred lashes the first time, stoning the second time: the corpse was not to receive sepulture, and it was to be left to rot and be eaten by foxes and condors). Stavig (1990, 78) also mentions pre-Columbian policies to deal with banditry.

22. Prescott states,

> The most emphatic testimony to the merits of the people is that afforded by Mancio Sierra Lejesama, the last survivor of the early Spanish Conquerors, who settled in Peru. In the preamble to his testament, made, as he states, to relieve his conscience, at the time of his death, he declares that the whole population under the Incas, was distinguished by sobriety and industry; that such things as robbery and theft were unknown; that far from licentiousness, there was not even a prostitute in the country; and that everything was conducted with the greatest order, and entire submission to authority. The panegyric is somewhat too unqualified for a whole nation, and may lead one to suspect that the stings of remorse for his own treatment of the natives goaded the dying veteran into a higher estimate of their deserts than was strictly warranted by facts. Yet this testimony by such a man at such a time is too remarkable, as well as too honorable to the Peruvians, to be passed over in silence by the historian. (1847, 2:102)

23. For an excellent account of Eleodoro Benel's uprising, as an expression of resistance against the advances of the Leguiísta state, see Taylor (1984).

24. For the purpose of this study, I will treat *Cuentos andinos* and *Nuevos cuentos andinos* as a single work. They are not, though. While the action of most of *Cuentos andinos* happens in the late nineteenth and early twentieth centuries,

the action of many of the stories in *Nuevos cuentos andinos* is clearly located in the 1920s ("Juan Ravines no perdona," for example, takes place well after the death of Eleodoro Benel). While the conflict of *Cuentos andinos* is centered on the Indian village of Chupán, Huánuco, *Nuevos cuentos andinos* moves away from it, to a reality that is populated with indexes of modernity (cars, highways, heavy machinery, mining enterprises, and foreign capital). This reality is more urban, and—to a degree—more individualistic.

25. The notion of heterogeneity, as Antonio Cornejo Polar (1994) proposed it in an intelligent and fruitful fashion, presupposes as its flip side the totalizing ambition of indigenist writers. It is precisely heterogeneity that ruins the totalizing effort. That is why, as Cornejo Polar indicates, the novel as artifact is the privileged instrument, and the indigenist classic project reaches its greatest achievements with Ciro Alegría as well as evidences its unsurpassable limits. In relation to the treatment of violence, this is shown in the dynamics of violence that indigenist novels usually enact: the novels contrast indigenous violence, under the form of the collective and failed uprising, with class violence, systematic and driven by economic interest (as in the case of Icaza's *Huasipungo*, or Alegría's *El mundo es ancho y ajeno*), or erratic and capricious (as evidenced in Arguedas's *Raza de bronce*). This functioning of violence, territorialized as class and ethnic violence, is what allows for the transformation of these narratives into undivided allegories.

26. In *Cuentos andinos*, there is a close connection between banditry and eye gouging (to the point that avengers are called *pishtacos*). In the last few decades, in particular during the time of Sendero Luminoso, narratives on eye gougers (pishtacos, or *sacaojos*) have acquired prominence both in the construction of social fears and as a topic of scholarly interest. However, Tschudi (1847, 139) bears witness to the presence of the practice and its association with banditry in early republican Peru:

> The zambo robbers are notorious for committing the most heartless cruelties. In June, 1842, one of them attacked the Indian who was conveying the mail to Huacho. 'Shall I,' said the robber, 'kill you or put out your eyes?' 'If I must choose,' replied the Indian, 'pray kill me at once.' The barbarian immediately drew forth his dagger and stuck it into the eyes of the unfortunate victim, and then left him lying on the Band. In this state a traveller, who conveyed him to a neighboring village, found the poor Indian.

The following anecdote was related to me by an Indian, in whose dwelling I passed a night, at Chancay: About half a league from the village he met a negro, who advanced towards him, with musket cocked, and commanded him to halt. My host drew out a large riding pistol and said, 'You may be thankful that this is not loaded or you would be a dead man.' The negro, laughing scornfully, rode up and seized the Indian, when the latter suddenly fired the pistol, and shot him dead.

27. In fact, López Albújar wrote and presented a scholarly piece on the "informal" (i.e., extralegal) systems of justice in Chupán, Huánuco ("Exégesis de la justicia penal chupana," 1942). His vision of these practices is mostly positive, in particular when compared to the painfully slow, indifferent, and corrupt Peruvian penal system.

28. The role of lawyers and judges in indigenist fiction should also be noted. For example, in Alegría's *El mundo es ancho y ajeno*, there are both corrupt *rábulas* who betray the Indians to the landowners (as in the case of Bismark) and honest, committed lawyers and activists, such as Arturo Correa Zavala and Pajuelo.

29. From the *Código penal del Perú* (1862, 80): "Art. 264. The female that were to commit adultery shall be punished with second-degree reclusion. The accomplice would suffer the same fate. Art. 265. The husband that were to commit adultery having a permanent mistress in a house provided by him, shall be punished with second-degree reclusion. The same punishment, but in the first degree, would apply in case of adultery with a female for which the husband has not provided a house."

30. This is abundantly expressed in "El Blanco."

CHAPTER 6: BORGES AND THE MELANCHOLIC
CULTOR DEL CORAJE

1. Also, as Cozarinsky (1981) and Aguilar and Jelicié (2010) have shown, Borges's relationship with gangster, Western, and adventure films is at the origin of his narrative enterprise: "Film, or better yet, a certain idea of film, appears in Borges closely associated to the practice of narrating, even to the very possibility of attempting to narrate" (Cozarinsky 1981, 13). Film heavily (and avowedly) influenced his first short stories, those later collected in *Historia universal de la infamia*. This influence is apparent in their themes (stories of larger-than-life

gangsters, samurai, pirates, gunslingers, confidence men), in their techniques (montage), and in the very notion of what kind of art form they should be (stories with an epic flavor in which the appeal of the hero does not correspond to his moral or political virtues; stories that do not necessarily pretend to be original, but are variations or rewritings of well-known stories; stories that have an unequivocal entertainment value). As Aguilar and Jelicié (2010, 12) put it, for Borges "the adventure of film is that of the eternal return of narrative, the Hollywood variations of 'ten or twelve plots,' just like the Greek tragedians did, a long time ago." And also: "At the beginning of the thirties, when he was writing his first pieces of fictional prose, [Borges] was intent upon the fact that his texts provoked a sense of entertainment and agility similar to the one that, in theaters all over the city, films were eliciting. A good story should be able to pass *the film test*" (20).

2. I suspect that the films bear more than a passing similarity to some Borgesian plots and themes. One of the screenwriters of *Once upon a Time in the West* was Bernardo Bertolucci, who shortly after *Once upon a Time* directed *Strategia del ragno*, based on Borges's short story "Tema del traidor y del héroe."

3. The narrative works that would compose this cycle include "Hombres pelearon" (*El idioma de los argentinos*, 1928); "Historias de jinetes" and "El desafío" (*Evaristo Carriego*, 1930); "Hombre de la esquina rosada" (*Historia universal de la infamia*, 1935); "La forma de la espada," "El fin," and "El Sur" (*Ficciones*, 1944); "El muerto," "Biografía de Tadeo Isidoro Cruz (1829–1874)," and "La espera" (*El Aleph*, 1949); "La intrusa," "El indigno," "Historia de Rosendo Juárez," "El encuentro," and "Juan Muraña" (*El informe de Brodie*, 1970); and "La noche de los dones" (*El libro de arena*, 1975). The poems are perhaps too numerous to list, but *Para las seis cuerdas* is perhaps the most sustained poetic effort around the figure of the dagger fighter. Also worthy of mention are his anthologies *El compadrito* (1945, with Sylvina Bullrich) and *El matrero* (1970), as well as *Los orilleros* (1955), a script written with Adolfo Bioy Casares.

4. The lines distinguishing the literary instances of the gaucho (rural) from the compadre (an urban or semiurban type) are fluid at best. Borges argues that "the literary primacy of the gaucho is probably only nominal: in the knife fighter Martín Fierro (as in Hormiga Negra and other champions of that ilk) people think that they admire a gaucho, but they basically admire the compadre, in the derogative sense of the term" (Borges and Bullrich 1945, 7). Some of Borges's

short stories play with this fluidity. In "El muerto," for example, the urban *com-padrito* from Buenos Aires becomes a member of a rural gang of smugglers in the Uruguayan backlands.

5. In the electoral goon, Borges emphasizes not the political aspects (i.e., the fact that he is a brutal enforcer of a corrupt political system), but his loyalty and personal attachment to his boss. This figure is, for Borges, primarily a man's man, one who does not "work for" a boss but is affiliated with him (like the jag-unços in *Grande Sertão: Veredas*). The archetype is Juan Moreira, bodyguard of Alsina (who gives him a horse and a dagger as a present) and later the electoral goon of Marañón, a man he truly loves (Gutiérrez [1879] 1999).

6. The *Diccionario de la real academia* provides these two definitions: "cultor, ra. (del lat. *cultor, -ōris*). 1. adj. cultivador. U. t. c. s. 2. adj. Que adora o venera algo" (1. Cultivator. 2. Somebody who worships or venerates something). These same two meanings are present in the Latin word, together with other ones that seem to have been lost in the evolution into Spanish: "Cultor—oris: 1. Husbandman / planter / grower; 2. inhabitant; 3. supporter; 4. who has interest; 5. worshiper."

7. The short story is a third-person narrative, but it is narrated from the exclusive point of view of Recabarren, whose rudimentary thought processes (which the narrator considers a plus) we are witness to. He cannot move, so he (and we) can only see what the narrow window of his room allows him to see, from the disadvantageous position on his cot. Recabarren's thoughts are mixed with the narrator's.

8. Nostalgia has, without a doubt, a crucial place in Borges's oeuvre. According to Beatriz Sarlo ([1993] 2003, 1999), Daniel Balderston (2000), and Alan Pauls (2004), nostalgia is the mark of the loss of a "Dionysian universe" (Sarlo 1999, 210), of which the narrator only imperfectly partakes through the mediation of literature. Thus, "the world of war and bravery has become an object of nostal-gia" (Pauls 2004, 30). The closing of "El incivil maestro de ceremonias Kotsuké no suké" would be one of the many formulations of that nostalgia: "This is the end of the story of the forty-seven loyal retainers—except that the story has no ending, because we other men, who are perhaps not loyal yet will never entirely lose the hope that we might one day be so, shall continue to honor them with words" (Borges 1998, 39). Other instances appear in the poem "Espadas," from *El oro de los tigres* ("Allow me, sword, to apply to you the rules of art; / Me, that was unable to use you" [Borges 1996a, 465]), and in the Tanka 6, in "Tankas,"

also in *El oro de los tigres* ("Not having fallen, / Like others of my blood, / In the midst of the battle. / To be, in the useless night, / The one who counts the syllables" [469]).

9. For an account of the circumstances of that rural frontier, see Chasteen (1995).

10. As Alejandra Laera has noted (and productively examined), the series of "popular novels with gauchos" began in 1879 with the publication of *Juan Moreira* as a serial in the newspaper *La patria Argentina*, and ended with the publication of *Pastor Luna* in 1885 as a serial and in 1886 as a book (Laera 2004, 289).

11. Even though, as I said above, *Juan Moreira* is the model for the series, there are significant differences among the novels. Prieto (1988) examines the distinctive nature of the Santos Vega cycle, whereas Laera (2003) draws enlightening comparisons (emphasizing the differences) between *Juan Moreira* and *Pastor Luna*.

12. In *Martín Fierro*, this series (offense, challenge, challenge, fight against the posse—which is a sort of challenge, since Fierro refuses to flee and refuses to surrender) is interrupted by the flight to the desert (a place outside both laws), where melancholy is replaced by lamentation for the loss (witness the two big tears running down Fierro's weathered cheeks).

13. Hegel, discussing vengeance, indicts precisely the potentially infinite character of the process (quoted in Courtois 1984, 9). This is a motif in bandit narratives, of course, present for example in *El mundo es ancho y ajeno*. Fiero Vásquez, after his first killing, would like to continue living in peace, but he cannot. And this is so not only because the law (or the local landowners, which in the novel are the same thing) will not let him, but because some people look for opportunities to fight him just to prove his reputation.

14. Consider this contrast: The gauchos in *Don Segundo Sombra* are also nomadic, but that nomadism is full of experience and learning. (In the case of Fabio, protagonist of the narrative, his years as a cattle driver are the school where he learns how to become a leader of men, once he is elevated to the position of landowner.) In *Huckleberry Finn* that nomadism is full of adventure, and is populated by remarkable characters. In *Kim*, the nomadism is full of human experience (Kim is the master of his identity, and he can move comfortably between languages, religions, or cultures—his nickname "The Little Friend of the Entire World" is sufficiently explicit in this regard). Also, in these three cases the point is not really about nomadism. Fabio, Kim, and Huck, even though they do not have a predetermined destination, follow the route of commodities in the con-

text of vast economies in cycles of expansion (the cattle routes for wintering or export in Buenos Aires Province, the products on the steamboats and rafts on the Mississippi, the "Grand Trunk" in the Punjab).

CHAPTER 7: DANGEROUS ILLUSIONS AND SHINING UTOPIAS

1. The bibliography on northeastern outlawry is extensive. Eric Hobsbawm devotes a significant portion of *Bandits* to cangaceirismo (see the section devoted to the variety of social bandit that he calls "the avenger" [(1969) 2000, 63–75]). Scholars who address banditry in the Northeast in the context of a widespread and well-established culture of violence are Pernambucano de Mello (2004), Pereira de Queiroz (1968), and De Lima (1965). Excellent articles on the topic include Lewin (1987), Chandler (1987), and Singelmann (1975). Biographies of Lampião, the most important cangaceiro together with Antônio Silvino, include Chandler (1978), Pernambucano de Mello (1993), and Grunspan-Jasmin (2001). These are not, by far, all the books of importance on the topic. Many others have been written about particular aspects of cangaceirismo, or about Lampião's career.

2. Nogueira Galvão (1972) places Amado within the "third regionalism" current, influenced by U.S. narrative (in particular the works of John Steinbeck). Fitz (2001) has developed, in detail, the comparison between Amado's *Seara Vermelha* and Steinbeck's *The Grapes of Wrath*.

3. For an account of the transformations of the PCB during the crucial years 1935–1945 (between the ALN rebellion and legalization), see Dulles (1983).

4. For a general consideration of the debate, from its Marxian roots to the dramatic shift represented by the Cuban Revolution, see Harris (1978) and Harding (1982).

5. A clear example of how this countermemory works is found in Engels's *The Condition of the Working Class in England* (a book that Amado probably read). In the section devoted to the education of working children, Engels quotes the *Children's Employment Commission's Report*. Commissioner Grainger brings up a startling discovery from Birmingham:

> The children examined by me are, as a whole, utterly wanting in all that could be in the remotest degree called a useful education. . . . Several boys

have never heard of London nor of Willenhall, though the latter was but an hour's walk from their homes. . . . Several have never heard the name of the Queen nor other names, such as Nelson, Wellington, Bonaparte; but it was noteworthy that those who have never heard even of St. Paul, Moses, or Solomon, were very well instructed as to the life, deeds, and character of Dick Turpin, the street robber, and especially of Jack Sheppard, the thief and gaol-breaker. ([1845] 1999, 123)

6. The 1930s was a period of relatively little activity for Lampião's gang (the 1920s were its heyday), but it was a period marked by intense public exposure, in particular through mass media such as illustrated magazines and film. Perhaps the most important of these interactions between Lampião and mass media was Benjamin Abrahão's film *Lampião, o rei do Cangaço* (1936), which features footage of the bandit, his legendary partner Maria Bonita, and his gang. It is said that the film so irritated President Getúlio Vargas that he ordered the persecution of Lampião to be intensified, ultimately resulting in the Angicos ambush in 1938.

7. This would also be the case in Scorza's *Redoble por Rancas* (1970), where banditry is the point of articulation between premodern, prepolitical Indian consciousness and full-fledged class consciousness (as depicted, for example, in the Indian assembly in his *La tumba del relámpago* ([1979] 1987). Amado would share this standing as Hobsbawm's precedent with the Turkish writer Yasar Kemal, whose *Memed, My Hawk* (1955) also enacts the various roles of banditry vis-à-vis peasant-landowner struggle. Set in the Taurus Mountains, the novel presents Memed, a peasant boy pushed into banditry by the ruthless Abdi Agha, boss of Deyirmenoluk village. (Hobsbawm quotes Kemal more than once. Oddly enough, he does not mention Amado.) The same link appears in some anarchist works, such as Alberto Ghiraldo's *Alma gaucha* (Argentina, 1906), where the protagonist, Cruz, is the son of a former outlaw (also named Cruz) who has fought with the Indians against whites in the nineteenth-century southern frontier area. The younger Cruz inherits the tradition of insurgency and rebellion from his father, whose lessons he has taken to heart.

8. For an illuminating account of the rise and zenith of the cocoa economy in Bahia, see Mahony (1996).

9. Valid comparisons could be drawn, for example, between *Terras do sem fim* and Louis L'Amour's *Silver Canyon* ([1951] 1956): the showdown of the two land-owners, the lovers caught in the middle of the conflict over land, and the smaller landowners being squeezed out by the competition between the dominant powers of the land.

10. In the Colombian *Violencia,* and in the Nicaraguan civil war, banditry was also a weapon in agrarian struggles, but the class struggle intersected with party conflicts (as well as local ones, making the whole picture more complicated).

11. I follow Stuart Hall's (1997) definition of naturalization as "a representational strategy designed to *fix* difference, and thus *secure it forever.* It is an attempt to halt the inevitable 'slide' of meaning and to secure discursive or ideological 'closure'" (245; italics in the original).

12. Miguel Angel Centeno (2002) examines the modernizing role of the army vis-à-vis peasants. This role appears in Alegría's *El mundo es ancho y ajeno,* in which Benito is drafted and returns to lead the uprising of the community; in López Albújar's "La bandera"; and also in Scorza's *La tumba del relámpago,* in which Hermógenes, elected representative of the community, has also been transformed by his stint in the army. This transformation is operative at the level of consciousness (with the transformation of community consciousness into class consciousness [Scorza (1979) 1987, 120]), but also at the level of the military organization, since he is able to organize the peasants as an army. The depiction of the revolt uses some facile symbols, denoting the blend between old and new tactics of popular revolt—the "Molotov sling," for example, in which the old rock-throwing device is repurposed for the mid-twentieth-century means of struggle (130). Once the community acquires class consciousness, the Ladrón de Caballos and the Abigeo come back from the dead, and they carry a flag that says "Land or Death" (146).

13. The character of Juvêncio is based on a real-life individual, the comrade Giocondo. Amado praises his exploits in "O camarada Dias," a nonfiction text included in *Homens e coisas do Partido Comunista* (1946). Some other episodes are taken from anecdotes pertaining to Amado's work with the PCB, such as the scene of the opening of the first legal headquarters of the party, narrated in the latter part of the novel (Amado [1946] 1999, 334), and, in more detail, in the text "Instalação da primeira sede legal do partido" (also in *Homens e coisas*). Also, there are episodes in both the novel (some of them narrated as pertaining

to Zé Tavares) and "O pai da gente" (also in *Homens e coisas*) that have as their sources the experiences of militants working with peasants in the short-lived Communist *ligas camponesas* (peasant leagues) in the Northeast.

14. Without entering into the thorny issue of deciding if the peasantry is a class, a transitional stage, or not a single class at all (but different ones), for the sake of our argument it suffices to say that *Seara Vermelha* narrates the transformation of peasants and sharecroppers into rural proletarians in an entirely modern agrarian context. This transformation accompanies or echoes the movement from the northeastern fazendas to the southern coffee plantations.

15. The contrast between the oral and the written word in the novel is very important. On the one hand, the oral word is the medium of the cultural pact between classes (as in the case of Inácio, as well as the pact—later betrayed— between Lucas Arvoredo and the Senator), and the medium of sertanejo culture (the songs, the poems, and the oral reputation). The written word, on the other hand, is an instrument of oppression: the ledger where Artur keeps track of debts, the letter in which Aureliano announces that he is selling the fazenda, and Jerônimo's clean bill of health whose signature Dr. Epaminondas uses to blackmail Marta into having sex with him.

16. Clearly, this picture of relentless exploitation (through one of its preferred symbols, the fazenda store) obscures a more complex reality. Johnson (1971) examines the case of sharecroppers in the Cariri area (Seara) in the 1960s, and provides a much more nuanced perspective on the role of the fazenda store (though for a later period in the twentieth century). Indebtedness, for example, is a means to secure (and coerce) a steady supply of labor, but, from the point of view of the peasant, it is also an insurance against all-too-likely catastrophes, such as crop failure, sickness, and so forth.

17. Lampião always insisted that the death of his father drove him to outlawry, and that he was an avenger and a social bandit, exacting money from the rich and giving it to the poor. His father's feud was indeed a cause. But both Chandler (1978) and Pernambucano de Mello (1993) note that the feud was not over land. The enemy was not a land-hungry colonel, and Lampião's father was never evicted. Plus, Lampião's father was killed when the Ferreira brothers were already outlaws. Lampião never really pursued his father's killers, and unlike real avengers, whose careers are limited in time and space (avengers have a specific objective that is confined to a limited region), Lampião acted for more than two decades, in six states. However, Lampião, in partic-

ular when out of his "original" territory, central Pernambuco, affected the manners and the practices of the noble robber (see Pernambucano de Mello 1993).

18. This seems to have been a rather widespread practice, not unique to Lampião. Schroeder (1996) transcribes depositions by survivors of massacres carried out by Conservative bandit Anastacio Hernández in 1927 in the Las Segovias area of Nicaragua, in which the same pattern is followed.

19. There are similar anecdotes pertaining to Villa: his taste for ice cream and peanut brittle, his tantrums, his shooting of paper effigies when the real target was unavailable. The naïf—the childish outlaw or criminal—is a trope that emphasizes his primal nature, or his underdeveloped one. The bandit shares with the prostitute this hybrid nature; many novels emphasize the childish tastes of prostitutes. One example is *Juana Lucero* (Augusto D'Halmar, Chile, 1902), in which the title character's colleague Bibelot spends all her ill-gotten money on knickknacks that she takes for high art (the same way that the pianist of the brothel takes Dumas for high drama).

20. The fact that a state senator conspires with a cangaceiro is not at all surprising—it was common practice, if frowned upon, and denied publicly whenever possible. Pernambucano de Mello (1993, 2004) mentions and transcribes numerous examples of correspondence between Lampião and members of the northeastern political and economic elite: colonels, representatives (*diputados*), and judges.

21. In fact, Lucas is crueler with Cândido, the old sertanejo soldier who aids the detachment sent after him. As a sertanejo, he knows the caatinga as well as Lucas does, and consequently he is a much more fearsome enemy than the Senator or Ezequiel da Silveira. Lucas's vengeance is, accordingly, harsher: he cuts off Cândido's tongue, and gouges out his eyes (though it is not clear whether this is torture or the desecration of a corpse).

22. There is only one genuine love relationship in this novel: the one between Juvêncio and his wife. The sertanejos are faithful husbands, for the most part. But the relationship is dry and rough, and this prevents a genuinely amorous relationship from flourishing (this is, of course, a statement on sertanejo culture). It goes without saying that there are gender inequalities and double standards that pollute these relationships.

23. On a different note, it is remarkable that Nenen's real son disappears from the narrative, as does his wife.

CHAPTER 8: THE HEART OF DARKNESS

1. These were not the only two occasions when Revueltas was imprisoned. The last (and most famous) of his stints in prison was that between 1969 and 1972, a direct result of Revueltas's participation in the events now known as Tlatelolco (both the student protests and the bloody government crackdown). By this time, however, Revueltas was no longer a member of the PCM.

2. An account of the controversy surrounding *Los días terrenales* and *El cuadrante de la soledad*, as well as a dossier on the controversy, can be found in the Archivos edition of the novel (coordinated by Evodio Escalante). Also, an account of the novel's reception and the deep emotional impact the controversy had on Revueltas can be found in Ruiz Abreu ([1992] 1993).

3. This characterization appears in practically every consideration of Revueltas's work. As far as I know, the most detailed examination is Ruiz Abreu ([1992] 1993), as well as Durán (2002).

4. This image was articulated in his novels, but also in the film adaptations of his more mainstream novels, such as *Dona Flor e seus dois maridos* (1976) and *Gabriela, cravo e canela* (1983), both directed by Bruno Barreto.

5. Ignacio Sánchez Prado (2007) argues persuasively that this influence was "emptied" of any ideological content (i.e., Communism), and based more upon Revueltas's prestige as a rebel and an uncompromising icon of the struggles of the 1930s.

6. Monsiváis (2010), with the impeccable credentials provided by his having been one of the young intellectuals connected with Revueltas in the 1960s and 1970s, is deeply aware of the fact that, for those outside the world of activists in the Marxist Left, many of the topics visited by Revueltas's narratives are now exotic, if not virtually incomprehensible. In this respect, Revueltas has not aged well, outside of certain intellectual and academic circles. It is startling that this is hardly noticed.

7. Bosteels (2007) carries out an interesting attempt to read Revueltas's narrative (specifically his novel *Los errores*) from the point of view of melodrama.

8. This contrast can also be explained (but not explained away) by mentioning the literary figures who influenced each author. John Steinbeck, and in particular *The Grapes of Wrath*, influenced Amado, while William Faulkner influenced *El luto humano*. This influence is apparent at the verbal level, in the plot, and in the larger symbolism that permeates both novels.

9. Gerald Martin (1989) compares Revueltas's prose to that of Roberto Arlt. I think the comparison is apt. Francisco Ramírez Santacruz (2007) ventures another comparison with another Argentine, Ernesto Sábato. While less flattering, at least according to the current critical consensus, this comparison is also apt.

10. In the piece that opens the Archivos edition of *Los días terrenales*, Zea (1991) reads both Revueltas's oeuvre and his artistic and political persona as essentially Dostoyevskian. The title of his contribution is telling: "Revueltas, el endemoniado" (Revueltas, the possessed), which is reminiscent of the title of Dostoyevsky's novel *Demons*, as it is usually translated into Spanish (*Los demonios, Los endemoniados*).

11. Of course, it has often been remarked that Marxism has a deep commonality with Christianity at the level of some basic tropes (humanity's fall, an emancipatory ideal, and so forth).

12. It seems that the episode is based on Revueltas's own experience organizing a strike in the irrigation system related to the San Martín dam in Araujo, Nuevo León. Revueltas was there in the early 1930s, during the presidency of Abelardo L. Rodríguez. His activities as representative of the Communist Party were responsible for his second stint in the Marías Islands (see Olea Franco 2010a, 204–5).

13. It is hard to ignore the commonalities between *El luto humano* and Graham Greene's *The Power and the Glory* (1940). Both novels deal with the Cristero War and its aftermath. Both novels' priests are loyal to Rome but are keenly aware of the differences between Mexican and Roman Catholicism. Both remain firm in their ministries, but are overwhelmed by the consciousness of their personal and political shortcomings. Both figures border on abjection. Both decide to die in a manner that touches both martyrdom, the ultimate exaltation of Catholic priesthood, and suicide, which condemns the soul to eternal perdition. Both die with mortal sins on their consciences. And both witness the collapse of their respective communities and are incapable of preventing it. From a different point of view, the priest of *El luto* could be compared to Padre Rentería, from Juan Rulfo's *Pedro Páramo*. Both are aware of (and tortured by) their moral shortcomings, in particular when it comes to their capacity to speak truth to power. But while Rentería seems to find a sort of redemption when joining the Cristiada, there is no redemption for the priest in *El luto*.

14. "Cecilia was the land, Úrsulo's fifteen hectares. . . . Natividad yearned to trans-

form the land and his doctrine needed a new man, a free man over a new, free land. That is why Cecilia, who was the land of Mexico, loved him, even though he did it unconsciously, and ignoring the deep, hidden forces that determined his love.... Calixto and Úrsulo were something entirely different. They were the transition toward something that waited in the future. They were a blind, deaf, complex, contradictory transition. They were the unspoken yearning; the confused hope that arises to find out about the best path. Chonita had died, many, many years before; she was the mysterious fruit of the hopeless land" (186–87).

15. Natividad is a paragon of all virtues, and those virtues shine through constantly and irresistibly. However, his charisma is stated but not narrated (for example, it is never explained how exactly Natividad, a relative newcomer to the area, becomes the inspiration for and leader of the strike), nor is it successfully transmitted (we are never convinced of Natividad's charisma). It seems that his revolutionary qualities command immediate obedience in men and love in women. But this remains highly unconvincing, a sort of throwback to romantic aesthetics in which the virtue of the hero or heroine is translated in his or her physical appearance and commands immediate, unexplained (and unnecessary-to-explain) love and allegiance.

16. Úrsulo thinks to himself, "Always a priest at the time of death. A priest who extracts the heart from the bosom with the stone knife of penance, to offer it, like the ancient priests before, in the stone of sacrifices, to God, to God in whose bosom the idols were pulverized, spreading their dust, now impalpable in the white body of the deity" (Revueltas [1943] 2003, 12).

17. This is similar to *The Power and the Glory*, where it is not clear who is really the martyr: José (the apostate priest), the "whisky priest" (who, poor and persecuted, keeps administering the holy sacraments), or Juan, the protagonist of the pious story that the anonymous woman reads (the most simple of martyrs, the novel seems to suggest).

CHAPTER 9: BORGES AND MOREIRA

1. This movie is based upon a crucial forgetting: that Fierro refused to be a proletarian. His becoming a cog in the machine of rural capitalism is the measure of his defeat. The sons of Fierro, on the other hand, proudly display a proletarian union identity. The signifier that allows this transference (which betrays the spirit of Hernández's poem, at least the first half) is that of "the people."

2. In the sixties, this identification was a phenomenon of hemispheric proportions. Perhaps the most important examples are Glauber Rocha's *Deus e o Diabo na Terra do Sol* (1964) and *Antônio das Mortes* (1969), also known as *O Dragão da Maldade contra o Santo Guerreiro*. The "other side" in the struggle used the identification between leftist insurgents and bandits as well (see, for example, the reactivation of the [Latin American] bandit motif in American film of the decade).

3. Montoneros was a leftist armed organization that fought for Perón's return from the late 1960s onward. In 1974, Perón (already in power) disowned them and opted for the right wing of his party, thus marking the beginning of the most vicious era of political violence in Argentina.

4. For example, in the Montoneros journal *El descamisado*, a comic strip appeared during those years in which "Juan" the paysano was the hero of Argentine popular history, in an arc that spanned from the popular resistance against the English invasions in 1806–1807 to the massacre in Ezeiza in 1974. The gaucho malo was also the emblem of the far-right group Tacuara, and of those that in 1963 (the centennial of Peñaloza's execution, ordered or at least allowed by Sarmiento—at the time the bête noire of nationalism of all stripes) vandalized Sarmiento's many statues (Luna 1966, 165).

5. Recent scholarship, perhaps aided by the publication after Borges's death of many of his pieces formerly scattered in periodicals and journals, has shown that Borges (and his work) was always involved in the political and cultural conflicts of his time. For the 1920s, see Sarlo ([1993] 2003). For an in-depth, enlightening analysis of how the ascendancy of fascism in Europe and authoritarian nationalism in Argentina impacted (and, to a degree, defined) Borges's writing, see Louis (2006, 2007).

6. Sandra Contreras (2009) carefully traces how Sarmiento's image as a cypher of the paradigm civilization/barbarism changes in different moments of the Borgesian oeuvre, in particular when it comes to the emergence and transformations of Peronism. For a history of the dyad in Argentine culture, see Svampa (1994).

7. The 1996 *Obras completas* (edited a decade after Borges's death) included this piece as an epilogue at the end of the fourth (and last) volume.

8. "I am Francisco Real, a man from the North. I am Francisco Real, the Corralero by another name. I have let these poor losers hit me because I am looking for a real man. There are some liars out there saying that in these godforsaken slums

there is a man with a reputation as a knife fighter and as a mean son of a bitch. They called him the Pegador. I want to find him, so that he can teach me, a perfect nobody, what it means to be a man of courage and skill" (Borges 2005a, 351).

9. On this "direct style" see Louis (2009).

10. Podestá was the actor who co-authored, with Gutiérrez, the adaptation of the novel for the circus and the popular theater. Podestá played the part of Moreira, and he followed in his impersonation Gutiérrez's description of the gaucho: full dark beard, flowing hair, piercing eyes. In the film version, Favio would also choose the mythical face of the gaucho (played by Rodolfo Bebán), as opposed to the more modest appearance of the historical gaucho, known because of the *filiaciones* (police descriptions) and the extant photograph of Moreira.

11. The use of this weapon had declined notoriously in the nineteenth century, with the advent of modern cartridges. Furthermore, the revolvers with multiple shots compared very favorably with the blunderbuss's hardly controllable spread of ammunition. However, it remained in use in the rural areas (as in the case of Moreira) into the twentieth century, in particular because it could shoot many things besides shot (such as rocks, nails, metal scraps, and even rock salt). The blunderbuss makes a memorable appearance in *Os sertões*, where the jagunços use them to fire stones propelled by homemade powder, and in *La guerra del fin del mundo*, where the blunderbuss is the weapon of choice of the bandit-turned-true-believer Pedrão. In *Moreira*, the use of the blunderbuss may serve to highlight Moreira's skill, since charging it after each shot, in the middle of a fight, was a complicated operation that required dexterity and nerve.

12. There was a reward on Moreira's head. Chirino tried to collect that money, but it seems that he was never able to do so.

13. Outside Argentina, Leonardo Favio was known as a popular singer of dubious prestige. Far less known was his long and celebrated career first as a film actor and later as a director, from the 1960s until his death (although within Argentina, and among those aware of Argentine film history, Favio is considered one of the most talented and distinctive directors in the history of Argentine film). Legend has it that Favio, after the critical success of his first movies—in particular *Crónica de un niño solo* (1965), *El romance del Aniceto y la Francisca* (1966), and *El dependiente* (1969)—started his career as a romantic songwriter and singer in order to raise the money to produce more movies, in color and with larger budgets. The first movie of this new period was *Juan Moreira*, followed

by *Nazareno Cruz y el lobo* (1975) and *Soñar, soñar* (1976).

14. Farina posits an implicit but direct relationship. He may have ignored the fact that "La noche," although collected in book form in 1975, was written and published before the movie was made. But beyond that, his intuition is, I think, correct and enlightening.

15. See Prieto (1988), in particular chapter 2, "Red textual y deslizamientos de lecturas: Martín Fierro, Juan Moreira, Santos Vega."

CHAPTER 10: LANGUAGE, THE DEVIL, AND THE (OUT)LAW

1. Many parts of the narrative register reactions by Riobaldo to things that the listener says or does. There are numerous dialogic indexes ("listen now," "pay attention to this," and so forth), as well as comments about the differences in education and outlook between the two interlocutors. For an examination of the interaction between them, see Pacheco (1992). Other important first-person bandit narratives (aside from the ones examined here) are *Eloy* (1959), by Carlos Drogett, and *La vida no tiene nombre* (1965), by Marcio Veloz Maggiolo.

2. Later on, Riobaldo discovers that Selorico Mendes may be his father (Guimarães Rosa [1956] 1986, 104). Selorico never acknowledges this fact officially (31), but he always shows affection for his "stepson" (94), taking him in after the death of his mother (93), and providing for his education (95). When Selrico dies, he bequeaths his two largest fazendas to Riobaldo (534).

3. Zé Bebelo had been defeated and taken alive by Joca Ramiro's forces not long before this. He is put on trial, so that Joca Ramiro's chieftains can decide what to do with him. He is sentenced to exile in Goiás. The benign verdict (reached in part because of Riobaldo's spirited speech at the trial) spares Zé Bebelo's life and honor, and wins his gratitude and ulterior loyalty. Thus, upon hearing the news of Joca Ramiro's murder, he comes back to lead the jagunços in the quest for retribution.

4. For example, in northeastern Brazil, the sertão is the arid or semiarid cattle frontier in the backlands of Bahia, Pernambuco, Alagoas, Sergipe, Piauí, and Rio Grando do Norte. The area was for centuries the westernmost limit of Portuguese (and later Brazilian) penetration from the coast into the interior. Since the reach of the state was tenuous and erratic, the areas enjoyed a large degree of self-determination, and were ruled by landowners who also had military,

judicial, and administrative prerogatives, the so-called "colonels" (an example of which appears in chapter 7 of this book).

5. The issue of the pact links with two long-standing cultural traditions: the bandit as the devil, and the bandit as having a covenant with the devil.

6. This also goes in another direction. A doctor on a trip (Guimarães Rosa [1956] 1986, 48) tells Riobaldo that God does not exist. That is terrible: God needs to exist. The devil, not at all.

CHAPTER 11: AN ABUNDANCE OF HATS AND A SCARCITY OF HEADS

1. It is important (and perhaps ironic) that this short story is dedicated to Victoria Ocampo, a person whose life and oeuvre were predicated upon her conviction that high culture had the ability (and mission) to keep violence at bay, and to eventually supersede it. The short story, to the contrary, shows the inextricable nature of culture and violence.

2. I do not say (absurdly) that Yu Tsun is a bandit. But he is a herald of this new order, that is, a new order of violence, but also an impossible moral order. Yu Tsun is a spy, efficient and dedicated, retained by the German Empire, one of the states that has come close, perhaps, to the ideal of the modern state, ruled by bureaucratic-instrumental reason. Yu Tsun, however, does not identify with that logic. Like his persecutor Madden (an Irishman in the service of the British Empire), Yu Tsun does not fight for a state, actual or ideal, but for a personal cause: the vindication of his identity (despised by his German boss), and his lineage (stained by the devotion of Ts'ui Pên to the labyrinth). He is like Otto Dietrich zur Linde in Borges's "Deutches Requiem" (originally published in 1946, collected in Borges 2005a), who is a minor but crucial cog in the genocidal Nazi bureaucracy, but who seeks with his participation in the Holocaust not a goal related to racial purity or the Reich, but a moral revelation, and a vindication of his declining family (his ancestors, he reminds us, were heroes in Germany's wars).

3. Like everything in the Library, the term "human race" does not mean the same as what it means in other worlds (ours, for example). Since there are only male librarians, how the species reproduces itself (and it does reproduce, since the narrator mentions his childhood memories) remains unexplained. One hypothesis is that there is some kind of artificial conception (as in "Las ruinas circulares") or some kind of parthenogenesis.

4. Sara Castro-Klarén links the novel (or some scenes within it) to "Hollywood's
   biblical and Western sagas or pirate movies" (1990, 166). On the other hand,
   Elmore (1997) links some episodes of the novel (primarily the fracas between
   Rufino and Gall) to the *novelas de caballería* to which Vargas Llosa is well
   known to be partial.

5. The opening sentences of the glowing 1982 review by Ángel Rama set the tone
   for the novel's critical success. He states, "After reading the 531 pages of *La
   guerra del fin del mundo,* two conclusions are unavoidable: it is a masterpiece,
   and it has achieved the consolidation of a genre: the high-popular novel in Latin
   America. It is not essential to be endowed with Cassandra's gift to foresee that
   it will have millions of readers and that a hundred years from now it will be
   mentioned as one of the key novels of the second half of the twentieth century,
   that witnessed the triumphant expansion of the genre in the continent." He
   adds, "The intensity, wide scope and coherence of the project, and the sovereign
   narrative mastery, should be credited with the fact that Latin America achieves
   its own *War and Peace,* although a century later, thus making of its author our
   biggest literary classic alive" (1982, 600).

   This is a rare accomplishment for several reasons. As a foreigner, Vargas
   Llosa was tackling a story central to (indeed, foundational for) the cultural
   imaginary of Brazil. He was venturing into a literary realm (that of the literature of the northeastern sertão) in which he would join some of the giants of
   Brazilian literature: Euclides da Cunha, José Lins do Rego, Jorge Amado, Ra-
   chel de Queiroz, and João Guimarães Rosa, among others. For a discussion and
   justification of Vargas Llosa's incursion into a foreign literary tradition, see
   Elmore (1997). Vargas Llosa repeated this incursion, with equal success, in *La
   fiesta del Chivo* (2000), another historical novel, this one focused on Dominican
   dictator Rafael Leónidas Trujillo (1891–1961). Vargas Llosa has fared extremely well on both accounts.

6. Leo Bernucci (1989) examines the intertextual relations of the novel with *Os
   sertões,* as well as with other works related to Canudos.

7. "Canudos," today, refers to different things at the same time. First, Canudos was
   the town erected deep in the Bahian backlands under the inspiration of Antonio Conselheiro. It was a town where the believers retired to live according to
   their faith. Second, it names the millenarian movement that erected the town,
   and enacted, albeit briefly, a social and cultural experiment that still fascinates
   and puzzles people. Finally, it names the bloody fights between the believ-

ers—"fanatics" and "bandits" according to the Republican press—and the state
and federal forces sent to destroy them. For a classic English-language consideration of Canudos, see Levine (1992). In Portuguese, see Pernambucano de
Mello (2007).

8. I leave the Baron aside. He is also an intellectual, but the novel considers him an
old-fashioned, irrelevant kind of intellectual. The Baron is a politician, a scientist, and an aesthete, but not really a professional in any of these endeavors. He
is too much of a gentleman to take any of them too seriously, or to compromise
his identity too wholly. He is above all a landowner, with the nice addition of a
sophisticated education and intellectual interests. Galileo Gall, the criminologists, and the nearsighted journalist are specialists and professionals, who live
from and for their professions. It is in this last sense that I refer to them as modern intellectuals.

9. Killing by knife (as opposed to firearm) implied dishonor and exclusion from
the afterlife. There is a long tradition of this in the West. In ancient Rome, as
Coleman (1990, 46) observes, modalities of execution or punishment were
aimed at humiliation, loss of status, and infamy. This infamy was not always
linked to the amount of pain delivered, or the visibility of the punishment. The
wheel, for example, perhaps one of the cruelest punishments ever conceived,
had a redeeming (even sacred) component to it (Merback 1999).

10. Nina Rodrigues's examination, to which the novel refers, actually took place. A
summary of its results can be read in his posthumous volume *As collectividades
anormaes*, as a sort of addendum to an earlier article, "A loucura das multidões,"
written while the fighting was still taking place.

11. Modern (American) examples of similar scandals and of the perhaps insurmountable difficulties in grappling with them in a coherent narrative fashion
include the struggle against the Vietcong guerrilla in Vietnam (which, just like
Canudos, has given us at least one masterpiece: *Apocalypse Now*, also the story
of a warrior community deep in the backlands, and its inscrutable leader) and
the fight against the Taliban in Afghanistan.

12. The novel reads,

Once the analysis of the bones was over, the problem arose of what to do
with them. Somebody proposed that the skull be sent to the National
Museum, as a historical curiosity. That proposal faced stiff opposition.
Who opposed it? The masons. They argued that Nosso Senhor do Bonfim

was enough as a center of pilgrimage. That skull in a showcase would make
the National Museum into a second Church of Bonfim, a heterodox shrine.
The Army agreed. It was imperative to prevent the skull from becoming a
holy relic, the seed of future uprisings. But how? How?

Obviously, not burying, murmured the Baron.

Obviously, since the fanatic crowd, sooner or later, would discover the
site. So, which place would be safer and more remote than the bottom of
the sea? The skull was placed in a sack full of rocks, the sack was sewn
and carried by an officer in a boat, under the cover of night, to a location
in the Atlantic equidistant from the Fort of San Marcelo and the Island of
Itapacarica. The sack was dropped to the bottom of the sea, to serve as an
anchor for corals. The officer in charge of the operation was Lieutenant
Pinto Souza: end of the story. (Vargas Llosa 1981, 433)

13. The saga of the head of Lampião and his gang after Angicos is perhaps the most
gruesome example of this. The heads, together with apparel pertaining to the
cangaceiros (hats, bags, rifles), were taken on a sort of traveling exhibition. The
famous picture of the heads of the late gang, neatly arranged on a staircase at
the entrance of a house and surrounded by cangaceiro memorabilia, pertains to
this episode.

14. On this (rather sudden) change from public, dramatic bodily punishment to
secret, bureaucratic punishment, see the opening sections of Foucault (1975).
In Latin America, and particularly when it came to rural insurgency, the dynamics of this transition were different, with public punishment surviving well into
the second half of the twentieth century. Probably the most famous (and most
recent) example is that of the pictures of Che Guevara dead in Bolivia, in 1967.
The posters in which the Bolivian government offered rewards for Guevara
and his group (reproduced in González and Sánchez Salazar 1969, 128) refer to
them as "castrocommunist bandits."

15. In *Polvo y ceniza*, by Eliécer Cárdenas, the bandit hunter Major Deifilio orders,
after executing Naún Briones, that his face be covered with a piece of cloth, so
that nobody will have a memory of the dead bandit. Once the corpse is carried to
Loja, no autopsy is performed, and the bandit is buried in an undisclosed location. This is the opposite of what bandit hunters usually did: cut off the head of
the bandit and take a picture in order to ensure maximum publicity of the fact.
But Major Deifilio's strategy is sound. These images, although part of a theater

of terror, tended to fix public attention on them. The Christlike quality of these images is unmistakable, because, in fact, the canonical symbol of Christianity (Christ hanging from the cross) is precisely the image of somebody who was executed in lieu of a bandit (Barabbas—although, significantly, the word used in the gospel is *lēstēs*, a word used for either bandits or insurgents of various stripes). Therefore, the pious image of Christ suffering on the cross is the exact equivalent of the image of Lampião, whose head (along with those of his accomplices) is displayed on the steps of some house or public building. Now, instead of a theater of the law, this image conveys all the lurid attractiveness of the outlaw. Major Deifilio shows how he is able to grasp the dynamics of social languages, and the subtle wars fought over images.

16. This identification is highlighted by the fact that when they die, they are hardly distinguishable from one another, because they fight in a tight embrace and are covered in mud.

17. Vargas Llosa's unequivocal turn toward liberalism, a turn that is announced by *La guerra*, was, in many sectors, in particular within the academic Left, the act that warranted his exile from the politically correct circles. Classic versions of this condemnation by the academic Left are the works of William Rowe (1992), Gerald Martin (1987), and Antonio Cornejo Polar (1982). More contemporary versions of this position can be found in the volume edited by Juan E. De Castro and Nicholas Birns (2012), in particular Birns's chapter on *La guerra* (71–83). One testimony (among others) to Vargas Llosa's continually controversial public persona are the protests triggered by the invitation to him to give the opening address at the 2011 Buenos Aires Book Fair.

18. "—All intellectuals are dangerous—Moreira César agreed. They are weak, sentimental, and capable of using the best ideas to justify the worst actions. The country needs them, but ought to handle them as circus animals" (Vargas Llosa 1981, 209). A previous episode (Moreira César's treatment of authorities and journalists when he arrives at Queimadas) further illustrates his contempt for men of letters.

19. Castro-Klarén notes that "his soft physique and stubborn intellectual demeanor seem to place him within a general scheme that Vargas Llosa uses for his journalists, scribblers, or well-intentioned souls such as Mayta in *The Real Life of Alejandro Mayta*, Pedro Camacho in *Aunt Julia*, or even Saúl Zurata in *El hablador*. These little men are singled out by an unmistakable physical defect: myopia, a birthmark, standing red hair, flat feet, or a big soft belly" (1990, 172).

20. Much has been made of what the shortsighted journalist "represents." In particular, it has been debated whether he is a fictional rewriting of Euclides da Cunha or not, Vargas Llosa or not. I follow Castro-Klarén (1990, 172) in thinking that the journalist, even though he certainly has traits that remind us of da Cunha, has no specific (individual) historical referent. He represents what he is: a modern intellectual.

21. The dominance of the visual dimension in the narrative, according to Castro-Klarén (1990, 164), has to do with the fact that the novel originated as a failed movie script on Canudos.

22. The fact that he is overcome with passion for Jurema, at an extreme point in his life, mirrors the event in which Gall, awash in lust after avoiding being assassinated by Epaminondas's jagunços, rapes Jurema (see Elmore 1997). However, while Gall tries to keep his distance (intellectual as well as affective) from the event, once it has happened (and he fails to do so), the journalist surrenders to it.

23. Two Brazilian examples can be found in the fact that both Antônio Silvino and Lampião cherished and used their mock titles of Governor of the Sertão and King of the Cangaço, respectively, and the fact that Lampião acted in many respects like a bureaucrat, issuing letters, passports, granting interviews, etc.

24. Perhaps the most telling case is the respect that Pajeú shows for Jurema. Pajeú, a fearsome warrior and hero of the New Jerusalem, is in love with Jurema. But he respects her desires, and does not impose himself upon her (the same cannot be said of the emancipator, Gall).

25. As Janes indicates in her brilliant work on decapitation,

> The lesson of the heads [decapitations during the Terror] is that there has been a fundamental change in social hierarchies and the distribution of power. Article 3 of the Declaration of the Rights of Man and Citizen declared that the people were "the source of sovereignty." Taking a head transforms the people from the passive "source of sovereignty" to the active executor of sovereign power. . . . When the people cut off and displayed the head of a "traitor," they made the "sovereignty of the people" more than a pretty compliment. They enacted that sovereignty by exercising a traditional prerogative of the sovereign. (2005, 21)

26. It is in this sense that I prefer to understand the trope of silence, as applied to Conselheiro (an interpretation originally put forward by Castro-Klarén [1986]).

Even though he is a public figure and a superb communicator, his motivations, his psychological life, his whole identity remain a mystery in the novel. But as the scene of the eschatological communion, or the conversions successively narrated (but not explained), seem to show, the jagunços partake of the secret (which, avoiding the trap of premodern transcendentalism, is never postulated as a secret).

27. Conselheiro's followers acknowledge those rights, or at least they acknowledge that the Baron belongs to the same world that they do (the rural world of Bahia), and that they can have a dialogue. This is why, when they are about to burn Calumbí to the ground, both as retaliation and "in order to let the land rest" (Vargas Llosa 1981, 238), they forewarn the Baron, and they allow him to flee the scene unharmed and carrying his valuables with him.

CHAPTER 12: BANDITRY, NEOLIBERALISM, AND THE DILEMMAS OF LITERATURE

1. The controversy had less to do with the novel itself than with the 1997 Premio Planeta award that, it was claimed, was improperly given to Piglia due to conflict of interest. The outcome of the protracted judicial battle that ensued tarnished Piglia's reputation in Argentina (see "Condenan a Ricardo Piglia" [2005], among other examples of the extensive press coverage of the fiasco). But it certainly did not hinder the overall commercial (and, to a point, critical) success of the novel. The 2003 Seix Barral edition notes that between 1997 and 2003 Planeta reprinted the novel twelve times. It was also made into an award-winning, star-studded movie directed by Marcelo Piñeyro, released in 2000.

2. The opening scene of the novel reads like the image on the poster of Tarantino's *Reservoir Dogs*: Dorda and Brignone, walking in dark suits. There are also other commonalities, such as a bank robbery gone awry that ends up with the robbers all dead or dying. Also, both narratives can be linked through their claustrophobic quality (most of the novel takes place in enclosed spaces).

3. In addition to Emilio Renzi's narrative voice, there is a third-person narrator, media accounts, and the direct and/or indirect speech (or thoughts) of many of the characters, such as Police Chief Silva, Malito, Nene, Dorda, Blanca, Martínez Tovar, et al. For an analysis of the very complex interplay of narrative voices in the novel, see Gutiérrez González (2003).

4. My reading of the novel dialogues with Joanna Page's (2004) excellent article. There is, however, a crucial difference (but not necessarily incompatibility) between the two: if I understand her article correctly, she reads *Plata quemada* as a reflection on state violence, and links that reflection to Argentina's dictatorial past. I read the novel as a reflection on more contemporary issues, and the demise of the nation-state.

5. For an examination of the role of money in Argentine fiction, see Laera (2002, 2014).

6. According to Piglia, "The only mystery that American detective novels propose—and never solve—is that of capitalist relationships: money that acts as the legislator of social ethics, and thus sustains the law, is the only 'logic' in these narratives where everything is for sale" ([1986] 2006, 62). Arlt, for his part, "does not construct his works using elements belonging to the immediate present, rather he addresses the laws that regulate society. . . . He takes as his point of departure certain core elements, such as the relations between power and fiction, between money and madness, between truth and conspiracy, and he transforms them in form and in narrative strategy, he transforms them into the foundation for his fiction" (22).

7. Delber Avelar (1999) proposes that this dual focus is a defining feature of all postdictatorial Latin American (or at least Southern Cone) narrative.

8. "At heart, he is only interested in literature, he experiences everything and he sees everything from the point of view of literature and in this sense, I use Renzi to poke irony at myself. Everything that is not literature bores me, as a czech would say. But I think that it would be better to say that Emilio Renzi is a sort of wandering Stephen Dedalus, a Quentin Compson who lives in Almagro, I mean, he is the young artist, the aesthetic character who considers the world with disdain" ([1986] 2006, 93). He adds, "For me literature is much more interesting than life. First, because literature has a much more elegant form, and second because it is a much more intense experience" (172).

9. Juan Pablo Canala has posited and examined a relationship between Arlt (in particular *El juguete rabioso*) and Gutiérrez's novels, specifically his novels on urban criminals such as Antonio Larrea (*Un capitán de ladrones en Buenos Aires*, 1879) and Serapio Boches. See Canala (2012, 2014).

10. The 1990s witnessed a deluge of work dealing with the most conflictive figures of the century: Eva Perón, Juan Perón, Jorge Luis Borges, and Che Guevara, the foremost icon of the 1960s. But in most cases the narrative surrounding these

characters is no longer articulated to any given conflict, as in the past; rather, it is resignified as Argentine (or Latin American) memory, thus erasing the dimension of conflict as an actual conflict from the historical or biographical narrative, even as the conflict itself is depicted.

11. In Fernando Vallejo's *La virgen de los sicarios* (1993), Jorge Franco's *Rosario Tijeras* (1999), and Paulo Lins's *Cidade de Deus* (1997)—some of the successful novels made into internationally celebrated films—the figures of the *sicario* (assassin), the drug dealer, and the *malandro* (con artist or petty criminal) are invoked to better attest to the demise of the nation-state as a social and cultural synthesis.

12. See Laera (2002) for an excellent assessment of the relationship between nonfiction and fiction as a distinct series in Argentine literature, from the nineteenth century (including Gutiérrez) to the present (including Piglia).

13. The same was not true of other areas of the country, such as the dry pampa (*pampa seca*, as opposed to the *pampa húmeda*), the Chaco region, Misiones, and Patagonia, where classic social banditry lasted well into the twentieth century and where social bandits of mythical status, such as Vairoletto, Mate Cosido, and the Velázquez brothers, were active.

14. Borges notes in "La poesía gauchesca" that "the true ethics of the criollo . . . maintains that to shed somebody else's blood is not that important, and that to kill is something that just happens to men. . . . 'Who did not owe a death in my time?' I heard one afternoon the mellow complaint of an elderly man. I will not forget, either, an orillero who once told me with utmost seriousness, 'Mr. Borges, it is true that I have been in jail many times, but always for murder'" (2005a, 207).

15. For an examination of the "infinite series" of challenges that make up the gaucho malo biography, see Laera (2004).

16. "The bravest and coolest guy that you have ever seen (according to Brignone). Once, with a 9 mm pistol, he made a stand against the pigs in Lanús and kept them at bay until Nene was able to break through, driving backward, and rescued him. It was awesome. He was just standing there, shooting, holding his gun with both hands, completely cool, boom, boom, with an elegance worth seeing, and all the cops shitting themselves" (Piglia 1997, 79).

17. "Dorda killed him for no reason at all. And certainly, he did not do it because the policeman represented a threat. He had killed him because he hated the police more than anything in the world, and he thought, in an utterly irrational fash-

ion, that each policeman that he killed was not going to be replaced. 'One less' was Gaucho's motto, as if he were diminishing the ranks of an enemy army that could not be renovated" (Piglia 1997, 40).

18. On Artigas, Sarmiento observes, "Had the Spaniards entered Argentina in 1811, it is possible to think that our Bolívar would have been Artigas" ([1845] 1979, 17). On Quiroga: "The first ray of the May sun illuminated for him the glorious career of military service to the fatherland. And there is no doubt that, with his strong temperament and his instincts bent toward destruction and butchery, moralized by disciplines and ennobled by the sublimity of the pursuit, Facundo would have returned one day from Peru, Chile, or Bolivia as one of the generals of the Republic" (83).

19. The episode in *Plata quemada* in which Malito sodomizes and kills a policeman who had tortured him is, I would argue, a direct rewriting of one of the best-known texts by Lamborghini, "El niño proletario" (included in *Sebregondi retrocede*, 1973): "Malito looked for [the cop] and kidnapped him one night when the guy was getting out of a bus in Varela. He drowned him in a ditch. He forced him on his knees and he submerged his face in the mud, and they say that he pulled the guy's pants down and he raped him while the cop shook with his head underwater" (Piglia 1997, 20).

20. Laera (2002) mentions the gratuitous act not in relation to the burning of the money, but in relation to Nene's "treason" to his own class.

21. Fernando Vallejo's *La virgen de los sicarios*, another runaway success of the 1990s (and also made into a disappointing movie), bears striking similarities to *Plata quemada* in many respects, including the gay outlaw and the man of letters, and subjects such as the dissolution of the political and the decadence of literature, as well as violence as the condition of possibility for love, and criminality as the condition of possibility for the experience of art. Also, it is significant that in order to become artists—and this becoming happens entirely outside any conscious decision—they have to betray all the codes of violence that define their practices (they kill at random).

CHAPTER 13: WHAT IS A BANDIT?

1. Another example is the sprawling *Une histoire de la violence* (2008), by Robert Muchembled. However, that book—which has many virtues—is somewhat simple in its thesis. The roles of elite bandit narratives are what they have usually

been considered to be: cautionary tales about the consequences of "breaking bad," told with an allure that vicariously keeps the passion for breaking bad alive (passion that is needed to persuade young men to fight the wars of the elite). Muchembled focuses on the generational conflict of which banditry (as a trope) is one of many symptoms: the anxiety in early modern societies about unattached, potentially violent and restless young men.

2. The same was true of Villa's movement, which was steeped in a culture of serrano violence against Apaches and rustlers in Chihuahua, Durango, and Sonora (Katz 1998); of the gavilleros' resistance in southeastern Dominican Republic, which was steeped in a caudillo tradition of party politics (Calder 2006; González Canalda 2008); of the cacos in the hinterland of Haiti (Schmidt 1995); and of the bandits in the southern islands of the Philippines archipelago who doggedly fought the Marines (Linn 2000).

3. The intervention happened before the current mixing up of the paradigms according to which "war" refers to domestic police operations (e.g., the war on drugs) and "police operation" refers to large-scale operations (e.g., the "security missions" in Asia, Africa, and the Balkans [Mansfield 2008]).

WORKS CITED

Adas, Michael. 1982. "Bandits, Monks, and Pretender Kings: Patterns of Peasant Resistance and Protest in Colonial Burma, 1826–1941." In *Power and Protest in the Countryside: Studies of Rural Unrest in Asia, Europe, and Latin America*, edited by Robert P. Weller and Scott E. Guggenheim, 75–105. Durham, NC: Duke University Press.

Agamben, Giorgio. (1995) 1998. *Homo Sacer: Sovereign Power and Bare Life*. Stanford, CA: Stanford University Press.

Agamben, Giorgio. (2003) 2005. *State of Exception*. Chicago: University of Chicago Press.

Aguilar, Gonzalo, and Emiliano Jelicié. 2010. *Borges va al cine*. Buenos Aires: Libraria Ediciones.

Aguilar Mora, Jorge. 1990. *Una muerte sencilla, justa, eterna: Cultura y guerra durante la Revolución Mexicana*. Mexico City: Ediciones Era.

Aguirre, Carlos. 1990. "Cimarronaje, bandolerismo y desintegración esclavista: Lima, 1821–1854." In Aguirre and Walker 1990, 137–82.

Aguirre, Carlos. 2005. *The Criminals of Lima and Their Worlds: The Prison Experience, 1850–1935*. Durham, NC: Duke University Press.

Aguirre, Carlos, and Ricardo Salvatore. 2001. Introduction to *Crime and Punishment in Latin America: Law and Society since Late Colonial Times*, edited by Ricardo Salvatore, Carlos Aguirre, and Gilbert Joseph, 1–33. Durham, NC: Duke University Press.

Aguirre, Carlos, and Charles Walker, eds. 1990. *Bandoleros, abigeos y montoneros: Criminalidad y violencia en el Perú, siglos XVII–XX*. Lima: Instituto de Apoyo Agrario.

Aguirre Benavides, Luis. 1964. *Las grandes batallas de la División del Norte al mando del General Francisco Villa*. Mexico City: Editorial Diana.

Aira, César. 1975. *Moreira*. Buenos Aires: Achával Solo.

Alarcón, Cristián. (2003) 2012. *Cuando me muera quiero que me toquen cumbia*. Buenos Aires: Santillana Argentina.

Alegría, Ciro. (1939) 1963. *Los perros hambrientos*. In *Novelas completas*, 175–326. Madrid: Aguilar.

Alegría, Ciro. (1941) 1963. *El mundo es ancho y ajeno*. In *Novelas completas*, 325–962. Madrid: Aguilar.

Alegría, Ciro. 1963. Prologue to *Memorias*, by Enrique López Albújar, 7–9. Lima.

Alegría, Ciro. 1980. *Mucha suerte con harto palo: Memorias*. Bogotá: Oveja Negra.

Almeida, Alfredo Wagner Berno de. 1979. *Jorge Amado, política e literatura: Un estudo sobre a trajetória intelectual de Jorge Amado*. Contribuições em ciências sociais 3. Rio de Janeiro: Editora Campus.

Almeida, José Américo de. (1928) 1972. *A bagaceira*. Rio de Janeiro: Livraria José Olympo Editora.

Almeida, José Américo de. (1935) 1979. *Coiteiros*. Rio de Janeiro: Editora Civilização Brasileira.

Alonso Cortés, Rodrigo. 1972. *Francisco Villa, el quinto jinete del Apocalipsis*. Mexico City: Diana.

Altamirano, Carlos, and Beatriz Sarlo. 1995. *Ensayos argentinos: De Sarmiento a la vanguardia*. Buenos Aires: Ariel.

Altamirano, Ignacio Manuel. 1901. *El Zarco*. Mexico City: Establecimiento Editorial de J. Ballescá.

Álvarez Barrientos, Joaquín, and Pilar García Moutón. 1986. "Bandolero y bandido: Ensayo de interpretactión." *Revista de dialectologia y tradiciones populares* 41: 7–58.

Amado, Jorge. 1933. *Cacau: Romance*. Rio de Janeiro: J. Olympio.

Amado, Jorge. (1935) 1965. *Jubiabá*. São Paulo: Livraria Martins Editôra.

Amado, Jorge. (1937) 1982. *Capitães da areia*. São Paulo: Livraria Martins Editôra.

Amado, Jorge. 1942. *Vida de Luiz Carlos Prestes, el caballero de la esperanza*. Buenos Aires: Editorial Claridad.

Amado, Jorge. (1943) 1995. *Terras do sem fim*. São Paulo: Livraria Martins Editôra.

Amado, Jorge. (1944) 1966. *São Jorge dos Ilhéus*. São Paulo: Livraria Martins Editôra.

Amado, Jorge. 1946. *Homens e coisas do Partido Comunista*. Rio de Janeiro: Edições Horizonte.

Amado, Jorge. (1946) 1999. *Seara Vermelha*. São Paulo: Livraria Martins Editôra.

Amado, Jorge. 2008. *Hora da guerra: A segunda guerra mundial vista da Bahia; Crônicas (1942–1944)*. São Paulo: Companhia das Letras.

Amir Habibullah [Bachchah-i Saqaw]. 1936. *From Brigand to King: Autobiography of Amir Habibullah*. London: S. Low, Marston.

Anderson, Benedict. (1983) 1996. *Imagined Communities*. London: Verso.

Anderson, Benedict. 1992. "El efecto tranquilizador del fratricidio: O de cómo las naciones imaginan sus genealogías." In *El nacionalismo mexicano*, edited by Cecilia Noriega Elio, 83–103. Mexico City: El Colegio de Michoacán.

Anderson, Mark. 2001. "Pancho Villa and the Marlboro Man: American-Style Charisma in the Marketplace of Ideas." *Media History* 7 (2): 171–80.

Anderson, Mark. 2007. "The Mythical Frontier, the Mexican Revolution, and the Press: An Imperial Subplot." *Canadian Review of American Studies* 37 (1): 1–22.

Andrade, Vera Lúcia. 1991. "Conceituação de jagunço e jagunçagem em *Grande Sertão: Veredas*." In *Guimarães Rosa*, edited by Eduardo F. Coutinho, 491–99. Rio de Janeiro: Civilização Brasileira.

Ángeles, Felipe. 1914. *Batalla de Zacatecas: Descripción tomada del diario del General Felipe Ángeles*. Chihuahua: Imprenta del Gobierno.

Antônio das Mortes (O Dragão da Maldade contra o Santo Guerreiro). 1969. Written and directed by Glauber Rocha. Rio de Janeiro: Mapa Films.

Aquézolo Castro, Manuel, ed. 1976. *La polémica del indigenismo*. Lima: Mosca Azul Editores.

Araújo, Antônio Amaury Corrêa de. 1984. *Lampião: As mulheres e o cangaço*. São Paulo: Traço Editora.

Archer, Christon. 1982. "Banditry and Revolution in New Spain, 1790–1821." *Bibliotheca Americana* 1 (1): 59–91.

Arévalo Cedeño, Emilio. 1936. *El libro de mis luchas*. Caracas: Tipografía Americana.

Arguedas, Alcides. (1919) 1945. *Raza de bronce*. Buenos Aires: Editorial Losada.

Arlt, Roberto. (1926) 1999. *El juguete rabioso*. Madrid: Cátedra.

Arráiz Lucca, Rafael. 2001. *Arturo Uslar Pietri: Ajuste de cuentas*. Caracas: Los Libros de El Nacional.

Arráiz Lucca, Rafael. 2005. *Arturo Uslar Pietri o la hipérbole del equilibrio*. Caracas: Fundación para la Cultura Urbana.

Assis Duarte, Eduardo de. 1996. *Jorge Amado: Romance em tempo de utopia*. Rio de Janeiro: Editora Record.

Augustine. (413–426) 1998. *The City of God against the Pagans*. Edited and translated by R. W. Dyson. Cambridge: Cambridge University Press.

Austin, John. 1962. *How to Do Things with Words: The William James Lectures Delivered at Harvard University in 1955*. Oxford: Clarendon Press.

Avelar, Idelber. 1994. "Os paradoxos do vazio e da ausência em *Grande Sertão: Veredas*." *Brasil/Brazil* 11: 9–23.

Avelar, Idelber. 1999. *The Untimely Present: Postdictatorial Latin American Fiction and the Task of Mourning*. Durham, NC: Duke University Press.

Azuela, Mariano. (1915/1916) 1996. *Los de abajo*. Edited by Jorge Ruffinelli. Nanterre, France: Colección Archivos.

Balderston, Daniel. 2000. *Borges: Realidades y simulacros*. Buenos Aires: Biblos.

Balderston, Daniel, Gastón Gallo, and Nicolás Helft. 1999. *Borges: Una enciclopedia*. Buenos Aires: Norma.

Baptista, Pedro. 1929. *Cangaceiros do nordeste*. Parahyba do Norte, Brazil: Librería S. Paulo.

Barczewski, Stephanie. 2000. *Myth and National Identity in Nineteenth-Century Britain: The Legends of King Arthur and Robin Hood*. Oxford: Oxford University Press.

Barkey, Karen. 1994. *Bandits and Bureaucrats: The Ottoman Route to State Centralization*. Ithaca, NY: Cornell University Press.

Barroso, Gustavo. (1912) 1962. *Terra de sol: Natureza e costumes do norte*. Fortaleza, Brazil: Imprensa Universitaria do Ceará.

Barroso, Gustavo. (1918) 1931. *Heróes e bandidos (os cangaceiros do nordeste)*. Rio de Janeiro: Livraria Francisco Alves.

Barthes, Roland. (1964) 2002a. "Le dernier des écrivains heureux." In *Oeuvres completes II*, 352–58. Paris: Seuil.

Barthes, Roland. (1964) 2002b. "Ecrivains et écrivants." In *Oeuvres completes II*, 403–10. Paris: Seuil.

Barthes, Roland. (1964) 2002c. "Tacite et le baroque funèbre." In *Oeuvres completes II*, 366–69. Paris: Seuil.

Bartra, Roger. (1987) 2003. *La jaula de la melancolía: Identidad y metamorfosis del mexicano*. Mexico City: Grijalbo.

Bauche Alcalde, Manuel. (1914) 2004. Prologue to *Pancho Villa: Retrato autobiográfico, 1894–1914*, by Francisco Villa, 67–71. Mexico City: Taurus-Alfaguara.

Baudrillard, Jean. (1990) 1999. *The Transparency of Evil: Essays on Extreme Phenomena*. Translated by James Benedict. London: Verso.

Bayer, Osvaldo. (1972) 1992. *La Patagonia rebelde I: Los bandoleros*. Buenos Aires: Editorial Planeta.

Bejel, Emilio. 2012. *José Martí: Images of Memory and Mourning*. New York: Palgrave Macmillan.

Bell, Edward. 1914. *The Political Shame of Mexico*. New York: McBride, Nast.

Benjamin, Thomas. 2000. *La Revolución: Mexico's Great Revolution as Memory, Myth, and History*. Austin: University of Texas Press.

Bernaldo de Quiros, Constancio. 1959. *El bandolerismo en España y México*. Mexico City: Editorial Jurídica Mexicana.

Bernucci, Leo. 1989. *Historia de un malentendido: Un estudio transtextual de "La guerra del fin del mundo" de Mario Vargas Llosa*. University of Texas Studies in Contemporary Spanish-American Fiction 5. New York: Peter Lang.

Beverley, John. 1997. "Siete aproximaciones al 'problema indígena.'" In *Indigenismo hacia el fin del milenio: Homenaje a Antonio Cornejo-Polar*, edited by Mabel Moraña, 269–84. Pittsburgh: Instituto Internacional de Literatura Iberoamericana.

Bhatia, Michael V. 2005. "Fighting Words: Naming Terrorists, Bandits, Rebels and Other Violent Actors." *Third World Quarterly* 26 (1): 5–22.

Billingsley, Phil. 1988. *Bandits in Republican China*. Stanford, CA: Stanford University Press.

Bioy Casares, Adolfo. *Borges*. 2006. Buenos Aires: Destino.

Birkbeck, Christopher. 1991. "Latin American Banditry as Peasant Resistance: A Dead-End Trail?" *Latin American Research Review* 26 (1): 156–60.

Birns, Nicholas. 2012. "Appropriation in the Backlands: Is Mario Vargas Llosa at War with Euclides da Cunha?" In De Castro and Birns 2012, 71–83.

Blanco, Eduardo. (1881) 1981. *Venezuela heroica*. Caracas: Ediciones de la Presidencia de la República.

Blanco, Eduardo. 1882. *Zárate*. Caracas: Impr. Bolívar.

Blanco Moheno, Roberto. 1969. *Pancho Villa, que es su padre*. Mexico City: Editorial Diana.

Blanco-Muñoz, Agustín. 1998. *Venezuela del 04F-92 al 06D-98: Habla el Comandante Hugo Chávez Frías*. Caracas: CEHA/IIES/FN-ES/UCV.

Blok, Anton. 1972. "The Peasant and the Brigand: Social Banditry Reconsidered." *Comparative Studies in Society and History* 14 (4): 494–503.

Blok, Anton. 1975. *The Mafia of a Sicilian Village, 1860–1960: A Study of Violent Peasant Entrepreneurs*. New York: Harper and Row.

Blok, Anton. 1983. "On Negative Reciprocity among Sicilian Pastoralists." *Production pastorale et sociètè* 13: 43–46.

Blok, Anton. 1998. "Bandits and Boundaries: Robber Bands and Secret Societies on the Dutch Frontier (1730–1778)." In *Challenging Authority: The Historical Study of Contentious Politics*, edited by Michael Hanagan, Leslie Page Moch, and Wayne te Brake, 91–106. Minneapolis: University of Minnesota Press.

Blood, Philip. 2008. *Hitler's Bandit Hunters: The SS and the Nazi Occupation of Europe*. Dulles, VA: Potomac Books.

Bolívar, Simón. 1939. *Proclamas y discursos del libertador, mandados publicar por el gobierno de Venezuela, presidido por el general Eleazar López Contreras*. Caracas: Litografía y Tipografía del Comercio.

Boot, Max. 2013. *Invisible Armies: An Epic History of Guerrilla Warfare from Ancient Times to the Present*. New York: Liveright.

Borges, Jorge Luis. 1970. *El matrero*. Buenos Aires: Edicom.

Borges, Jorge Luis. 1979. *Obras completas en colaboración*. Buenos Aires: Emecé.

Borges, Jorge Luis. 1996a. *Obras completas*. Vol. 3. Buenos Aires: Emecé.

Borges, Jorge Luis. 1996b. *Obras completas*. Vol. 4. Buenos Aires: Emecé.

Borges, Jorge Luis. 1997. *Textos recobrados, 1919–1929*. Buenos Aires: Emecé.

Borges, Jorge Luis. 1998. *Collected Fictions*. Translated by Andrew Hurley. New York: Penguin.

Borges, Jorge Luis. 2001. *Textos recobrados, 1931–1955*. Buenos Aires: Emecé.

Borges, Jorge Luis. 2003. *Textos recobrados, 1956–1986*. Buenos Aires: Emecé.

Borges, Jorge Luis. 2005a. *Obras completas*. Vol. 1. Buenos Aires: Emecé.

Borges, Jorge Luis. 2005b. *Obras completas*. Vol 2. Buenos Aires: Emecé.

Borges, Jorge Luis, and Adolfo Bioy Casares. (1955) 1979. *Los orilleros*. In Borges 1979, 199–253.

Borges, Jorge Luis, and Sylvina Bullrich. 1945. *El compadrito: Su destino, sus barrios, su música*. Buenos Aires: Emecé.

Borges, Jorge Luis, and Margarita Guerrero. (1953) 1979. "El Martín Fierro." In Borges 1979, 513–68.

Bosteels, Bruno. 2007. "Marxismo y melodrama: Reflexiones sobre *Los errores*, de José Revueltas." In Ramírez Santacruz and Oyata 2007, 121–46.

Botello, Oldman. 2005. *Historia documentada del legendario Pedro Pérez Delgado, Maisanta*. Caracas: Catalá, Editor; El Centauro.

Bowman, Glenn. 2005. "Constitutive Violence and the Nationalist Imaginary: The Making of 'The People' in Palestine and 'Former Yugoslavia.'" In *Populism and the Mirror of Democracy*, edited by Francisco Panizza, 118–42. London: Verso.

Boym, Svetlana. 2010. *Another Freedom: The Alternative History of an Idea*. Chicago: University of Chicago Press.

Bracewell, Catherine Wendy. 2011. *The Uskoks of Senj: Piracy, Banditry, and Holy War in the Sixteenth-Century Adriatic*. Ithaca, NY: Cornell University Press.

Braudel, Fernand. (1949) 1972. *The Mediterranean and the Mediterranean World in the Age of Philip II*. 2 vols. New York: Harper Colophon.

Bravo, Víctor. 2004. *El orden y la paradoja: Jorge Luis Borges y el pensamiento de la modernidad*. Rosario: Beatriz Viterbo Editora.

Brooks, Peter. 1976. *The Melodramatic Imagination: Balzac, Henry James, Melodrama, and the Mode of Excess*. New Haven, CT: Yale University Press.

Brown, Nathan. 1990. "Brigands and State Building: The Invention of Banditry in Modern Egypt." *Comparative Studies in Society and History* 32 (2): 258–81.

Burga, Manuel, and Alberto Flores Galindo. 1979. *Apogeo y crisis de la república aristocrática (oligarquía, aprismo y comunismo en el Perú 1895–1932)*. Lima: Ediciones "Rikchay Perú."

Burns, Bradford. 1993. *A History of Brazil*. New York: Columbia University Press.

Bush, Matthew Robert. 2008. "Poetic Justice: Melodrama and the Articulation of Political Identities in Modern Latin American Fiction." PhD diss., University of Colorado at Boulder.

Byron, George Gordon (Lord Byron). (1812–1818) 2008. *Childe Harold's Pilgrimage*. In *Lord Byron: The Major Works*, edited by Jerome J. McGann, 19–206. Oxford: Oxford University Press.

Caballero, Manuel. 1993. *Gómez, el tirano liberal*. Caracas: Monte Avila.

Caballero, Manuel. 2004. "Maisanta: Godo, derrotado y cuatrero." *El universal*, June 21.

Calder, Bruce J. 2006. *The Impact of Intervention: The Dominican Republic during the U.S. Occupation of 1916–1924*. Princeton, NJ: M. Wiener.

Campobello, Nellie. (1931) 2005. *Cartucho: Relatos de la lucha en el norte de México*. Mexico City: Era.

Campobello, Nellie. 1940. *Apuntes sobre la vida militar de Francisco Villa*. Mexico City: Ediapsa.

Canala, Juan Pablo. 2012. "Las aspiraciones de Silvio Astier: Fama, delito y lectura en *El juguete rabioso* de Roberto Arlt." *Orbis Tertius* 17 (18). http://www.orbistertius.unlp.edu.ar/article/view/OTv17n18a07/4882.

Canala, Juan Pablo. 2014. "La traición como tradición: Lectura y escritura en la novela inaugural de Roberto Arlt." Unpublished manuscript.

Candido, Antônio. 1969. *Formação da literatura brasileira*. Vol. 2, *1836–1880*. São Paulo: Livraria Martins Editora.

Candido, Antônio. 1970. "Jagunços mineiros de Cláudio a Guimarães Rosa." In *Vários escritos*, 133–60. São Paulo: Livraria Duas Cidades.

Carballo, Emmanuel. 1965. *Diecinueve protagonistas de la literatura mexicana del siglo XX*. Mexico City: Empresas.

Cárdenas, Eliécer. (1979) 1986. *Polvo y ceniza*. Quito, Ecuador: Editorial el Conejo.

Cárdenas, Eliécer. 2008. *El árbol de los quemados*. Quito, Ecuador: Libresa.

Carr, Barry. 1992. *Marxism and Communism in Twentieth-Century Mexico*. Lincoln: University of Nebraska Press.

Carri, Roberto. (1968) 2001. *Isidro Velázquez: Formas prerrevolucionarias de la violencia*. Buenos Aires: Colihue.

Carriego, Evaristo. (1908) 1913. "El guapo." In *Poesías de Evaristo Carriego*, 89–91. Barcelona: Establecimiento Tipográfico de Auber y Pla.

Carrillo, Francisco. 1967. "Los aciertos indigenistas de Enrique López Albújar." *Revista peruana de cultura* 11–12: 147–58.

Carrillo-Ramírez, Alberto. 1976. *Luis Pardo, "el gran bandido": Vida y hechos del famoso bandolero chiquiano que acaparó la atención pública durante varios años*. 2nd ed. Lima.

Cartwright, Cecilia Altuna. 1973. "The Cangaceiro as a Fictional Character in the Novels of Franklin Távora, Rodolfo Teófilo, and José Lins do Rêgo." PhD diss., University of Wisconsin.

Cassá, Roberto. 1998. "Movimientos sociales durante la intervención." *Ecos* 6 (8): 177–206.

Castellanos, Rosario. (1962) 1977. *Oficio de tinieblas*. New York: Penguin.

Castro Urioste, José. 2006. "Ambigüedades, mestizaje y tensiones irresueltas en la narrativa indigenista de Enrique López Albújar." In *De Doña Bárbara al neolib-*

eralismo: Escritura y modernidad en América Latina, 52–69. Lima: Latinoamericana Editores.

Castro-Klarén, Sara. 1986. "Santos and Cangaceiros: Inscription without Discourse in *Os Sertões* and *La guerra del fin del mundo*." *MLN* 101 (2): 366–88.

Castro-Klarén, Sara. 1990. "Cinematography and *The War of the End of the World*." In *Understanding Mario Vargas Llosa*, 163–88. Columbia: University of South Carolina Press.

Centeno, Miguel Angel. 2002. *Blood and Debt: War and the Nation-State in Latin America*. University Park: Pennsylvania State University Press.

Cerqueira, Nelson. 1988. *A política do Partido Comunista e a questão do realismo em Jorge Amado*. Coleção Casa de Palavras. Salvador: Fundação Casa de Jorge Amado.

Cervantes, Federico. 1959. *Francisco Villa y la revolución*. Mexico City: Ediciones Alonso.

Chamberlain, Samuel E. 1956. *My Confession: The Recollections of a Rogue*. New York: Harper.

Chandler, Billy Jaynes. 1978. *The Bandit King: Lampião of Brazil*. College Station: Texas A&M University Press.

Chandler, Billy Jaynes. 1987. "Brazilian *Cangaceiros* as Social Bandits: A Critical Appraisal." In Slatta 1987, 97–112.

Chandler, Billy Jaynes. 1988. *King of the Mountain: The Life and Death of Giuliano the Bandit*. DeKalb: Northern Illinois University Press.

Chasteen, John Charles. 1995. *Heroes on Horseback: A Life and Times of the Last Gaucho Caudillos*. Albuquerque: University of New Mexico Press.

Chávez Alfaro, Lizandro. 1963. *Los monos de San Telmo*. Havana: Casa de las Américas.

Chevalier, Louis. 1973. *Laboring Classes and Dangerous Classes in Paris during the First Half of the Nineteenth Century*. New York: H. Fertig.

Chumbita, Hugo. 2000. *Jinetes rebeldes: Historia del bandolerismo social en Argentina*. Buenos Aires: Editorial Vergara.

Clausewitz, Carl von. (1832) 1982. *On War*. London: Penguin.

Código penal: Ley no. 4868. 1924. Lima: E. Moreno.

Código penal del Perú. 1862. Lima: Imprenta Calle de la Rifa.

Código penal Santa-Cruz del Estado Nor-Peruano. 1836. Lima: Imprenta de Eusebio Aranda.

Coelho Fontes, Oleone. 1999. *Lampião na Bahia*. Petrópolis, Brazil: Editora Vozes.

Cohen, Jeffrey Jerome, ed. 1996. *Monster Theory: Reading Culture*. Minneapolis: University of Minnesota Press.

Colas, Alejandro, and Bryan Mabee, eds. 1999. *Mercenaries, Pirates, Bandits and Empires: Private Violence in Historical Context*. Oxford: Oxford University Press.

Coleman, Kathleen. 1990. "Fatal Charades: Roman Executions Staged as Mythological Enactments." *Journal of Roman Studies* 80: 44–73.

"Condenan a Ricardo Piglia y a la editorial por el Premio Planeta." 2005. *Clarín*, March 1. http://www.clarin.com/diario/2005/03/01/sociedad/s-03015.htm.

Contador, Ana María. 1998. *Los Pincheira: Un caso de bandidaje social, Chile, 1817– 1832*. Santiago, Chile: Bravo y Allende Editores.

Contreras, Sandra. 2009. "Breves intervenciones con Sarmiento: A propósito de 'Historias de Jinetes.'" In *Borges: Políticas de la literatura*, edited by Juan Pablo Dabove, 77–101. Pittsburgh: Instituto Internacional de Literatura Iberoamericana.

Cornejo, Raúl Estuardo. 1961. *López Albújar, narrador de América: Trayectoria vital*. Madrid: Anaya.

Cornejo Polar, Antonio. 1982. Review of *La guerra del fin del mundo*, by Mario Vargas Llosa. *Revista de crítica literaria latinoamericana* 8 (15): 219.

Cornejo Polar, Antonio. 1994. *Escribir en el aire: Ensayo sobre la heterogeneidad sociocultural en las literaturas andinas*. Lima: Editorial Horizonte.

Cornejo Polar, Antonio. 2004. *La "trilogía novelística clásica" de Ciro Alegría*. Lima: Centro de Estudios Literarios "Antonio Cornejo Polar"—Latinoamericana Editores.

Cornejo Polar, Antonio. 2005. *Literatura y sociedad en el Perú: La novela indigenista*. Lima: Latinoamericana Editores.

Coronado, Jorge. 2009. *The Andes Imagined: Indigenismo, Society, and Modernity*. Pittsburgh: University of Pittsburgh Press.

Coronil, Fernando. 1997. *The Magical State: Nature, Money, and Modernity in Venezuela*. Chicago: University of Chicago Press.

Corral de Villa, Luz. (1949) 1976. *Pancho Villa en la intimidad*. Chihuahua: Centro Librero la Prensa.

Courtois, Gérard. 1984. "La vengeance, du désir aux institutions." In *La vengeance: Etudes d'ethnologie, d'histoire et de philosophie*, edited by Gérard Courtois, 7–45. Paris: Editions Cujas.

Coutinho, Eduardo de Faria. 1991. *The "Synthesis" Novel in Latin America: A Study of João Guimarães Rosa's "Grande Sertão: Veredas."* Chapel Hill: University of North Carolina Press.

Cova García, Luis. 1955. *El bandolerismo en Venezuela (el estudio psicológico, antropológico, psiquiátrico y social del bandolero venezolano que actuó como caudillo en nuestras guerras civiles).* Alcalá de Henares, Spain: Imprenta Talleres Penitenciarios.

Covarrubias Orozco, Sebastián de. (1611) 1994. *Tesoro de la lengua castellana o española.* Edited by Felipe Maldonado. Revised by Manuel Camarero. Madrid: Editorial Castalia.

Cozarinsky, Edgardo. 1981. *Borges en/y/sobre cine.* Madrid: Fundamentos.

Creelman, James. 1908. "President Díaz, Hero of the Americas." *Pearson's Magazine,* March, 231–77.

Crespi, Roberto Simon. 1979. "José Revueltas (1914–1976): A Political Biography." *Latin American Perspectives* 6 (3): 93–113.

Crummey, Donald. 1986. "The Great Beast." Introduction to *Banditry, Rebellion and Social Protest in Africa,* edited by Donald Crummey, 1–24. London: James Curie–Heinemann.

Cueto, Sergio. 1995. "Sobre el humor melancólico." In *Borges, ocho ensayos,* 17–24. Rosario: Beatriz Viterbo Editora.

Curran, Mark. 1995. "*Grande Sertão: Veredas* e a literatura de cordel." *Brasil/Brazil* 14: 9–49.

Dabove, Juan Pablo. 2003. "La fiesta popular, la banda de bandidos, la 'bola': La revolución y sus metáforas en *Los de abajo.*" In *Heterotropías: Narrativas de identidad y alteridad latinoamericana,* edited by Carlos Jáuregui and Juan Pablo Dabove, 167–95. Pittsburgh: Instituto Internacional de Literatura Iberoamericana.

Dabove, Juan Pablo. 2007. *Nightmares of the Lettered City: Banditry and Literature in Latin America, 1816–1929.* Pittsburgh: University of Pittsburgh Press.

Dabove, Juan Pablo. 2009. "'La cosa maldita': Leopoldo Lugones y el gótico imperial." *Revista Iberoamericana* 75 (228): 773–92.

Dabove, Juan Pablo, and Susan Hallstead. 2009. "Pasiones fatales: Consumo, bandidaje y género en *El Zarco.*" *A contracorriente* 7 (1): 168–87.

da Cunha, Euclides. (1902) 1995. *Os sertões: Campanha de Canudos.* In *Obra completa,* vol. 2, 97–516. Rio de Janeiro: Editora Nova Aguilar.

Danker, Uwe. 1988. "Bandits and the State: Robbers and the Authorities in the Holy Roman Empire." In *The German Underworld*, edited by Richard Evans, 75–107. London: Routledge.

Darwin, Charles. (1839) 2001. *The Voyage of the Beagle*. New York: Modern Library.

Daus, Ronald. 1982. *O ciclo épico dos cangaceiros na poesia popular do nordeste*. Rio de Janeiro: Fundação Casa de Rui Barbosa.

Davis, William B. 1920. *Experiences and Observations of an American Consular Officer during the Mexican Revolutions*. Chula Vista, CA: privately printed.

Dawe, John, and Lewis Taylor. 1994. "Enrique López Albújar and the Study of Peruvian Brigandage." *Bulletin of Latin American Research* 13 (3): 247–80.

De Castro, Juan E., and Nicholas Birns, eds. 2012. *Vargas Llosa and Latin American Politics*. New York: Palgrave Macmillan.

De la Fuente, Alejandro. 2001. *A Nation for All: Race, Inequality, and Politics in Twentieth-Century Cuba*. Chapel Hill: University of North Carolina Press.

De Lima, Estácio. 1965. *O mundo estranho dos cangaceiros*. Salvador: Itapoã.

Della Cava, Ralph. 1970. *Miracle at Joaseiro*. New York: Columbia University Press.

Deus e o Diabo na Terra do Sol. 1964. Written and directed by Glauber Rocha. Rio de Janeiro: Copacabana Films.

Días Fernandes, Carlos. 1914. *Os cangaceiros: Romance de costumes sertanejos*. Parahyba do Norte, Brazil: Imprensa Official.

Díaz Rodríguez, Manuel. (1901) 1982. *Ídolos rotos*. In *Narrativa y ensayo*, 3–161. Caracas: Biblioteca Ayacucho.

Díaz Rodríguez, Manuel. (1902) 1982. *Sangre patricia*. In *Narrativa y ensayo*, 163–232. Caracas: Biblioteca Ayacucho.

Droguett, Carlos. (1960) 1993. *Eloy*. Santiago, Chile: Editorial Universitaria.

Drumond, Josina Nunes. 2008. *As dobras do sertão: Palavra e imagem; O neobarroco em "Grande Sertão-Veredas," de Guimarães Rosa, e em "Imagens do Grande Sertão," de Arlindo Daibert*. São Paulo: Annablume.

Dulles, John W. F. 1983. *Brazilian Communism, 1935–1945: Repression during World Upheaval*. Austin: University of Texas Press.

Duncan-Baretta, Silvio, and John Markoff. 1978. "Civilization and Barbarism: Cattle Frontiers in Latin America." *Comparative Studies in Society and History* 20 (4): 587–620.

Duque, José Roberto, and Boris Muñoz. 1995. *La ley de la calle*. Caracas: Fundarte Alcaldía de Caracas.

Durán, Javier. 2002. *José Revueltas: Una poética de la disidencia*. Xalapa, Mexico: Universidad Veracruzana.

Ebelot, Alfredo. (1889–1890) 2001. *La pampa: Costumbres argentina*. Buenos Aires: Taurus.

Echeverría, Esteban. (1871) 1993. *El matadero: La cautiva*. Madrid: Cátedra.

Elizalde, Rosa, and Luis Báez. 2007. *Chávez nuestro*. Hondarribia, Spain: Hiru.

Elmore, Peter. 1993. *Los muros invisibles: Lima y la modernidad en la novela del siglo XX*. Lima: Mosca Azul; El Caballo Rojo.

Elmore, Peter. 1997. *La fábrica de la memoria: La crisis de la representación en la novela histórica hispanoamericana*. Mexico City: Fondo de Cultura Económica.

Encinas, José Antonio. 1919. *Causas de la criminalidad indígena en el Perú: Ensayo de psicología experimental*. Lima: Facultad de Jurisprudencia de la Universidad Mayor de San Marcos de Lima.

Engels, Friedrich. (1845) 1999. *The Condition of the Working Class in England in 1844*. Translated by Florence Kelley-Wischnewetsky. Oxford: Oxford University Press.

Engels, Friedrich. 1926. *The Peasant War in Germany*. Translated by Moissaye J. Olgin. New York: International Publishers.

Escajadillo, Tomás. 2007. *La narrativa de López Albújar*. Lima: Universidad Ricardo Palma.

Escalante, Evodio. 1979. *José Revueltas, una literatura del "lado moridor."* Mexico City: Era.

Escalante, Evodio. 1991. "Circunstancia y genesis de *Los días terrenales*." In Revueltas (1949) 1991, 191–214.

Escalante, Evodio. 2010. "El tema filosófico del 'mundo invertido' en las novelas de Revueltas." In Olea Franco 2010b, 83–100.

Facó, Rui. 1972. *Cangaceiros e fanáticos: Gênese e lutas*. Rio de Janeiro: Editora Civilizaçao Brasileira.

Farina, Alberto. 1993. *Leonardo Favio*. Buenos Aires: Centro Editor de América Latina.

Fernández de Lizardi, José Joaquín. (1816/1830) 1996. *El periquillo sarniento*. 5 vols. Mexico City: Porrúa.

Fielding, Henry. (1743) 2010. *Jonathan Wild*. Oxford: Oxford University Press.

Fitz, Earl E. 2001. "The Vox Populi in the Novels of Jorge Amado and John Steinbeck." In *Jorge Amado: New Critical Essays*, edited by Keith H. Brower, Earl E. Fitz, and Enrique Martínez-Vidal, 111–23. New York: Routledge.

Fló, Juan, ed. 1978. *Contra Borges*. Buenos Aires: Galerna.

Flores Galindo, Alberto. (1986–1994) 2005. *Buscando a un Inca: Identidad y utopía en los Andes*. Lima: Sur Casa de Estudios del Socialismo.

Flores Galindo, Alberto. 1990. "Bandidos de la costa." In Aguirre and Walker 1990, 57–68.

Fornet-Betancourt, Raúl. 2001. *Transformaciones del marxismo historia del marxismo en América Latina*. Mexico City: Universidad Autónoma de Nuevo León.

Foucault, Michel. (1974) 1994. "La verité et les formes juridiques." In *Dits et écrits*, vol. 2, *1970–1975*, 538–646. Paris: Gallimard.

Foucault, Michel. 1975. *Surveiller et punir: Naissance de la prison*. Paris: Gallimard.

Fradkin, Raúl. 2006. *La historia de una montonera: Bandolerismo y caudillismo en Buenos Aires, 1826*. Buenos Aires: Siglo Veintiuno Editores.

Franco, Jean. 2002. *The Decline and Fall of the Lettered City: Latin America in the Cold War*. Cambridge, MA: Harvard University Press.

Franks, Julie. 1995. "The Gavilleros of the East: Social Banditry as Political Practice in the Dominican Sugar Region, 1900–1924." *Journal of Historical Sociology* 8 (2): 158–81.

Frazer, Chris. 2006. *Bandit Nation: A History of Outlaws and Cultural Struggle in Mexico, 1810–1920*. Lincoln: University of Nebraska Press.

Fuentes Morúa, Jorge. 2001. *José Revueltas: Una biografía intelectual*. Mexico City: UNAM-Unidad Iztapalapa.

Gallant, Thomas W. 1999. "Brigandage, Piracy, Capitalism, and State-Formation: Transnational Crime from a Historical World-Systems Perspective." In Heyman 1999, 25–61.

Gallegos, Rómulo. (1929) 1997. *Doña Bárbara*. Madrid: Cátedra.

Gálvez Cancino, Felipe. 2004. "Manuel Bauche Alcalde confesó a Pancho Villa a punta de estilográfica." In *Anuario de investigación 2003*, 43–65. Mexico City: Universidad Autónoma Metropolitana Unidad Xochimilco, Departamento de Educación y Comunicación.

Gambetta, Diego. 1993. *The Sicilian Mafia: The Business of Private Protection*. Cambridge, MA: Harvard University Press.

Garabano, Sandra. 2003. "Homenaje a Roberto Arlt: Crimen, falsificación y violencia en *Plata quemada*." *Hispamérica: Revista de literatura* 32 (96): 85–90.

García Calderón, Ventura. 1924. *La venganza del cóndor*. Paris: Casa Editorial Garnier Hermanos.

García Canclini, Néstor. 1990. *Culturas híbridas: Estrategias para entrar y salir de la modernidad*. Mexico City: Editorial Grijalbo.

García Canclini, Néstor. 1995. *Consumidores y ciudadanos: Conflictos multiculturales de la globalización*. Mexico City: Editorial Grijalbo.

García Márquez, Gabriel. (1967) 2000. *Cien años de soledad*. Madrid: Cátedra.

García Ponce, Guillermo. 1965. *Las armas en la Guerra de la Independencia*. Caracas: Ediciones La Muralla.

Garner, Paul. 2001. *Porfirio Díaz: Profiles in Power*. London: Longman.

Gerassi-Navarro, Nina. 1999. *Pirate Novels: Fictions of Nation Building in Spanish America*. Durham, NC: Duke University Press.

Ghiraldo, Alberto. 1906. *Alma gaucha*. Madrid: Renacimiento.

Giddens, Anthony. 1985. *A Contemporary Critique of Historical Materialism*. Vol. 2, *The Nation-State and Violence*. Oxford: Polity.

Girón, Nicole. 1976. *Heraclio Bernal, bandolero, cacique o precursor de la Revolución?* Mexico City: Instituto Nacional de Antropología e Historia, SEP, Departamento de Investigaciones Históricas.

Gomes de Almeida, José Mauricio. 1981. *A tradição regionalista no romance Brasileiro (1857–1945)*. Rio de Janeiro: Achiané.

Gómez de Avellaneda, Gertrudis. (1841) 2005. *Sab*. Madrid: Cátedra.

Gonzáles, Luis J., and Gustavo A. Sánchez Salazar. 1969. *The Great Rebel: Che Guevara in Bolivia*. New York: Grove.

González Canalda, María. 2008. *Los gavilleros 1904–1916*. Santo Domingo: Archivo General de la Nación.

González de Cascorro, Raúl. 1975. *Aquí se habla de combatientes y de bandidos*. Havana: Casa de las Américas.

González Echevarría, Roberto. 1998. *Myth and Archive: A Theory of Latin American Narrative*. Durham, NC: Duke University Press.

González Prada, Manuel. (1894/1908) 1985. *Páginas libres. Horas de lucha*. 2 vols. in one. Caracas: Biblioteca Ayacucho.

Gott, Richard. 2000. *In the Shadow of the Liberator: Hugo Chávez and the Transformation of Venezuela*. London: Verso.

Greene, Graham. (1940) 1990. *The Power and the Glory*. New York: Viking.

Grünewald, Thomas. (1999) 2004. *Bandits in the Roman Empire: Myth and Reality*. London: Routledge.

Grunspan-Jasmin, Élise. 2001. *Lampião: Vies et morts d'un bandit brésilien*. Paris: PUF.

Guerrero, Emilio Modesto. 2012. *¿Quién inventó a Chávez?: Un ensayo biográfico.* Caracas: Fundación Editorial El Perro la Rana.

Guerrero, Emilio Modesto. 2013. *Chávez: El hombre que desafió a la historia.* Buenos Aires: Continente.

Guha, Ranajit. (1983) 1999. *Elementary Aspects of Peasant Insurgency in Colonial India.* Durham, NC: Duke University Press.

Guha, Ranajit. 1988. "The Prose of Counter-Insurgency." In *Selected Subaltern Studies,* edited by Ranajit Guha and Gayatri Chakravorty Spivak, 45–87. New York: Oxford University Press.

Guimarães Rosa, João. (1946) 1971. *Sagarana.* Rio de Janeiro: Livraria José Olympio Editora.

Guimarães Rosa, João. (1956) 1986. *Grande Sertão: Veredas.* Rio de Janeiro: Nova Fronteira.

Güiraldes, Ricardo. (1926) 2002. *Don Segundo Sombra.* Madrid: Cátedra.

Gutiérrez, Eduardo. (1879) 1999. *Juan Moreira.* Buenos Aires: Editorial Perfil.

Gutiérrez, Miguel. 1988. *Hombres de caminos.* Lima: Editorial Horizonte.

Gutiérrez González, Josué. 2003. "Notas para un mapa de voces en *Plata quemada.*" *Palabra y el hombre: Revista de la Universidad Veracruzana* 125 (January–March): 115–26.

Guzmán, Martín Luis. (1928) 1961. *El águila y la serpiente.* In *Obras completas I,* 201–507. Mexico City: Fondo de Cultura Económica.

Guzmán, Martín Luis. (1936–1951) 1961. *Memorias de Pancho Villa.* In *Obras completas II.* 9–763. Mexico City: Fondo de Cultura Económica.

Hale, Charles. 1990. *The Transformation of Liberalism in Late Nineteenth-Century Mexico.* Princeton, NJ: Princeton University Press.

Hale, Charles. 2008. *Emilio Rabasa and the Survival of Porfirian Liberalism: The Man, His Career, and His Ideas, 1856–1930.* Stanford, CA: Stanford University Press.

Hall, Stuart. 1997. "The Spectacle of the 'Other.'" In *Representation: Cultural Representation and Signifying Practices,* edited by Suart Hall, 225–79. London: Sage.

Harding, Timothy F. 1982. "Critique of Vanden's 'Marxism and the Peasantry.'" *Latin American Perspectives* 9 (4): 99–106.

Hardt, Michael, and Antonio Negri. 1994. *Labor of Dionysus: A Critique of the State-Form.* Minneapolis: University of Minnesota Press.

Harries, Jill. 1999. *Law and Empire in Late Antiquity*. Cambridge: Cambridge University Press.

Harris, Richard L. 1978. "Marxism and the Agrarian Question in Latin America." *Latin American Perspectives* 5 (4): 2–26.

Hart, John Mason. (1987) 1997. *Revolutionary Mexico: The Coming and Process of the Mexican Revolution*. Berkeley: University of California Press.

Hay, Douglas. 1975. "Property, Authority and the Criminal Law." In *Albion's Fatal Tree: Crime and Society in Eighteenth-Century England*, edited by Douglas Hay, Peter Linebaugh, John G. Rule, E. P. Thompson, and Cal Winslow, 17–63. New York: Pantheon.

Hayden, Tom, ed. 2002. *The Zapatista Reader*. New York: Avalon.

Heaney, Seamus, trans. 2000. *Beowulf: A New Verse Translation*. New York: W. W. Norton.

Hernández, José. (1872/1879) 2001. *El gaucho Martín Fierro (La ida) and La vuelta de Martín Fierro*. 2 vols. in one. Nanterre, France: Colección Archivos.

Hernández, Pablo. 1999. *Compañeros: Perfiles de la Militancia Peronista*. Buenos Aires: Biblos.

Herrera, Celia. (1939) 1964. *Pancho Villa ante la historia*. Mexico City.

Herrera, Yuri. 2011. *Los trabajos del reino*. Mexico City: Periférica.

Herrera Luque, Francisco. (1972) 1980. *Boves, el urogallo*. Buenos Aires: Pomaire.

Heyman, Josiah McC., ed. 1999. *States and Illegal Practices*. Oxford: Berg.

Hobsbawm, Eric. (1959) 1965. *Primitive Rebels*. New York: Norton Library.

Hobsbawm, Eric. (1969) 1981. *Bandits*. 3rd ed. New York: Pantheon Books.

Hobsbawm, Eric. (1969) 2000. *Bandits*. 4th ed. New York: Pantheon Books.

Hobsbawm, Eric. 1973. "The Rules of Violence." In *Revolutionaries: Contemporary Essays*, 209–15. New York: Random House.

Hobsbawm, Eric. 1988. Review of *Bandidos: The Varieties of Latin American Banditry*, edited by Richard W. Slatta. *Hispanic American Historical Review* 68 (1): 135–36.

Hobsbawm, Eric. 1992. "Introduction: Inventing Traditions." In *The Invention of Tradition*, edited by Eric Hobsbawm and Terence Ranger, 1–14. Cambridge: Cambridge University Press.

Holguín, José de la O. 2000. *Tomás Urbina, el guerrero mestizo*. Durango: Instituto de Cultura del Estado de Durango.

Horsley, Richard, and John S. Hanson. 1985. *Bandits, Prophets, and Messiahs: Popular Movements in the Time of Jesus*. Minneapolis: Winston.

Howard, Harvey James. (1927) 1932. *Ten Weeks with Chinese Bandits*. New York: Dodd, Mead.

Hudson, William Henry. (1885) 1979. *The Purple Land*. Berkeley: Creative Arts.

Huerta, Victoriano. 1975. *Yo, Victoriano Huerta*. Mexico City: Editorial Contenido.

Hugo, Victor. (1862) 1992. *Les Misérables*. New York: Modern Library.

Icaza, Jorge. (1934) 1994. *Huasipungo*. Madrid: Cátedra.

Iglesia, Alvaro de la. 1901. *La bruja de Atarés, o, Los bandidos de a Havana: Novela cubana*. Havana: La Moderna Poesía.

Inclán, Luis G. (1865) 1984. *Astucia: El jefe de los Hermanos de la Hoja o los charros contrabandistas de la Rama; Novela histórica de costumbres mexicanas con episodios originales*. Mexico City: Porrúa.

Irving, Washington. 1975. *The Complete Tales of Washington Irving*. Garden City, NY: Doubleday.

Isaacs, Jorge. (1867) 2000. *María*. Madrid: Cátedra.

Izard, Miguel. 1981. "Ni cuatreros ni montoneros: Llaneros." *Boletín Americanista* 31: 83–142.

Izard, Miguel. 1982. "Oligarcas temblad, viva la libertad: Los llaneros del Apure y la Guerra Federal." *Boletín Americanista* 32: 227–77.

Izard, Miguel. 1983. "Sin domicilio fijo, senda segura, ni destino conocido: Los llaneros del Apure a finales del periodo colonial." *Boletín Americanista* 33: 13–83.

Izard, Miguel. 1984. "Ya era hora de emprender la lucha para que en el ancho feudo de la violencia reinase algún día la justicia." *Boletín Americanista* 34: 75–125.

Izard, Miguel. 1987. "Sin el menor arraigo ni responsabilidad: Llaneros y ganadería a principios del siglo XIX." *Boletín Americanista* 37: 109–42.

Izard, Miguel. 1988. "Cimarrones, cuatreros e insurgentes." In *Los llanos: Una historia sin fronteras*, 247–55. Bogotá: Academia de Historia del Meta.

Izard, Miguel, and Richard Slatta. 1987. "Banditry and Social Conflict on the Venezuelan Llanos." In Slatta 1987, 33–48.

Jackson, Joseph Henry. 1955. Introduction to *The Life and Adventures of Joaquín Murieta, the Celebrated California Bandit*, by Yellow Bird (John Rollin Ridge), xi–l. Norman: University of Oklahoma Press.

Jameson, Fredric. 1981. *The Political Unconscious: Narrative as a Socially Symbolic Act*. Ithaca, NY: Cornell University Press.

Janes, Regina. 2005. *Losing Our Heads: Beheadings in Literature and Culture*. New York: NYU Press.

Jáuregui, Carlos A. 2008. *Canibalia: Canibalismo, calibanismo, antropofagia cultural y consumo en América Latina*. Madrid: Iberoamericana.

Jaurrieta, José María. 2009. *Con Villa (1916–1920), memorias de campaña*. Mexico City: Conaculta.

Jeffery, Catherine. 1986. *El arte narrativo de Rafael Felipe Muñoz*. Madrid: J. Porrúa Turanzas.

Johnson, Alan. 2000. "Labeling Theory." In *The Blackwell Dictionary of Sociology*, 167–68. Malden, MA: Blackwell.

Johnson, Allen W. 1971. *Sharecroppers of the Sertão*. Stanford, CA: Stanford University Press.

Jones, Bart. 2007. *¡Hugo!: The Hugo Chávez Story from Mud Hut to Perpetual Revolution*. Hanover, NH: Steerforth.

Jones, David. 1986. *History of Criminology: A Philosophical Perspective*. New York: Greenwood.

Jones, Timothy S., ed. and trans. 1998. "The Outlawry of Earl Godwin from the *Vita Aedwardi Regis*." In *Medieval Outlaws: Ten Tales in Modern English*, edited by Thomas H. Ohlgren, 1–11. Thrupp, Stroud, Gloucestershire: Sutton.

Juan Moreira. 1973. Directed by Leonardo Favio. Buenos Aires: Centauro Films. DVD, Buenos Aires, International DVD Group S.A., 2001.

Katz, Friedrich. 1984. "Presentación." In Terrazas (1936) 1984, 11–14.

Katz, Friedrich. 1998. *The Life and Times of Pancho Villa*. Stanford, CA: Stanford University Press.

Keen, Maurice. (1961) 1987. *The Outlaws of Medieval Legend*. New York: Dorset.

Kemal, Yaşar. (1955) 1961. *Memed, My Hawk*. New York: Pantheon Books.

Kennedy, Capt. 1916. *The Life and History of Francisco Villa, the Mexican Bandit*. Baltimore, MD: I and M. Ottenheimer.

King, John. 2000. *Magical Reels: A History of Cinema in Latin America*. London: Verso.

Klarén, Peter. (2000) 2005. *Nación y sociedad en la historia del Perú*. Lima: IEP.

Kleist, Heinrich von. (1808) 1978. *Michael Kohlhaas*. In *The Marquise of O and Other Stories*, translated by David Luke and Nigel Reeves, 114–213. London: Penguin.

Knight, Alan. 1985. "El liberalismo mexicano desde la Reforma hasta la Revolución (una interpretación)." *Historia Mexicana* 35 (1): 59–91.

Knight, Alan. (1986) 1990. *The Mexican Revolution*. 2 vols. Lincoln: University of Nebraska Press.

Kokotovic, Misha. 2006. *La modernidad andina en la narrativa Peruana: Conflic-*

to social y transculturación. Berkeley: Centro de Estudios Literarios "Antonio Cornejo Polar."

Koliopoulos, John. 1987. *Brigands with a Cause: Brigandage and Irredentism in Modern Greece 1821–1912*. Oxford: Oxford University Press.

Kolokotrōnēs, Theodoros. 1969. *Memoirs from the Greek War of Independence, 1821–1833*. Chicago: Argonaut.

Koui, Théophile. 1991. "*Los días terrenales*, la novela de la herejía." In Revueltas (1949) 1991, 215–42.

Krauze, Enrique. 1987. *Porfirio Díaz: Místico de la autoridad*. Mexico City: Fondo de Cultura Económica.

Laclau, Ernesto. 1996. *Emancipation(s)*. London: Verso.

Laclau, Ernesto. 2000. "Identity and Hegemony." In *Contingency, Hegemony, Universality: Contemporary Dialogues on the Left*, edited by Judith Butler, Ernesto Laclau, and Slavoj Žižek, 44–89. London: Verso.

Laclau, Ernesto, and Chantal Mouffe. (1985) 1999. *Hegemony and Socialist Strategy*. London: Verso.

Laera, Alejandra. 2002. "Piglia—Eloy Martínez: Contribuciones a la relación entre realidad y ficción en la literatura argentina." *Milpalabras (letras y artes en revista)* 3: 47–55.

Laera, Alejandra. 2004. *El tiempo vacío de la ficción: Las novelas argentinas de Eduardo Gutiérrez y Eugenio Cambaceres*. Buenos Aires: Fondo de Cultura Económica.

Laera, Alejandra. 2014. *Ficciones del dinero*. Buenos Aires: Fondo de Cultura Económica.

Lamborghini, Osvaldo. 1973. *Sebregondi retrocede*. Buenos Aires: Ediciones Noé.

Lamnek, Siegfried. (1977) 2002. *Teorías de la criminalidad: Una confrontación crítica*. Mexico City: Siglo XXI.

L'Amour, Louis. (1951) 1956. *Silver Canyon*. New York: Avalon.

Landis, Erik C. 2008. *Bandits and Partisans: The Antonov Movement in the Russian Civil War*. Pittsburgh: University of Pittsburgh Press.

Lane, Frederic C. 1979. *Profits from Power: Readings in Protection Rent and Violence-Controlling Enterprises*. Albany: State University of New York Press.

Langer, Erick D. 1987. "Andean Banditry and Peasant Community Organization, 1882–1930." In Slatta 1987, 113–30.

Laqueur, Walter, ed. 2004. *Voices of Terror: Manifestos, Writings, and Manuals of Al*

Qaeda, Hamas, and Other Terrorists from around the World and throughout the Ages. New York: Reed.

Lauer, Mirko. 1997. *Andes imaginarios: Discursos del indigenismo-2*. Lima: CBC-Sur; Casa de Estudios del Socialismo.

Leal, Luis. 1999. Introduction to *Vida y aventuras del más célebre bandido sonorense Joaquín Murieta: Sus grandes proezas en California*, by Ireneo Paz, 1–95. Houston: Arte Público.

Lecuna, Vicente. 1923. "La guerra de independencia en los llanos de Venezuela." *Boletín de la Academia Nacional de la Historia* 12 (21): 1017–35.

Legrand, Catherine C. 1995. "Informal Resistance on a Dominican Sugar Plantation during the Trujillo Dictatorship." *Hispanic American Historical Review* 75 (4): 555–96.

Legrás, Horacio. 2009. *Literature and Subjection: The Economy of Writing and Marginality in Latin America*. Pittsburgh: University of Pittsburgh Press.

Leps, Marie-Christine. 1992. *Apprehending the Criminal: The Production of Deviance in Nineteenth-Century Discourse*. Durham, NC: Duke University Press.

Levi, Margaret. 1988. *Of Rule and Revenue*. Berkeley: University of California Press.

Levine, Robert. 1970. *The Vargas Regime: The Critical Years, 1934–1938*. New York: Columbia University Press.

Levine, Robert. 1992. *Vale of Tears: Revisiting the Canudos Massacre in Northeastern Brazil, 1893–1897*. Berkeley: University of California Press.

Lewin, Linda. 1979. "Oral Tradition and Elite Myth: The Legend of Antônio Silvino in Brazilian Popular Culture." *Journal of Latin American Lore* 5 (2): 157–202.

Lewin, Linda. 1987. "The Oligarchical Limitations of Social Banditry in Brazil: The Case of the 'Good' Thief Antônio Silvino." In Slatta 1987, 67–96.

Lewis, Matthew. (1796) 1995. *The Monk*. Oxford: Oxford University Press.

Lihn, Enrique, ed. 1972. *Diez cuentos de bandidos*. Santiago, Chile: Empresa Editora Nacional Quimantu Limitada.

Linn, Brian McAllister. 2000. *The Philippine War, 1899–1902*. Lawrence: University Press of Kansas.

Llamozas, José Ambrosio. (1815) 1921. "Memorial presentado al rey en Madrid por el doctor José Ambrosio Llamozas, vicario y capellán primero del ejército de Boves." *Boletín de la Academia Nacional de la Historia* 5 (17): 515–27.

Lombardi, John. 1982. *Venezuela: The Search for Order, the Dream of Progress*. New York: Oxford University Press.

Lomnitz, Claudio. 2008. *Death and the Idea of Mexico*. New York: Zone Books.

López Albújar, Enrique. (1920) 2005. *Cuentos andinos*. Lima: Peisa.

López Albújar, Enrique. (1926) 1976. "Sobre la psicología del indio." In Aquézolo Castro 1976, 15–21.

López Albújar, Enrique. (1928) 2004. *Matalaché*. Lima: Peisa.

López Albújar, Enrique. 1936. *Los caballeros del delito: Estudio criminológico del bandolerismo en algunos departamentos del Perú*. Lima: Compañía de Impresiones y Publicidad.

López Albújar, Enrique. 1937. *Nuevos cuentos andinos*. Santiago, Chile: Ediciones Ercilla.

López Albújar, Enrique. 1942. "Exégesis de la justicia penal chupana." In *Actas y trabajos científtcos del XXVII Congreso Internacional de Americanistas*, vol. 2, 75–77. Lima.

López de San Miguel, Mercedes. 2013. "Ni las mentiras ni el odio pudieron con él." *Página/12*, March 9. http://www.pagina12.com.ar/diario/elmundo/4-215435-2013-03-09.html.

López Ortega, Antonio. 1994. "Venezuela: Historia, Política y Literatura (Conversación con Arturo Uslar Pietri)." *Revista Iberoamericana* 60 (166–67): 397–413.

López y Fuentes, Gregorio. 1931. *Campamento: Novela mexicana*. Madrid: Espasa-Calpe.

Louis, Annick. 2006. *Borges face au fascisme 1: Les causes du present*. Montreuil: Aux Lieux d'Etre.

Louis, Annick. 2007. *Borges face au fascisme 2: Les fictions du contemporain*. Montreuil: Aux Lieux d'Etre.

Louis, Annick. 2009. "El testamento: Formas del realismo en *El informe de Brodie*." In *Borges: Políticas de la literatura*, edited by Juan Pablo Dabove, 331–54. Pittsburgh: Instituto Internacional de Literatura Iberoamericana.

Lowenthal, Abraham F. 1995. *The Dominican Intervention*. Baltimore: Johns Hopkins University Press.

Loyola, Hernán. 1991. "Canudos: Euclides da Cunha y Mario Vargas Llosa frente a Calibán." *Casa de las Américas* 32 (185): 64–80.

Ludmer, Josefina. 1988. *El género gauchesco: Un tratado sobre la patria*. Buenos Aires: Editorial Sudamericana.

Ludmer, Josefina. 1999. *El cuerpo del delito: Un manual*. Buenos Aires: Perfil Libros.

Lugones, Leopoldo. (1905) 1995. *La guerra gaucha*. Mexico City: Conaculta.

Lugones, Leopoldo. (1916) 1972. *El payador*. Buenos Aires: Huemul.

Lukács, György. (1937) 1983. *The Historical Novel*. Lincoln: University of Nebraska Press.

Luna, Félix. 1966. *Los caudillos*. Buenos Aires: A Peña Lillo Editor.

Lunenfeld, Marvin. 1970. *The Council of the Santa Hermandad: A Study of the Pacification Forces of Ferdinand and Isabella*. Coral Gables, FL: University of Miami Press.

Lynch, John. 1992. *Caudillos in Spanish America, 1800–1850*. Oxford: Clarendon.

MacAulay, Neill. (1967) 1998. *The Sandino Affair*. Micanopy, FL: Wacahoota.

MacLachlan, Colin. 1974. *Criminal Justice in Eighteenth-Century Mexico: A Study of the Tribunal of the Acordada*. Berkeley: University of California Press.

Madero, Francisco. (1910) 1976. "Plan de San Luis Potosí." In *Documentos fascimilares*, 7–16. Mexico City: Partido Revolucionario Institucional, Comisión Nacional Editorial.

Magaña-Esquivel, Antonio. 1974. *La novela de la revolución*. Mexico City: Porrúa.

Magdaleno, Mauricio. 1937. *El resplandor, novela*. Mexico City: Ediciones Botas.

Mahony, Mary Ann. 1996. "The World Cacao Made: Society, Politics, and History in Southern Bahia, Brazil, 1822–1919." PhD diss., Yale University.

Maia, João Roberto. 2007. "Sobre a crítica de Guimarães Rosa." *Espéculo: Revista de estudios literarios* 37 (November 2007–February 2008). http://www.ucm.es/info/especulo/numero37/guimaro.html.

Mallon, Florencia. 1995. *Peasant and Nation: The Making of Postcolonial Mexico and Peru*. Berkeley: University of California Press.

Mansfield, Nick. 2008. *Theorizing War: From Hobbes to Badiou*. New York: Palgrave Macmillan.

Mantecón Pérez, Adán. 1967. *Recuerdo de un villista: Mi campaña en la revolución*. Mexico City.

Marcano, Cristina, and Alberto Barrera Tyszka. 2007. *Hugo Chávez*. New York: Random House.

Mariátegui, José Carlos. (1928) 1979. *Siete ensayos de interpretación de la realidad peruana*. Mexico City: Era.

Marín, Rufino. 1933. *Hablan desde la cárcel los hijos de Martín Fierro: Reportajes hechos en el penal de Viedma, a los más famosos bandoleros del Sud*. Buenos Aires: Librerías Anaconda.

Marksman, Herma. 2004. *Habla Herma Marksman: Hugo Chávez me utilizó*. Caracas: Cátedra Pío Tamayo.

Marlowe, Christopher. (c. 1590) 1998. *Tamburlaine the Great*. In *Doctor Faustus and Other Plays*, edited by David Bevington and Eric Rasmussen, 1–136. Oxford: Oxford University Press.

Marotti, Giorgio. 1988. *Santi e banditti nel romanzo brasiliano*. Rome: Bulzoni.

Márquez Rodríguez, Alexis. 1990. *Historia y ficción en la novela venezolana*. Caracas: Monte Avila Editores.

Martin, Gerald. 1987. "Mario Vargas Llosa: Errant Knight of the Liberal Imagination." In *On Modern Latin American Fiction*, edited by John King, 205–33. New York: Hill and Wang.

Martin, Gerald. 1989. *Journeys through the Labyrinth*. London: Verso.

Martínez Estrada, Ezequiel. 1948. *Muerte y transfiguración del Martín Fierro: Ensayo de interpretación de la vida argentina*. 2 vols. Buenos Aires: Fondo de Cultura Económica.

Masotta, Oscar. 1982. *Sexo y traición en Roberto Arlt*. Buenos Aires: Centro Editor de América Latina.

Mayer, Eric. 1990. "Ecología, crimen y rebelión en los Andes (Ayacucho, 1852–1929)." In Aguirre and Walker 1990, 183–212.

McCarthy, Cormac. (1985) 2001. *Blood Meridian; or, The Evening Redness in the West*. New York: Modern Library.

Meadows Taylor, Philip. (1839) 1933. *Confessions of a Thug*. Oxford: Oxford University Press.

Melgarejo Acosta, María del Pilar, and Joshua Lund. 2006. "Altamirano's Demons." *Colorado Review of Hispanic Studies* 4: 49–63.

Melville, Herman. (1856) 1985. "Bartleby, the Scrivener: A Story of Wall Street." In *Pierre, Israel Potter, The Piazza Tales, The Confidence-Man, Billy Budd, Uncollected Prose*, edited by G. Thomas Tanselle, 635–72. New York: Library of America.

Merback, Mitchell. 1999. *The Thief, the Cross and the Wheel: Pain and the Spectacle of Punishment in Medieval and Renaissance Europe*. Chicago: University of Chicago Press.

Merrim, Stephanie. 2006. "*Grand Sertão: Veredas* (João Guimarães Rosa, Brazil, 1956)." In *The Novel: Volume 1; History, Geography, and Culture*, edited by Franco Moretti, 862–69. Princeton, NJ: Princeton University Press.

Meyer, Jean. 1984. *Esperando a Lozada*. Zamora, Mexico: El Colegio de Michoacán.

Meyer, Jean. 1989. *La tierra de Manuel Lozada*. Guadalajara: Universidad de Guadalajara.

Meyer, Michael C. 1967. *Mexican Rebel: Pascual Orozco and the Mexican Revolution, 1910–1915*. Lincoln: University of Nebraska Press.

Meyer, Michael C. 1972. *Huerta: A Political Portrait*. Lincoln: University of Nebraska Press.

Miliani, Domingo. 1993. "Introducción." In Uslar Pietri (1931) 1993, 11–116.

Miró Quesada, Oscar. *Breves apuntes de mesología criminal peruana*. Lima.

Molloy, Silvia. (1979) 1994. *Signs of Borges*. Durham, NC: Duke University Press.

Monsiváis, Carlos. 1975. "Clasismo y Novela en México." *Latin American Perspectives* 2 (2): 164–79.

Monsiváis, Carlos. 2010. "Revueltas: Crónica de una vida militante." In Olea Franco 2010b, 15–63.

Montalvo, Juan. (1880–1882) 1985. *Las catilinarias*. Caracas: Biblioteca Ayacucho.

Montejo, Esteban. 1968. *Biografía de un cimarrón*. Edited by Miguel Barnet. Barcelona: Ediciones Ariel.

Moore, Barrington. 1966. *Social Origins of Dictatorship and Democracy: Lord and Peasant in the Making of the Modern World*. Boston: Beacon.

Moreiras, Alberto. 1999. *Tercer espacio: Literatura y duelo en América Latina*. Santiago, Chile: LOM; Arcis.

Moreta, Salustiano. 1978. *Malhechores-Feudales: Violencia, antagonismos y alianzas de clases en Castilla, siglos XII–XIV*. Madrid: Cátedra.

Moss, David. 1979. "Bandits and Boundaries in Sardinia." *Man* 14 (3): 477–96.

Moya Pons, Frank. 1998. *The Dominican Republic: A National History*. Princeton, NJ: Markus Wiener.

Muchembled, Robert. 2008. *Une histoire de la violence, de la fin du Moyen Âge à nos jours*. Paris: Éditions du Seuil.

Muñoz, Rafael F. (1931) 1999. *¡Vámonos con Pancho Villa!* Mexico City: Espasa-Calpe.

Muñoz, Rafael F. 1936. *Santa Anna: El que todo lo ganó y todo lo perdió*. Madrid: Espasa-Calpe.

Muñoz, Rafael F. 1941. *Se llevaron el cañón para Bachimba*. Buenos Aires: Espasa-Calpe.

Muñoz, Rafael F. 1955. *Pancho Villa, rayo y azote*. Mexico City: Populibros "La Prensa." Originally published in 1923 as *Memorias de Pancho Villa* by El Universal Gráfico.

Muñoz, Rafael F. 1967. *Obras incompletas, dispersas o rechazadas*. Mexico City: Ediciones Oasis.

Muñoz, Rafael F. 1985. *Relatos de la revolución: Cuentos completos*. Mexico City: Grijalbo.

Negri, Antonio. 1999. *Insurgencies: Constituent Power and the Modern State*. Translated by Maurizia Boscagli. Minneapolis: University of Minnesota Press.

Neruda, Pablo. (1950) 2006. *Canto general*. Madrid: Cátedra.

Neruda, Pablo. 1966. *Fulgor y muerte de Joaquín Murieta, bandido chileno injusticiado en California el 23 de julio de 1853*. Santiago, Chile: Zig-Zag.

Neruda, Pablo. (1966) 1972. *Splendor and Death of Joaquín Murieta*. Translated by Ben Belitt. New York: Farrar, Straus and Giroux.

Nina Rodrigues, Raimundo. 1939. *As collectividades anormaes*. Rio de Janeiro: Civilização Brasileira.

Nogueira Galvão, Walnice. 1972. *As formas do falso: Um estudo sôbre a ambigüidade no "Grande Sertão: Veredas."* São Paulo: Editôra Perspectiva.

Obregón, Alvaro. (1917) 1989. *Ocho mil kilómetros de campaña*. Mexico City: Editorial del Valle de Mexico.

O cangaceiro. 1953. Directed by Lima Barreto. Veracruz, Mexico: Companhia Cinematográfica Vera Cruz.

Olea Franco, Rafael. 2010a. "El género novela en *El luto humano*: Pasión y religion." In Olea Franco 2010b.

Olea Franco, Rafael, ed. 2010b. *José Revueltas: La lucha y la esperanza*. Mexico City: El Colegio de Mexico.

Olivier, Florence. 2007. "Estravíos novelescos y justificaciones teóricas de una realidad marxista." In Ramírez Santacruz and Oyata 2007, 247–60.

O'Malley, Ilene. 1986. *The Myth of the Revolution: Hero Cults and the Institutionalization of the Mexican State, 1920–1940*. New York: Greenwood.

O'Malley, Pat. 1979. "Social Bandits, Modern Capitalism, and the Traditional Peasantry: A Critique of Hobsbawm." *Journal of Peasant Studies* 6 (4): 489–501.

Orlove, Benjamin S. 1980. "The Position of Rustlers in Regional Society: Social Banditry in the Andes." In *Land and Power in Latin America: Agrarian Economies and Social Processes in the Andes*, edited by Benjamin S. Orlove and Glynn Custred, 179–94. New York: Holmes and Meier.

O'Rourke, Shane. 2008. *The Cossacks*. Manchester: Manchester University Press.

Ortiz, Fernando. 1995. *Los negros curros*. Havana: Editorial de Ciencias Sociales.

Osorio, Nelson. 1985. *La formación de la vanguardia literaria en Venezuela (antecedentes y documentos)*. Caracas: Biblioteca de la Academia Nacional de la Historia.

Osorio, Rubén, ed. 2006. *La correspondencia de Francisco Villa: Cartas y telegramas de 1911 a 1923*. Chihuahua: Ediciones del Gobierno del Estado de Chihuahua.

Oubiña, David, and Gonzalo Moisés Aguilar. 1993. *De cómo el cine de Leonardo Favio contó el dolor y el amor de su gente, emocionó al cariñoso público, trazó nuevos rumbos para entender la imagen y otras reflexiones.* Buenos Aires: Nuevo Extremo.

Pacheco, Carlos. 1992. *La comarca oral: La ficcionalización de la oralidad cultural en la narrativa latinoamericana contemporánea.* Caracas: Ediciones La Casa de Bello.

Páez, José Antonio. (1867) 1888. *Autobiografía.* Caracas: Tipografía de Espinal e Hijos.

Page, Joanna. 2004. "Crime, Capitalism, and Storytelling in Ricardo Piglia's *Plata quemada.*" *Hispanic Research Journal* 5 (1): 27–42.

Paiva, Antonio J. 1957. *Motivos llaneros.* Valencia, Venezuela: Tipografía "Fénix."

Palamartchuk, Ana Paula. 2003. *Os novos bárbaros: Escritores e comunismo no Brasil (1928–1948).* Campinas, São Paulo: Biblioteca Digital da Unicamp. http://libdigi.unicamp.br/document/?code=vtls000296054.

Palma, Ricardo. (ca. 1908) 1957. "Un negro en el sillón presidencial." In *Tradiciones peruanas completas,* 1075. Madrid: Aguilar.

Palti, Elías. 1994. "Literatura y política en Ignacio M. Altamirano." In *La imaginación histórica en el siglo XIX,* edited by Lelia Area and Mabel Moraña, 73–103. Rosario: UNR.

Palti, Elías. 2010. *La invención de una legitimidad: Razón y retórica en el pensamiento mexicano del siglo XIX. (Un estudio sobre las formas del discurso político).* Mexico City: FCE.

Parra, Max. 2005. *Writing Pancho Villa's Revolution: Rebels in the Literary Imagination of Mexico.* Austin: University of Texas Press.

Parra, Max. 2007. "Violencia, pueblo indígena y nación: *El luto humano* de José Revueltas y la tradición de la novela en México." In Ramírez Santacruz and Oyata 2007, 84–94.

Parra, Teresita. 1993. *Visión histórica en la obra de Arturo Uslar Pietri.* Madrid: Editorial Pliegos.

Pauls, Alan. 2004. *El factor Borges.* Barcelona: Anagrama.

Payno, Manuel. (1891) 2000. *Los bandidos de Río Frío.* Mexico City: Porrúa.

Paz, Octavio. (1950) 1997. *El laberinto de la soledad y otras obras.* New York: Penguin.

Paz Sánchez, Manuel de, José Fernández Fernández, and Nelson López Novegil. 1993. *El bandolerismo en Cuba (1800–1933): Presencia canaria y protesta rural.* Santa Cruz de Tenerife, Spain: Centro de Cultura Popular Canaria.

Pereira de Queiroz, Maria Isaura. 1968. *Os cangaceiros: Les bandits d'honneur brésiliens*. Paris: Julliard.

Perez, Louis A., Jr. 1986. "The Pursuit of Pacification: Banditry and the United States' Occupation of Cuba, 1889–1902." *Journal of Latin American Studies* 18 (2): 313–32.

Perez, Louis A., Jr. 1989. *Lords of the Mountain: Social Banditry and Peasant Protest in Cuba, 1878–1918*. Pittsburgh: University of Pittsburgh Press.

Pérez-Mundaca, José. 1997. *Montoneras, bandoleros y rondas campesinas (violencia política, abigeato y autodefensa en Cajamarca 1855–1990)*. Cajamarca: Municipalidad Provincial de Cajamarca.

Pérez Rul, Enrique [Juvenal, pseud.]. 1916. *¿Quién es Francisco Villa?* Texas: Gran Imprenta Políglota.

Pernambucano de Mello, Frederico. 1993. *Quém foi Lampião*. Recife: Editora Stahli.

Pernambucano de Mello, Frederico. 2004. *Guerreiros do sol: Violência e banditismo no Nordeste do Brasil*. São Paulo: A Girafa.

Pernambucano de Mello, Frederico. 2007. *A guerra total de Canudos*. São Paulo: A Girafa.

Phillips, Dretha M. 1987. "Latin American Banditry and Criminological Theory." In Slatta 1987, 181–90.

Piglia, Ricardo. (1980) 2002. *Respiración artificial*. Buenos Aires: Seix Barral.

Piglia, Ricardo. 1986. *Crítica y ficción*. Santa Fe, Argentina: Universidad Nacional del Litoral.

Piglia, Ricardo. (1986) 2006. *Crítica y ficción*. Buenos Aires: Anagrama.

Piglia, Ricardo. (1988) 1998. *Prisión perpetua*. Buenos Aires: Seix Barral.

Piglia, Ricardo. 1997. *Plata quemada*. Buenos Aires: Planeta.

Piglia, Ricardo. 2002. "Teoría del complot." *Ramona: Revista de artes visuales* 23: 4–14.

Pilares Polo, Víctor. 1936. "Interpretacion biológica de la criminalidad en la raza indígena." *Revista universitaria: Órgano de la Universidad del Cuzco* 70: 127–33.

Pino Iturrieta, Elías. 1988a. "Ideas sobre un pueblo inepto: La justificación del gomecismo." In Pino Iturrieta 1988b, 187–201.

Pino Iturrieta, Elías, ed. 1988b. *Juan Vicente Gómez y su época*. Caracas: Monte Ávila.

Pino Iturrieta, Elías. 2003. *El divino Bolívar: Ensayo sobre una religión republicana*. Caracas: Los Libros de la Catarata.

Pino Iturrieta, Elías. 2007. *Nada sino un hombre: Los orígenes del personalismo en Venezuela*. Caracas: Editorial Alfa.

Pinto Rodríguez, Jorge. 1991. "El bandolerismo en la frontera, 1880–1920: Una aproximación al tema." In *Araucania*, edited by Sergio Villalobos and Jorge Pinto Rodríguez, 101–23. Concepción, Chile: Ediciones Universidad de la Frontera.

Pitt-Rivers, Julian. (1954) 1971. *The People of the Sierra*. Chicago: University of Chicago Press.

Plata quemada. 2000. Directed by Marcelo Piñeyro. Buenos Aires: Oscar Kramer SA; Cuatro Cabezas.

Pocaterra, José Rafael. 1990. *Memorias de un venezolano de la decadencia*. Caracas: Biblioteca Ayacucho.

Poe, Edgar Allan. (1843) 1975. "The Tell-Tale Heart." In *The Complete Tales and Poems of Edgar Allan Poe*, 303–6. New York: Vintage Books.

Pollak-Eltz, Angelina. 2000. *La esclavitud en Venezuela: Un estudio histórico-cultural*. Caracas: Universidad Católica Andrés Bello.

Poma de Ayala, Felipe Huamán. 1980. *Nueva Corónica y buen gobierno*. Caracas: Biblioteca Ayacucho.

Poole, Deborah. 1988. "Landscapes of Power in a Cattle-Rustling Culture of Southern Andean Peru." *Dialectical Anthropology* 12: 367–98.

Poole, Deborah. 1990. "Ciencia, peligrosidad y represión en la criminología indigenista peruana." In Aguirre and Walker 1990, 335–67.

Popoca y Palacios, Lamberto. 1912. *Historia del bandalismo en el estado de Morelos: ¡Ayer como ahora! ¡1860! ¡1911! ¡Plateados! ¡Zapatistas!* Puebla, Mexico: Tipografía Guadalupana.

Portinaro, Pier Paolo. (1999) 2003. *Estado: Léxico de política*. Buenos Aires: Nueva Visión.

Poumier-Taquechel, Maria. 1986. *Contribution à l'étude du banditisme social à Cuba*. Lille, France: Atelier National.

Prado Alvarado, Agustín. 2007. "Bandoleros y aventuras." *El Comercio*, July 28.

Prassel, Frank Richard. 1993. *The Great American Outlaw: A Legacy of Fact and Fiction*. Norman: University of Oklahoma Press.

Prescott, William H. 1847. *History of the Conquest of Peru, with a Preliminary View of the Civilization of the Incas*. 2 vols. Paris: Baudry's European Library.

Prieto, Adolfo. 1988. *El discurso criollista en la formación de la Argentina moderna*. Buenos Aires: Editorial Sudamericana.

Puente, Ramón. 1919. *Vida de Francisco Villa, contada por él mismo*. Los Angeles: O. Paz y Compañía, Editores.

Puente, Ramón. 1937. *Villa en pie*. Mexico City: Editorial "México Nuevo."

Queiroz, Maria Isaura Pereira de. 1968. *Os cangaceiros, les bandits d'honneur brésiliens*. Paris: Julliard.

Quesada, Ernesto. 1902. *El "criollismo" en la literatura Argentina*. Buenos Aires: Imprenta y Casa Editora de Coni Hermanos.

Quintero Montiel, Inés Mercedes. 2009. *El ocaso de una estirpe: La centralización restauradora y el fin de los caudillos históricos*. Caracas: Editorial Alfa.

Rama, Ángel. 1982. "*La guerra del fin del mundo*: Una obra maestra del fanatismo artístico." *Eco: Revista de Cultura de Occidente* 40 (6): 600–640.

Rama, Ángel. 1984. *La ciudad letrada*. Hanover, NH: Ediciones del Norte.

Rama, Ángel. 1988. "*La guerra del fin del mundo*: Mario Vargas Llosa y el fanatismo por la literatura." *Antípodas* 1: 88–104.

Ramírez Santacruz, Francisco. 2007. "De ratas, rateros y antropofagia inquisitorial: Los errores, una historia de horror." In Ramírez Santacruz and Oyata 2007, 315–43.

Ramírez Santacruz, Francisco, and Martín Oyata, eds. 2007. *El terreno de los días: Homenaje a José Revueltas*. Puebla, Mexico: Benemérita Universidad Autónoma de Puebla.

Ramos, Julio. 1989. *Desencuentros de la modernidad en América Latina: Literatura y política en el siglo XIX*. Mexico City: FCE.

Reed, John. (1914) 1999. *Insurgent Mexico*. New York: International.

Rêgo, José Lins do. 1953. *Cangaceiros*. Rio de Janeiro: J. Olympio.

Reis, Roberto. 1997. "João Guimarães Rosa, 1908–1967." In *Encyclopedia of Latin American Literature*, edited by Verity Smith, 739–45. London: Routledge.

Renan, Ernest. (1882) 1990. "What Is a Nation?" In *Nation and Narration*, edited by Homi Bhabha, 8–22. London: Routledge.

Revueltas, José. (1941) 2001. *Los muros de agua*. Mexico City: Era.

Revueltas, José. (1943) 2003. *El luto humano*. Mexico City: Era.

Revueltas, José. (1944) 2006. *Dios en la tierra*. Mexico City: Era.

Revueltas, José. (1949) 1991. *Los días terrenales*. Nanterre, France: Colección Archivos.

Revueltas, José. 1964. *Los errores*. Mexico City: Fondo de Cultura Económica.

Revueltas, José. 1967. *Obras literarias*. 2 vols. Mexico City: Empresas Editoriales.

Revueltas, José. (1969) 2005. *El apando*. Mexico City: Era.

Robinson, Amy. 2006. "Manuel Lozada and the Politics of Mexican Barbarity." *Colorado Review of Hispanic Studies* 4: 77–94.

Robinson, Amy. 2009. "Mexican Banditry and Discourses of Class: The Case of Chucho el Roto." *Latin American Research Review* 44 (1): 5–31.

Rodríguez, José Angel. 1986. *Los paisajes neohistóricos cañeros en Venezuela*. Caracas: Academia Nacional de la Historia.

Rojas, Ricardo. (1917–1923) 1948. *Historia de la literatura Argentina: Ensayo filosófico sobre la evolución de la cultura en el Plata*. 8 vols. Buenos Aires: Editorial Losada.

Romo, David Dorado. 2005. *Ringside Seat to a Revolution: An Underground Cultural History of El Paso and Juárez; 1893–1923*. El Paso, TX: Cinco Puntos.

Rosa, Nicolás. 1997. "El paisano ensimismado." In *La lengua del ausente*, 149–73. Buenos Aires: Biblos.

Rowe, William. 1992. "Liberalism and Authority: The Case of Mario Vargas Llosa." In *On Edge: The Crisis of Contemporary Latin American Culture*, edited by George Yúdice, Jean Franco, and Juan Flores, 45–64. Minneapolis: University of Minnesota Press.

Rubione, Alfredo, ed. 1983. *En torno al criollismo: Textos y polémica*. Buenos Aires: Cedal.

Ruff, Julius R. 2001. *Violence in Early Modern Europe 1500–1800*. Cambridge: Cambridge University Press.

Ruiz Abreu, Alvaro. (1992) 1993. *José Revueltas: Los muros de la utopía*. Mexico City: Cal y Arena.

Rulfo, Juan. (1953) 2001. *El llano en llamas*. Madrid: Cátedra.

Rulfo, Juan. (1955) 1992. *Pedro Páramo*. In *Toda la obra*, 179–307. Nanterre, France: Colección Archivos.

Russell, John. 2005. "Terrorists, Bandits, Spooks and Thieves: Russian Demonisation of the Chechens before and since 9/11." *Third World Quarterly* 26 (1): 101–16.

Said, Edward. (1978) 1994. *Orientalism*. New York: Vintage Books.

Salazar, Alonso. 1990. *No nacimos pa' semilla: La cultura de las bandas juveniles de Medellín*. Bogotá: Cinep.

Sampson, Steven. 2003. "'Trouble Spots': Projects, Bandits, and State Fragmentation." In *Globalization, the State, and Violence*, edited by Jonathan Friedman, 309–42. London: Altamira.

Sánchez, Fernando Fabio. 2010. *Artful Assassins: Murder as Art in Modern Mexico*. Nashville: Vanderbilt University Press.

Sánchez, Gonzalo, and Donny Meertens. (1983) 1984. *Bandoleros, gamonales y campesinos: El caso de la violencia en Colombia*. Bogotá: El Ancora.

Sánchez Prado, Ignacio. 2007. "'Bienaventurados los marginados porque ellos recibirán la redención': José Revueltas y el vaciamiento literario del marxismo." In Ramírez Santacruz and Oyata 2007, 147–73.

Sant Cassia, Paul. 1993. "Banditry, Myth, and Terror in Cyprus and Other Mediterranean Societies." *Comparative Studies in Society and History* 35 (4): 773–95.

Sant Cassia, Paul. 2005. "'Better Occasional Murders than Frequent Adulteries': Discourses on Banditry, Violence, and Sacrifice in the Mediterranean." In *States of Violence*, edited by Fernando Coronil and Julie Skurski, 219–68. Ann Arbor: University of Michigan Press.

Sarlo, Beatriz. (1993) 2003. *Borges, un escritor en las orillas*. Buenos Aires: Seix Barral.

Sarlo, Beatriz. 1994. *Escenas de la vida posmoderna: Intelectuales, arte y videocultura en Argentina*. Buenos Aires: Ariel.

Sarlo, Beatriz. 1999. "Un mundo de pasiones." In *Borges: Desesperaciones aparentes y consuelos secretos*, edited by Rafael Olea Franco, 207–24. Mexico City: El Colegio de México.

Sarmiento, Domingo Faustino. (1845) 1979. *Facundo, o civilización y barbarie*. Caracas: Ayacucho.

Sasturain, Juan. 1995. *El domicilio de la aventura*. Buenos Aires: Ediciones Colihue.

Scarlett, Campbell. 1838. *South America and the Pacific: Comprising a Journey across the Pampas and the Andes, from Buenos Ayres to Valparaiso, Lima, and Panama*. London: Henry Colburn.

Schiller, Friedrich. (1781) 1981. *The Robbers and Wallenstein*. Translated by Francis J. Lamport. London: Penguin.

Schmidt, Friedhelm. 2000. "Literaturas heterogéneas y alegorías nacionales: ¿Paradigmas para las literaturas poscoloniales?" *Revista Iberoamericana* 66 (190): 175–85.

Schmidt, Hans. 1995. *The United States Occupation of Haiti, 1915–1934*. Camden, NJ: Rutgers University Press.

Schmitt, Carl. (1922/1934) 1985. *Political Theology: Four Chapters on the Concept of Sovereignty*. Cambridge, MA: MIT Press.

Schroeder, Michael J. 1996. "Horse Thieves to Rebels to Dogs: Political Gang Violence and the State in the Western Segovias, Nicaragua, in the Time of Sandino, 1926–1934." *Journal of Latin American Studies* 28 (2): 383–434.

Schroeder, Michael J. 2005. "Bandits and Blanket Thieves, Communists and Terrorists: The Politics of Naming Sandinistas in Nicaragua, 1927–36 and 1979–90." *Third World Quarterly* 26 (1): 67–86.

Schwartz, Rosalie. 1989. *Lawless Liberators: Political Banditry and Cuban Independence*. Durham, NC: Duke University Press.

Schwarz, Roberto. (1973) 1992. "Misplaced Ideas: Literature and Society in Late-Nineteenth-Century Brazil." In *Misplaced Ideas: Essays on Brazilian Culture*, 19–32. London: Verso.

Scorza, Manuel. (1970) 2002. *Redoble por Rancas*. Madrid: Cátedra.

Scorza, Manuel. (1979) 1987. *La tumba del relámpago*. Lima: Peisa.

Scott, James C. 1976. *The Moral Economy of the Peasant: Rebellion and Subsistence in Southeast Asia*. New Haven, CT: Yale University Press.

Scott, James C. 1985. *Weapons of the Weak: Everyday Forms of Peasant Resistance*. New Haven, CT: Yale University Press.

Scott, James C. 1990. *Domination and the Arts of Resistance: Hidden Transcripts*. New Haven, CT: Yale University Press.

Scott, Sir Walter. (1817) 1995. *Rob Roy*. London: Penguin.

Scrunton, Roger. (1982) 1996. *Dictionary of Political Thought*. London: Macmillan.

Seal, Graham. 1996. *The Outlaw Legend: A Cultural Tradition in Britain, America, and Australia*. Cambridge: Cambridge University Press.

Serra, Tania Rebelo Costa. 1990. *Riobaldo Rosa: A vereda junguiana do "Grande Sertão."* Brasília: Thesaurus.

Sharpe, James. (2004) 2005. *Dick Turpin: The Myth of the English Highwayman*. London: Profile Books.

Shaw, Brent. 1984. "Bandits in the Roman Empire." *Past and Present* 105: 3–52.

Sigal, Silvia, and Eliseo Verón. (1986) 2003. *Perón o muerte: Los fundamentos discursivos del fenómeno peronista*. Buenos Aires: Eudeba.

Singelmann, Peter. 1975. "Political Structure and Social Banditry in Northeast Brazil." *Journal of Latin American Studies* 7 (2): 59–83.

Singelmann, Peter. 1991. "Establishing a Trail in the Labyrinth." *Latin American Research Review* 26 (1): 152–55.

Slater, Candace. 1989. *Stories on a String: The Brazilian Literatura de Cordel*. Berkeley: University of California Press.

Slatta, Richard. 1980. "Rural Criminality and Social Conflict in Nineteenth-Century Buenos Aires Province." *Hispanic American Historical Review* 60 (3): 450–72.

Slatta, Richard. 1983. *Gauchos and the Vanishing Frontier*. Lincoln: University of Nebraska Press.

Slatta, Richard, ed. 1987. *Bandidos: The Varieties of Latin American Banditry*. New York: Greenwood.

Slatta, Richard. 1991. "Bandits and Rural Social History: A Comment on Joseph." *Latin American Research Review* 26 (1): 145–51.

Slatta, Richard. 1994. "Banditry." In *Encyclopedia of Social History*, edited by Peter N. Stearns, 76–78. New York: Garland.

Solana, Rafael. 1964. "Rafael Munoz, al medio siglo de su actividad literaria." *El libro y el pueblo* 4 (10): 1–5.

Solanas, Fernando E., Edgardo Pallero, José Hernández, Julio Troxler, Martíniano Martínez, Tito Almerjeiras, Roberto Lar, and Alfredo Zitarrosa. (1975) 1990. *Los hijos de Fierro*. Buenos Aires: Colección Solanas.

Sommer, Doris. 1991. *Foundational Fictions: The National Romances in Latin America*. Berkeley: University of California Press.

Somoza, Anastasio. (1936) 1976. *El verdadero Sandino; o, El calvario de las Segovias*. 2nd ed. Managua: Editorial y Litografía "San José."

Souza, Paulo de. 2006. "*Seara Vermelha*: Discurso ideológico / partidário e suas implicações no estético." PhD diss., Universidade Federal de Alagoas.

Spierengurg, Pieter. (1984) 2008. T*he Spectacle of Suffering: Executions and the Evolution of Repression*. Cambridge: Cambridge University Press.

Spraggs, Gillian. 2001. *Outlaws and Highwaymen: The Cult of the Robber in England from the Middle Ages to the Nineteenth Century*. London: Pimlico.

Stavig, Ward. 1990. "Ladrones, cuatreros y salteadores: Indios criminales en el cusco rural a fines de la colonia." In Aguirre and Walker 1990, 69–104.

Stein, William. 1988. *El levantamiento de Atusparia*. Lima: Mosca Azul.

Stiles, T. J. 2002. *Jesse James: Last Rebel of the Civil War*. New York: Alfred A. Knopf.

Supiot, Alain. (2005) 2012. *Homo juridicus: Ensayo sobre la función antropológica del derecho*. Buenos Aires: Paidós.

Svampa, Maristella. 1994. *El dilema argentino: Civilización o barbarie; De Sarmiento al revisionismo Peronista*. Buenos Aires: Ediciones el Cielo por Asalto.

Taibo, Paco Ignacio, II. (2006) 2010. *Pancho Villa: Una biografía narrativa*. Mexico City: Planeta.

Tapia, José León. 1974. *Por aquí pasó Zamora*. Caracas: Editorial Fuentes.

Tapia, José León. (1974) 1976. *Maisanta: El último hombre a caballo*. Caracas: Ediciones Centauro.

Taunay, Alfredo Maria Adriano d'Escragnolle (Vizconde de Taunay). (1872) 1999. *Inocência*. São Paulo: L and PM Editores.

Taussig, Michael. 1997. *The Magic of the State*. London: Routledge.

Taylor, Lewis. 1984. "Literature as History: Ciro Alegría's View of Rural Society in the Northern Peruvian Andes." *Ibero-Amerikanisches Archiv* 10 (1): 349–78.

Taylor, Lewis. 1987. *Bandits and Politics in Peru: Landlord and Peasant Violence in Hualgayoc, 1900–30*. Cambridge: Centre of Latin American Studies.

Taylor, Lewis. 1990. "Los orígenes del bandolerismo en Hualgayoc, 1870–1900." In Aguirre and Walker 1990, 213–47.

Taylor, William. 1982. "Bandit Gangs in Late Colonial Times: Rural Jalisco, Mexico, 1794–1821." *Bibliotheca Americana* 1 (1): 29–58.

Terrazas, Silvestre. (1936) 1984. *El verdadero Pancho Villa, el Centauro del Norte . . . sus heroicas batallas y sus acciones revolucionarias*. Mexico City: Era.

Teskey, Gordon. 1996. *Allegory and Violence*. Ithaca, NY: Cornell University Press.

Thompson, E. P. 1974. "Patrician Society, Plebeian Culture." *Journal of Social History* 7 (4): 382–405.

Thompson, E. P. 1975. *Whigs and Hunters: The Origins of the Black Act*. New York: Pantheon Books.

Thomson, Janice. 1994. *Mercenaries, Pirates, and Sovereigns: State Building and Extraterritorial Violence in Early Modern Europe*. Princeton, NJ: Princeton University Press.

Thornton, Bruce. 2003. *Searching for Joaquín: Myth, Murieta, and History in California*. San Francisco: Encounter Books.

Tilly, Charles. 1975. Foreword to *The Mafia of a Sicilian Village, 1860–1960: A Study of Violent Peasant Entrepreneurs*, by Anton Blok. New York: Harper and Row.

Torres, Ana Teresa. 2009. *La herencia de la tribu: Del mito de la independencia a la Revolución Bolivariana*. Caracas: Alfa.

Torres, Elías. 1934. *20 vibrantes episodios de la vida de Villa (Fragmentos de la vida revolucionaria del general Francisco Villa)*. Mexico City: Editorial Sayrois.

Torres, Elías. (1938) 1963. *La cabeza de Pancho Villa*. Mexico City: El Libro Español.

Torres, Elías. 1975. *Vida y hechos de Francisco Villa*. Mexico City: Editorial Epoca.

Tristán, Flora. 1838. *Les pérégrinations d'une paria: 1833–1834*. Paris: Arthus Bertrand.

Tschudi, Jacob von. 1847. *Travels in Peru, during the Years 1838–1842, on the Coast, in the Sierra, across the Cordilleras and the Andes, into the Primeval Forests.* Translated by Thomasina Ross. New York: Wiley and Putnam.

Turner, John Kenneth. 1911. *Barbarous Mexico.* Chicago: Charles H. Kerr.

Turner, John Kenneth. 1915. *¿Quién es Pancho Villa?* El Paso, TX: Imprenta "El Paso del Norte."

Tutino, John. 1989. *From Insurrection to Revolution in Mexico: Social Bases of Agrarian Violence, 1750–1940.* Princeton, NJ: Princeton University Press.

Ulloa, Francisco. (1893) 1927. *Astucias de Pancho Falcato: El más famoso de los bandidos de América.* Valparaiso, Mexico: Imprenta Franco-Chilena de C. Hubel e Hijos.

Urbaneja, Diego Bautista. 1988. "El sistema político gomecista." In Pino Iturrieta 1988b, 59–79.

Urteaga, Horacio. 1928. *La organización judicial en el imperio de los Incas: Contribución al estudio del derecho peruano.* Lima: Librería e Imprenta Gil.

Uslar Pietri, Arturo. (1931) 1993. *Las lanzas coloradas.* Edited by Domingo Miliani. Madrid: Cátedra.

Uslar Pietri, Juan. 1962. *Historia de la rebelión popular de 1814, contribución al estudio de la historia de Venezuela.* Caracas: Edime.

Utley, Robert M. 1989. *Billy the Kid: A Short and Violent Life.* Lincoln: University of Nebraska Press.

Valadés, Edmundo. 1990. "La revolución y las letras." In *La revolución y las letras: Dos estudios sobre la novela y el cuento de la Revolución Mexicana*, edited by Luis Leal and Edmundo Valadés, 9–88. Mexico City: Conaculta.

Valcárcel, Luis. 1927. *Tempestad en los Andes.* Lima: Minerva.

Valdizán, Emilio. 1919. *Locos de la Colonia.* Lima: Sanmarti.

Valenzuela Márquez, Jaime. 1991. *Bandidaje rural en Chile central: Curicó, 1850–1900.* Santiago, Chile: Dirección de Bibliotecas, Archivos y Museos.

Vallejo, Fernando. 1994. *La virgen de los sicarios.* Bogotá: Alfaguara.

Vallenilla Lanz, Laureano. (1919) 1989. *Cesarismo democrático y otros textos.* Caracas: Ayacucho.

¡Vámonos con Pancho Villa! 1936. Directed by Fernando de Fuentes. Mexico City: Clasa Films.

Vanderwood, Paul J. 1992. *Disorder and Progress: Bandits, Police, and Mexican Development.* Rev. ed. Wilmington, DE: Scholarly Resources.

Van Young, Eric. 2001. *The Other Rebellion: Popular Violence, Ideology, and the*

Mexican Struggle for Independence, 1810–1821. Stanford, CA: Stanford University Press.

Varallanos, José. 1937. *Bandoleros en el Perú: Ensayos*. Lima: Edt. Altura.

Vargas Arreola, Juan Bautista. (1988) 2010. *A sangre y fuego con Pancho Villa*. Mexico City: FCE.

Vargas Llosa, Mario. 1981. *La guerra del fin del mundo*. Barcelona: Seix Barral.

Vasconcelos, José. (1937) 2000. *La tormenta*. Mexico City: Linterna Mágica.

Vega Billán, Rodolfo. 2003. *Enrique López Albújar: Juez reformador del derecho penal*. Huánuco: Universidad Nacional Hermilio Valdizán.

Veloz Maggiolo, Marcio. (1965) 2002. *La vida no tiene nombre*. Santo Domingo, Dominican Republic: Editora Cole.

Verani, Hugo. 1986. *Las vanguardias literarias en Hispanoamérica (Manifiestos, proclamas y otros escritos)*. Rome: Bulzoni Editore.

Vezzetti, Hugo. (2009) 2013. *Sobre la violencia revolucionaria: Memorias y olvidos*. Buenos Aires: Siglo Veintiuno.

Viana Moog, Clodomir. (1954) 1994. "Bandeirantes and Pioneers." In *Where Cultures Meet: Frontiers in Latin American History*, edited by David Weber and Jane Rausch, 74–97. Wilmington, DE: Scholarly Resources.

Vidaurre, Manuel Lorenzo de. 1828. *Proyecto de un código penal*. Boston: Hiram Tupper.

Videla de Rivero, Gloria. 1994. *Direcciones del vanguardismo hispanoamericano*. Pittsburgh: Instituto Internacional de Literatura Iberoamericana.

Viggiano, Alan. (1974) 2007. *Itinerario de Riobaldo Tatarana: Geografia e toponimia em "Grande Sertão: Veredas."* Belo Horizonte, Brazil: Crisalida Livraria e Editora.

Villa, Francisco. 2004. *Pancho Villa: Retrato autobiográfico, 1894–1914*. Edited by Guadalupe and Rosa Helia Villa. Mexico City: Taurus-Alfaguara.

Villa, Guadalupe. 2004. Introduction to *Pancho Villa: Retrato autobiográfico, 1894–1914*, by Francisco Villa, 19–42. Mexico City: Taurus-Alfaguara.

Villanueva, Graciela. 2005. "Avatares de Moreira." *Revista Iberoamericana* 71 (213): 1167–77.

Villavicencio, Víctor Modesto. 1930. *Algunos aspectos de nuestra sociología criminal*. Lima.

Viñas, David. 1973. *La crisis de la ciudad liberal*. Buenos Aires: Editorial Siglo XX.

Viñas, David. 1982. *Literatura Argentina y realidad política*. Buenos Aires: Cedal.

Viñas, David. 1996. *Literatura Argentina y política*. 2 vols. Buenos Aires: Editorial Sudamericana.

Volkov, Vadim. 2002. *Violent Entrepreneurs: The Use of Force in the Making of Russian Capitalism*. Ithaca, NY: Cornell University Press.

Wagner, Kim. 2007. *Thuggee: Banditry and the British in Early Nineteenth-Century India*. London: Palgrave.

Wahloxten, Gustavo. 1992. *Maisanta en caballo de hierro*. Caracas: Fuentes Editores.

Wald, Elijah. 2001. *Narcocorrido: A Journey into the Music of Drugs, Guns, and Guerrillas*. New York: Rayo.

Walker, Charles. 1990. "Montoneros, bandoleros, malhechores: Criminalidad y política en las primeras décadas republicanas." In Aguirre and Walker 1990, 105–36.

Weber, David, and Jane Rausch, eds. 1994. *Where Cultures Meet: Frontiers in Latin American History*. Wilmington, DE: Scholarly Resources.

Welsome, Eileen. 2006. *The General and the Jaguar: Pershing's Hunt for Pancho Villa; A True Story of Revolution and Revenge*. Lincoln: University of Nebraska Press.

Williamson, Edwin. 2004. *Borges: A Life*. New York: Viking.

Wilson, Stephen. 1988. *Feuding, Conflict, and Banditry in Nineteenth-Century Corsica*. Cambridge: Cambridge University Press.

Wolf, Eric. (1969) 1999. *Peasant Wars of the Twentieth Century*. Norman: University of Oklahoma Press.

Woll, Allen L. 1987. "Hollywood Bandits, 1910–1981." In Slatta 1987, 171–80.

Womack, John, Jr. (1968) 1970. *Zapata and the Mexican Revolution*. New York: Vintage Books.

Wordsworth, William. (1803–1807) 1932. "Rob Roy's Grave." In *The Complete Poetical Works of Wordsworth*, edited by Andrew J. George, 300. Boston: Houghton Mifflin.

Yánez, Agustín. (1947) 1996. *Al filo del agua*. Nanterre, France: Colección Archivos.

Yarrington, Doug. 1997. *A Coffee Frontier: Land, Society, and Politics in Duaca, Venezuela, 1830–1936*. Pittsburgh: University of Pittsburgh Press.

Yellow Bird [John Rollin Ridge]. (1854) 1955. *The Life and Adventures of Joaquín Murieta, the Celebrated California Bandit*. Norman: University of Oklahoma Press.

Yoo, John. 2003. "Military Interrogation of Alien Unlawful Combatants Held outside the United States." Memorandum for William J. Haynes II, General Counsel of the Department of Defense. Washington, DC: US Department of Justice, Office of Legal Counsel, Office of the Deputy Assistant Attorney General. https://www.aclu.org/memo-regarding-torture-and-military-interrogation-alien -unlawful-combatants-held-outside-united.

Zapata Cesti, Víctor. 1966. *La delincuencia en el Perú*. Lima: Imprenta del Departamento de Prensa y Publicaciones de la Guardia Civil.

Zea, Leopoldo. 1991. "Revueltas, el endemoniado." In Revueltas (1949) 1991, xv–xx.

Zehr, Howard. 1976. *Crime and the Development of Modern Society: Patterns of Criminality in Nineteenth-Century Germany and France*. Totowa, NJ: Rowman and Littlefield.

Ziems, Ángel. 1988. "Un ejército de alcance nacional." In Pino Iturrieta 1988b, 138–67.

INDEX

"A hora e vez de Augusto Matraga" (Guimarães Rosa), 221

Abade, João, 231, 239, 241

Acordada, xvii, 5, 38

Act to Suppress Robbery and House-breaking and the Harboring of Robbers and Housebreakers, An, 309n10

Adán, 103, 176, 177; body of, 182; characterization of, 180; as messenger, 179; Natividad and, 179; social bandits and, 180; Úrsulo and, 178; violence and, 181–82

aesthetics, 82, 173, 195, 298n1, 324n15

Agha, Abdi, 318n7

Agostinho, 151, 159

agrarian conflict, 154, 163

Aguilar, Gonzalo, 127, 313n1

Aguinaldo, Emilio: guerrilla warfare and, 283n2

Al-Qaeda, xv, 20

Albert, Stephen, 228, 229

Albuquerque, Honorato Nepomuceno de, 231, 232, 233

Alegría, Ciro, 34, 105, 115, 116, 117, 118, 121, 152, 298n3, 307n1, 312n25, 313n28, 319n12

Algunos aspectos de nuestra sociología criminal (Modesto Villavicencio), 111

Allende, Salvador, xvii, xviii

Alsina, Adolfo, 206, 207, 315n5

Altamirano, Ignacio Manuel, 6, 94, 299n3

Amado, Jorge, 13, 144–45, 148, 149, 150, 152, 153, 159, 161, 162–63, 164, 166, 193, 214, 216, 236, 317n2, 317n5, 318n7, 319n13, 329n5; Arvoredo and, 162; Badarós/Horácio and, 157; Christian tropes/motifs and, 172, 173; class conflict and, 154; cultural ethnography and, 155; influence on, 322n8; *letrado* and, 175; literary production of, 143–44; melodramas by, 172; Mexican Marxism and, 174; outlaw violence and, 145; politics and, 165; and Revueltas compared, 170–72; sertanejo culture and, 158; work of, 171, 172

Amenábar y Roldán, Álvaro, 117, 121, 152

Anderson, Benedict, 66–67, 235, 286n13

Andrade, Ignacio, 52, 200, 201, 253

Ángeles, Felipe, 96, 306n11

Angicos, 8, 318n6, 331n13

anti-imperialism, 10, 50

anti-Peronism, 129, 192

Antônio das Mortes (Rocha), 164, 325n2

Apaches, 24, 338n2

Arango Arámbula, Doroteo. *See* Villa, Francisco "Pancho"

Arcedos, 67, 73

Arévalo Cedeño, Emilio, 59, 296n15

Arguedas, José María, 118, 312n25

Arlt, Roberto, 247, 249, 255, 335n6, 335n9; Revueltas and, 322n9

Arráiz Lucca, Rafael, 301n10, 301n11, 302n18

Artigas, José Gervasio de, 69, 193, 195, 253; Sarmiento on, 337n18

Artur, 155, 156, 157, 158, 159, 320n15

Arvoredo, Lucas, 161, 162, 163–64, 177, 180, 320n15, 321n21; logic of, 163; nomadism of, 165; saga of, 162; spaces of, 163; symbolism and, 164

Aureliano, Colonel, 155, 156, 168, 320n15; cultural prestige of, 165; fazenda of, 151, 153, 155, 157, 165

Avelar, Idelber, 216, 35n7

avengers, 7, 20, 21, 31, 37, 41, 88, 94, 115, 124, 130, 131, 144, 201, 206, 208, 211, 268, 269, 287n17, 288n20, 290n37, 312n26, 317n1, 320n17

Aztecs, 184, 287n16

Azuela, Mariano, 33, 90

Bahia, 143, 146, 148, 160, 212, 213, 235, 236, 241, 242

Bahiano, Zé, 173, 174

Bandeira, Azevedo, 126, 132–33, 134

Bandeira gang, 132–33

Bandera, 177, 183

bandido, 56, 271, 281n2

bandit narratives, 10, 32, 33, 107, 137, 228, 268; Borgesian, 129; classic, 253

bandit studies, 1, 9, 283n8

banditry, 66, 104, 108, 112, 152, 161, 162, 165, 168, 229, 235, 262, 272, 273, 288n20, 309n11; accusations of, 29; as act of language, 266–67; baroque, 280n11; capitalism and, 150; co-opting, xvi; criminal nature of, 269; as cultural capital, 4, 145; cultural imagery and, 12; dealing with, 310n15; debates about, 1; definition of, xxiv, 263, 264; degeneration into, 230; end of, xvi, 223; endemic of, xxiii, 308n6; Latin American culture and, 261, 263; law against, 272; manifestations of, 263, 264, 265; metaphorical uses of, 268; Mexican, 106–7; and millenarianism compared, 166; offenses related to, 263; patrician, 37; penal codes and, 106; Peruvian, 108, 112; politics and, 12, 266, 269; potential of, 166; resistance and, 270, 271–72; revolution and, 28; rise of, 154; rural, xvi, 154, 261, 281n2; social cohesion and, 111; social/political nature of, 269; specter of, xv–xvi; state and, xix; studying, 263; as trope, xvii, xxi, xxv, 2, 3, 4, 10–11, 23, 266, 267, 268; understanding, 264 bandits, xx, xxi, 9, 15, 24, 30, 54, 66, 100, 149, 228, 231, 266, 272, 273, 289n28, 309n14; aegis of, 108; black, 109; Borgesian, 132; execution of, 234–35; fallen comrades and, 281n3; fanatics and, 329n7; guerrilla, 68; historical, 265; humankind and, 230; inside/outside and, 262; journalists and, 15; leftist, 325n2; life of, 38; llaneros and, 51; man of letters and, 2, 5, 11, 248, 260; memories of, 270; mestizo, 121; mythical, xxiii; noble, 28, 116; professional, 287n17; profiteering, 27; real, 1; revolutionaries as, 23, 281n16; robin-hoodization of, 29; Roman, 289n26; rural, 233, 251; terrorists and, 20; thriving of, 275; urban, 245; voice of, 30. *See also* social bandits

Bandits (Hobsbawm), 278n2, 282n8, 317n1

bandolerismo, 263

bandolero, 56, 228, 271, 281n2

Barbadura, 232, 236

Barczewski, Stephanie, 267, 268

Barinas, 50, 53, 57, 292n1, 296n14, 297n19

Barthes, Roland, 145, 170, 175, 301n14

Bartra, Roger, 179, 180

Bastião, 156, 157

Battle of Celaya (1915), 25, 87, 286n12

Battle of La Victoria, 66, 69, 74, 83, 84, 299n4

Battle of Las Queseras (1819) del Medio, 296n17

Battle of Léon (1915), 25, 87

Battle of Paredão, 214, 215

Battle of Rellano (1912), xx, 280n14

Battle of Torreón (1913), xx, 27, 87, 92, 289n29

Battle of Zacatecas (1914), 27, 94, 95

Bauche Alcalde, Manuel, 10, 26, 35, 285nn9–11, 286n14, 287n16; editing by, 286n12; memoirs and, 285n12; Vasconcelos and, 27; Villa and, 26, 27, 28, 29

Beatito, 232, 239, 241

beatos, 143, 161, 162

Bebelo, Zé, 215, 327n3; organizational skills of, 213, 225; Riobaldo and, 212, 225

Becerrillo, 91, 92, 93, 96, 99

Bedouins, 110, 111

Beggar's Opera, The (Gay), 7, 32

Benel, Eleodoro, 105, 112, 113, 262, 311n23, 312n24

Beowulf, 122, 127

Bernardo, 73, 75

bildungsroman, 72, 152, 305n8

Billy the Kid, 34, 202

"Biografía de Tadeo Isidoro Cruz" (Borges), 126, 200

Biografía de un cimarrón (Montejo), 29–30, 32, 58

Bioy Casares, Adolfo, 134, 191, 192

Blake, William, 4, 211, 226

Blanco, Eduardo, 34, 301n14

Blanco-Muñoz, Agustín, 297n22

blancos de orilla, 51, 68

Blok, Anton, 241, 290n33

Blood Meridian (McCarthy), 32, 288n22

Bolívar, Simón, 49, 60, 67, 75, 296n13, 299n5, 337n18; Boves and, 74; Chávez and, 69, 76, 77; death of, 70; Decreto de Guerra a Muerte and, 68; Espíritu Santo and, 74; as historical nemesis, 77; Nation and, 72; nature/culture and, 70; as pivotal figure, 71; Presentación and, 66, 73–74, 77–78; statue of, 70

Bonaparte, Napoleon, 124, 126, 318n5

Borges, Jorge Luis, 13, 123, 129, 130,
134, 136, 137, 138, 198, 199, 201,
202, 208, 209, 210, 221, 227, 228,
233, 244, 248, 252, 328n2, 335n10,
336n14; death of, 325n5, 325n7;
duels narrated by, 196; electoral
goon and, 315n5; on epic, 122; films
and, 313n1; gauchos and, 12, 14,
132; on gauchos/orilleros, 126–27;
Gutiérrez and, 205; life of, 194–95;
melancholy and, 135; Moreira and,
14, 204, 206; narratives of, 193;
oeuvre of, 315n8; orillero fights and,
252; prediction by, 192–93; quote of,
122, 191; short stories by, 135, 314n4;
work of, 11–12, 204
Botello, Oldman, 53, 55, 58, 96, 296n16,
297n20; death of, 92
Boves, José Tomás, 68, 69, 74–75, 81,
82, 87, 96, 296n13, 299n6, 302n15,
303n22; army of, 76, 79; Bolivar and,
74; Presentación and, 76, 83, 84
Brazilian Communist Party, 144,
172
Brignone ("El nene"), 245, 246, 255,
334n2, 336n16, 337n20; sexual escapades of, 253
Briones, Naún, 236, 331n15
Buenos Aires, 132, 195, 199, 315
Buenos Aires Province, 30, 130, 199,
317n14
Bunge, Carlos Octavio, 247, 252, 259
Bush, George W., 50, 95, 295n7; Chávez
and, 46–48, 49; criticism of, 46–47,
48; as man of the people, 44

caatinga, 146, 160, 162, 166, 172, 237
Cacau (Amado), 144, 146, 147, 152
"Cachorro de tigre" (López Albújar),
113, 118, 307n2, 307n4

Cain, 179, 180
Calixto, 177, 178, 324n14
Calumbí, 238, 241, 334n27
Camarão, Zé, 147, 151, 152
Campaña Admirable, 299n4
Campobello, Nellie, xx, 25
Campos, Presentación, 62, 68, 71, 85,
177, 299n4, 299nn7–8, 302n17,
303nn19–20; Bolívar and, 66, 73–74,
77–78; Boves and, 76, 83, 84; David
of, 81, 82; as hero, 75; on land, 83;
political motivations and, 80; rape
by, 69, 73, 300n9; Venezuela and, 78;
war and, 78, 79, 80, 81
Cañabrava, Baron of, 231, 234, 238, 242,
330n8, 331n12, 334n27; Canudos
and, 242
Candido, Antônio, 214, 220, 321n21
cangaceiros, 34, 148, 157, 161, 163,
164, 173, 231, 232, 281n2, 287n17,
288n20, 317n1, 331n13
Canudos, 15, 155, 223, 232, 234–37, 240,
242, 243, 246, 262, 272, 329nn6–7,
330n7, 330n11, 333n21; burning of,
241; defeat of, 8, 238; piety of, 239;
story of, 230–31; territorialization
and, 233
Capitães de areia (Amado), 146, 147, 152
capitalism, 117, 168, 261, 278n2; agrarian, xvi, 148, 150, 153, 159, 173, 278n2;
banditry and, 150; dominant version
of, 159; free-market, 158; triumphant, 248
Caracas, 49, 296n13, 303n22
Cárdenas, Eliecer, 56, 88, 105, 174,
331n15
Carrancistas, 23, 26, 87, 90, 95, 98, 101,
286n12
Carranza, President, 21, 23, 88, 94, 95,
164, 284n4; assassination of, 89;

break with, 27; nationalism of, 89; Villa and, 22

Carriego, Evaristo, 128, 129, 137

Castro, Cipriano, 49, 52, 57, 60

Castro-Klarén, Sara, 328n4, 332n19, 333nn20–21, 333n26

cattle rustling, 104, 262, 273

caudillos, xii, xvi, 52, 59, 67, 208, 284n4, 303n22

cautiva, 199, 202, 209

Centeno, Miguel Angel, 262, 264, 319n12

César, Moreira, 231, 232, 332n17; corpse of, 240; death of, 238; head of, 239, 241–42; revenge of, 239

Chandler, Billy Jaynes, 144–45, 263, 317n1

Chávez, Hugo, 52, 57, 61, 193, 292n1, 293nn2–3, 294n6, 295nn9–10, 297nn18–19; agenda of, 10, 56; authoritarian populism of, 50; Bolívar and, 69, 76, 77; Bush and, 46–48, 49; charisma of, 2, 42, 46, 60; Constitution and, 43; democracy and, 43; discourse of, 39, 45, 46, 47; Guaicaipuro and, 295n9; historical drama of, 49, 59; insurrection and, 43; Jean Valjean and, 46; lancer graduation and, 54; literacy of, 44; llaneros and, 53, 55; loyalty to, 42; Maisanta and, 53–54, 55, 59, 60–61, 184, 297n18; as man of the people, 43, 44; narrative of, 43, 45, 50; Obama and, 48; orality of, 44, 58, 294n5; People and, 49; public imagination and, 45; public interventions by, 2; rule of, 47, 56; style of, 54; Tapia and, 56; Uslar Pietri and, 302n18

Chavismo, 45, 59, 60, 292n1

Chinese Revolution (1949), 13, 144, 278n2

Chirino, Víctor, 209, 326n12; Moreira and, 200, 202, 203, 204

Chonita, 177, 178, 324n14

Cirilo, 71, 79

citizenship, 74, 250, 270

civil wars, 20, 25, 51, 279n2, 309n7

class struggle, 147, 154, 155, 158, 160, 162, 216, 319n10

code of honor, 39, 97, 124, 125, 237

Código Penal Santa-Cruz del Estado Nor-Peruano, 307n5

coiteiros, 162, 164

Colorados, xx, 99, 304nn3–4

Columbus, New Mexico: attack on, 32, 87, 98

communism, 166, 168, 170, 173, 186

Communist Party, 12, 13, 143, 146, 152, 154, 169

community, 37–38; codes of, 79; cultural, 137; moral, xxi, 34, 36, 37; national, 67; outlawry and, 37; premodern, 117; rural, 31, 163, 201, 205

"Cómo se hizo pishtaco Calixto" (López Albújar), 113

compadres, 37, 132, 314n4

condottieri, xxii, 24

Confessions of a Thug (Taylor), 32, 108

conquistadors, 66, 291n36

Conrad, Joseph, 124, 131

consciousness, 260, 323n9; absence of, 102; class, 158, 159, 163, 167, 319n12; community, 319n12; national, 179; negative, 163; peasant, 173, 270; self-, 8

Conselheiro, Antônio, 8, 147, 155, 161, 216, 231, 233, 239, 329n7, 333n26; Conservatives, 273; corpse of, 240; death of, 241; head of, 234–35; jagunços of, 232; Liberals and, 271

Corisco, Captain, 143, 147

Cornejo Polar, Antonio, 117, 120, 298n3, 312n25, 332n17

coronéis forces, 262, 280n11

Corral Villa, Luz, 285n12, 288n24

"Corrido de caballería" (Eloy Blanco), 53, 54

Corrientes, Diego, 249, 291n36

corte de chaleco, 265, 273

Count of Monte Cristo, The (Dumas), 107, 131

Creelman, James, xiii, xvii

Creoles, 66, 72, 73, 104, 296n13, 300n9; colonial aristocracy and, 68; segmentation, 84

Crime and Punishment (Dostoyevsky), quote from, xi, 19

criminality, 111, 269, 270; factions out of power and, 246

criminals, xv, 37, 256, 291n33, 310n19; Indian, 116, 310n19; political, 246; urban, 4

Cristero Rebellion, 88, 89, 174, 279n2

Cristeros, 178, 180–81, 182, 225

Cristiada, 180, 272, 323n13

Cruz, Artemio, 23, 34, 126, 199, 253, 318n7

Cuban Revolution (1959), 144, 193, 278n2, 317n4

Cuentos andinos (López Albújar), 11–12, 13, 105, 113, 115, 117, 118–19, 307nn3–4, 311n24, 312n26; Vargas Llosa and, 118

Cuerudo, 202, 208; Moreira and, 209

cultor, 128, 129, 136

cultor del coraje, 12, 126, 128, 136, 138, 139, 194, 198; melancholy of, 129, 130

cultural capital, 43, 254

cultural memory, 205, 266

cultural synthesis, 49, 336n11

culture, 2, 83, 89; Afro-Brazilian, 147;

Argentine, 193, 198; Brazilian, 216; Chicano, 8; Cuban, 69; elite, 49; frontier, 8, 248; Latin American, 3–4, 261, 263, 275; leather, 215; nature and, 70; popular, 49; postcolonial, 5; rural, 156, 282n8; sertanejo, 158, 321n15, 321n21; Venezuelan, 69; Western, 30

Da Cunha, Euclides, 214, 232, 233, 329n5, 333n20

Dantès, Edmond, 107, 131

David, Captain, 73, 75, 79, 301n15, 302n16; Presentación and, 81, 82

De Castro, Juan E., 332n17

De la Huerta, Adolfo, 22, 39, 41, 88; attack on, 27; Madero and, 31; political ambitions of, 306n12

Decreto de Guerra a Muerte (War to the Death decree), 68, 85

Deus e o Diabo na Terra do Sol (Rocha), 143, 324n2

D'Hubert, Armand, 124, 125

Diadorim, 220, 221; Riobaldo and, 212–13, 214, 215

Díaz, Porfirio, xix, 22, 297n20; banditry and, xvxvi, xvii; exile for, 278n1, 279n9; Mexican People and, xii, xiv–xv, xvii; praise for, 279n7; on rebellion, xiii; regime of, 279n6; resignation of, xi, xiii–xiv, xvii, xviii, xxiv, 277n1

Die Räuber (Schiller), xix, 78–79

Dionisio Cisneros, José, 68, 74

División del Norte, xxii, 22, 87, 92, 93, 94, 95, 98, 285n9, 306n9, 306n12; joining, 99; smallpox for, 96–97

Doña Bárbara (Gallegos), 11, 48, 52, 65, 73, 83, 149

Dorda, Marcos ("El gaucho rubio"), 245, 246, 251, 252, 255, 256, 258, 259, 260, 334nn2–3, 336n17; identity of, 253

Dostoyevsky, Feodor, xi, xix, 19, 172, 323n10

drug dealers, 4, 336n11

Duellists, The (film), 124, 126

Dumas, Alexandre, 26, 105, 321n19

economic issues, xvi, 84, 89, 104, 156, 195, 241, 257

economy: Andean, 309n7; oil, 56, 58; Venezuelan, 56

education, xiii, 89, 168, 212, 286n13; classical/modern, 227; criminal, 249; levels of, 27; literary, 249

El águila y la serpiente (Guzmán), 23, 25, 90, 164, 287n16

El Altar, 67, 68, 73, 82, 299n7, 303n19, 304n23; destruction of, 69; uprising at, 79

"El Blanco" (López-Albújar), 113, 120, 313n30

El compadre Mendoza (film), xxi, 304n3

El cuadrante de la soledad, (Revueltas), 171, 322n2

"El desafío" (Borges), 126, 137, 196; quote from, 122

"El fin" (Borges), 130, 131, 133, 138, 139, 191, 196, 200

El gaucho Martín Fierro (Hernández), 34, 131, 136, 199, 207

"El general Quiroga va en coche a la muerte" (Borges), 199

"El indigno" (Borges), 195, 197, 208–9, 210

El informe de Brodie (Borges), 194, 195

El juguete rabioso (Arlt), 249, 335n9

El libro de arena (Borges), 194, 199, 209

El luto humano (Revueltas), 89, 103, 171–176, 178, 182, 323n13; influence on, 322n8

El matadero (Echeverría), 3, 199

El Mentao, Pedro, 196, 197

"El muerto" (Borges), 126, 132, 314n3, 314n4

El mundo es ancho y ajeno (Alegría), 34, 105, 116, 117, 118, 120, 152, 307n1, 312n25, 313n28, 316n13, 319n12

El oro de los tigres (Borges), 199, 315n8

El Pensador Mexicano, 6, 9

El periquillo sarniento (Fernández de Lizardi), 5, 6

El último hombre a caballo (Tapia), 53, 58, 93; Chávez and, 61; Maisanta and, 59

El Zarco (Altamirano), xix, 6, 94

Engels, Friedrich, 155, 167, 317n5

Epaminondas, Dr., 152, 160, 161, 233, 236, 237, 242, 320n15, 333n22

epic, 23; Borgesian, 129–30; emancipatory, 75; poetry and, 122; shortcuts of, 103

Espíritu Santo, 74, 301n12

Estevão, 159, 161, 162, 166, 167

Facundo, o civilización y barbarie (Sarmiento), 15, 193, 194, 199, 248

fanatics, 161; bandits and, 329n7

Farina, Alberto, 204, 326n14

fascism: rise of, 175; struggle against, 161

Favio, Leonardo, 200, 204, 206, 326n13

fazendas, 151, 153, 154, 155, 157, 158, 159, 163, 164, 165, 168, 213, 214, 215, 216, 225, 320n14, 320n16, 327n2

Federal Army, 26, 27, 94, 281n16, 287n15

Federales, 92, 288n23, 305n5

Federalism, 30, 49

Feraud, Gabriel, 124, 125, 126

Fernández de Lizardi, José Joaquín, 4, 9, 282n4, 291n35; nom de plume of, 6; primal scene and, 4

Fernando, 67, 68, 69, 71, 72–73, 76, 81, 300n9, 301n12, 302n15; death of, 299n4

Ferrari, Francisco, 197, 198; Santiago and, 210

Ficciones (Borges), 130, 209

Fidel, 177, 183, 187, 188

Fiero Vásquez, 34, 121, 307n1, 316n13

Fierro, Martín, 39, 87, 126, 127, 128, 129, 132, 191–92, 197, 206, 207, 209, 253, 314n4, 316n12; as avenger, 201; death of, 131, 133; Moreno and, 131, 138–39; story of, 199

Fischbein, Santiago (Jacobo), 197, 198

Fontas, 67, 73

Foucault, Michel, 267, 281n17, 331n14

4-F. *See* insurrection of February, 4, 1992

Francisco, Don, 33–34, 201, 205

Frank, 123–24, 125

fratricide, 50, 66, 75, 299n4

Fuentes, Fernando de, xxi, 97, 304n3

Fulgor y muerte de Joaquín Murieta (Neruda), 6, 7, 9, 145

Galeano, Blanca, 253, 253, 334n3

Gall, Galileo, 231, 232, 233, 329n4, 333n22, 333n24; Epaminondas and, 237; outlaw violence and, 242; problems for, 236–37; profession of, 235; rape by, 237

Gallegos, Rómulo, 11, 48, 65, 149, 298n2

gamonal, 116, 120, 152

gangs, xv, 122, 273, 308n5, 313n1; markers for, 291n33; millenarian armed, xii

García Calderón, Ventura, 105–6, 117

gaucho genre, 251, 252, 253

gaucho malo, 14, 15, 118, 136, 193, 194, 205, 248, 251, 252, 336n15; politics of, 209

gauchos, 11, 14, 126, 126–27, 193, 195, 198, 201, 252, 253, 254, 316n10, 316n14, 326n10, 337n17; compadres and, 314n4; real, 251

gavilleros, 56, 283n2

Gay, John, 7, 32

Giuliano, Salvatore, 29, 287n18

God, 231; devil and, 221

Goethe, Johann Wolfgang von, 194, 229

Gómez, Juan Vicente, 49, 52, 53, 56, 57, 297n20; dictatorship of, 10, 51

González, Abraham, xx, xxiii, 41, 95, 281n15, 287n15, 331n14; letter to, 19; Villa and, 23, 33

González Prada, Manuel, 110, 111

Grande, João, 231, 239

Grande Sertão: Veredas (Guimarães Rosa), 13, 144, 211, 214, 215, 218, 221, 231, 315n5

Grapes of Wrath, The (Steinbeck), 317n2, 322n8

Gray, Dorian, 14–15, 238

Gregorio, 157, 158, 159, 176, 177–78, 182–83, 184, 188; classical art and, 185; ethics/politics and, 178; Fidel and, 183; gonorrhea for, 187; as Other, 187; Ventura and, 186

Grünewald, Thomas, 267–68, 280n13

Guadalupe, 180, 182

Guaicaipuro, 49, 50, 60, 295n9

guapos, 12, 128, 138

Guerrero, Emilio Modesto, 294n5, 294n6, 297n18

guerrillas, 26, 68, 162, 193, 272, 283n2, 284n5, 284n7

Guevara, Ernesto (Ché), 8, 55, 250, 331n14, 335n10

Guha, Ranajit, 163, 164, 207–8, 241, 269

Guimarães Rosa, João, 13, 15, 215, 219, 220, 222, 328n6; language of, 217–18; sertão of, 214

Gutiérrez, Eduardo, 12, 14, 34, 118, 122, 136, 137, 191, 200, 202, 248, 326n10, 335n9, 336n12; Borges and, 205; gauchos and, 201, 252; Piglia and, 251; serial novels of, 252

Gutiérrez, Miguel, 105, 116

Guzmán, Martín Luis, 23, 27, 28, 90, 305n4; books by, 25; Villa and, 287n16

Habão, Seó, 213, 219, 225

hacendados, 35, 38, 120, 262, 270

Hart, John Mason, 278n2

Hermógenes, 215, 219, 220, 225, 226, 319n12; assassination by, 213; death of, 214; fazenda of, 213, 216; Riobaldo and, 217, 221, 223

Hernández, José, 34, 118, 192, 202, 324n1

Hernández, Mocho, 52, 57

Herrera, Celia, 21, 284n6, 290n29

Herrera Luque, Francisco, 75, 296n13

Hidalgo y Costilla, Miguel, 39, 68

"Historia de Rosendo Juárez" (Borges), 126, 195–96, 197, 200

Hobsbawm, Eric, 12, 28, 37, 144, 149, 269, 274, 278n2, 282n8, 284n5, 290n33, 318n7; bandits and, xvi, 317n1; on Lampião, 146; Marxist thought and, 145

"Hombre de la esquina rosada" (Borges), 126, 128, 137, 138, 195, 196, 197, 203–4, 211

"Hombres pelearon" (Borges), 137, 138, 196, 314n3

Horácio, Colonel, 148, 149–50

Hormiga Negra, 122, 205, 206, 314n4

Hormiga Negra (Gutiérrez), 14, 122, 137, 205, 206, 214n4

hostes, 20, 268

House of Bourbon, 20, 268

Huánuco, 113, 118, 119, 312n24, 313n27

Huasipungo (Icaza), 118, 120, 149, 312n25

Huckleberry Finn (Twain), 316n14

Huerta, Victoriano, 21, 281n16; counterrevolutionary coup and, 279n9; Villa and, xxii

Icaza, Jorge, 118, 149, 312n25

identity, 76, 186, 253; bandit, 25; bourgeois, 282n4; civil, 99, 175; cultural, 13, 151; functions and, 271; Italian, 266; making, 250; metaphors, 85; national, 82, 262; political, xv; popular, 36; Venezuelan, 50, 55; violence and, 229

ideology, 4; racial, 267; Stalinist, 182

imperialism, 58, 272

Inácio, Colonel, 151, 155, 156, 161, 320n15

Inca Empire, banditry in, 111–12

Indian problem, 11, 105, 113, 115, 118, 120

indigenism, 11, 105, 113, 115, 117, 298n1

indigenismo, 105, 113, 298n1

individualism, 102, 159, 286n13

Inés, 67, 72, 302n15; David and, 302n16; rape of, 69, 73, 77, 300n9

insurgents, xx–xxi, 66, 274, 325n2

insurrection of February 4, 1992 (4-F), 43, 45

ISIL, xv, xviii, 20, 229, 235

Ivanhoe, xxiii, xxiv

jagunços, 13, 15, 26, 51, 120, 144, 147, 164, 173, 211, 212, 213, 215, 216, 219–20, 223, 232, 236, 241, 262, 281n2, 315n5, 334n26; decapitations by, 239; military and, 239; real, 231

James, Jesse, 8, 30, 34, 202

Janes, Regina, 8, 282n6, 333n25

Januario, 9, 182, 282n4; Perico and, 5, 6

Jelicié, Emiliano, 127, 313n1

Jerônimo, 151, 152, 154, 159, 161, 162, 165, 166, 168, 178

Joaquim, Father, 231, 236, 239

Joaquín Murieta (Neruda), 236

Joca Ramiro, 211, 215, 217, 220, 327n3; leadership by, 213

José María El Tempranillo, 291n36, 291n38

Juan Jorge, 114, 115

Juan Moreira (film), 200, 204

Juan Moreira (Gutiérrez), 14, 15, 34, 136, 137, 200, 201, 202, 204, 205, 206, 207, 208, 210, 252, 289n28, 316nn10–11, 326n13; reading, 209

Juárez, Rosendo, 39, 94, 126, 128, 182, 185, 197, 198; Real and, 195, 196; revolutionaries and, 277n1

Jubiabá (Amado), 146, 147, 152

Jucundina, 151, 152, 159–61, 166, 167

Judas, 39, 129, 176, 198, 209, 213, 221

Jurema, 333n24; rape of, 237, 333n22

justice, 269; law and, xix

Kafka, Franz, 131, 135, 139, 223

Katz, Friedrich, 20, 28, 285n10, 286n13, 290n30; Bauche Alcalde and, 285n12; epic legend and, 23; outlaw past and, 25; Villa and, 306n12; on Villismo, 21

Kemal, Yasar, 289n28, 318n7

Kirchner, Néstor, 249, 250

Kleist, Heinrich von, xix, 283n1

Knight, Alan, 174, 264; liberalism and, 279n6; on social banditry, 25; state consolidation and, 279n3; Villa and, 25; on Villismo, 25

knowledge, 167; criminological, 246; local, 168; thesis on, 199

Kohlhaas, Michael, 79, 265

"La biblioteca de Babel" (Borges), 139, 224, 230

"La escritura del Dios" (Borges), 129, 135

Laera, Alejandra, 136, 316nn10–11, 336n12

La Estrella, 199, 200, 201, 202, 208, 253

La guerra del fin del mundo (Vargas Llosa), 14–15, 230, 241, 243, 246, 251, 326n11, 329n5, 332n17

"La intrusa" (Borges), 126, 130, 195, 197

La invasión (Piglia), 247, 248

"La lotería de Babilonia" (Borges), 135, 224

La Marqueseña, 56, 297n19

Lamborghini, Osvaldo, 253, 337n19

Lampião, 7, 29, 148, 155, 281n3, 287n17, 317n1, 318n6, 320n18, 321n20, 332n15, 333n23; banditry and, 288n20; commission for, 173–74; death of, 147; gang of, 173–74; head of, 8; life/legend of, 162; outlawry and, 320n17; saga of, 331n13; Volta Seca and, 146

landowners, 154, 273; capital statutes and, 280n12; peasants and, 156, 290n33, 320n16

landscape, 70; as metaphor, 83

"La noche de los dones" (Borges), 14, 126, 194, 199–200, 201, 203, 204, 205, 206, 207, 327n14; passions of the multitude and, 210; paysanos and, 208; reading, 209

Las lanzas coloradas (Uslar Pietri), 11, 52, 66, 67, 70, 72, 77, 82, 85, 87, 88, 96,

105, 153, 176, 295n11, 299n6, 301n13; described, 65

"Las ruinas circulares" (Borges), 135, 138, 226, 233

La tormenta (Vasconcelos), 23, 90, 284n4

latro, 20, 268, 281n2

latrocinium, 20, 268

La tumba del relámpago (Scorza), 318n7, 319n12

La vida no tiene nombre (Veloz Maggiolo), 145, 327n1

La virgen de los sicarios (Vallejo), 336n11, 337n21

La vuelta de Martín Fierro (Hernández), 128, 130–31, 137, 192, 197, 202, 206

law, 223, 225; breaking with, 79; international, 47; jagunço, 241; justice and, xix; theater of, 235

leadership, 96, 213, 217, 225, 226, 277n1

Leones de San Pablo, 11, 92, 93, 94, 99; code of honor and, 97; joining, 99; Villa and, 87, 91

Les Misérables (Hugo), 46, 61

Lewin, Linda, 263, 317n1

liberalism, 279n3, 309n7; corporatism versus, 79; Porfirian, 279n6; prerevolutionary, 279n6; savage, 303n18

Lins do Rêgo, José, 34, 329n5

llaneros, 10, 56, 68, 75, 83, 85, 193, 296n13; bandits and, 51; identity of, 76; insurgency by, 11, 51, 55; martial prowess of, 11; outlaws and, 51; violence and, 229

llanos, 10, 24, 50, 78, 79, 83, 84, 303n22; cattle ranching in, 51; geographical position of, 51; history of, 53

López Albújar, Enrique, 11–12, 105, 111, 115, 120, 121, 127, 307nn3–4, 311n20, 319n12; Andean outlaw violence and, 116; Andean Western and, 105; Andes of, 120; criticism of, 112–13; extralegal systems and, 213n27; fictional work of, 105; indigenism and, 117; narrative by, 118; passionate Indian and, 116–17; Peruvian verosimile and, 118

López Negrete, Don Agustín, 33, 41, 288n25; criticism of, 290n30; Martina and, 35; rape by, 289n29

Los caballeros del delito (López Albújar), 111, 112

Los de abajo (Azuela), 33, 90

Los días terrenales (Revueltas), 171, 175, 176, 182, 322n2, 323n10; quote from, 170

Los errores (Revueltas), 171, 322n7

Los orilleros (Borges), 134–35, 191, 314n3

loyalty, 31, 39, 40, 42, 53, 56, 68, 92, 97, 101, 103, 133, 171, 286n12, 306n12, 315n5, 327n3

Lozada, Manuel, 50, 280n10

Lucas, Don, 134, 135

Ludmer, Josefina, 132, 207, 248, 251

Lukács, György, 72, 247

lumpenproletariat, 143, 147, 161

Maderista, xx, 26, 40, 41

Madero, Emilio, xiv, xvii, xx, xxi, 21, 23, 26, 89, 281n15, 306n12; betrayal of, 39; coup against, 40; death of, xxiv, 31, 41; Díaz and, xxiii; Huerta and, 31; leadership by, 277n1; murder of, 279n9; narrative of, xiv; Parral and, xxii; People and, 10; Plan de San Luis Potosí and, xxi; treason and, 39; Villa and, xxii, xxiii, 39, 40–41, 53, 277n1, 292n39

Maduro, Nicolás, 60, 292n1

Maisanta: El último hombre a caballo (Tapia), 45, 52, 59

malandros, 143, 336n11

malevos, 12, 127, 197, 198

Malito, Mario, 245, 246, 252, 254, 334n3, 337n19

man of letters, 4, 175; bandits and, 2, 5, 11, 248, 260; literature's place/authority and, 2; production of, 6; writer and, 175, 176

Man with the Harmonica, 123–24, 125, 130

mantuano, 11, 66, 296n13

María (Isaacs), 82, 202

Mariátegui, José Carlos, 11, 13, 105, 115, 307n3

Marksman, Herma, 53, 54–55

Marta, 151, 152, 160, 167, 320n15

Martín Fierro (Hernández), 127, 136, 191, 192, 194, 197, 206, 208, 252, 316n12

Martin, Gerald, 322n9, 332n17

Marxism, 12, 13, 14, 147, 186, 188, 193, 278n2, 322n6; Christianity and, 323n11; Latin American, 145; Mexican, 174

masculinity, 40, 47, 97, 99, 177

Maupassant, Guy de, 11, 105, 307n4

Maya, Tiburcio, 11, 92, 95, 96, 175, 177, 180, 232, 305n4, 306n9; attitude of, 101, 306n11; death of, 102, 103; desertion by, 97; destiny of, 101; emergence of, 94; loyalty of, 103; reenlistment of, 98; refusal by, 101, 102; Villa and, 87, 93, 98, 99, 100–101

McCarthy, Cormac, 32, 288n22

media, 257; American, 277n1; international, 277n1

melancholy, 130, 135–36, 179

Melitón, 87, 305n4

melodramas, 30, 31, 33, 39, 41, 66, 152, 172

Memed, My Hawk (Kemal), 131, 289n28, 318n7

Memorias de Pancho Villa (Guzmán), 25, 27

Mendes, Selorico, 212, 214, 223, 327n2

Mendoza, Macario, 176, 177, 185, 186

Menem, Carlos Saúl, 44, 249

Mereles ("El cuervo"), 153, 245, 246, 253, 254

Mexican-American War, xvi, 24

Mexican Communist Party (PCM), 170–71, 174, 175, 178, 182, 186, 322n1

Mexican Constitution (1857), xiv

Mexican Constitution (1917), 23, 89

Mexican People, xii, xiii, xiv, xvii

Mexican Revolution, 10, 13, 94, 172, 174, 185, 228, 264, 311n19; image of, 92; influenza pandemic and, 971 peasant wars and, 279n21 success with, 278n21 Villa and, 19–20

Michael Kohlhaas (Kleist), xix, 283n1

migration, 128, 152, 168

Miguel Ángel, 87, 91

Miliani, Domingo, 82, 301n11

millenarianism, 161, 162, 166, 168

Mix, Tom, 163, 164

modernista literature, 2, 112

modernity, 112, 186, 233, 236, 238, 312n24; Latin American, 261, 262; Western, 228

Monsiváis, Carlos, 172, 304n2, 322n6

Montoneros, 108, 112, 283n1, 309n12, 310n17, 325n3; journal of, 325n4; logo, 193; politics and, 309n13

Moor, Karl von, 78–79, 79

Morales, 134, 135

Moreira, Juan, 33, 39, 122, 126, 137, 251,

262, 315n5, 326nn10–12, 327n15; alliances of, 206; as avenger, 201; as bandit, 206; Borges and, 14; courage of, 206; cruelty of, 204; Cuerudo and, 209; as cultural signifier, 198; death of, 39, 200–204, 208, 252; as gaucho, 201; last fight of, 253–54; Matanzas and, 208; paysanos and, 206, 207; praise for, 204–5; rewritings of, 205; rural community and, 201; sexual escapades of, 253; as showoff, 209; as sociopath, 202; story of, 199; superiority of, 209; treason of, 202; violence of, 204–5

Moreno, 39, 129, 130, 133, 136, 197; destiny of, 132; Fierro and, 131, 138–39; social banditry and, 131

Moss, David, 268; banditry and, 266–67

Muchembled, Robert, 337n1

Muñoz, Rafael, 90, 92, 93, 127, 175, 305n7; novels of, 304n3; short stories of, 305n5; Villa and, 11, 91, 98; writing of, 103

Murieta, Joaquín, 7–8, 9, 33

Musolino, Giuseppe ("King of Aspromonte"), 111, 310n18

naming, politics of, 37, 266, 272

Napoleon, xi, 20, 105, 126

narcos, 4, 25, 34

narratives, xiv, 5, 33, 35, 43, 45, 50, 75–76, 89, 92–93, 193, 202, 224, 228, 322n6; cultural, 66; frontier, 113, 114–15, 118; historical/biographical, 336n10; Homeric, 215; *indigenista*, 116; Latin American, 335n7; national, 46, 177; official, 89; revolutionary, 177; self-justifying, 90; Western, 118. *See also* bandit narratives

Natera, Pánfilo, 90, 95

Nation, xv, 83, 279n5; Bolívar and, 72; embodiment of, 78

nation-state, 4, 51, 75, 76, 84, 229, 235, 252, 261, 304n24, 335n4; building, xi, xvii; demise of, 251; notion of, 104; system/opt out of, 265

national culture, 3; conflict and, 66; literature and, 2

national problem, 11, 105

nationalism, 11, 50, 89, 208, 278n2; ethnic, 283n1; state-sponsored, 14, 193

nationhood, 65, 293n3

Natividad, 74, 79, 177, 178, 180, 182, 314n15, 323n14; Adán and, 179

Natuba, Léon de, 231, 239

nature, 70, 83

Nenen, 152, 155, 162, 166, 167, 321n23

neoliberalism, 247, 249, 250, 251

Neruda, Pablo, 6, 7, 145, 236, 282n5; Murieta and, 8, 9

Nielsens, 126, 130

Nietzsche, Friedrich, 134, 233, 267, 271

Noca, 151, 159

Nogueira Galvão, Walnice, 216, 218, 317n2

nominalist approach, 1, 263

Northern Division, 29, 98

"Nuestros tigres" (González Prada), 110, 111

Nuevos cuentos andinos (López Albújar), 105, 113, 311n24

Obama, Barack, 44, 48, 95

Obras completas (Borges), 194, 325n7

Obregón, Alvaro, 21, 95, 284n4; assassination of, 88, 89; reconstruction and, 23; Villa and, 89

O'Malley, Ilene, 20, 89, 304n2

Once upon a Time in the West (film), 123, 314n2

Orbegoso y Moncada, Luis José de, 109, 308n5

orillas, 196, 132, 197, 198

orilleros, 12, 14, 126–27, 134, 201, 209, 252

Orozco, Pascual, xxi, xxiii, xxiv, 39, 41, 304n3; Colorados of, xx, 304n4; División del Norte and, xxii; as Judas, 39; Madero and, xx, 277n1; Torreón and, xx; uprising of, 91; Villa and, xx

Os sertões (da Cunha), 144, 214, 233, 326n11, 329n6

Otálora, 132, 133, 134

Other, 220, 275, 304n2

outlawry, 40, 104, 113, 147, 271, 320n17; community and, 37; llanero, 46; rural popular, 37

"Outlawry of Earl Godwin, The" (Jones), 292n40

outlaws, 148, 149, 211, 265, 287n17; historical/fictional autobiographies of, 32; llanero, 77; llanos and, 51; meaning of, 100; network of, 107; peasant, 176; refractory, 177; retribution by, 241; revolutionaries and, 28; rural, 194, 262; violence by, 177

Outlaws of the Marsh, 282n7, 289n26

Pacto de Punto Fijo, 43, 49, 60

Páez, José Antonio, 49, 68, 84, 85, 296n13; coming of age moment for, 36

Pajeú, 231, 239, 241, 333n24

Palma, Ricardo, 109, 110

Pancho Villa: Retrato autobiográfico, 1894–1914 (Villa), 10, 26, 27, 29, 30, 32, 36, 37, 41, 57, 280n15, 283n3, 285nn8–9, 287n16, 288n25, 290n30, 291n36; impact of, 26; traitors in, 39

Parra, Max, 20, 89, 90, 99, 269, 286n13; bandit life and, 38

Parral, xx, xxiii, 7, 38, 39, 52, 202; extraction from, xxiv; fall of, xxi; Madero and, xxii; sacking of, xxii

Partido Comunista do Brazil (PCB), 144, 145, 151, 154, 161, 167, 168, 317n3, 319n13

partisans, 39, 181, 262, 272

Passion, 209, 221

Patagonia, 274, 336n13

patria, 31, 35, 293n3

paysanos, 127, 136, 192, 206–8, 325n4

Paz, Octavio, 173, 175

PCB. *See* Partido Comunista do Brazil

PCM. *See* Mexican Communist Party

peasant leagues, 167, 319n13

peasantry, 154, 172, 267, 319n14; agrarian capitalism and, 278n2; culture of, 158; landlords and, 156, 290n33, 320n16; precipitating, 154

Pedrão, 231, 239, 326n11

Pedro Páramo (Rulfo), 149, 214, 323n13

penal codes, 106, 119, 263

Peñaloza, Ángel Vicente ("Chacho"), 193, 325n4

People, xv, 35, 39, 57, 93, 103, 279n5; as armed gangs, xv; in arms, 95; mimicry of, xv; passions of, 49; Villa and, 10

Perea, Máximo, 87, 96, 306n11

Pereira de Queiroz, Maria Isaura, 263, 317n1

Pérez, Carlos Andrés, 45, 56

Pérez Delgado, Pedro (Maisanta), 10, 294n5, 296nn15–16, 297n19, 297nn21–22; Chávez and, 53–54, 55, 59, 60–61; death of, 52, 54; history of, 60; legacy of, 45; Macías and, 57; rural Venezuela and, 58; Tapia and, 54; uprising and, 52–53

Pérez Rul, Enrique, 25, 285n9, 289n29

Perico, 5, 6, 9, 282n4, 291n35

Pernambucano de Mello, Federico, 29, 146, 263, 287n17, 288n20, 317n1, 320n17, 321n20, 327n4; landless colonel and, 164

Perón, Juan Domingo, 56, 192, 193, 195, 204, 283n1, 294n6, 325n3, 335n10

Peronism, 14, 192, 193, 246, 250, 325n6

Peronismo de la Resistencia, 250, 258

Pershing, John: Punitive Expedition of, 22, 87

Piglia, Ricardo, 3, 13, 46, 247, 249, 250, 334n1, 335n6, 336n12; Gutiérrez and, 251; journalists/bandits and, 15; nationalist imaginary and, 251; work of, 248

Pilares Polo, Víctor, 117

Pinochet, Augusto: coup by, xvii–xviii

"Plan de San Luis Potosí" (Madero), xiv, xxi

Plata quemada (Piglia), 15, 245, 246, 247, 248, 250, 251, 253, 254, 258, 259, 260, 335n4, 337n19, 337n21

Plateados, 270, 279n10

Poe, Edgar Allan, 181, 188

poietic potency, 43, 50, 293n4

politics, xiv, xvii, xix, 146, 164, 165, 182, 195, 271; banditry and, 12, 163, 266, 269; defining, 269, 270; ethics and, 177; liberal, 309n13; nationalist-statist notion of, 270; peasant, 270; policy and, xxiv; populist, 250; radical, 267; sense of, 102

Polvo y ceniza (Cárdenas), 105, 236, 331n15

Popular Front, 144, 155

populism, xiii, 103, 160, 192, 208; authoritarian, 50; nationalist, 14; postmodern cultural, 250; state, 56, 161

Porfirian press, xiv, xx, 278n1

Porfirian regime, xvii, 278n1, 279n6

Porfiriato, xi, 24

Prescott, William H., 112, 311n22

Prestes Column, 29, 155, 174

PRI, 90, 103

Prieto, Adolfo, 201, 316n11, 327n15

property: crime against, 264; taking, 264–65

prostitution, 143, 151, 160, 172, 177, 186, 254, 311n22, 321n19

Proyecto de un código penal (Vidaurre), 110, 308n5

Puente, Ramón, 27, 34, 285n8, 289n29

pulpería, 130, 136, 207, 252

Punitive Expedition (1916–1917), 22, 87, 100

Quiroga, Facundo, 199, 253, 337n18

racism, 9, 42, 311n19

Rama, Ángel, 4, 251, 329n5

rape, 35, 66, 69, 73, 77, 162, 163

Raskolnikov, xi, xix, 19, 172

Real, Francisco 197; death of, 203; Rosendo and, 195, 196

realism, 1, 195, 263; socialist, 173, 247

Recabarren, 130, 132, 315n7

Redoble por Rancas (Scorza), 145, 307n1, 318n7

Rentería, Austreberta, 90, 285n12

Renzi, Emilio, 246, 247, 248, 257–59, 260, 334n3, 335n8; evolution of, 256

Republican China, 228; as bandit country, 107

resistance, xxi, 15, 108, 145, 150, 152, 154, 158, 161, 166, 206, 207, 212, 250, 254, 268, 311n23, 325n4, 338n2; banditry and, 270

Respiración artificial (Piglia), 15, 247, 248, 258, 259

revenge, 29, 34, 41, 73, 79, 93, 98, 115,

121, 131, 132, 177, 178, 216, 235, 239,
    256, 258, 289n29, 307n4
Revolución Libertadora, 52, 57, 192
revolution, xviii; banditry and, 28; tran-
    sition to, 154
revolutionaries, xv, 1–2, 89, 278n2;
    bandits and, 23, 281n16; outlaws
    and, 28
Revueltas, José, 13, 89, 103, 145, 174,
    225, 322nn2–3, 322n5, 323n10,
    323n12; and Amado compared, 170–
    72; Christian tropes/motifs and, 172,
    173; empowering denial and, 180;
    imprisonment of, 321n1; Mexican
    Marxism and, 174; Mexican Revo-
    lution and, 174, 185; narratives of,
    322n6; novels by, 175; participation
    in, 322n1; PCM and, 170; prose of,
    322n9
Ribas, José Félix, 77, 83, 84, 301n14
Riobaldo, 13, 14, 217–18, 219, 220,
    327nn1–2, 328n6; Bebelo and, 212,
    225; Diadorim and, 212–13, 214, 215;
    exploits of, 211–12; hagiographies
    and, 223; Hermógenes and, 217,
    221, 223; language and, 224–25;
    leadership of, 217, 226; narrative of,
    222, 224; reincarnation and, 222; as
    Urutú Branco, 213, 225; victory of,
    216; violence of, 217, 223
River Plate, 69, 126, 132, 253, 254, 264,
    293n4
robbery, xviii, 37, 38, 263, 265, 269, 274,
    281n2, 308n5, 312n26; filial love and,
    38; highway, 1, 104, 262, 273, 308n5;
    life of, 108; necessity of, 38
Rob Roy, 129, 253; Rob Roy, 9; "Rob
    Roy's Grave" (Wordsworth), 253
Robin Hood, 20, 37, 38, 40, 129, 208,
    267, 288n20, 291n37. See also
    self-Robin-Hoodization

Rocha, Glauber, 164, 324n2
Rodrigues, Nina, 231, 232, 234, 330n10
Rosas, Juan Manuel de, 110, 194, 248,
    253, 293n4
Roso, Colonel, 71, 75, 83, 84
Rufino, 199, 235, 237, 242, 329n4
Ruiz Abreu, 173, 322nn2–3
Rulfo, Juan, 149, 172, 303n21, 323n13
Rumi, 105, 117, 121, 152
Rurales, xvi, 33, 38, 290n29
Russian Revolution (1917), 144, 228,
    278n2, 311n19

Saint Augustine, divine justice and,
    xviii–xix
Salaverry, Felipe Santiago, 109, 110
Sánchez Prado, Ignacio, 171, 173, 322n5
Sandino, Augusto César, 1, 262, 272,
    274; assassination of, 273, 275; as
    bandit, 54, 271, 273, 275
Santa Fe, 205, 251, 252
Santiago, Don, 210, 300n9
Santos Luzardo, 83, 149
Santos Vega, 253, 316n11
São Francisco River, 159, 160
São Jorge dos Ilhéus (Amado), 148, 150,
    157
Sardetti, 201, 205, 208
Sarlo, Beatriz, 248, 315n8, 325n5
Sarmiento, Domingo Faustino, 3,
    15, 110, 193, 194, 199, 253, 293n4,
    304n24, 325n4, 325n6; on Artigas,
    337n18
Schiller, Friedrich, xix, 78–79
Schroeder, Michael, 268–69, 271, 273,
    274, 320n18
Scorza, Manuel, 116, 145, 307n1, 318n7,
    319n12
Scott, James, 152, 156, 164; adulation/
    deference and, 207–8; banditry and,
    269

Se llevaron el cañón para Bachimba (Muñoz), 90–91, 99, 304n4, 305n8

Seara Vermelha (Amado), 146, 150, 151, 152, 154, 155, 157, 162, 167, 168, 172, 173, 214, 236, 317n2, 320n14, 320n16

Second Republic, 68, 74, 296n13

self-Robin-Hoodization, 29, 148

Sendero Luminoso, 308n6, 312n26

Sergipe, 146, 327n4

serranos, 92, 120, 338n2

sertanejo, 14, 151, 160, 168, 169, 231, 237; ethics, 153; morality, 158

sertão, 14, 15, 24, 146, 147, 150, 151, 153, 166, 167, 168, 169, 212, 214, 221, 233, 237, 243; peasantry of, 154; violence in, 126

sicarios, 26, 336n11

Siete ensayos (Maríategui), 13, 115

Silva, Police Chief, 258, 334n3

Silvino, Antônio, 34, 317n1, 333n23

Singelmann, Peter, 263, 317n1

Slatta, Richard, xxiv, 263, 264

slavery, 68, 69, 79, 104, 112, 272

social bandits, 10, 12, 25, 43, 121, 144, 180, 205, 206, 269, 290n33, 317n1; mythical status of, 336n13; narratives of, 202; urban version of, 249; varieties of, 37

social bonds, 25, 111

social fabric, 76, 215

social life, 144, 147, 247

social mobility, 155, 157, 159

social reality, 46, 154

social realm, 4, 294n4

social transformation, xi, 263

society, 247; against any, 256; class-based, 161; criminal, 256; entire, 256

Sombra, Don Segundo, 128–29, 199, 209

Sommer, Doris, 35, 298n3

Somoza, Anastasio 272, 275

sovereignty, xiii, xvi, 4, 22, 40, 43, 51, 79, 82, 112, 214, 223, 242, 252, 261, 274, 333n25

Stalinism, 12, 182

Steinbeck, John, 317n2, 322n8

symbolism, 164, 181–82, 238, 260

Tacuara, 193, 325n4

Taibo, Margarita (Giselle), xxii, 97, 253, 285n9, 286n12; on Villa, 28

Taliban, 229, 330n11

Tape Burgos, 128, 129

Tapia, José León, 45, 93, 296n14, 296n16, 297n22; bandit label and, 57; book by, 52, 53, 55; Chávez and, 56; death of, 52; Maisanta and, 52, 54; Premio Nacional de Literatura and, 54; testimonials and, 58

Tarantino, Quentin, 202, 246, 334n2

Taylor, Philip Meadows, 32, 108

Tempestad en los Andes (Valcárcel), 116, 118

Terras do sem fim (Amado), 144, 148, 149, 150, 157, 164, 318n9

Terrazas clan, xx, 24, 90

terrorists, 4, 20, 266, 283n1

Tilly, Charles, 262, 270

Tonho, 151, 167–68

Torres, Ana Teresa, 46, 294n5, 305n6

Torres, Elías, 27, 91

transcendentalism, 13, 334n27

treason, 59, 229; fear of, 98; as moral pitfall, 39–40; obsession with, 60; revenge and, 41; trope of, 39

"Tres versiones de Judas" (Borges), 209, 221

Trevoada, Zé, 161, 162, 165, 166, 167

trickster, 33, 37, 291n37

Trillo, Manuel, 285n10, 287n14

truth, 75; power and, 281n17; strategic use of, 29, 288n20; tests, 266

Tschudi, Jacob von, 107, 108, 112,

308n5, 310n16, 312n26; banditry and, 106

Tsun, Yu, 227, 228, 229, 231, 328n2

Tuerto Ventura, 177, 183, 184, 185, 186

Turner, John Kenneth, 21, 290n29

Turpin, Dick, 32, 282n3, 318n5

Urbina, Tomás, xxiii, 92, 96, 97, 262

Úrsulo, 177, 179, 180, 182, 323n14, 324n14, 324n16; Adán and, 178

Uslar Pietri, Arturo, 11, 52, 66, 69, 70, 83, 127, 299n6, 301n10, 301n13; book by, 65; Chávez and, 302n18; on independence war, 300n9; public persona of, 298n2; quote of, 65; reconstruction of, 74

utopia, 117, 145, 166, 250

Valcárcel, Luis, 116, 118

Vallejo, Fernando, 336n11, 337n21

Vámonos con Pancho Villa! (film), 175, 304n3

Vámonos con Pancho Villa! (Muñoz), 87, 88, 90, 91, 93, 98, 99, 105, 176; *Vámonos-1,* 91, 92, 93–94, 95, 98, 99, 101, 102; *Vámonos-2,* 98, 99, 102, 175, 306n9; Villismo and, 96

Vampa, Luigi, 26, 107

Vanderwood, Paul, xvi, 56, 263

Varallanos, José, 111, 112, 311n20

Vargas, Getúlio, 56, 59, 144, 161, 318n6

Vargas Llosa, Mario, 13, 14–15, 118, 230, 234, 236, 237, 238, 242, 243, 246, 251, 329nn4–5, 332n17, 332n19, 333n20

Vasconcelos, José, 23, 90, 175, 284n4; Bauche Alcalde and, 27

Vaz, Medeiro, 213, 219, 220

Veloz Maggiolo, Marcio, 145, 327n1

vengeance, 94, 106, 113, 114, 115, 118, 121, 125, 131, 132, 133, 213, 220, 237, 241, 263, 305n4, 316n13, 321n21

Veredas Mortas, 218, 219

victimization, trope of, 31, 35–36, 39, 290n32

Vietnam War, 144, 278n2

Villa, Francisco "Pancho," xx, xxi, 1–2, 19, 20–21, 26, 41, 42, 52, 57, 69, 90, 109, 110, 177, 202, 262, 283n3, 284nn3–4, 285n9, 286n12, 286n14, 287n18, 288n22; anecdotes pertaining to, 320n19; arrest of, xxii, 290n30; as bandit, 10, 20, 22, 23, 25, 28, 30, 37, 54, 91; biographies of, 2, 21, 33, 285n8; bravery of, 40; charisma of, 59–60, 97; community and, 37–38; Conventionistas and, 95; criminal feats of, 37; defeat of, 87; Fatherland and, 10; guerrilla warfare and, 284n5; horsemanship/ marksmanship of, 31, 288n18; individualism of, 286n13; as innocent hero, 40; interpellation of, 97–98; intervention by, 26; killings by, 38; leadership of, 96; legends of, 32, 103; marriages of, 31, 32; memory of, 88, 94; as Mexican Other, 286n13; military strategy of, 25; murder of, 88, 91, 305n4, 305n6; mystique of, 89; name adoption by, 20; narrative of, 33, 35, 92–93; nation/fatherland and, 36; outlaw past of, 24, 25, 29, 36; People and, 10, 35, 39; rehabilitation of, 98; reputation of, 23, 27, 284n5; retaliation by, 39; revolution and, 19–20, 28, 29, 33, 38; revolutionary pantheon and, 89; robberies by, 37,

38; robin-hoodization of, 29; status of, 22; success for, 28; supporters for, 24–25; treason and, 39; as victim, 30–31; voice of, 28; white legend and, 28; words/tropes of, 287n16

Villa, Guadalupe, 26–27, 285nn9–10, 286n12

Villismo, xx, 21, 25, 95, 96, 97, 304n3; Villa and, 11, 98

Villistas, xx, 11, 21, 26, 27, 90, 284n4, 304n3, 305n5

violence, xv, xvi, 175, 177, 181, 204–5, 266; Andean, 113, 116, 121; backlands, 237; capitalist, 168; class, 162, 237, 312n26; as commodity, 269; Corsican, 105; criminal, 251; culture of, 162; economy of, 39, 117; entropic, 217; ethnic, 312n25; germ of, 112; growth of, 195; identity and, 229; indigenous, 312n25; lawful, 271; mapping, 120; Mediterranean, 105; Mexican, 181–82; monopoly of, 261–62; national, 120; nonstate, 261; outlaw, 113, 116, 143, 144, 145, 148, 232, 242, 271, 275; paradoxes of, 217; performances of, 265; political, 94; regulating, 24; revolutionary, 94; rural, 88, 104, 261, 273; school of, 177; serrano, 338n2; state, 335n4; traditions of, 309n10; transformation of, 94

Viriatus, 33, 273

Vitor, Antônio, 149, 150

war, 270; alternative vision of, 78; Dionysian experience of, 80, 81, 82, 88; ideological, 79

War of Independence, xvi, 49, 51, 68, 69, 79, 87, 300n9

War of the Pacific, 106, 112

War to the Death decree, 68, 85

Water Margin, The, 274, 282n7

Westerns, 122; Andean, 113–14; as frontier narrative, 114–15; Peruvian, 114–15; spaghetti, 123

Wild, Jonathan, 34, 280n13

Wilde, Oscar, 14, 238, 243

Yellow Bird, 33

Zacatecas, 87, 92, 306n11

Zamora, Ezequiel, 10, 49, 60, 297n19; legacy of, 45

Zapata, Emiliano, 54, 88, 89, 262

Zapatismo, 184, 304n3

Zastrozzi (Shelley), 19, 40

Zefa, 51, 152, 159, 161